D0213417

Writing the Image After Roland Barthes

New Cultural Studies

Series Editors

Joan DeJean
Carroll Smith-Rosenberg
Peter Stallybrass
Gary A. Tomlinson

A complete list of books in the series is available from the publisher.

Writing the Image After Roland Barthes

Edited by Jean-Michel Rabaté

Whitaker Library
Chowan College
Murfreesboro, North Carolina

PENN

University of Pennsylvania Press

Philadelphia

118646

Copyright © 1997 University of Pennsylvania Press
All rights reserved
Printed in the United States of America on acid-free paper

10 9 8 7 6 5 4 3 2 1
Published by
University of Pennsylvania Press
Philadelphia, Pennsylvania 19104-6097

Library of Congress Cataloging-in-Publication Data
Writing the image after Roland Barthes / edited by Jean-Michel Rabaté.
p. cm. — (New cultural studies)
"The chapters collected here were originally presented as papers during the conference 'After Roland Barthes,' which took place at the University of Pennsylvania in April 1994"—Introd.
Includes bibliographical references and index.
ISBN 0-8122-3369-7. — ISBN 0-8122-1596-6 (pbk.)
1. Photography—France—Philosophy. 2. Barthes, Roland—Criticism and interpretation. 3. Photographic criticism—France. I. Rabaté, Jean-Michel, 1949- II. Series.
TR183.W73 1997
770'.1—dc21

97-9579
CIP

Contents

List of Abbreviations

Throughout the present volume, references to works by Roland Barthes are provided parenthetically in the text of each selection. A bibliography is provided at the end of the volume.

With the exception of the recently published three volumes of the *Œuvres complètes*, abbreviations refer to available English translations of books by Barthes. Some contributors, however, have chosen to provide alternative translations. In such cases, and for those works for which no English translation exists, original sources are indicated in the notes of the given selection.

BR	*A Barthes Reader*
CE	*Critical Essays*
CL	*Camera Lucida*
CT	*Criticism and Truth*
EL	*Elements of Semiology*
ES	*The Empire of Signs*
ET	*The Eiffel Tower and Other Mythologies*
FS	*The Fashion System*
GV	*The Grain of the Voice*
IMT	*Image-Music-Text*
IN	*Incidents*
LD	*A Lover's Discourse*
MI	*Michelet*
MY	*Mythologies*
NCE	*New Critical Essays*
OC1, OC2, OC3	*Œuvres complètes 1, 2, 3*
OR	*On Racine*
PT	*The Pleasure of the Text*
RB	*Roland Barthes by Roland Barthes*
RF	*The Responsibility of Forms*

RL	*The Rustle of Language*
SC	*The Semiotic Challenge*
SFL	*Sade/Fourier/Loyola*
SZ	*S/Z*
WDZ	*Writing Degree Zero*

Introduction

Jean-Michel Rabaté

Roland Barthes died in 1980: seventeen years should provide enough time to assess his lingering and pervasive influence on critical theory and move beyond the mere anecdote to witness how his figure has taken on the more momentous contours provided by fate. Barthes's "fate" can appear to have been determined in part by the fact that his last published work was a treatise devoted to photography. The photographic image achieves exactly the effect I have described when mentioning "fate": it freezes a development, eternalizes what is an essentially mobile object under a figure. Although one ought to be wary of the retrospective illusion that automatically metamorphoses a last book into a testament, this last word forced on him by death is not attributable to mere contingency. Barthes always wished to understand History—a term he systematically capitalized—as a series of snapshots, of immobile yet unstable exposures. From his earlier investigations into the works of the French historian Michelet, who endowed universal history with the mythological elements needed to transform his nineteenth-century bourgeois ideology into an epic, to his later encounter with an Eastern otherness so fascinated by the click of a camera, Barthes's trajectory exhibits a constant and deep concern for the image.

Initially, Barthes's position in the face of images seems to be a very suspicious or critical one: he stated his reluctance or hostility to "analogical" forms of thought and art many times, always preferring the ethical cleanliness of discursive—therefore, discrete, digital, articulated, and codified—formations. Language can demystify because it never adheres to reality; its arbitrary nature introduces a differential space in which one can really think. The almost Sartrian terms I have just used still account for Barthes's convergence with Lacan's early condemnation of the "Imaginary" realm as that of the ego's subjective illusions. For both Sartre and Lacan, the stickiness of the subject's identification produces unwholesome coalescences between signifiers and signifieds; this imaginary projection is the first lure to be debunked. Barthes's career can thus be described as going from one "Imaginary"—the Sartrian consciousness, which underpins existentialist or neo-Marxist phenomenology—to another, the Lacanian "image-repertoire," which has to be squeezed between the logical structure of the symbolic and encounters with a real that resists language.

That Barthes died the same year as Sartre is ominous. Barthes said in the 1970s that when World War II ended he was a Marxist and a Sartrian. His last book, *Camera Lucida*, is thus not dedicated to a cherished mother who had just died, and who is its acknowledged inspiration, but to one of Sartre's early essays, *L'Imaginaire.* I will return to this curious convergence of these two major French thinkers who entertained deep and hidden affinities although they were associated with doctrines and movements as radically antipodal as existentialism and structuralism. This accounts for the fact that the main focus and general starting point for this collection[1] are texts that analyze the photographic image, whether inscribed under the heading of demystification, semiology, poststructuralist multiple decodings, or phenomenology. Our agenda is less to engage with a recapitulative survey of the works of a famed and versatile theoretician than to scrutinize the concepts used today in the context of broader multicultural issues.

Since Barthes's death in March 1980, his influence has continued to grow in France as well as in English-speaking countries. One might even say that today's developments in cultural studies and neo-Marxist theories of the media and popular culture derive in great part from his essays. The later Barthes fascinated wide audiences with his mixture of theoretical radicality, urbane skepticism, and delightful wit. He has rightly been called a master of the essay, writing in the tradition of Montaigne and Gide, but he is also a contemporary who clearly belongs to a century that has seen radical innovations in the field of critical theory. Like Walter Benjamin, Barthes as essayist and theoretician of culture exhibits a degree of intellectual complexity and stylistic fastidiousness. While Barthes's texts are credited with introducing students to structuralism and semiology in domains as varied as film studies, the analysis of advertisement, modern rhetorics of the image, the semiology of fashion, and the structural analysis of narrative, his later work shows a marked tendency to return to questions of history and biography.

These questions seem to have been bracketed by the strict linguistic model taken as the paradigm of scientificity that dominated the first phase of Barthes's research. Barthes's genius has always lain in his ability to adapt specific scientific models to classical studies of the humanities. This approach caused a number of conflicts with the traditionally minded scholars of the Sorbonne, who took a long time to accept the idea of interdisciplinary studies promoted so vigorously by Barthes, but who, as Antoine Compagnon shows, were not completely misled in their strictures. What distinguished Barthes was less his pseudoscientific tone than his immense curiosity, which led him to constantly broaden the scope of his investigations, moving from the reading of texts to the debunking of contemporary mythologies, from the interpretation of popular culture to personal accounts of his encounters with music, painting, and photography. The later Barthes, as much a novelist as a versatile critic, seemed ready to qualify or even dismiss his prophecy of a coming "death of the author," in order to stress the individual enjoyment one is expected to derive from literature and art (*The Pleasure of the Text*). He described his experiences when he discovered Japan as identical to the experience of reading a text. Barthes's wonderful awareness of the values at stake in these apparent random encounters with a world of signs founded on different beliefs led him to launch into his "moralities," such as his famed meditation on the nature of love (*A Lover's Discourse*) and his reflexive aphorisms on his own teachings (*Roland Barthes by Roland Barthes*). This culminated with *Camera Lucida*, Barthes's last book before many posthumous collections of essays, a moving autobiographical disclosure of his love for his mother under the guise of a study of photography. The autobiographical approach, which may appear to contradict all the tenets of Barthes's previous semiological approaches, nevertheless yields invaluable insights that can be generalized to other fields.

Whereas in former essays on the image Barthes had emphasized the artificial nature of the medium and the ideological function it could serve, *Camera Lucida* explores the phenomenological concept of photography. Photography is defined as producing an image for a consciousness that essentially mourns an absent object or person rather than relishing its presence. Photography provides an image of actual people and places that become "certified" as having really been there. If photography bespeaks a past presence, it also ultimately refers to death, and each photograph appears as a little poem, a Japanese haiku, forcing us to stare more directly at reality. As several of the critics in this volume show in greater detail, Barthes opposes the *studium*, or scientific approach, which risks missing the very point of the photograph, to the *punctum*, the small "point," which is likely to capture the eye of the beholder. The term *punctum* is used to justify an apparently subjective selection of photographs, all chosen and lovingly described because of some minor but revealing element that varies from picture to picture. Such a Zen-like meditation on the struggle between death and appearance is a fitting testament to Barthes and shows him to be a writer of immense integrity and almost magical verbal power. Above all, photography as understood in *Camera Lucida*—that is, essentially reduced to a melancholic viewer's fascination for dead people's portraits—acquires a strategic function: it is there that universal history meets a private history at the locus of one particular body.

An investigation of the role of photography in Barthes's works is crucial, for it not only permits a fresh and unprejudiced reexamination of the medium itself but also provokes a reappraisal of what seems to have baffled most commentators: the shift between the first Barthes, who demystifies messages by exposing their hidden codes before embracing a more systematic structuralist methodology, and the later Barthes, who seems more concerned with personal "ecstasies." As a recent commentator states, "The first ecstasy inaugurates a poststructuralism, the second a postmodernism."[2] Photography, or perhaps more broadly, the technological or historicized image, can be situated at the hinge between structuralism and what has been called poststructuralism.

The recent publication of the three volumes of Barthes's *Œuvres complètes* puts into perspective what really took place between 1966, when Barthes was still promoting the structural analysis of narrative as the tool of modernity, and 1973, when he launched into an erotics of writing, replacing the "political and psychoanalytical policemen" with a radical hedonism and allowing the terms *pleasure* and *bliss* to provide a new couple and new wedge for dislocating scientific reductionism. In less than ten years an apparently radical shift or split occurred. *S/Z* clearly marks a turning point, since the 1968–69 seminar on Balzac's tale is still announced in its second calendar year as "Structural Analysis of a Narrative: 'Sarrasine' by Balzac" but is presented as "an attempt at a pluralistic mode of criticism" (*OC2*, 549).

The reference to the "events" of May 1968 should not be taken as a watershed: all the interviews given by Barthes between 1966 and 1969 suggest that the major discovery that imposed itself as a real break was the discovery of Japan. In the summer of 1968, Barthes wrote eloquently of the Bunraku theater (*OC2*, 485–90) while noting that after May 1968 most of his work seems to belong to the "past" (*OC2*, 524). The first trip to Japan, followed by a few others, took place in May 1966. If May 1968 is indeed an important moment, it is because it accelerated a dissatisfaction with the then dominant mode of structuralism. As early as March 1967, Barthes predicted that, as far as structuralism was concerned, "the time of separations is near" (*OC2*, 459), alluding to a split he foresaw between Lacan and Lévi-Strauss. He located the widening rift in the way these thinkers use writing: here again, the term "writing" keeps its differential impact.

New names, new friends, such as Sollers and Kristeva, brought a spate of original departures and concerns between 1963 and 1967. The second volume of the *Œuvres complètes* sheds new light on Derrida's influence on Barthes; Barthes acknowledges his eminence quite regularly after 1967 as a groundbreaking thinker of writing (*OC2*, 440, 506, 524). One short, hitherto unpublished monograph, written in 1973 for an Italian encyclopedia, testifies to the depth of Barthes's research into the problematic of writing. Titled "Variations on Writing" (*OC2*, 1535–71), the text provides the previously unknown scientific backing or historical basis for *The Pleasure of the Text*, published in 1973. "Variations on Writing" follows a more complex classification than an alphabetical listing of entries, since the essay surveys all the forms of writing known to man. It begins by stressing that if writing was the "first object" met by Barthes in his critical work, he used it in a metaphorical sense. Now he wishes to address it in a physical sense, as manuscript "scription" engaging the whole body, but also history. Interestingly enough, Derrida is not mentioned in this very learned essay, which comes closer to an anthropology of culture; however, it is clear that if Barthes does not feel confident in the domain of philosophy, he does wish to come to terms with the illusions of linguists who systematically base their research on a phonological model of language. Against this reduction, Barthes alludes to Van Ginneken's theory according to which "*writing would have occurred before spoken language*" (*OC2*, 1545), only to dismiss all the myths of origins, showing that writing exceeds not only what he calls "alphabetical prejudice" but the whole concept of language when reduced to communication.

More space would be necessary to deal with this fascinating essay completely. Since I merely wish to document the shift in Barthes's thinking, I would like to mention another text, which has not yet been published in English. It is an early lecture, the first in which Barthes actually alludes to Derrida and in which he describes for the first time the shock of his encounter with Tokyo. "Semiology and Urbanism," a conference read in 1967 (*OC2*, 439–46), shows Barthes still donning the mask of the semiotician, but turning his attention to a relatively new object for him—the city. He points out that few urban sociologists have tackled the issue of urban signs and quotes Victor Hugo as the author who has best perceived the signifying function of cities. In *Notre-Dame de Paris*, Hugo announces that the book will ultimately destroy the city: he means that soon men will write only in print and not in stone. The equivalence between urban planning and writing appears very illuminating to Barthes, who then refers to Derrida's philosophy of writing (*OC2*, 440). Throughout the lecture, Barthes refers to Tokyo as the privileged example of such a post-Derridian urban writing: the city holds a center, but it is an empty center—one of the major insights of *The Empire of Signs*. He connects this with Hugo's idea: "Here we find again Hugo's ancient intuition: the city is a writing; he who walks in the city [. . .]

is a sort of reader" (*OC2*, 444). The reader is now confronted with an open text, such as Queneau's poetic combinatory that generates "*One hundred thousand billions of poems*": "Whether we know it or not, we are a little like this avant-garde reader when we move in a city" (*OC2*, 444). The avant-garde reader learns to explore or combine signs. He writes as much as he reads, and both activities are playful and erotic. Moving on to an analysis that borrows terms from Lacan's psychoanalytic system, Barthes finally links eroticism and sociability (*OC2*, 445). Thus, in this short 1967 essay, one finds the lineaments of not only *The Empire of Signs* but also *The Pleasure of the Text* and all Barthes's later autobiographical "drifts" through language and culture.

Derrida's name does not appear in the 1973 essay on writing. Barthes seems to prefer mentioning themes and motives provided by forerunners of Derrida such as Blanchot and Bataille (as Arkady Plotnitsky's chapter suggests) or to an earlier mode of phenomenology—similar to the "vague, casual, even cynical phenomenology" alluded to in *Camera Lucida* (*CL*, 20). More useful to Barthes than either Lacan or Derrida (who both seem to frighten him somewhat, perhaps because he cannot tinker with their concepts so easily), Sartre's early essays allow him to move more freely between his own body, taken as the foundation of his critical discourse, and a return to ontological notions. This move is indeed parallel with Barthes's decision to stop appearing "modern" at any cost (indeed, Sartre's early essays were completely outmoded, even in their author's eyes, by the late 1970s).

Thus, *L'Imaginaire*, published in 1940, can be taken as the philosophical foundation for *Camera Lucida*.[3] In it, Sartre systematically analyzes what happens to his memory of a friend he calls Peter, whom he considers under three aspects: first as a mental image provided by memory, then through a photograph, then as caricatured by a street artist. He explains that a caricature, which concentrates on just a few expressive or revealing features, can "give back" Peter more accurately than an exact but lifeless likeness. A photograph exists for the subject only insofar as he or she "animates it" (*I*, 55), whereas a mental image's main characteristic is a "certain way for the object to be absent in the midst of presence" (*I*, 144). One of Sartre's interesting conclusions is that the "imaging (or image-producing) consciousness" is not radically distinct from a "desiring consciousness" since "desire is a blind effort to possess as a representation what has already been given in an affective fashion" (*I*, 142). However, despite an apparent convergence with the psychoanalytical approach, Sartre remains extremely critical of the crudely reductive solutions provided by French psychiatrists such as Janet, Lagache, or Clérambault to the problem of the image in the unconscious. Typically, Sartre refuses to leave the realm of consciousness—for him, "obsession is a type of consciousness" (*I*, 296)—but this phenomenological bias allows him to describe the role of images in dreams in a very subtle and innovative way. He gives as an example a dream in which he is a slave running for his life, pointing out that the link between the slave and his consciousness is not merely a relation of representation but a relation of "emanation" (*I*, 332)—a key concept in Barthes's own "note on photography."

The dreamer can retrieve his dream as an unreal affective quality, remembering how he was not merely "seeing" a slave but had identified with his fear and despair, emotions that become emblematic as fictional passions. Interestingly, Sartre alludes to Hugo's *Les Misérables* and refers to both Jean Valjean's goodness and Ténardier's evil nature. These novelistic equivalents allegorize the noematic structure of intentionality through which a subject can believe in the reality of oneiric terror and fascination. The Sartrian dreamer, both transcendent and immanent to his dream, becomes Barthes's model of eidetic projection in *Camera Lucida.* Almost identical expressions describe the viewer of images, caught up in a fascination that exerts itself all the more since he does not know where it comes from, but remaining relatively free to evaluate and contextualize the imaginary nature of photographs.

This phenomenological analysis would not in itself suffice to account for Barthes's dedication of his book to *L'Imaginaire.* The conclusion of Sartre's treatise proves even more relevant to the aesthetics of *Camera Lucida.* Going beyond demonstrating the structural identity between the consciousness of an image and a desiring consciousness, Sartre points out the insufficiency of saying that some natural spectacles are more beautiful than others: they are beautiful only insofar as they are imagined, but the imagination remains at a remove from reality. It even has to kill, destroy reality, to create its own level of autonomy: "Reality is never beautiful. Beauty is a value which can only apply to imaginary productions and which implies a complete annihilation [*néantisation*] of the world in its essential structure" (*I*, 371). This is why, as Sartre explains in the last pages of *L'Imaginaire,* a woman's extreme beauty kills the desire for physical possession (*I*, 372). The reality of physical possession will never exactly tally with the unreality of an aesthetic experience. The imaging or imagining consciousness, which transforms the object into an analogon of itself, is therefore primarily a negating consciousness that has to empty the world of its ordinary qualities in order to transform it into an aesthetic image. Such negativity makes it impossible, for instance, to move logically from the domain of aesthetics to the realm of ethics (*I*, 371). This is the tragic dimension of the imaginary experience, as revisited by Barthes: no easy Hegelian conceptual contortion could elicit the dialectical impetus toward mourning an image. The beholder remains caught or "glued," to use a familiar Sartrian term, in his or her vision, deprived of any possibility of dialectical sublimation. The dedication of *Camera Lucida* to *L'Imaginaire* is an oblique acknowledgment of this tragic limitation. A novel about Barthes's mother's death, the essay is also a theoretical piece documenting the impossibility of writing a novel about the mother's death.

As Nancy Shawcross has shown in her comprehensive study of Barthes and photography, photography allows Barthes to envisage himself as a novelist precisely because he does not consider the technique to be an art.[4] In *Camera Lucida* at least, photography is only a technology, not a *techné*. By stressing the ontological nature of the apparent mystery by which real past objects or people leave an "emanation" as a visual trace of their presence in the world, rather than the authorial or ideological manipulations by which an operator transforms or frames a material that is still plastic and malleable, Barthes deprives photography of its productive transitivity. As a pure technology of traces, photography enacts the "death of the author" in the classical sense, a death that "authorizes" the critic or the reader. Photography, described in earlier essays as producing "messages without a code," becomes a technology whose functioning cannot be explained. Its messages refer only to an absolute loss. The mourning for this loss is what makes us wish to speak or write about it. This is why the first half of the diptych made up of the essays that follow considers the written status of Barthesian discourse on the image. Its title, "Reflections on Photography," could also have been called "Rhetorics of the *Punctum*," since most of its essays start from this difficult term. The second half of the diptych engages broader issues of literary theory and history as fundamentally redefined by the later Barthes.

Starting with Barthes's very personal essay describing the peculiar drowsiness he feels when leaving a theater after a film, Victor Burgin defines Barthes's main quality as an exemplary "discretion" facing images: halfway between critical vigilance and passive enjoyment, the flickering gaze of the viewer or *flâneur* among urban spectacles bridges the gap between the diffuse eroticism of our consumer society and Baudelaire's aesthetics of modernity. The well-known plea for photographic images that Barthes mounts against the encroachment of the cinema places the critical gaze midway between narcissistic enthrallment and a more active discernment. "Discretion" evokes all these enmeshed meanings, allowing for a rereading of the contemporary relevance of the medieval notion of *acedia*.

By pairing off a contemporary French artist's photographic series and the theses of *Camera Lucida*, Marjorie Perloff questions the ontology Barthes presupposes as a substratum for photography while expanding his main idea that Death constitutes the eidos of Photography. When

Christian Boltanski puts together photo albums showing people he does not know in order to play the role of an anthropologist interpreting and classifying strange rituals, he clearly destroys the notion of a stable referentiality: he invents names and stories, and the singleness of an event that should have happened only once is replaced by a series of simulations. While pointing to the difficulty met by Barthes's project of a science of the unique being, and sending back singularities to communities and to cultural discourse, Boltanski nevertheless appears haunted by death and catastrophe. His postmodernist mode of exposure is skillfully contrasted with Barthes's modernist position.

Returning to the same confrontation between Barthes and Boltanski, Nancy Shawcross's essay refers to the way *Mythologies* criticized Edward Steichen's photographic exhibition *The Family of Man*. What was denounced in 1956 as a sentimental and mythical view of a supposedly "eternal" human nature free from all historical context reverts to a private mythology when Barthes refuses to reproduce his mother's photograph. From this point of view, Barthes's later work contains a refutation of the ironic ethnography offered by Boltanski. Photographs cannot be organized as a narrative, nor do they function as a private or collective memory. While Boltanski subverts the filter of culture that orchestrates the public response to photography, Barthes simply surpasses it.

The notion that reality exceeds the frame we impose on it and that an ontological mystery is revealed by visual traces of people or events also underpins Colin MacCabe's essay on Barthes and Bazin. MacCabe is the first critic to stress a bewildering similarity between the approach of André Bazin, the founder of the famous *Cahiers du Cinéma*, which provided the *Nouvelle Vague* with new models and new concepts, and Barthes's last essay on photography. Bazin's celebrated essay on the ontology of the photographic image seems to haunt the margins of *Camera Lucida*: thirty-five years before Barthes, Bazin stressed the essential link between the image and the object, but his praise of realism is not reductive, for his "fingerprints" theory of the image is used to promote the notion of photography as a "true hallucination," which finds its paradigm in surrealism as much as Italian realism.[5] The only illustration Bazin adds to his brief yet dense piece (which ends with an abrupt and tantalizing sentence that seems to announce the early Barthes, "Moreover, the cinema is a language") is a reproduction of the Holy Shroud of Turin, one of the images to which *Camera Lucida* constantly refers.

The hidden reference to an unfashionable theoretician could help explain Barthes's strong opposition of a study of images and the poignant effect they have on us. *Camera Lucida* finds a crucial articulation in the opposition of *studium* and *punctum*, and both Derek Attridge and Jolanta Wawrzycka question the concept of the *punctum* used in a nonsystematic way by Barthes. While Attridge explores the links with Derrida's deconstruction, Wawrzycka notes how one is compelled to present a private mythology to deal with Barthes's analyses. How can the fiercely personal experience of death and mourning that Barthes sees inherent to any photograph become collective? If all the names provided in Barthes's definitions are contradictory, they ultimately tend to function as proper names. Attridge points to the deconstructive logic of supplementarity that inhabits the rational discourse of *Camera Lucida.* Barthes was aware of the impossible nature of his project, while achieving a degree of sublimity in the very presentation of this impossibility.

The experience of an undialectic death nevertheless belongs to our culture, and its fascination with images of alienation exemplifies this. Carol Shloss's essay starts from a moving sequence of images about homeless children in Seattle, *Streetwise,* to apply not only Barthes's notions of *punctum* and *studium* but also his narratological strategies. By showing that the counterpoint of the children's images and voices calls up the central opposition, Shloss suggests that both the text and the visual sequence confirm a dialogue between the homeless children and the cultural codes that surround them. In their exclusion from the symbolic realm, in their fragile immaturity, one can verify how the "signs of dispossession are also the signs of mass culture." In Mary Ellen Mark's book, photography indeed functions as a wound and provides a grim parody of Barthes's adoration for the image of his mother as a little girl. The photo-essay thus proves Barthes's central thesis with a vengeance: the homeless children are also motherless, but their exclusion and attendant exploitation proves that the mean streets are not culture's opposite but its "apotheosis."

Meditating on a similar site of loss and mourning, Liliane Weissberg relates Barthes's insistence on singularity to Benjamin's idea of the loss of the aura, an idea that introduces the "optical unconscious," intimately connected with a certain type of economy or circulation. Photography belongs to a commodity culture and reduplicates a capitalist system, but it also condenses psychic processes and rituals. Beginning with a contrastive analysis of Benjamin's and Barthes's theses on photography, Weissberg shows how the *punctum*'s aureatic uniqueness nevertheless postulates a genealogy, even if it is to invert the order of precedence in the mother-son relationship. Because they are still circulating as meaningful markers, Barthes's family photographs are not altogether unlike the portrait of Freud that today circulates as an Austrian banknote.

Barthes reproduces a curious IOU note from a paternal grandfather in the photo section of *Roland Barthes by Roland Barthes.* Using such personal documents and sharing a concern with literary or familial genealogies—which may imply the inversion of a supposedly natural order of generation—Diana Knight and Beryl Schlossman both link Barthes's quest for a lost mother through an investigation into the essence of photography to an interrogation on the links between his writing and his own sexuality. This leads them to explore differently the Proustian overtones of Barthes's last "family romance." Using the myth of the Woman Without a Shadow (according to Hofmannsthal and Strauss) and the myth of Orpheus and Eurydice (especially as rephrased by Blanchot), these critics point to the way language meets photography when the inherited sterility is transformed into an exceedingly fertile shadow.

These essays thus conclude the first part "Reflections on Photography" (to call up Barthes's subtitle to *Camera Lucida*) with considerations of Barthes's own language, which tries to emulate the image and also exceeds it. The second part of the diptych, "Seeing Language, Seeing Culture," focuses on the connections established between language, history, and culture.

Steven Ungar, the author of a major study of Barthes's works,[6] opens with Barthes's description of his particular ability or disease, which we chose as a title for this collection of essays: "I see language." Ungar analyzes the particular format of *Michelet*—an "explosion of index cards" and many reproductions—to show how Barthes experienced language visually. Just as he read Michelet's historical works and filed them into discrete linguistic categories, Barthes contemplated all the extant portraits of Michelet in order to understand him. The same productive interplay of word and image is found in the book's illustrations, which announce those of *Camera Lucida*, with the famous bas-relief of Michelet's tomb as a major allegory. Barthes concludes that Michelet, who literally "eats" history, also links it with his own body. History is thus more than a resurrection; it reconstitutes an androgynous body in which the excess of the signifier appears as a visible counterpart.

In a similar fashion, Philippe Roger, the author of an influential essay, *Roland Barthes, roman*,[7] explores the theme of history from the point of view of Marxism. Roger focuses on the 1950s, ten very productive years during which Barthes claimed he was a Marxist and attacked Camus' *The Plague* and defended Sartre's propaganda play *Nekrassov* by invoking historical materialism and class struggle as the main forces determining history. For all this activity, Barthes never appeared as a simple "fellow traveler" of Marxism but rather as "accompanied" by Marx or Marxian discourse (to which he had been introduced by a dissident Trotskyite) through these years. His original position, which led him to criticize proletarian literature in *Writing Degree Zero*, explains his enthusiasm for Brecht's theater. What Barthes admired in Brecht was fundamentally the spirit of the Enlightenment more than his Marxism. Brecht's dialectical theater was both the place of an exploration of society's conflicts and the utopian space of a new sociability.

The same dialectical nimbleness gives Pierre Force a point of departure when he explores Barthes's "science of degrees." *Bathmology*, meaning the discourse on the gradation of all phenomena, appears very close to Pascal's mystical ordering of different types of discourse. The concept replaces an older term, with which Barthes had played until it collapsed—the notion of *metalanguage*. The need to go beyond the logic of *doxa* (common opinion) negated by paradox and superseded by a return to the deeper meaning gives birth to endless conceptual vortices. By alluding to the French novelist Renaud Camus, who systematized this notion in a playful manner, Force is able to show how Barthes could remain an intellectual trendsetter while always staying out of reach, beyond any comprehensive or reductive statement.

Compagnon investigates a bathmology that he applies to its own inventor. Noting that there may have been as many Roland Bartheses as books or projects, Compagnon, a close friend and collaborator of Barthes, attempts to account for Barthes's relentless race after the new, which no doubt made him set trends in French critical theory.[8] Often guilty of reconstituting an authorial coherence (with Racine or Michelet, for instance) when he tried to do away with the author as a principle of explanation, Barthes would shift the issue in following publications, moving on to textuality, intertextuality, and other wider contexts of reading, until he reached the idea that all languages could be called "fascistic" insofar as they are made up of codes. Compagnon questions this idea, pointing out that the very fact that one can use language to denounce it as fascistic proves it to resist totalitarian codification. What has to be stressed, therefore, are the possibilities of enjoyment provided by language, Barthes's unique source of bliss.

Marjorie Welish gives a precious account of one source of bliss; painting. Noting that Barthes rarely wrote about painting, and only when he felt a special compulsion to do so, painter, poet, and art critic Welish explores the "poetic nonnarrative" produced by Barthes on Cy Twombly. True to his own sensualist and symbolist bias, the *littérateur* turned art historian sees in Twombly's work an enactment of his own late poetics, or the material inscription of "transfigured dissolution." Beyond the impressionistic nature of Barthes's remarks one can observe a deep fascination for Twombly's gesture, both in a concretely physical and in a generalized sense. Barthes admires the way Twombly could force himself to draw and write with his left hand, putting acculturation at a distance while miming deliberate clumsiness. What fascinates Barthes above all in Twombly is the topos of production, to the point that he wonders aloud whether he might not be tempted to imitate the painter. Barthes's insights could thus be parallel both to Twombly's structuralist approach to mythical history (with his *Fifty Days at Ilium*) and to his minimalist chalked blackboards series that present painting as some sort of half-erased, half-illegible handwriting or signature. This later poetics of genesis also has important consequences for literary criticism in general.

If Barthes is associated with structuralism as often as with what has been called poststructuralism outside France, he has also been instrumental in promoting a more recent trend that concentrates on explorations of the genetic properties of writing. Daniel Ferrer, current director of the ITEM, shows how Barthes not only paved the way for this type of genetic investigation but also became actively engaged in it, when he analyzed writing as rhythm and gesture during the 1970s.[9] Barthes is credited with having brought the term *writing* to the fore of the critical scene as early as the 1950s with his influential *Writing Degree Zero* (1953). His later stress on the material and historical aspects of writing illustrates how he remained ahead of his time.

Barthes continually emphasized the physical enjoyment provided by the activity of writing, comparing it to some sort of oriental calligraphy. This leads us to the famous "detours" he took to Japan, China, and Morocco, three privileged places upon which he founded his theory of exotic drifting. Dalia Kandiyoti explores the links between Barthes and contemporary multiculturalism. Kandiyoti uses the preface to Loti's Turkish novel, *Aziyadé*, to show how the fin de siècle fascination with exotic paradises is both mirrored and questioned by Barthes. The twentieth-century critic reduplicated Loti's quest for a purely aesthetic perception of an "otherness" that blended erotic perversity and a regression to meaninglessness or "exemption of meaning." Kandiyoti reveals how Barthes allows an exotic otherness to write itself onto him (at least in Japan and Morocco, since China remained unerotic, colorless, and ultimately foreign to him). A detached but sensuous observer can traverse another culture in a devious mapping that follows no guidebook.

Similarly, without attempting to assign a precise place on the philosophical map to a writer whose main asset is his mobility and multiplicity, Arkady Plotnitsky sees in Barthes's desire to be exempted from meaning a vital and critical relation to philosophy as such. Focusing on the concept of the "scriptible" as developed in *S/Z*, Plotnitsky wonders whether Barthes's notion of writing approaches Derrida's *écriture*, or whether it may not be more intimately related to Bataille's vision of excess and loss. While acknowledging Derrida's influence on Barthesian strategies during the 1970s, Plotnitsky proves Bataille to be a more productive model, at least insofar as he oriented the basic approach to Balzac's famous story *Sarrasine*. Alluding also to Nietzsche and Blanchot,

Plotnitsky replaces Barthes in the intellectual landscape of his time and throws new light on the transition from structuralism to poststructuralism. Barthes's insistence on a plural writing that demands to be read yet resists description and conceptualization reaches its main objective—which is to let texts "think."

Finally, in a playful "envoi," poet and critic Bob Perelman imagines a postmortem confrontation between Barthes and Frank O'Hara. Taking up Roger's point that there was some "Haddockism" in Barthes[10]—a reference to the cartoon character Captain Haddock who always rescues Tintin from danger in the most unlikely circumstances—Perelman depicts O'Hara and "Herbé" (as he wanted to be called) engaged in a hilarious discussion during which they broach the difference between penises and phalluses, the essentialism of the word, and the regressive semiological systems used by postmodernist poetry. Perelman suggests a fundamentally poetic status for Barthes's writings: not only is he heir to a distinctively modernist tradition, but in his emphasis on the pleasure of the text, on the obtuse meaning perceived outside any code, he transcends the old opposition between formalism and realism and allows for a reawakening of language in everyday usage.

I have tried to show elsewhere how Barthes's apparent reversal of values, his return to a so-called naive phenomenology had in fact been prepared by his earlier essays.[11] A good example can be found in one of the *Mythologies* essays devoted to "Shock-Photos" (translated in *ET*, 71–73). Barthes has very harsh comments for an exhibition of political photographs shown at the Galerie d'Orsay. They describe repression in Guatemala, but the images of tortured prisoners and heaps of skulls cannot touch the viewer, according to Barthes, because the horror is too deliberate, calculated, overconstructed. The thinking and the emotion have already been spent, never leaving a space for the viewer to shudder, commiserate, or condemn. This becomes a "synthetic nourishment" (*ET*, 72) and falls into the category of what Barthes later called *studium*: we know what to expect, we are not startled into emotion or thought. This essay subsequently attacks all photographs that aim at surprising the viewer with trick effects, strange angles, frozen movements. The "scandal" that any successful portrait should in itself represent disappears from such contrived images in which everything has been devoted to technical ingenuity. Against this, Barthes alludes to the way certain painters of the empire managed to dramatize Napoleon on a rearing horse: ". . . painters have left movement the amplified sign of the unstable, what we might call the *numen*, the solemn shudder of a pose nonetheless impossible to fix in time . . ." (*ET*, 72). The positive term *numen* announces the *punctum*: both present this strange "photogeny" in which art meets a brute reality precisely because it does not attempt to reduce it to some signification.

In the conclusion to "Shock-Photos," Barthes opposes the art of Brecht, who demands that art produce a "critical catharsis," to the naive and well-meaning wish of the photographers of the Galerie d'Orsay to be committed, when the best intentions in the world remain just that—intentions. He warns against the danger that lies in wait in this reduction of art's materiality to "interpretations" (in the sense used by Susan Sontag[12]): the photographs then appear "alien, almost calm, inferior to their legend" (*ET*, 73). I would like, as a conclusion, to apply these remarks to both Barthes and this book. My hope is that after these essays, which describe a changing, contradictory, and perplexing yet always thought-provoking writer, and which attempt to write an exact caption under his photograph to do justice to the living myth he embodies, Barthes will never be inferior to his legend.

Notes

1. The chapters collected here were originally presented as papers during the conference "After Roland Barthes," which took place at the University of Pennsylvania in April 1994. It was planned by Nancy Shawcross, Craig Saper, and me. I express my gratitude to the Research Foundation of the University of Pennsylvania, which made this international venue possible through a generous grant.

2. Mary Bittner Wiseman, *The Ecstasies of Roland Barthes* (New York: Routledge, 1989), p. xiv.

3. Jean-Paul Sartre, *L'Imaginaire: Psychologie phénoménologique de l'imagination* [1940], rev. A. Elkaïm-Sartre (Paris: Gallimard, 1986). Hereafter cited in the text as *I*. Barthes first mentioned this book in 1967, in the *Fashion System* (see *OC2*, 146), where he remarks in a footnote "From photography to a drawing, from a drawing to a schema, from a schema to language, there is a progressive investment of knowledge" and then refers to Sartre's *L'Imaginaire.* The notion of the "Imaginary" looms even larger in *Roland Barthes by Roland Barthes*—in which, strangely enough, the term *l'imaginaire* is variously translated as "image-system," "image-repertoire," and "imaginary" by Richard Howard.

4. Nancy Shawcross, *Roland Barthes on Photography: The Critical Tradition in Perspective* (Gainesville: University Press of Florida, 1996).

5. Bazin defines photography as a "true hallucination" in the seminal essay "Ontology of the Photographic Image" (first published in 1945, reprinted in *Qu'est-ce que le cinéma?* [Paris: Cerf, 1975]), p. 16.

6. Steven Ungar, *Roland Barthes: The Professor of Desire* (Lincoln: University of Nebraska Press, 1983).

7. Philippe Roger, *Roland Barthes, roman* (Paris: Grasset, 1986).

8. Antoine Compagnon organized and edited the first Cerisy conference devoted to Roland Barthes in 1977; see *Contexte: Roland Barthes* (Paris: 10/18/Union générale d'éditions, 1978).

9. The Institut des Textes et Manuscrits Modernes (ITEM) is a research unit

of the CNRS. The main journal disseminating its views is *Genesis* (Paris: Editions du CNRS).

10. Roger, *Roland Barthes, roman*, p. 283.

11. Jean-Michel Rabaté, *La Pénultième est morte* (Seyssel: Champ-Vallon, 1993), pp. 71–85, and *The Ghosts of Modernity* (Gainesville: University Press of Florida, 1996), pp. 67–83.

12. Susan Sontag, "Against Interpretation" [1964], in *Against Interpretation* (New York: Doubleday, 1990), pp. 3–14.

I
Reflections on Photography

1

Barthes's Discretion

Victor Burgin

Film has finally attracted its own Muse. Her name is Insomnia.
—Hollis Frampton[1]

In *La Paresse,* Jean-Luc Godard's fifteen-minute contribution to the film *Sept péchés capitaux,* Eddie Constantine plays a B-movie actor who turns down an offer of sex from an ambitious young starlet.[2] He refuses, he tells her, because he cannot bear the thought of having to get dressed all over again afterward. In a note on this short film, Alain Bergala observes: "Eddie Constantine marvelously embodies that very special state given by an immense lassitude, an apparent inertia which is in fact a state of great porosity to the strangeness of the world, a mixture of torpor, of loss of reality and of a somewhat hallucinatory vivacity of sensations. [. . .] Godard speaks to us of this very special way of being in the world, on the edge of sleep [. . .]."[3] That such a somnolently receptive attitude might be the basic condition of all cinematic spectatorship was first suggested in a special issue of the journal *Communications* devoted to psychoanalysis and cinema. Published in 1975, the issue has five photograms on its cover—arranged vertically, in the manner of a filmstrip. The top and bottom frames are both from the same film, *The Cabinet of Dr. Caligari.* They show the face of the somnambulist Cesare—first with eyes staring open, then with eyes closed. To look quickly from one frame to the other produces a rudimentary animation: Cesare appears to blink. The image of the cinema audience as waking somnambulists, blinking as they emerge from the auditorium into the light, may be found in more than one of the essays in this issue of *Communications.* Christian Metz, for example, writes that "spectators, on leaving, brutally expelled from the black interior of the cinema into the vivid and unkind light of the lobby, sometimes have the bewildered face [. . .] of people just waking up. Leaving the cinema is a bit like getting out of bed: not always easy [. . .]."[4] Metz notes that the subject who has fallen prey to the "filmic state" feels "as if numb" (*engourdi*). Roland Barthes describes his own feelings on leaving the cinema in much the same terms.[5] He feels "a little numb [*engourdi*], a little awkward, chilly, in brief sleepy: *he is sleepy*, that's what he thinks; his body has become something soporific, soft, peaceful: limp as a sleeping cat" ("En sortant," 104; *RL*, 345).

Barthes's short essay of 1975, "En sortant du cinéma," may be read as a reprise of his 1973 essay "Diderot, Brecht, Eisenstein." The theme of "representation"—defined as a structure that guarantees the imaginary capture of a subject by an object—is central to both essays, but is developed differently in each. The earlier essay points to an irresolvable problem in any politically inspired attempt to free the spectator from the grasp of the spectacle *from within the spectacle itself*. Barthes acknowledges that the "tableau," the "epic scene," and the "shot" all work against narrative mimesis and identification. Framing the mutely eloquent "social gest," the tableau may produce the effect of "distanciation" (*Verfremdung*). The spell is broken, the spectator's eyes are opened—but onto what? "In the long run," Barthes observes, "it is the Law of the Party which cuts out the epic scene, the filmic shot; it is this Law which looks, frames, enunciates" (*IMT*, 76–77). It takes a "fetishist subject," Barthes writes, to "cut out the tableau" from the diegesis. He cites a lengthy passage from Diderot's defense of the tableau, which concludes: "a painting made up of a large number of figures thrown at random on to the canvas, [. . .], no more deserves to be called a *true composition* than scattered studies of legs, nose and eyes [. . .], deserve to be called a *portrait* or even a *human figure*." Barthes comments that it is this transcendental figure "which receives the full fetishistic load" (*IMT*, 71–72). But Diderot's unification of a "body in pieces" within the bounds of a "figure" might be assimilated to Lacan's account of the mirror stage as well as to Freud's account of fetishism. In his later paper, Barthes writes: "I stick my nose, to the point of squashing it, to the mirror of the screen, to this imaginary 'other' with whom I narcissistically identify myself" ("En sortant," 106; *RL*, 348). To pass from Barthes's earlier paper to the later one is to watch a scene of fetishistic fascination cede prominence to one of narcissistic identification—but as if in a filmic cross-dissolve, where neither scene may yet be clearly distinguished from the other. What remains in focus, in both the 1973 and the 1975 essays, is the question of the autonomy of the subject of civil society in modern, media-saturated democracies. But whereas "Diderot, Brecht, Eisenstein" explicitly takes up the question of how to awaken the hypnotized subject of this society of the spectacle, "En sortant du cinéma" implicitly raises the question of whether somnolence itself may not be the spectator's best defense before the spectacle of the law.

As often as he may go to the cinema to see this or that movie, Barthes confesses that he also goes for the darkness of the auditorium. The necessary precondition for the projection of a film is "the color of a diffuse eroticism." Barthes remarks on the spectators' postures in the darkness, often with their coats or legs draped over the seat in front of them, their bodies sliding down into their seats as if they were in bed. For Barthes, such attitudes of idle "availability" represent what he calls the "modern eroticism" peculiar to the big city. He notes how the light from the projector, in piercing the darkness, not only provides a keyhole for the spectator's eye but also turns that same spectator into an object of specular fascination, as the beam "illuminates—from the back, from an angle—a head of hair, a face." Just as Metz speaks of *l'état filmique* of the spectator, Barthes posits a fundamental *situation de cinéma.* But whereas Metz speaks of this torpidly receptive state as produced by a visit to the cinema, for Barthes it is a precondition of the visit: "[T]he darkness of the movie theater is prefigured by the 'twilight reverie' (preliminary to hypnosis, according to Breuer-Freud) which precedes this darkness and leads the subject, from street to street, from poster to poster, finally to engulf him in a dark cube, anonymous, indifferent, where must be produced this festival of affects we call a film" ("En sortant," 104; *RL*, 346).[6]

About watching the film, Barthes writes: "It is necessary for me to be in the story (the *vraisemblable* requires it), but it is also necessary for me to be *elsewhere*: an imaginary slightly unstuck [*décollé*], that is what, as a scrupulous fetishist [. . .] I require of the film and of the situation where I go to look for it" ("En sortant," 105–6; *RL*, 347). Barthes unsticks himself from the screen by allowing his attention to peel away, to "take off," to "get high."[7] His act of ideological resistance—for all that it proceeds from an ethical attitude—takes the route of pleasure rather than denial. He responds to the fetishistic and ideologically suspect visual pleasure of narrative cinema not by resisting the perversion but by doubling it. Barthes suggests a culturally dissident way of going to the cinema other than "armed by the discourse of counter-ideology"; it is

> in allowing oneself to be fascinated *two times*: by the image and by what surrounds it, as if I had two bodies at the same time: a narcissistic body which looks, lost in the close mirror, and a perverse body, ready to fetishise, not the image, but precisely that which exceeds it: the grain of the sound, the theater itself, the darkness, the obscure mass of other bodies, the rays of light, the entrance, the exit: in brief, to distance myself, "unstick", I complicate a "relation" by a "situation." ("En sortant," 106; *RL*, 349)

We leave the movie theater, Barthes suggests, only to reenter an *other* cinema, that of civil society. He writes: "The historical subject, like the spectator in the cinema I am imagining, is also *stuck* to ideological discourse. [. . .] the Ideological would be at bottom the Imaginary of a time, the Cinema of a society; [. . .] it even has its photograms: the stereotypes with which it articulates its discourse [. . .]" ("En sortant," 106; *RL*, 348). These remarks suggest the question, What relation, if any, have the means by which Barthes "unsticks" himself from the imaginary in the movie theater to the situation of the historical subject glued to the ideological in society? It might appear that Barthes "distracts" himself from the film by behaving in the cinema much as he might in the street. In its early history, cinema was more often integrated into everyday urban *flânerie* than it is today. For example, in a chapter appropriately titled "Streetwalking Around Plato's Cave," Giuliana Bruno has described the peripatetic forms of spectatorship—and their attendant erotics—that accompanied the introduction of cinema to Italy in the final years of the nineteenth century, most explicit in the practice of projecting films in the open air of Naples's main shopping arcade.[8] Or again, we may recall the later practice of André Breton and Jacques Vaché, who would visit as many cinemas in Nantes as they could within the space of a single afternoon—entering and leaving with no regard for any narrative development other than that of their own *dérive.* Today, our everyday passage through the "cinema" outside the movie theater takes us through television, advertising, and glossy magazines. These arts are today appreciated—like architecture, in Benjamin's description—"in a state of distraction." However, the distraction that typically accompanies an evening's television viewing—answering telephone calls, fixing drinks, chatting, "zapping," flipping through newspapers and magazines, and so on—has nothing to do with the distance Barthes finds in the movie theater. When watching television, Barthes remarks, anonymity is lost; the surrounding bodies are too few. Worst of all, "the darkness is erased," and we are "*condemned* to the Family." As a consequence, "the *eroticism* of the place is foreclosed" ("En sortant," 105; *RL*, 346). In an essay about a Paris dance hall, Barthes confesses: "I admit to being incapable of interesting myself in the beauty of a place, if there are no people in it [. . .]; and reciprocally, to discover the interest of a face, a silhouette, an item of dress, to savor an encounter, I need the place of this discovery, also, to have its interest and its savor."[9] This simultaneity of fascination by both people and place, he remarks later, amounts to "that which one calls Festival, and which is quite different from Distraction" ("Au Palace ce soir," 68).

We may recall that Barthes refers to the film as a "festival of affects." He goes to the cinema, he says, only in the evening. The city at night is a form of organization of general darkness, and Barthes sees the darkness of the cinema as a particular organization of the darkness of the city at large. The movie auditorium, for him, condenses the "modern eroticism" of the big city. It is as if what Barthes calls "the eroticism of the place" were a modern equivalent of the eighteenth-century *genius loci*, the "genius of the place." Like the attendant spirit, the erotic effect may be unpredictably fleeting in its appearances. In *Le Plaisir du texte*, Barthes writes: "it is intermittence, as psychoanalysis has so well stated, which is erotic: [. . .] the staging of an appearance-disappearance."[10] The eroticism that may accompany what Barthes calls "the Cinema of society," like the "dancing ray of the projector" of which he speaks, *flickers*. Baudelaire chose precisely this term to describe the pleasures of the crowded city street, speaking of "the flickering grace of all the elements of life."[11] The photograms of Barthes's biphasic cinema—his festival for two bodies, narcissistic and perverse—appear abruptly, detaching themselves from the phenomenal flux in the manner of the fragment of which he speaks in *Roland Barthes par Roland Barthes*—in "a yawning [*bâillement*] of desire."[12] If desire "yawns," it may have more than a little to do with the alert torpidity of the somnambulist, or of someone on his way home to bed.

In a passage in "Soirées de Paris," Barthes recounts flickering chance encounters during his walk home at the end of an evening spent in cafés—as if reversing the itinerary "from street to street, from poster to poster," he describes as leading him to the cinema. In the rue Vavin he crosses the path of a beautiful and elegant young woman, behind whom trails "a delicate scent of muguet." On a column in the rue Guynemer he comes across a film poster, with the names of two actresses—Jane Birkin and Catherine Spaak—printed in huge letters (as if, Barthes remarks, the names alone were "incontestable bait"). In front of a house in the rue de Vaugirard appears "an attractive silhouette of a boy."[13] The film poster clearly may represent what Barthes calls a "photogram" of the ideological. Along with other forms of publicity, film posters mainly show stereotypical individuals and objects, in stereotypical relations and situations. In *Mythologies* and subsequent texts, Barthes gave us the means to demystify and dismantle such "rhetoric of the image" in terms of counterideological analyses such as Marxism and semiology. In "En sortant du cinéma," Barthes uses a Lacanian vocabulary. In these terms, what constitutes the imaginary exceeds what an ordinary taxonomy of objects of daily use may classify as "images." The beautiful woman and the attractive boy not only have their counterparts in actual film posters; they may serve as living photograms—ideologemes—in Barthes's cinema of society. In "En sortant du cinéma," Barthes asks in passing, "Do we not have a dual relation to the common place [*lieu commun*]: narcissistic and maternal?"[14] The woman trails behind her "a scent of muguet." In France, by long tradition, sprigs of muguet—a small, white, bell-shaped flower—are sold on the streets on the first of May. Small children—raised in their mother's shadow—learn the division of common time through such traditions. This woman who casts the shadow of time itself might be assimilated to the maternal side of the "dual relation" Barthes invokes. The "attractive silhouette" of the boy—whose fugitive character elicits what Benjamin called "love at last sight" (prompted by Baudelaire's verses *A une passante*)—might be assimilated to the other, narcissistic side.

Another evening in Paris Barthes follows a route that will eventually lead to the "dark cube" of a movie theater. He first visits a gay bathhouse, then moves on to what seems to be some sort of brothel. Here Barthes notes: "about to leave is a beautiful Moroccan who would really like to hook me [*m'accrocher*] and gives me a long look; he will wait in the dining room until I come down again, seems disappointed that I don't take him right away (vague *rendez-vous* for the following day). I leave feeling light, physically good [. . .]."[15] The image of Barthes on the stair, exchanging glances with the "beautiful Moroccan," reminds me of another image. Bergala's note on *La Paresse* is part of a Godard filmography in a special issue of *Cahiers du Cinéma.* A band of photograms runs horizontally along the bottom of each page of the filmography—less like a filmstrip than a comic strip, or *photo roman.* One of the images is from *La Paresse.* Eddie Constantine appears to have just descended a carpeted staircase, which winds up and out of frame behind him. He is immaculately dressed in suit and tie and is wearing a hat. He is looking at the starlet—who is standing close by him, dressed only in her underwear. Barthes traces Brecht's idea of the "social gest" to Diderot's concept of tableau. The tableau has a history prior to Diderot. In the mid-sixteenth century, humanist scholars gave advice to painters in which two ideas were essential: first, the painter should depict human action in its most exemplary moral forms; second, since the "history painter" could show only a single moment from a moral fable, that moment should be the *peripateia*—the "decisive moment" when all hangs in the balance.[16] The images of Barthes and Constantine on the stairs both have something about them of a motif that appears throughout the history of Western European painting: "Hercules at the Crossroads." To a "counterideological discourse," the inequitable distribution of material authority across the lines of, respectively, race and gender is obvious in both of these modern *mise-en-scènes.* My particular interest here is in what this image condenses of Bergala's description of Godard's film and what, in turn, this description condenses of Barthes's remarks on "*la situation de cinéma.*" The woman in the diegesis is making a spectacle of herself; in French one might say "*elle fait son cinéma.*" Constantine on the stair, much like Barthes on the stair, responds with, to repeat Bergala's words, "an apparent inertia which is in fact a state of great porosity to the strangeness of the world, a mixture of torpor, of loss of reality and of a somewhat hallucinatory vivacity of sensations."

The expression "hallucinatory vivacity" may remind us of Barthes's description of the photograph. The photograph, he says, represents "an anthropologically new object" in that it constitutes "a new form of hallucination: false at the level of perception, true at the level of time."[17] The film, on the other hand, is "always the precise opposite of an hallucination; it is simply an illusion [. . .]." The film "can present the cultural signs of madness, [but] is never mad by nature" (*CC*, 181). To the contrary, the photograph is an authentically "mad image, rubbed by the real" (*CC*, 177). Nevertheless, the abrasion of image against real, which Barthes finds and values in photography, is at least structurally similar to his readiness, when in the cinema, "to be fascinated *two times*: by the image and by what surrounds it." In *Roland Barthes par Roland Barthes*, he writes: "The dream displeases me because one is entirely absorbed by it: the dream is *monological*; and the fantasy pleases me because it remains concomitant to the consciousness of reality (that of the place where I am); thus is created a double space, dislocated, spaced out [. . .]" (90). These men on the stairs are not sleepwalkers, but they are "spaced out." In "En sortant du cinéma," it is as if Barthes is urging a practice of spectatorship that will pull the filmic experience toward the side of fantasy and away from the shore of the dream. Barthes's inclination to phenomenology leads him to seek mutually exclusive "essences" of film and photography. But such oppositions fade as he steers closer to semiology and psychoanalysis. Barthes himself admits as much, even in one of his more "phenomenological" texts. On the first page of *La Chambre claire*, he writes: "I declared that I liked Photography *against* the cinema—from which, however, I never managed to separate it" (*CC*, 13). Here then is another site of abrasion: where photography touches cinema. Barthes's well-known interest in the film still is often mentioned to exemplify his preference for the photograph over the film. The "photogram," however, is strictly neither photograph nor film. It is the material trace of that moment of arrest that establishes a space between the photograph and the film. In terms of Lacan's discussion of the gaze, to which Barthes explicitly gestures in "En sortant du cinéma," this time of arrest is that of the "lure."

The filmic image, says Barthes, is "a *lure.*" He adds: "This word must be understood in the analytical sense" ("En sortant du cinéma," 106; *RL*, 347). Lacan uses the word *leurre* with the full range of meanings it takes in French: "lure," "bait," and "decoy"; "allurement" and "enticement";

"trap," "delusion," and "deceit." The analytical sense Lacan brings to it comes most specifically from what he makes of Roger Caillois's remarks on the "three functions of mimicry."[18] In the animal and insect behaviors named by Caillois as travesty, camouflage, and intimidation, Lacan says, "the being gives of itself, or it receives from the other, something which is mask, double, envelope, detached skin, detached to cover the frame of a shield."[19] The frame from *La Paresse* depicts just such a meeting of masks—as beautiful as the chance encounter, on a staircase, of some undergarments with a business suit. "Without any doubt," Lacan remarks, "it is by the intermediary of masks that the masculine, the feminine, meet in the most pointed, the most ardent, way (99)." However, Lacan notes a difference between human behavior and the behaviors described by Caillois: "Only the subject—the human subject, the subject of desire [. . .]—is not, unlike the animal, entirely held by this imaginary capture. He takes his bearings in it (*Il s'y repère*). How? To the extent that he isolates the function of the screen, and plays with it. Man, in effect, knows how to play with the mask, as being that beyond which there is the gaze. The screen is here the place of mediation (99)."

Christian Vincent's film *La Discrète* is a story of seduction and betrayal set in modern-day Paris.[20] It takes its title, however, from a seventeenth-century practice. Fashionable women of that period would wear a "beauty spot"—usually a dot of black taffeta—on their faces. Worn on the forehead it was called a *majestueuse*; placed by the eye it was a *passionnée*; by the lips, a *galante*; and on the chin, a *discrète*. In eighteenth-century Venice, the *moretta* was one of only two masks worn at carnival time, and it was worn only by women. The *moretta* was held in position by means of a button gripped between the teeth; in order to speak, the woman had to unmask, quite literally to "reveal herself." Both practices exemplify a play with the mask in the field of the gaze. As in all play—productive of spacing, difference—meaning is created. A fascination beyond words is at the same time a potentially garrulous semiotic system. For the human animal, the lure is a place of passage between imaginary and symbolic, between the drive and the contractual regulation of sexuality. What flickers on the screen of the lure is the dance of desire and the law. Barthes emphasizes that the filmic image, which so often stages the scene of lure, is itself a lure. However, so—potentially—is any other image in the "Cinema of society." Barthes himself recognizes this in the very terms of his exasperation at the film poster he comes across in the rue Guynemer, the actresses' names printed large, "as if they were incontestable bait" (*appâts*). The looks given by the actresses emerge from within an image-product of a visual cultural institution—here, the cinema—of the cinema of society. That is to say, the look emerges from within the gaze.

Among the various functions of the gaze is the subjection of what Barthes calls the "historical subject." Lacan gives the example of the mural paintings that adorn the great hall of the Palace of the Doges, in Venice: "Who comes to these places? Those who form that which Metz calls *the people*. And what do the people see in these vast compositions? The gaze of those persons who—when they are not there, they the people—deliberate in this hall. Behind the painting, it is their gaze which is there."[21] Today, the environment of images from what we call "the media" has taken the place and the function of those murals in the Palace of the Doges. Lacan does not mention it, but the paintings—like the products of the media today—would also have been an object of wonder and delight, of fascination, for those subjected to the authority of those who commissioned the images. The long history of the multiple forms of decoration and pageant in society demonstrates the inseparability of power from visible display: the element of hypnotic fascination in voluntary submission. However, such means of control are unstable, and the history of authority is also one of struggle for mastery of the "twilight reverie."

Lassitude, inertia, torpor; a body become soporific, soft, limp; a loss of reality, a porosity to the strangeness of the world, a hallucinatory vivacity of sensations. A "very special way of being in the world," known for centuries of Western Christianity as *acedia*—a state of mortal sin. In his book on the concept of *acedia* in medieval thought and literature, Siegfried Wenzel traces the notion of the "sin of sloth" to the fourth Christian century and the milieu of Egyptian desert monks who lived near Alexandria.[22] For these monks, Acedia was the name of a demon with whom they frequently fought. A stealthy drowsiness would announce the demon's arrival. An assault of impressions, thoughts, and feelings that could overwhelm devotional duty would follow. Monks became melancholy; they found it difficult to remain in their cells and would wander out in search of the secular world they had renounced. By the twelfth century, *acedia*—sloth—was firmly established as one of the "seven deadly sins." Its most "modern" description, however, was given at the inception of the concept. Wenzel writes that, in the early Christian moral theology of Clement of Alexandria, *acedia* was judged to be the product of "affections of the irrational part of man's soul, which originate in sense impressions or in memory and are often accompanied by pleasure." In the soporific state of *acedia*, "reason is [. . .] subjected to the ebb and flow of affections, which tyrannize it and keep it in a state of turmoil—the master has become a slave (13–14)."

Acedia, then, threatens the hierarchical order of things: the theocentric order of Christianity, certainly, but also the secular world order of Western capitalism that succeeded it. The religious education of the industrial proletariat continued to stress that "the devil finds work for idle hands." Common soldiers in imperialist armies, when neither fighting nor training, were put to such work as whitewashing lumps of coal. Fundamental to the instrumental logic of slave ownership was the category of the "lazy slave"; in the logic of the colonialist it was the "lazy native." Clearly the threat of lassitude was less to production than to authority—whether that of God or Mammon. Lassitude can be highly productive, but it produces insubordination and syndicalism, mutinies and revolutions. At this point, however, we may no longer distinguish between the corrosive consequences of lassitude and the products of a counterideological reason honed through leisure.

Until about the twelfth century, *acedia* was considered to be mainly a monastic vice, one that attacked those devoted to the contemplative life.[23] In "Soirées de Paris," Barthes confesses to his difficulty in remaining in his cell: "Always this difficulty in working in the afternoon, I went out around six-thirty, looking for adventure."[24] It would not have surprised a desert monk to learn that Barthes wound up soliciting a male prostitute on the rue de Rennes, giving him money on the promise of a rendezvous an hour later. "Naturally," Barthes writes, "he wasn't there." Barthes acknowledges how barely credible his action must seem, in exchanging money for such a promise. But he also recognizes that, whether or not he had gone to bed with this man, "at eight o'clock I would have found myself again at the same point in my life; and, as the simple contact of the eyes, of the promise, eroticises me, it is for this *jouissance* that I had paid (87)." In this particular sector of the libidinal economy, sexual tension is perversely spent in the exchange not only of promises but of temporal location—here coined in a grammatical tense, the future anterior: "I shall have had." Constantine, spaced-out, refuses sex with the starlet because he speaks to her from a different time—the aftermath of the afterglow. *Acedia* is a complex vice. The fourth century treatises on spiritual life that established the concept of *acedia* also inaugurated the practice, followed in medieval handbooks, of identifying the "daughters" to whom this or that of the seven capital sins had given birth. Disobedience was only one of the daughters of *acedia*; among the many others was Deferment.

Metz refers to the "novelistic film" as "a mill of images and sounds which overfeed our zones of shadow and irresponsibility."[25] Barthes defers feeding—like a recalcitrant infant who turns from the breast in search of adjacent pleasures, even, or especially, those "not good for it." He asks: "could there be, in the cinema itself (and in taking the word in its etymological profile), a possible *jouissance* of *discretion*?" ("En sortant," 107; *RL*, 349). In exercising his discretion, Barthes is at the same time at the discretion of something else. His presence in the cinema is impulsive. In *Le Plaisir du texte,* he speaks of "that moment when my body goes to follow its own ideas—for my body does not have the same ideas as I do" (30). The pressures of a "twilight reverie" impel Barthes "from street to street, from poster to poster," to immerse himself in darkness. Freud spoke of "somnambulistic certainty" to characterize the unerring confidence with which, under certain circumstances, a long-lost object is found.[26] All that is certain in our compulsion to repeat, however, is that the object will elude us. ("Naturally," Barthes writes, having kept the rendezvous, "he wasn't there.") As to the source of our need to keep keeping, in Lacan's words, "an appointment [. . .] with a real that escapes us,"[27] we are all in the dark. Clement of Alexandria found *acedia* to be the product of "affections of the irrational part of man's soul, which originate in sense impressions or in memory [. . .] often accompanied by pleasure." This psychoanalytic judgment *avant la lettre* suggests that "this special way of being in the world, on the edge of sleep" steers us closer to the shores of that "other locality" where Freud first took his bearings: "another space, another scene, *the between perception and consciousness.*"[28]

Between the spectator totally enthralled by the narrative and the critic who sits analyzing shots, there is a continuum of degrees of alertness. Barthes, however, sliding down into his seat, adopts a posture toward the film that cannot be assigned to a simple position on a scale between enthrallment and vigilance. "I am hypnotized by a distance," he writes, "and this distance is not critical (intellectual); it is, if one can say this, an amorous distance." A *jouissance* of discretion. A pleasure in differences, distances. A tactful delight in heterogeneity: the "flickering grace of all the elements of life" that Baudelaire found on the streets of Paris, now revealed by the flickering light of the projector in the auditorium. The café-frequenting spectator's glass of Kir and dish of olives have given way to Coca-Cola and buttered popcorn, but the society is no less utopian. In American cities, where "street life" so often gives way to "street death," the citizen is almost certainly safer in the movie theater than at home, at work, or in prison. In a world riven by violent factional and fractional conflict, the cinema is peaceful. The cinema audience—a totally aleatory conglomeration of alterities—sleeps together in a space of finely judged proximities, a *touching* space.

On leaving the cinema, the cinema of society, we reenter a global cinema, where cultural and ideological differences come together in intimate electronic proximity. In this cinema, too, the image is a lure. Flickering on the hook is the alternative the mirror relation presents: narcissistic identification or aggressive rivalry. Here also, Barthes seems to suggest, we may defer taking the bait—but not in order to calculate a fine scale of "correct distances" between fusion and abjection. The distance that hypnotizes him, Barthes says, is not intellectual but "amorous." The territory of this distance is claimed in the name of lassitude. Exercising a somnolent discretion, from within a state of great porosity to the strangeness of the world, Barthes embraces that daughter of *acedia* whom we can only name—in the full sense of the word—*dissipation*.

Notes

1. Hollis Frampton, "For a Metahistory of Film: Commonplace Notes and Hypotheses" [1971], in *Circles of Confusion: Film, Photography, Video, Texts, 1968–1980* (Rochester, N.Y.: Visual Studies Workshop, 1983), p. 116.

2. Jean-Luc Godard, *La Paresse*, episode of *Sept péchés capitaux* (1961). Eddie Constantine (Eddie Constantine), Nicole Mirel (the Starlet). [Other episodes by Claude Chabrol, Edouard Molinaro, Jacques Demy, Roger Vadim, Philippe de Broca, Sylvain Dhomme.]

3. Alain Bergala, note on *La Paresse, Cahiers du Cinéma: Godard, trente ans depuis* (1990): 114.

4. Christian Metz, "Le Film de fiction et son spectateur," *Communications* 23 (1975): 119.

5. Roland Barthes, "En sortant du cinéma," *Communications* 23 (1975): 104–7. Translations are mine, although the piece appears in English translation as "Leaving the Movie Theater," in *RL*, pp. 345–49.

6. Breuer and Freud refer to "the semi-hypnotic twilight state of daydreaming, auto-hypnoses, and so on." *The Standard Edition of the Complete Psychological Works of Sigmund Freud*, vol. 2 (London: Hogarth, 1955), p. 11.

7. Barthes plays on various senses of the verb *décoller*, which can mean not only to "unstick" but also to "take off" (in the aeronautical sense) and to "get high" (in the drug-use sense).

8. Giuliana Bruno, *Streetwalking on a Ruined Map: Cultural Theory and the City Films of Elvira Notari* (Princeton, N.J.: Princeton University Press, 1993), chapter 3.

9. Roland Barthes, "Au Palace ce soir," in *Incidents* (Paris: Seuil, 1987), p. 65 (translation mine).

10. Roland Barthes, *Le Plaisir du texte* (Paris: Seuil, 1973), p. 19.

11. Charles Baudelaire, "The Painter of Modern Life," in *The Painter of Modern Life and Other Essays* (New York: Garland, 1978), p. 10.

12. Roland Barthes, *Roland Barthes par Roland Barthes* (Paris: Seuil, 1975), p. 98.

13. Barthes, *Incidents*, p. 86.

14. In French, a *lieu commun* is a platitude (cf. English "commonplace"); at the same time, taken word for word, it may mean "common place," in the sense of "public space."

15. Barthes, *Incidents*, p. 104.

16. See Victor Burgin, "Diderot, Barthes, *Vertigo*," in *The End of Art Theory: Criticism and Postmodernity* (London: Macmillan, 1986).

17. Roland Barthes, *La Chambre claire* (Paris: Cahiers du cinéma, 1980), p. 177. Hereafter abbreviated as *CC* in the text.

18. Roger Caillois, *Méduse et Cie* (Paris: Gallimard, 1960), 71 ff.

19. Jacques Lacan, *Le Séminaire, livre 11, Les Quatres concepts fondamentaux de la psychanalyse* (Paris: Seuil, 1973) p. 98.

20. Christian Vincent, *La Discrète* (1990), with Fabrice Luchini and Judith Henry.

21. Lacan, *Le Séminaire,* livre 11, p. 104.

22. Siegfried Wenzel, *The Sin of Sloth: Acedia in Medieval Thought and Literature* (Chapel Hill: University of North Carolina Press, 1960).

23. Ibid., p. 35.

24. Barthes, *Incidents,* p. 87.

25. Christian Metz, "Le Film de fiction et son spectateur," p. 112.

26. Sigmund Freud, *The Standard Edition of the Complete Psychological Works of Sigmund Freud,* vol. 6 (London: Hogarth, 1960), pp. 140, 142, 150.

27. Lacan, *Le Séminaire,* livre 11, p. 53.

28. Ibid., p. 55.

2

"What has occurred only once"

Barthes's Winter Garden/Boltanski's Archives of the Dead

Marjorie Perloff

I begin with two photographs, both of them family snapshots of what are evidently a young mother and her little boy in a country setting (Figures 2.1 and 2.2). Neither is what we would call a "good" (i.e., well-composed) picture. True, the one is more "expressive," the anxious little boy clinging somewhat fearfully to his mother (Figure 2.1), whereas the impassive woman and child look straight ahead at the camera (Figure 2.2).

The second pair of photographs are class pictures (Figures 2.3 and 2.4): The first, an end-of-the-year group photo of a smiling high-school class with their nonsmiling male teacher in the first row, center; the second, a more adult (postgraduate?) class, with their teacher (front row, third from the left) distinguished by his white hair, and smiling ever so slightly in keeping with what is evidently the collegial spirit of the attractive young group.

Both sets may be used to illustrate many of the points Barthes makes about photography in *Camera Lucida.* First, these pictures are entirely ordinary—the sort of photographs we all have in our albums. Their appeal, therefore, can only be to someone personally involved with their subjects, someone for whom they reveal the "that-has-been" (*ça a été*) that is, for Barthes, the essence or *noème* of photography. "The photographic referent," we read in #32, "[is] not the *optionally* real thing to which an image or a sign refers but the *necessarily* real thing which has been placed before the lens, without which there would be no photograph. [. . .] [I]n Photography I can never deny that *the thing has been there*" (*CL*, 76). And again, "The photograph is literally an emanation of the referent" (*CL*, 80). In this sense, "every photograph is a certificate of presence" (*CL*, 87).

Figure 2.1. "La Demande d'amour." Anonymous photograph (1923), in *Roland Barthes par Roland Barthes* (Paris: Seuil, 1975), p. 7 ("The Demand for Love," in *Roland Barthes by Roland Barthes*, trans. Richard Howard [New York: *Farrar, Straus, and Giroux*, 1977], unpaginated photo section preceding text). Courtesy of Editions du Seuil.

Figure 2.2. (below) Christian Boltanski, from *Album de photos de la famille D, 1939–1964.* Artist's book of 150 black-and-white photographs (self-published, 1971). Courtesy of Marian Goodman Gallery, New York.

Figure 2.3. Christian Boltanski, from *Classe terminale du Lycée Chases en 1931.* Artist's book of 38 black-and-white photographs (Saint-Etienne: Maison de la culture et de la communication de Saint-Etienne, 1987). Courtesy of Marian Goodman Gallery, New York.

Figure 2.4. "L'espace du séminaire . . . [de l'Ecole des Hautes-Etudes]." Photograph by Daniel Boudinet (1974), in *Roland Barthes par Roland Barthes,* p. 173 ("The Space of the Seminar . . . ," in *Roland Barthes by Roland Barthes,* p. 171). © Ministère de la Culture–France.

But "presence," in this instance, goes hand in hand with death. "What the Photograph reproduces to infinity has occurred only once: the Photograph mechanically repeats what could never be repeated existentially" (*CL*, 4). As soon as the click of the shutter has taken place, what was photographed no longer exists; subject is transformed into object, "and even," Barthes suggests, "into a museum object" (*CL*, 13). When we look at a photograph of ourselves or of others, we are really looking at the return of the dead. "Death is the *eidos* of the Photograph" (*CL*, 15).

Christian Boltanski, whose photographs I have paired with two of the illustrations in *Roland Barthes by Roland Barthes*, shares Barthes's predilection for the ordinary photograph, the photograph of everyday life. Like Barthes, he dislikes "art photography," photography that approaches the condition of painting. For him, too, the interesting photograph provides the viewer with testimony that the thing seen *has been*, that *it is thus*. In Barthes's words, "the Photograph is never anything but an antiphon of 'Look,' 'See,' 'Here it is'; it points a finger at certain *vis-à-vis*, and cannot escape this pure deictic language" (*CL*, 5). But, in Boltanski's oeuvre, as we shall see, this pure deictic language, this pointing at "what has occurred only once" (4), takes on an edge unanticipated in the phenomenology of *Camera Lucida*.

Consider the mother-and-child snapshots above. Both foreground the "real" referent of the image, the outdoor scene that the camera reproduces. But in what sense are the photographs "certificates of presence"? Figure 2.1 portrays Roland Barthes, age five or six, held by his mother, who stands at some distance from a house (her house?) in a nonspecifiable countryside. The mother's clothes and hairdo place the photograph somewhere in the 1920s; the long-legged boy in kneesocks, shorts, and sweater seems rather big to be held on his mother's arm like a baby. The caption on the facing page accounts for this phenomenon: it reads, "The demand for love [*la demande d'amour*]" (*RB*, 5).

The second photograph (Figure 2.2) is part of a work (similarly published in the early 1970s) called *Album de photos de la famille D, 1939–64*, which depicts a "family" (are they a family?) Boltanski did not know. He borrowed several photo albums from his friend Michel Durand-Dessert (hence the *D*), reshot some 150 snapshots from these albums, and tried to establish their chronology as well as the identities of their subjects using what he called an ethnological approach: for example, "the older man who appeared only at festive occasions must be an uncle who did not live in the vicinity."[1] But the sequence he constructed (see Figure 2.5) turned out to be incorrect: "I realized," the artist remarked, "that these images were only witnesses to a collective ritual. They didn't teach us anything about the Family D. [. . .] but only sent us back to

Figure 2.5. Christian Boltanski, "24 photographies extraites de *L'Album de la famille D, 1939–64*" (1971). Courtesy of Marian Goodman Gallery, New York.

our own past."[2] And, since the snapshots in the sequence date from the French Occupation and its immediate aftermath, the viewer begins to wonder what this bourgeois provincial family was doing during the war. Were these men on the battlefield? Were they Nazi collaborators or resistance fighters? Did these women have to harbor the enemy? And so on. What, in short, is it that *has been* in the snapshot of the young woman and small boy resting in a shady meadow?

Similar questions are raised by the second Boltanski photograph above. Again, the two class pictures make an interesting pair. In Figure 2.4, we have one of the "*S*" entries in *Roland Barthes by Roland Barthes*: a photograph of Barthes's seminar, taken sometime in the 1970s. The caption reads: "The space of the seminar is phalansteric, i.e., in a sense, fictive, novelistic. It is only the space of the circulation of subtle desires, mobile desires; it is, within the artifice of a sociality whose consistency is miraculously extenuated, according to a phrase of Nietzsche's: 'the tangle of amorous relations' " (*RB*, 171). The "real," "referential" photograph thus becomes an occasion for pleasurable erotic fantasy.

In contrast, the other class photograph (Figure 2.3) is a picture Boltanski came across by chance. It portrays the 1931 graduating class of the Lycée Chases (Chases Gymnasium), the Jewish high school in Vienna, which was shut down shortly after this end-of-the-year group photograph was taken. If, as Barthes posits, the photograph is coterminal with its referent, here the "death" of its subjects produced by the camera may well have foreshadowed their real death in the camps. For his 1986 installation *Lycée Chases*, Boltanski rephotographed the individual smiling faces in this "ordinary" class photograph, enlarging them until they lost any sense of individuality and began to look like skeletal X rays or, better yet, death masks (Figures 2.6 and 2.7). Yet this version is no more "real" than the other, since Boltanski never learned what actually happened to the members of the class of 1931. When *Lycée Chases* was shown in New York in 1987, one of the students in the photograph, now in his late sixties, came forward and identified himself to Boltanski. But this Chases graduate, who had emigrated to the United States in the early 1930s, knew nothing of the fate of the other students.[3]

"Every photograph," says Barthes, "is somehow co-natural with its referent" (*CL*, 76). But what is the referent of the Chajes graduation picture? What "evidential force" does it possess and for whom? To answer this question, we might begin with Barthes's famed Winter Garden photograph, the photograph whose *punctum* (the prick, sting, or sudden wound that makes a particular photograph epiphanic to a particular viewer) is so powerful, so overwhelming, so implicated in Barthes's anticipation of his own death that he simply cannot reproduce it in *La Chambre claire.*

(I cannot reproduce the Winter Garden Photograph. It exists only for me. For you, it would be nothing but an indifferent picture, one of the thousand manifestations of the "ordinary"; it cannot in any way constitute the visible object of a science; it cannot establish an objectivity, in the positive sense of the term; at most it would interest your *studium*: period, clothes, photogeny; but in it, for you, no wound). (*CL*, 73)

Figure 2.6. Christian Boltanski, from *Le Lycée Chases* (1987). Courtesy of Marian Goodman Gallery, New York.

The Winter Garden photograph thus becomes the absent (and hence more potent) referent of Barthes's paean to presence, a paean that takes the form of an elegiac *ekphrasis*.

"One November evening, shortly after my mother's death," Barthes recalls, "I was going through some photographs. I had no hope of 'finding' her. I expected nothing from these 'photographs of a being before

Figure 2.7. Christian Boltanski, from *Le Lycée Chases* (1987). Courtesy of Marian Goodman Gallery, New York.

which one recalls less of that being than by merely thinking of him or her' " (*CL*, 63). And Barthes puts in parentheses following the quote the name of the writer who is the tutelary spirit behind his own lyric meditation—Proust. Like the Proust of *Les Intermittences du coeur*, Barthes's narrator has learned, from the repeated disillusionments of life, to expect nothing. The mood is autumnal, sepulchral, and the image of the dead mother cannot be recovered—at least not by the voluntary memory. Different photographs capture different aspects of her person but not the "truth of the face I had loved": "I was struggling among images partially true and therefore totally false" (*CL*, 66).

As in Proust, the miraculous privileged moment, the prick of the *punctum*, comes when least expected. The uniqueness of the Winter Garden photograph—an old, faded, album snapshot with "blunted" corners—is that it allows Barthes to "see" his mother, not as he actually saw her in their life together (this would be a mere *studium* on his part), but as the child he had never known in real life, a five-year-old girl standing with her seven-year-old brother "at the end of a little wooden bridge in a glassed-in conservatory" (*CL*, 67). We learn that brother and sister are united "by the discord of their parents, who were soon to divorce" (*CL*, 69). But in Barthes's myth, this little girl is somehow self-born. "In this little girl's image I saw the kindness which had formed her being immediately and forever, without her having inherited it from anyone; how could this kindness have proceeded from the imperfect parents who had loved her so badly—in short, from a family?" (*CL*, 69). In an imaginative reversal, the mother-as-child in the Winter Garden photograph now becomes his child: "I who had not procreated, I had, in her very illness, engendered my mother" (*CL*, 72). The tomblike glass conservatory thus becomes the site of birth.

"The unknown photographer of Chennevières-sur-Marne," Barthes remarks, "had been a mediator of a truth" (*CL*, 70)—indeed, of *the* truth. His inconsequential little snapshot "achieved for me, utopically, *the impossible science of the unique being*" (*CL*, 71)—impossible because the uniqueness of that being is, after all, only in the eye of the beholder. Like Proust's Marcel, the Barthesian subject must evidently purge himself of the guilt prompted by the unstated conviction that his own "deviation" (sexual or otherwise) from the bourgeois norms of his childhood world must have caused his mother a great deal of pain. Like Marcel, he therefore invents for himself a perfect mother, her goodness and purity deriving from no one (for family is the enemy in this scheme of things). Gentleness is all: "during the whole of our life together," writes Barthes in a Proustian locution, "she never made a single 'observation'" (*CL*, 69). Thus perfected, the mother must of course be dead; the very snapshot that brings her to life testifies to the irreversibility of her death.

Barthes understands only too well that the *punctum* of this photograph is his alone, for no one else would read the snapshot quite as he does. The "emanation of the referent," which is for him the essence of the photograph, is thus a wholly personal connection. The intense, violent, momentary pleasure (*jouissance*) that accompanies one's reception of the photograph's "unique Being" is individual and "magical," for unlike all other representations, the photograph is an image without a code (*CL*, 88), the eruption of the Lacanian "Real" into the signifying chain, a "*satori* in which words fail" (*CL*, 109).

As an elegy for his mother and as a kind of epitaph for himself, *Camera Lucida* is intensely moving. But what about Barthes's insistence on the "realism" of the photograph, his conviction that it bears witness to what has occurred only once? "From a phenomenological viewpoint," says Barthes, "in the Photograph, the power of authentication exceeds the power of representation" (*CL*, 89). Authentication of what and for whom? Here Boltanski's photographic representations of everyday life raise some hard questions. Indeed, the distance between Barthes's generation and Boltanski's—a distance all the more remarkable in that such central Boltanski photo installations as *La Famille D*, *Le Club Mickey*, and *Détective* date from the very years when Barthes was composing *Roland Barthes by Roland Barthes*, *A Lover's Discourse*, and *Camera Lucida*—can be measured by the revisionist treatment Boltanski accords to the phenomenology of authentication practiced by the late Barthes.

Roland Barthes was born in the first year of World War I (26 October 1915); Christian Boltanski, in the last year of World War II, specifically on the day of Paris's liberation (6 September 1944)—hence his middle name, Liberté. Barthes's Catholic father was killed in October 1916 in a naval battle in the North Sea; the fatherless child was brought up in Bayonne by his mother and maternal grandmother in an atmosphere he described as one of genteel poverty and narrow Protestant bourgeois rectitude. Boltanski's father, a prominent doctor, was born a Jew but converted to Catholicism; his mother, a writer, was Catholic, and young Christian was educated by the Jesuits. To avoid deportation in 1940, the Boltanskis faked a divorce and pretended the doctor had fled, abandoning his family, whereas in reality he was hidden in the basement of the family home, in the center of Paris, for the duration of the Occupation. The death of Barthes's father, an event his son understood early on as being only too "real," may thus be contrasted to the simulated "death" of Dr. Boltanski at the time of his son's birth. Indeed, this sort of simulation, not yet a central issue in World War I when battlelines were drawn on nationalistic rather than ideological grounds, became important in the years of the resistance, when simulation and appropriation became common means of survival. For example, in his fictionalized autobiography *W or the Memory of Childhood*, Georges Perec (a writer Boltanski greatly admires and has cited frequently) recalls that his widowed mother, who was to die at Auschwitz, got him out of Paris and into the Free Zone by putting him on a Red Cross convoy for the wounded en route to Grenoble. "I was not wounded. But I had to be evacuated. So we had to pretend I was wounded. That was why my arm was in a sling."[4]

Under such circumstances, *authentication* becomes a contested term. How does one document what has occurred only once when the event itself is perceived to be a simulation? And to what extent has the experience of *studium* versus *punctum* become collective, rather than the fiercely personal experience it was for Barthes? In a 1984 interview held in conjunction with the Boltanski exhibition at the Centre Pompidou in Paris, Delphine Renard asked the artist how and why he had chosen photography as his medium. "At first," he replied, "what especially interested me was the property granted to photography of furnishing the evidence of the real [*la preuve du réel*]: a scene that has been photographed is experienced as being true. [. . .] If someone exhibits the photograph of an old lady and the viewer tells himself, today, she must be dead, he experiences an emotion which is not only of an aesthetic order."[5]

Here Boltanski seems to accept the Barthesian premise that the "photographic referent" is "not the *optionally* real thing to which an image or a sign refers but the *necessarily* real thing which has been placed before the lens, without which there would be no photograph. [. . .] [I]n Photography I can never deny that *the thing has been there.*" But for Boltanski, this "reasonable" definition is not without its problems:

> In my first little book, *Tout ce qui reste de mon enfance* of 1969, there is a photograph that supplies the apparent proof that I went on vacation to the seashore with my parents, but it is an unidentifiable photograph of a child and a group of adults on the beach. One can also see the photograph of the bed I slept in when I was five years old; naturally, the caption orients the spectator, but the documents are purposely false. [. . .] In most of my photographic pieces, I have utilized this property of the proof one accords to photography to expose it or to try to show that *photography lies, that it doesn't speak the truth but rather the cultural code.* (*BOL*, 75; emphasis added)

Such cultural coding, Boltanski argues, characterizes even the most innocent snapshot (say, the Winter Garden photograph). The amateur photograph of the late nineteenth century was based on a preexisting image that was culturally imposed—an image derived from the painting of the period. Even today the amateur photographer "shows nothing but images of happiness, lovely children running around on green meadows: he reconstitutes an image he already knows" (*BOL*, 76). Tourists in Venice, for example, who think they are taking "authentic" photographs of this or that place, are actually recognizing the "reality" through the lens of a set of clichés they have unconsciously absorbed; indeed, they want these pictures to resemble those they already know. So Boltanski creates an experiment. Together with Annette Messager he produces a piece called *Le Voyage de noces à Venise* (1975), composed of photographs taken elsewhere (*BOL*, 76). And in another book, *10 portraits photo-*

graphiques de Christian Boltanski, 1946–1964 (1972), the temporal frame (the boy is depicted at different ages) is a pure invention; all the photographs were actually taken the same day (Figure 2.8). "This little book," says the artist, "was designed to show that Christian Boltanski had only a collective reality . . . [that of] a child in a given society" (*BOL*, 79). In a related book, *Ce dont ils se souviennent*, we see what looks like an updated version of a Proustian scene in which the narrator and Gilberte play together in the Champs-Elysées (Figure 2.9); here, ostensibly, are young Christian's friends playing on the seesaw in the park. This simple little photograph is enormously tricky. There are actually three seesaws, as evident from the three horizontal shadows stretching across the ground in the bottom of the frame.[6] The two little girls next to one another on parallel seesaws on the left look normal enough, but what is happening at the other end? The slightly crouching boy in the center (his legs straddling a third seesaw) seems to be staring at what looks like an extra leg, its knee bent on the board opposite—a leg that suggests a body on the rack rather than a child at play. The impression is created by the photograph's odd lighting: the figure on the far right, who is evidently holding down one seesaw in balance, blocks the second figure (feet dangling) and the head and torso of the third. Moreover, the ropelike thin line of the third seesaw extends from that bent leg on the right to the head of the little girl at its opposite pole, creating the illusion that she is chained to it. Thus the little playground scene takes on an aura of isolation and imprisonment. Is it winter (the white area could be snow) or a scorchingly sunny summer? The more one looks at this "ordinary" photograph (actually, Boltanski tells us, a found photograph taken from the album of a young woman), the less clear the "emanation of the referent" becomes.

But Boltanski's is by no means a simple reversal of the Barthesian *noème*. For the paradox is that, like Barthes and even more like Perec, he finds nothing as meaningful as the ordinary object, the trivial detail. Photography for him is a form of ethnography. Boltanski has spoken often of his early fascination with the displays in the Musée de l'Homme, not so much the displays of large pieces of African sculpture but of everyday objects—Eskimo fishhooks, arrows from the Amazon valley, and so on:

> I saw large metal boxes in which there were little objects, fragile and without signification. In the corner of the case there was often a small faded photograph representing a "savage" in the middle of handling these little objects. Each case presented a world that has disappeared: the savage of the photograph was no doubt dead, the objects had become useless, and, anyway, no one knew how to use them any more. The Musée de l'Homme appeared to me as a great morgue. Numerous artists have here discovered the human sciences (linguistics, sociology, archeology); here there is still the "weight of time" which imposes itself

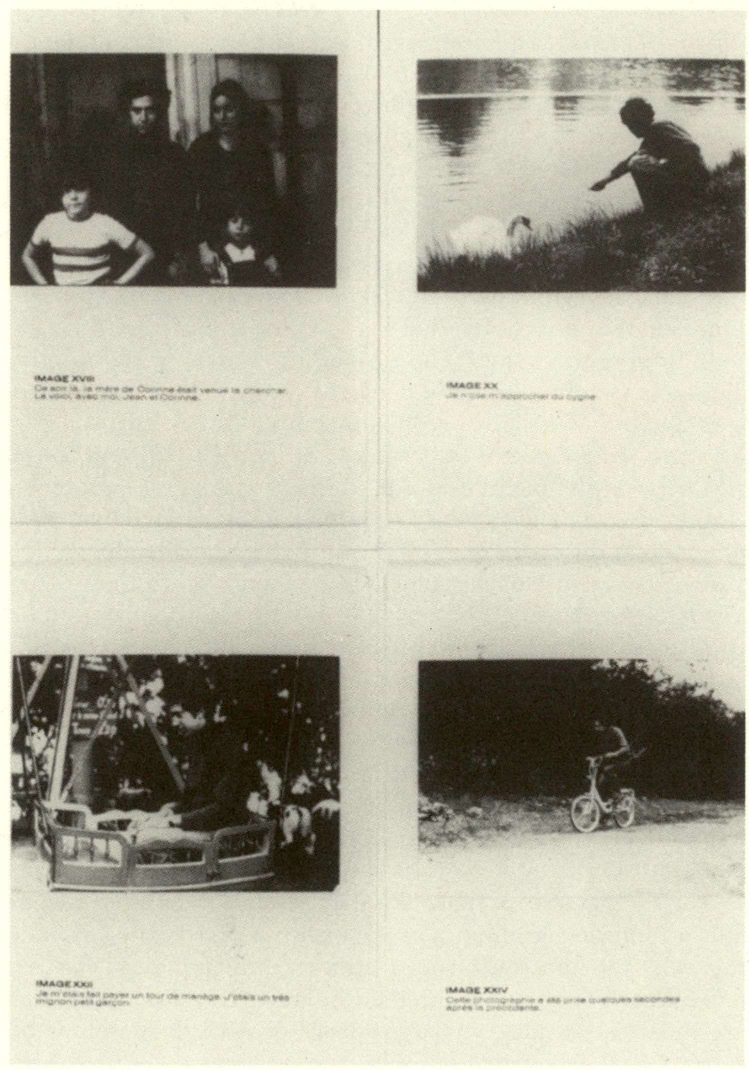

Figure 2.8. Christian Boltanski, from *10 portraits photographiques de Christian Boltanski, 1946–1964*. Artist's book (Paris: Editions Multiplicata, 1972). Courtesy of Marian Goodman Gallery, New York.

Figure 2.9. Christian Boltanski, *Ce dont ils se souviennent,* #86. Artist's book (self-published, 1972). Courtesy of Marian Goodman Gallery, New York.

on artists. . . . Given that we have all shared the same cultural references, I think we will all finish in the same museum. (*BOL*, 71)

Does this mean that art discourse can be no more than a cultural index, that the individual artwork is no longer distinguished from its family members? On the contrary. For whereas Barthes posits that what he calls "the impossible science of the unique being" depends on a given spectator's particular reading of an "ordinary" photograph, Boltanski enlarges the artist's role: it is the artist who creates those images "imprecise enough to be as communal as possible"—images each viewer can interpret differently. The same holds true, the artist posits, for captions, the ideal situation being one, for example, in which a picture from an elementary school history book every child has used is reproduced, bearing a caption like "Ce jour-là, le professeur entra avec le directeur [That day, the teacher entered with the principal]" (*BOL*, 79).

One of Boltanski's favorite genres is thus the inventory. If many of his albums use "fake" photos to tell what are supposedly "true" stories, the *Inventaire* series work the other way. Consider, for example, the *Inventaire des objets ayant appartenus à un habitant d'Oxford* of 1973 (Figures 2.10,

Figure 2.10. Christian Boltanski, from *Inventaire des objets ayant appartenu à un habitant d'Oxford* (1973). Courtesy of Marian Goodman Gallery, New York.

2.11a, and 2.11b). Boltanski had read of the untimely death of an Oxford student and wrote to his college asking if his personal effects, "significant" or otherwise, could be sent to him. Photographed against a neutral background, these objects take on equal value: the pope's photograph, a folded shirt, a suit jacket on a hanger, a set of pamphlets, a toothbrush. The question the inventory poses is whether we can know someone through his or her things. If the clothes make the man, as the adage has it, can we re-create the absent man from these individual items? Or does the subject fragment into a series of metonymic images that might relate to anyone? Is there, in other words, such a thing as identity?

Here again Barthes offers an interesting *point de repère.* One of the sections in *Roland Barthes by Roland Barthes* is called "*Un souvenir d'enfance*— A Memory of Childhood" and goes like this:

> When I was a child, we lived in a neighborhood called Marrac; this neighborhood was full of houses being built, and the children played in the building sites; huge holes had been dug in the loamy soil for the foundations of the houses, and one day when we had been playing in one of these, all the children climbed out except me—I couldn't make it. From the brink up above, they teased me: lost! alone! spied on! excluded! (to be excluded is not to be outside, it is to be *alone in the hole,* imprisoned under the open sky; *precluded*); then I saw my mother running up; she pulled me out of there and took me far away from the children—against them. (*RB,* 121–22)

We could obviously submit this text to a psychosexual reading and discuss its Freudian symbolism. But what interests me here is less the content than Barthes's assumption that the *souvenir d'enfance* has meaning; that memory can invoke the past, revive the fear, panic, and sense of release the boy felt when his mother rescued him. However painful the memory, the little filmic narrative implies, it relates past to present and creates Barthes's sense of identity.

Memory plays no such role in Boltanski's work. "I have very few memories of childhood," he tells Delphine Renard, "and I think I undertook this seeming autobiography precisely to blot out my memory and to protect myself. I have invented so many false memories, which were collective memories, that my true childhood has disappeared" (*BOL,* 79). Again, Perec's *W or the Memory of Childhood* comes to mind: "I have no childhood memories. Up to my twelfth year or thereabouts, my story comes to barely a couple of lines" (6). For writers and artists born in World War II France, and especially for Jewish artists like Perec and Boltanski, the Proustian or Barthesian *souvenir d'enfance* seems to have become a kind of empty signifier, a site for assumed identities and invented sensations.

Take the installation *Détective* (a first version was mounted in 1972,

Figures 2.11a–b. Christian Boltanski, from *Inventaire des objets ayant appartenu à un habitant d'Oxford* (1973). Courtesy of Marian Goodman Gallery, New York.

Kleenex
Tide
Tide

a more extensive one in 1987), which consists of four hundred black-and-white photographs, one hundred ten metal boxes with magazine articles, and twenty-one clamp-on desk lamps (Figures 2.12 and 2.13). "These photographs," we read in the headnote, "originally appeared in the magazine *Détective.* A weekly specializing in news items, it presents an indiscriminate blend of assassins and victims, the unintentional heroes of forgotten dramas."[7] The immediate occasion, Boltanski explains, was the 1987 trial in Lyons of the Nazi war criminal Klaus Barbie. "Barbie has the face of a Nobel Peace Prize Winner," Boltanski remarked. "It would be easier if a terrible person had a terrible face" (see *LE,* 81). And in an interview for *Parkett* called "The White and the Black," Boltanski explains that his ideas of original sin and grace stem from his Christian upbringing even as his longing for a lost Jerusalem is part of Jewish mythology. "My work is caught between two cultures as I am."[8]

The mystery of *Détective* is that one cannot tell the criminals from the victims. Inevitably, when told that this is the case, one tries to rise to the challenge by distinguishing between the two. The bald man whose head and cheeks have been cropped (top row, third from the left) is surely a killer, isn't he? Or could he be an innocuous person, the local butcher or pharmacist, perhaps, who is one of the murdered? Is he a mental patient? And what about the little boy with blond curls (second row, third from the right); surely he is an innocent victim? Or is it a baby picture of someone who turned out to be an ax murderer? The pictures do not reveal anything. Each and every photograph can be read both ways and there are all sorts of metonymic linkages: compare the woman (if it is a woman) with glasses (bottom row, second from the right) to the man in the top row referred to above. The cropping, lighting, and pose are similar. One wears glasses, the other does not. One is probably female, the other definitely male. Throughout the sequence, each person looks a bit like someone else (e.g., the young girls in bathing suits). Just so, the sequence implies, the middle-class Nazis and Jews of prewar Berlin, for example, were quite indistinguishable.

What sort of evidence, then, does the photograph supply? I have already mentioned the students of *Lycée Chases,* whose faces Boltanski cropped, enlarged, and placed under transparent paper so that they resembled death masks. But the same phenomenon can be found much closer to home: in 1973, in the foyer of a junior high school in Dijon, Boltanski installed the portrait photographs of each of the students attending the school who were then between the ages of ten and thirteen (see Figure 2.14). Thirteen years later he produced an installation using the same photographs, which had been supplied by the children's parents. As Günter Metken explains, "[Boltanski] tightened the format, closing in on the subject, so that the clothing, hairstyle and background

Figure 2.12. Christian Boltanski, from *Les Archives—Détective* (1987). Installation of 400 photographs, 110 metal boxes with magazine articles, and 21 clamp-on desk lamps. Photographs 18 × 24 cm (7" × $9\frac{1}{2}$"). Collection of the Ydessa Art Foundation, Toronto. Courtesy of Marian Goodman Gallery, New York.

Figure 2.13. Christian Boltanski, from *Réserve-Détective* (1972). Courtesy of Marian Goodman Gallery, New York.

Figure 2.14. Christian Boltanski, from *Portraits des élèves du C.E.S. des Lentillères [Dijon] en 1973* (1973). Courtesy of Marian Goodman Gallery, New York.

disappeared, and only the faces, standardized by their identical presentation remained" (*COL*, 155). In the case of the girl in question, Boltanski enhanced the black-and-white contrast and added glasses—a logical development for a woman now in her mid-twenties (Figure 2.15). As in the case of *Lycée Chases*, the artist merely brings out what is already there.

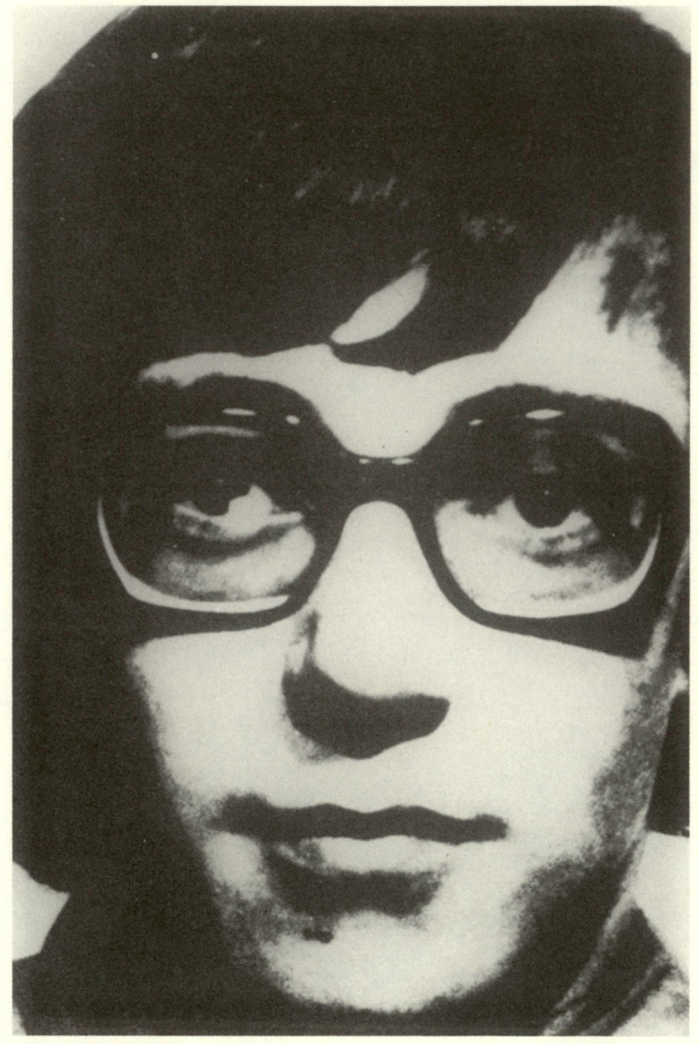

Figure 2.15. Christian Boltanski, from *Monument: Les Enfants de Dijon* (1986). Courtesy of Marian Goodman Gallery, New York.

The figurative "death" of the Dijon schoolgirl, reborn a plain woman in glasses, prefigures death itself, which is for Boltanski, as for Barthes, the very essence of photography. In 1991 Boltanski produced a piece called *Les Suisses morts* (see Figures 2.16 and 2.17) that can be read as an interesting public counterpart to Barthes's very private Winter Gar-

Figure 2.16. Christian Boltanski, from *Les Suisses morts* (1991). Courtesy of Marian Goodman Gallery, New York.

Figure 2.17. Christian Boltanski, from *Les Suisses morts* (1991). Courtesy of Marian Goodman Gallery, New York.

den. The "subjects" are some three thousand dead Swiss citizens as depicted in the obituary announcements published in the Swiss regional newspaper *Le Nouvelliste du Valais.* Why Swiss? "Because," Boltanski explains, "Switzerland is neutral. There is nothing more neutral than a dead Swiss. Before, I did pieces with dead Jews but 'dead' and 'Jew' go too well together. It's too obvious. There is nothing more normal than the Swiss. There is no reason for them to die, so they are more terrifying in a way. They are us" (*PAR,* 36). The "normalcy" of the three thousand Swiss is further heightened by the conventions of the obituary photograph: "The thing about pictures of dead people is that they are always taken when the subjects are alive, all tanned, muscular, and smiling. The photo replaces the memory. When someone dies, after a while you can't visualize them anymore, you only remember them through their pictures" (*PAR,* 36).

What exactly does one remember? One looks in vain at these obituary photos of men and women, some old, some younger, and even a child or two, for clues about the meaning of their lives. Is theirs a national identity? At moments the viewer persuades herself that these white Aryan Europeans look stolid and bourgeois—the representatives of a country that has never known war, genocide, famine, natural disaster. But what about their private lives? Was the pretty woman in the second row, far left, happily married? Was the man to her right a successful businessman? And what were all these people doing when not smiling at the camera?

"Why," asks Georgia Marsh in the *Parkett* interview, "this delectation of the dead?" Boltanski answers:

> I don't really know myself. We are all so complicated and then we die. We are a subject one day, with our vanities, our loves, our worries, and then one day, abruptly, we become nothing but an object, an absolutely disgusting pile of shit. We pass very quickly from one stage to the next. It's very bizarre. It will happen to all of us, and fairly soon too. Suddenly we become an object you can handle like a stone, but a stone that was someone. There is no doubt something sexual about it. (*PAR,* 36)

This linkage of sexuality and death takes us back to Barthes's elegy for his mother-turned-child in *Camera Lucida.* "What is always fascinating," says Boltanski, "is that every being is interchangeable, and at the same time each one has had a very different life with different desires" (*PAR,* 37). For Barthes, still writing as an interpreter in the late modernist tradition, the reception of the photograph is a kind of rescue operation: the *punctum* of the Winter Garden photograph is achieved when its viewer (Barthes) is able to turn the object back into a subject, a sentient and sexual being.

For Boltanski, such individual transcendence is no longer possible. The referent, to paraphrase Barthes, adheres all right, but that referent is *they*, not *she*, and the shock of recognition comes when the viewer recognizes the interchangeability of human beings—an interchangeability paradoxically born out of difference, since each of us has different desires, problems, goals. Personal tragedy—the loss of an adored mother—gives way to a more collective scene of mourning; individuality matters less than positionality (the *à côté de*) in the larger space of inscription. Thus glass, as in glass conservatory (winter garden), gives way to mass, and what has occurred only once may recur again and again. Or it may not have occurred at all.

Notes

1. See Lynn Gumpert, "The Life and Death of Christian Boltanski," in *Christian Boltanski: Lessons of Darkness*, ed. L. Gumpert and Mary Jane Jacob (Chicago: Museum of Contemporary Art, 1988), p. 59. This catalog is subsequently cited in the text as *LE*.

2. Christian Boltanski, interview with Suzanne Pagé in *Christian Boltanski—Compositions*, exhibition catalog (Paris: A.R.C./Musée d'art moderne de la Ville de Paris, 1981), p. 7; cited in Lynn Gumpert's translation, in *LE*, p. 59.

3. See *Christian Boltanski: Catalogue, Books, Printed Matter, Ephemera, 1966–91*, ed. Jennifer Flay, with commentaries by Günter Metken (Cologne: Walther König, 1992), p. 155. This catalog is subsequently cited as *COL*.

4. Georges Perec, *W or the Memory of Childhood* [1975], trans. David Bellos (Boston: David Godine, 1988), pp. 54–55. The story about the sling turns out to have been fabricated. In the very next paragraph Perec admits that, according to his aunt, his arm was not in a sling; rather, "It was as a 'son of father deceased', a 'war orphan', that I was being evacuated by the Red Cross, entirely within regulations" (55). See also David Bellos, *Georges Perec: A Life in Words* (Boston: David Godine, 1993), pp. 55–59.

5. Delphine Renard, "Entretien avec Christian Boltanski," in *Boltanski* (Paris: Centre Georges Pompidou, 1984), p. 75. This catalog is subsequently cited as *BOL*. Translations are my own.

6. In the first version of this essay (*Artes* 2 [1995]: 110–25) I read this photograph as containing two, rather than three, seesaws (see p. 118). The presence of the third (the thin, ropelike one at the furthest distance) was pointed out by Gérard Malanga in a letter to the editor in *Artes* 3 (1996): 146. Malanga discovered (and his interpretation is quite convincing) that the shadows demonstrate the existence of a third seesaw. I am very grateful for his correction, which actually corroborates my reading of the sinister potential of the lighting in this complex image.

7. See *LE*, p. 14. The entire run of photographs is reproduced in this catalog (see pp. 15–48).

8. Georgia Marsh, "The White and the Black: An Interview with Christian Boltanski," *Parkett* 22 (1989): 37. This issue of *Parkett* is subsequently cited as *PAR*.

3

The Filter of Culture and the Culture of Death

How Barthes and Boltanski Play the Mythologies of the Photograph

Nancy M. Shawcross

Culture, states Roland Barthes, is "a contract arrived at between creators and consumers" (*CL*, 28). Contract implies expectations between its participants; expectations, however, limit and direct interpretation and response and act, so to speak, as a filter. Through his ruminations on the photograph in *Camera Lucida*, Barthes ruptures the "filter of culture." Specifically, he breaches the limits of semiology—the science of the sign that was his principal methodology in the 1950s and 1960s. As a contract sustained by culture, semiology may encompass and elucidate a large realm of human knowledge and experience, but ultimately Barthes understands that it remains incomplete as a philosophical construct or methodology.

The sense of trying to "go beyond" the walls and ceiling of structuralism and semiology pervades Barthes's texts of the 1970s. More often than not this attempt is described in relation to "the texture of desire, the claims of the body" (*RB*, 71) and to the "exemption of meaning," a world of which Barthes dreams and "in which is imagined 'the absence of every sign' " (*RB*, 87). As early as 1961, in his essay "The Photographic Message," Barthes senses that the medium of photography does not properly conform to the philosophical and analytical assumptions of semiology or, more precisely, linguistics. He introduces in this essay and repeats in the 1964 piece "Rhetoric of the Image" the concept that the photograph is a "message without code," echoing sentiments that have haunted the medium since its inception while also signaling a profound turn of the screw in the discourse on photography.

The consideration given photography in Barthes's earliest pieces on the subject (collected in *Mythologies*) uniformly resides within the dialectic heralded by Charles Baudelaire in his Salon of 1859 review and formally argued by Walter Benjamin in the 1930s in essays such as "A Short History of Photography" and "The Work of Art in the Age of Mechanical Reproduction." "Photography and Electoral Appeal," for example, examined the use of photographs as iconographic tokens or symbols used to sell values to an undiscriminating public and argued that photography "constitutes an anti-intellectual weapon" that "tends to restore the paternalistic nature of elections" (*MY*, 91). In 1956 Barthes dismissed Edward Steichen's photographic exhibition *The Family of Man* as cultural propaganda. The exhibit, billed as "the greatest photographic exhibition of all time," comprised 503 pictures from sixty-eight countries and traced the seemingly eternal realities of human life—birth, childhood, marriage, work, play, war, death. To Barthes, however, the removal of the images' historical context yields sentimentality and a diffusion of the accountability of individual, as well as societal, action: "if one removes History from [the photographs], there is nothing more to be said about them; any comment about them becomes purely tautological. The failure of photography seems to me flagrant in this connection: to reproduce death or birth tells us, literally, nothing" (*MY*, 101). Benjamin had also written of the diminution of value—the loss of aura—that has accompanied the proliferation of the mechanically reproduced image. The arguments of Baudelaire in the Salon of 1859, of Benjamin in his writing on mechanical reproduction, and of Barthes in *Mythologies* rest on the cultural implications of photography with regard to art, politics, and social issues. The filter of culture is precisely what generates the disquieting power and their nascent loathing of the medium of photography.

The words *culture* and *cultural* permeate Part I of *Camera Lucida* but recede to a scant few in Part II. Yet except for the photograph in Part II captioned "The Stock," all the images in *Camera Lucida* have been extensively mediated by culture. That is to say, they have appeared in newspapers, journals, on exhibition, and in numerous histories and anthologies of photography, as well as catalogs of a photographer's work. All but one photograph, therefore, may fairly be described as "public" images—public not only because of their previous publication and exhibition venues but also because of their iconographic imprint on our cultural memory. One color polaroid precedes the primary text of *Camera Lucida*—a sultry image recently on exhibition in Paris. It conveys a sense of mystery, intimacy, and the erotic. The curtains suggest that something is already hidden (private) or to be hidden, yet the triangular separation between the two parts of the curtain or drapery is inviting, provocative. This photograph—among the twenty-five that are reproduced in the book—carries the barest of dispassionate information: that of the photographer, the photographic medium, and the year created. This image is the only one not captioned by Barthes himself. Its appearance and style of presentation play off the apparent contradictions about to be brought forth in the text itself. The ironies prompted by the predominantly blue polaroid derive from the following particulars: it is a color photograph (Barthes states, "I am not very fond of Color" in *Camera Lucida* [81]); it is an "art" photograph (Barthes claims making photography into an art is one of two ways society has to tame the photograph [*CL*, 117]); it is a photograph devoid of humans ("there are moments when I detest Photographs: what have I to do with Atget's old tree trunks" [*CL*, 16]); and, quite simply, it bears no apparent particularity of time and place (unless perhaps it does for Barthes, a fact that would be outside most readers' scope of knowledge). Where, one might be tempted to ask, is the history? This photograph, one could argue, tells us literally nothing.

Obviously, a new or differing relation to the photograph (than that discussed by Barthes in "The Great Family of Man" essay) informs *Camera Lucida*. An alternate note or tone is struck; Barthes reanimates the myth that the unique phenomenon of the photograph lies with the magic associated with alchemy (where the metals of alchemy like the silver metal of photography are "alive" [*CL*, 81]). This sensibility was not uncommon in the early years of photography; in *Cousin Pons*, for example, Balzac suggests that daguerreotypy proves that "a building or a figure is at all times and in all places represented by an image in the atmosphere, that every existing object has a spectral intangible double which may become visible."[1] The ruminations in *Camera Lucida* appraise photography as a magic, not an art, thus circumventing much of the rhetoric of art criticism. Yet many of the photographic choices that appear in the book have traditionally been evaluated as works of art—in particular, the prints of Nadar, Alfred Stieglitz, André Kertész, Richard Avedon, and Robert Mapplethorpe. All but two of the remaining images—by Charles Clifford, Alexander Gardner, G. W. Wilson, August Sander, James Van Der Zee, Lewis Hine, William Klein, and Koen Wessing—can be categorized as journalistic or documentary works. Both sets of pictures signify the commodities of culture. Part I of *Camera Lucida* essentially reworks this theoretical ground.

With culture Barthes becomes "docile" in the face of those photographic images that speak to him (*CL*, 43). He is "sympathetically interested" in certain photographs for their ability to convey information regarding society and its mores. Photographs stimulate Barthes's historical curiosity and enhance his knowledge of the past. He terms this field of interest *studium*. "The *studium* is that very wide field of unconcerned desire, of various interest, of inconsequential taste" (*CL*, 27). The world of the *studium* is "polite" and "of the order of liking"; it is what makes so many encounters with photographs homogenous. Culture and its counterpart, *studium*, represent the common ground among individuals within a given society. As comprehensible, productive, or comforting as community may be, culture risks subsuming what is particular and unique in its quest for collective understanding. Without culture, however, Barthes claims that certain photographs achieve "utopically, *the impossible science of the unique being*" (*CL*, 71). Part II of *Camera Lucida* explores this speculative ground. Led by an image of his mother and uncle as children (therefore preceding his own birth), Barthes confronts the reality of his mother's physical as well as spiritual existence. The Winter Garden photograph not only attests to her legal and hereditary identity but to her air. "The *air* of a face is unanalyzable [. . .]. The air is not a schematic, intellectual datum, the way a silhouette is. Nor is the air a simple analogy—however extended—as is 'likeness.' No, the air is that exorbitant thing which induces from body to soul—*animula*, little individual soul, good in one person, bad in another" (*CL*, 107, 109). The air is precisely that which culture can neither explain nor absorb. To confront it yields only a cry—"There she is!"—"that cry [which is] the end of all language" (*CL*, 109).

Discussed formally in Part II, the concept of public versus private delineates well the difference between the reflections proffered in Part I and Part II of *Camera Lucida*. Although all but one image in the book can be classified as "public," the public images of Part I retain their cultural stamp, whereas those of Part II seem to have transcended or exceeded their cultural imprinting and reemerged as "pure" or direct experience. For example, Stieglitz's "The Horse-Car Terminal" appears as the first reproduction in the body of the text. No analysis is provided beyond the traditional description available in any history of photography. The reader is simply told that no other photograph by Stieglitz delights Barthes. The two succeeding photographs, by the photojournalist Koen Wessing, depict scenes from the politically controversial rebellion in Nicaragua. Although the concept of the *punctum* is introduced at this point to explain how these photographs offer more than the common image of war, this preliminary sense of the *punctum* focuses on the duality of content in the photograph—a juxtaposition that breaks from the expected without veering into the whimsical or contrived. Barthes refers to the *punctum* as a personal or individual response, one that "pierces" or "pricks" him (*CL*, 26–27). In the latter half of Part I he comes to recognize that the photographic *punctum* may also be what awakens desire. Photographs by Charles Clifford and Robert Mapplethorpe stimulate these meditations. But such ponderings remain comfortable or reasonable as public responses to these public images.

Part II ventures into the sphere of private photographs, specifically family photographs, and keeps the most precious image private. The remaining public prints are reconfigured: the presence/nonpresence of the Winter Garden photograph redirects Barthes's attention and returns what is private—personal and individual—to the very public, cultural images by Nadar, Kertész, and Avedon. The image of Lewis Payne by Alexander Gardner, for example, exceeds its function as a visual record of an attempted assassin: it incarnates the paradox of him who is dead and him who is going to die. The horror of "an anterior future of which death is the stake" (*CL*, 96) becomes an essential part of Barthes's realization of the photographic *punctum*. The *punctum* is especially legible, he contends, in historical photographs because "there is always a defeat of Time in them" (*CL*, 96). This insight makes manifest the hollowness for Barthes at the center of Steichen's most famous exhibition, for time has been effaced in *The Family of Man*. The articulation of the laceration of time in the photograph is interwoven with the wound reopened by viewing the photograph of a loved one who has died. The potential for losing the beloved "twice over" punctuates every family photograph. Yet not only family portraits or images of those one knows prick the spectator in the ways described in Part II. A portrait of Ernest, for example, taken by Kertész in 1931, prompts neither artistic nor sociological speculation. Instead, Barthes sees only a real boy whose individual life opens onto a realm of possibilities while the photograph (given its date) concomitantly represents a closed field of prospects: Ernest's life to 1979 has already been lived, but his image at age six or seven stands as an arrested moment that leaves open the question—asserts the intrigue—of what will be. "What a novel!" Barthes exclaims, but this expression is metaphorical. Barthes is the "reference of every photograph" (*CL*, 84); he, therefore, is like a novelist who can perceive the dimensions that stretch out in time and space of a face, a name, a character, a life.

The photographic *punctum* is double-edged: death triumphant and defeated at the same time. As the reference of every photograph, Barthes "sees" the "imperious sign of my future death" in each photograph. This challenge is capable of piercing through the banality—the tame, civilized, domesticated effects—that the mediation of culture has provided for photographs almost since the beginning of the medium's existence. This challenge can be expressed as that which allows for and even exalts the participation and identification of individual over collective identity—the private and personal over the public and universal. In *Camera Lucida* Barthes is arguing from the spectator's perspective; he empowers the spectator to retrieve from the insulation of culture the madness—the pain and ecstasy—of the photograph. He found his way through this labyrinth by means of a private family photograph; his studious interest or evaluation of the photograph, however, was reconfigured because of the pangs of love. No culture can "speak" the grief and suffering that he experiences by his mother's death; the Winter Garden photograph, nonetheless, opens the wound of that death and "*fills the sight by force*" (*CL*, 91). Instead of offering a transformation of his grief—which to Barthes would be a diminution of his pain—the photograph affirms the existence or reality of his mother and affirms or keeps desire "alive" (metaphorically speaking).

In many museum and exhibition installations Christian Boltanski has relied on photography to carry his message, to incarnate his art. Among these events are *Album de photos de la famille D, 1939–64*, *Le Club Mickey*, *Détective*, *Lycée Chases*, and *Les Suisses morts*. Significant and common to these five shows is Boltanski's appropriation of photographic images produced by others. Although Boltanski may "reshoot" the images, enlarge or crop them, and most certainly recontextualize them, the faces and scenes that make up these shows serve as pawns in Boltanski's conceptual game. The power of Boltanski's presentations—in addition to the power of his layout or physical configuration—rests with letting the audience know the origin of the images on display. The filter of culture is essential to any "play" that Boltanski might seek regarding cultural stereotypes and photography. His working mythologies of the photograph reside firmly in the public uses and sociological analyses that have become commonplace concerning the medium. In *Camera Lucida* Barthes asserts that in considering the photograph he "wanted to be a primitive, without culture": he wants "to dismiss such sociological commentary" as the "Amateur Photograph" being "nothing but the trace of a social protocol of integration, intended to reassert the Family, etc."; he does not dare "to reduce the world's countless photographs" (*CL*, 7). Boltanski, on the other hand, most definitely does care about society's myths and categories for the photograph. His art exists because he dares to reconsider the validity of what we take for granted. A work such as *La Famille D* makes visually and conceptually concrete the sentimentality and fiction that inform an exhibition like Steichen's. Through anonymous photographs (in the sense that the subjects are anonymous) Steichen reaches to "make universal" the apparent signifying moments of individual experience. Beginning with the premise that the family photograph album has become an essentially "universal" phenomenon in modern life, Boltanski—in contradistinction to Steichen—breaks the contract between creators and consumers (the "culture" of family and its rituals) by dismantling what has become accepted as "real" and replacing it with a fiction he creates. This play gains its vigor through photography because the "authority" of the ordinary photograph has remained generally unchallenged in our lives.

Part of the impulse or phenomenon that informs much of Boltanski's photographic reassemblages concerns the "fancy turned obsession" at the heart of Michelangelo Antonioni's 1966 film, *Blow-Up*. In *Camera Lucida* Barthes notes the " 'detective' anguish" of *Blow-Up*; he describes it as a "distortion between certainty and oblivion" that yields a "kind of vertigo" (*CL*, 85). Photographs represent figuratively and literally what existed in reality, but just because a photograph "proclaims" or certifies that someone (or thing) has been there (the "there" depicted in the photograph) does not mean that the spectator can recollect or rediscover that reality. Boltanski relies on the conviction of the photograph's certainty not only in *La Famille D*, but most assuredly in *Détective*. He removes the captions and accompanying text that the magazine *Détective* provides for the photographs of crime victims and perpetrators and challenges the exhibition viewer to "make sense" of these now anonymous figures. Barthes would very much agree that this exercise will prove futile: the photograph (even a series of photographs) is not a narrative (although an image may prompt speculation) and—phenomenologically speaking—does not belong to the realm of memory. In attempting to "scrutinize" the Winter Garden photograph, Barthes at first naively believes that by enlarging the face of his mother he will see it better, understand it better, know its truth, and ultimately reach his mother's very being (*CL*, 99). "The Photograph justifies this desire [to *know*], [. . .] [but] it does not satisfy it" (*CL*, 99). In *Détective* Boltanski teases us by revealing just a little information: that the images derive from the magazine of the same name. A realm of possibilities regarding the particularity of the people depicted (their occupations, dreams, marital status, family members, hometowns, education, etc.) is thereby reduced to the categorization of these individuals as either crime victims or criminals. Boltanski manipulates our response to the photographs and initiates the direction of our questions concerning the faces on view.

In *Lycée Chases* and *Les Suisses morts* a somewhat different phenomenon predominates. Although all of Boltanski's photographic exhibitions present death in the sense that Barthes addresses in *Camera Lucida* (the photograph as "the living image of a dead thing" [*CL*, 79]), the intellectual or textual underpinning in *Lycée Chases* and *Les Suisses morts* centers on either the likelihood of literal death in the former or the certainty of it in the latter. Barthes argues that "Death must be somewhere in a society," and since "it is no longer (or less intensely) in religion," it may perhaps lie "in this image [the Photograph] which produces Death while trying to preserve life" (*CL*, 92). *Le Nouvelliste du Valais*, the Swiss regional newspaper that originally printed the pictures of people who had recently died in the area, would appear to confirm Barthes's theory. The obituary offers both a written and visual record of life and death. Boltanski re-presents the images but discards the text, which traditionally identifies an individual to strangers (giving her name and biographical statistics such as year and place of birth). On one level, *Les Suisses morts* is an elaborate verbal witticism: Boltanski contends that Switzerland's traditional neutrality is most perfectly made manifest through the confrontation with Swiss dead ("nothing more neutral than a dead Swiss"). Boltanski came to realize that the association of death and European—particularly German and Austrian—Jews had become too obvious, had become, in fact, practically synonymous. The expectation of imminent death informs present-day response to an exhibition like *Lycée Chases*, because the class picture from which Boltanski derived the individual enlarged photographs depicts the graduating seniors of a Jewish high school in Vienna in 1931. The "neutral" Swiss, on the other hand, represent the commonality and absurdity of death to humankind in general.

Somewhat akin to Barthes's stance in *Camera Lucida*, in which he asserts his individuality to the subject at hand, are Boltanski's comments regarding his own work. He admits his personal obsession with death and with his past and sense of personal identity. He suggests that the anonymity of *La Famille D* leads us not to the "real" family but to ourselves. Although Barthes and Boltanski circle over similar territory touched by the photograph, they part significantly in terms of the phenomenology articulated and apparently experienced in the face of the unique medium of photography. Whereas Boltanski subverts the filter of culture that orchestrates public response to the medium, Barthes exceeds it. To anyone who senses the madness of photography as articulated by Barthes, Boltanski's "photographic" exhibitions harbor the potential for a similar response. The lingering laceration and unresolved paradox of the photograph to which Barthes testifies in *Camera Lucida* also invest Boltanski's work with that which remains uncomfortable and unresolvable. The photographs of the dead Swiss, for example, are of real people, who did live. Even if one were to learn that Boltanski lied and did not take the images from the journal he said, they remain photographs of real people at some point in time that we witness contemporaneously, in a manner of speaking. That madness adheres (to use a Barthesian term) and will punctuate Boltanski's work unremittingly, not as a lyricism as Steichen intended in his exhibition but as a wound.

In *Les Suisses morts* Boltanski manipulates the association society has made between the photograph and death in order to reexamine his own emotions and concerns regarding the subject, but the consideration of death has been present throughout his lifetime of artistic work (another "conspicuous" case in point being the *Inventaire des objets ayant appartenu à un habitant d'Oxford*). For Barthes the culture of death has also been present in his writings from the beginning. And Barthes has linked the concepts of death, photography, and history from the beginning. Patrizia Lombardo notes in her book *The Three Paradoxes of Roland Barthes* that one of Barthes's first references to photography appears in his 1952 article "Michelet, l'histoire et la mort." " 'Thus the flesh of men who follow each other preserves the obscure trace of the incidents of History, until the day when the historian, like a photographer, *reveals* through a chemical operation that which has previously been experienced.' "[2] This incipient sense of the historian's task is repeated in his 1954 book *Michelet par lui-même* in a passage written by Michelet but selected by Barthes.

> Each soul, among vulgar things, possesses certain special, individual aspects which do not come down to the same thing, and which must be noted when this soul passes and proceeds into the unknown world.
>
> Suppose we were to constitute a guardian of graves, a kind of tutor and protector of the dead?
>
> I have spoken elsewhere of the duty which concerned Camoëns on the deadly shores of India: *administrator of the property of the deceased.*
>
> Yes, each dead man leaves a small property, his memory, and asks that it be cared for. For the one who has no friends, the magistrate must supply one. For the law, for justice is more reliable than all our forgetful affections, our tears so quickly dried.
>
> This magistracy is History. And the dead are, to speak in the fashion of Roman Law, those *miserabiles personae* with whom the magistrate must be concerned.
>
> Never in my career have I lost sight of that duty of the Historian. I have given many of the too-forgotten dead the assistance which I myself shall require.
>
> I have exhumed them for a second life. [. . .] Now they live with us, and we feel we are their relatives, their friends. Thus is constituted a family, a city shared by the living and the dead. (*MI*, 101–2)

In *Camera Lucida*, specifically in Part II, Barthes assumes the role of "magistrate" for his mother. Barthes willingly—beseechingly—accepts the responsibility of "protector of the dead" for his mother. He does so in an age (unlike Michelet's) that questions the very nature of "family" and community. But Michelet's sensibility is not entirely lost in today's world. Maxine Hong Kingston, for example, in *The Woman Warrior: Memoirs of a Girlhood Among Ghosts* interweaves the literal and figurative loss of an aunt with the shape and quality of her own (Kingston's) life.[3] In China in 1924 Kingston's aunt transgressed the mores of her community: she became pregnant by someone other than her husband. The ostracism and belittlement by that community prompted her suicide and the concomitant murder of her child. Her community and, most especially, her family treat her life and death "as if she had never been born" (3). The failure to acknowledge the existence of this life through family narratives, photographs, and memorabilia haunts the family and Kingston herself. Her aunt is a ghost who has been denied protection not only in life but also in death.

> People who can comfort the dead can also chase after them to hurt them further—a reverse ancestor worship. The real punishment was not the raid swiftly inflicted by the villagers, but the family's deliberately forgetting her. Her betrayal so maddened them, they saw to it that she would suffer forever, even after death. Always hungry, always needing, she would have to beg food from other ghosts, snatch and steal it from those whose living descendants give them gifts. [. . .] My aunt remains forever hungry. Goods are not distributed evenly among the dead. (16)

Although prompted by the injustice of a society (as opposed to the injustice of death's inherent absurdity or finality), Kingston declares that if we fail to exhume the "second life" for the dead we poison our own lives. "My aunt haunts me—her ghost drawn to me because now, after fifty years of neglect, I alone devote pages of paper to her, though not origamied into houses and clothes" (16). By following her family's silence regarding her aunt, Kingston claims that she is participating in her aunt's punishment. Silence—even a generation later—is not "innocent."

Kingston's confrontation with the culture of death stands at the other extreme from Boltanski's, with Barthes's position somewhat between the two. Boltanski insinuates that the dead remain nothing more than the fictitious "pictures" derived from what is left behind either in photographs or in possessions (the Oxford student, for example). Kingston, on the other hand, was nurtured in a culture that tried to make a fiction of a real existence. She becomes (through her mother's admission) the guardian of her aunt's grave. Ironically, she is afforded no resources to concretize the reality of her aunt's life: all Kingston can do is speculate what happened to her aunt, blend sympathy (and empathy) with logic in order to begin to account for her death, and affirm her aunt's existence, her *reality*. Barthes's link with the dead and his sense of reanimating the dead rest with love. Like Kingston, he knows that the written pages he publishes will, in one sense, make his mother's memory "last at least the time of my own notoriety" (*CL*, 63). But history, as practiced even by the master, Michelet, is double-edged. "It is constituted only if we consider it, only if we look at it—and in order to look at it, we must be excluded from it" (*CL*, 65). History, therefore, embodies separation, seemingly defeating in advance the integration or resurrection Barthes figuratively seeks. The photograph that "advenes" (like the Winter Garden photograph) arrests history's phenomenological stance while simultaneously certifying historical reality. This state that precedes history is made possible for Barthes through the animation of love and desire and stimulates pathos.

In our modern or postmodern age the culture of death teeters on spiritual and emotional bankruptcy. Boltanski's installations suggest that death has become dislodged in culture, that it is somehow adrift in our cultural awareness: death is not only a meaningless event but a phantom reality for the living. In seeking her own identity as a Chinese-American woman, Kingston needs to confront the culture of death and choose the role she will assume in that culture. Death and its meaning are not a game but a serious enterprise. Her life and death hinge on penetrating the silence that seeks to make her aunt dead "twice-over." The same fate may well await Kingston. Barthes asks to dismiss the filter of culture that diminishes pain, love, desire, and the individual. Unlike Boltanski, however, the "fiction" of a person's life that may emerge from the physical tokens that remain are contradicted by the photograph and by love.

> Here again is the Winter Garden Photograph. I am alone with it, in front of it. The circle is closed, there is no escape. I suffer, motionless. Cruel, sterile deficiency: I cannot *transform* my grief, I cannot let my gaze drift; no culture will help me utter this suffering which I experience entirely on the level of the image's finitude (this is why, despite its codes, I cannot *read* a photograph): the Photograph—my Photograph—is without culture: when it is painful, nothing in it can transform grief into mourning. And if dialectic is that thought which masters the corruptible and converts the negation of death into the power to work, then the photograph is undialectical: it is denatured theater where death cannot "be contemplated," reflected and interiorized; or again: the dead theater of Death, the foreclosure of the Tragic, excludes all purification, all *catharsis*. (*CL*, 90)

In works such as *10 portraits photographiques de Christian Boltanski, Tout ce qui reste de mon enfance, Le Voyage de noces à Venise, La Famille D,* and *Lycée Chases* Boltanski plays with society's ritual of photographing one's family and the events of its members' lives. He intentionally compiles false documents and parades them as stand-ins for the real images and the original context. This luxury of invention has been denied Kingston, because she has been denied choice through her family's silence. She must "imagine" her aunt, because no traditional tokens of her aunt's life have been preserved. Supporting the works created by Boltanski is the possibility to contrast the assemblage (the fiction) with the data available through historical research. Kingston has no property of the dead to administer, yet feels responsible for serving as her aunt's guardian in death. Barthes locates his culture of death in the photograph. For Barthes photographic culture offers more than Boltanski's exploits. Like Kingston and Michelet, who maintain or at least attest to the umbilical cord that literally connects mother and child and figuratively connects the living and the dead, Barthes argues that the photograph links the "body of the photographed thing to my gaze: light, though impalpable, is here a carnal medium, a skin I share with anyone who has been photographed" (*CL*, 81). Yet Barthes chooses not to reproduce the Winter Garden photograph and allow his readership to "gaze"—a final lack of faith in the visual over the verbal in a public setting.

Notes

1. Honoré de Balzac, *The Works of Honoré de Balzac*, vol. 11 (1901; reprint, Freeport, N.Y.: Books for Libraries Press, 1971), pp. 112–13.
2. Patrizia Lombardo, *The Three Paradoxes of Roland Barthes* (Athens: University of Georgia Press, 1989), p. 139.
3. Maxine Hong Kingston, *The Woman Warrior: Memoirs of a Girlhood Among Ghosts* (New York: Alfred A. Knopf, 1990).

4

Barthes and Bazin

The Ontology of the Image

Colin MacCabe

The last decade has witnessed a veritable avalanche of work around the recently dead. Not just Barthes but Foucault and Lacan look set to be buried underneath a mudslide of biographies and studies. How is one to account for this mountain of print, a mountain for which I can think of no historical parallels? The most cynical reason is the professional. The injunction to publish or perish is so deeply engraved within the academic system through annual salary review and research selectivity that there is now no alternative; we perish by publishing. But when publishing has become the vacuous activity that it now so often is, when many books arc read only by those who referee them for an academic press, when these same books provide pleasure only to those who review them for an academic journal, it becomes obvious why so much of that print is devoted to academic thinkers.

Even when one has discounted this academic self-interest, this vain preening where material ambition finds itself perfectly reflected in false judgment, there is still a surplus to be explained. I suspect that part of the answer is to be found with death itself. One of the most profound inadequacies of a secular society is its total inability to find forms that relate it to the dead—unless they have died in violent combat. If the tomb of the unknown soldier is the monument around which modern nations take form, all secular pantheons are simply testimonies to the folly of their builders. I feel sure that part of the impulse that has motivated the contributors to this volume and the idea of the volume itself is part of a work of mourning.

Barthes was undoubtedly one of my most important intellectual influences. It is difficult, even now, to convey his importance to me—the pleasure that I found in his writing and the time that I devoted to a full understanding of his texts. Over a period of two years at the beginning of the 1970s, I must have read *S/Z* some ten times—copiously annotating each reading. I feel confident that almost all the contributors to this volume would attest to similar experiences and feelings even though the examples would be different. In that sense I feel that this volume functions as a kind of memorial—and perhaps all the more for those who knew Barthes well. One of the attractions of Barthes's writing, and one that exceeded any particular intellectual content, was a kind of wisdom that avoided (even in the heat of polemic) the fixity of intellectual position, the dogmatism of certitude that is the bane of so much theoretical and academic discourse.

My own very brief acquaintance with Barthes, when I was a student in Paris in the 1972–73 academic year, confirmed this impression of wisdom very strongly. I am sure that this volume is in part an attempt to remember and to bear witness to that wisdom. If this is true, then perhaps this volume should have taken a less conventional form. We should perhaps have selected readings, photos, and interviews and in their juxtaposition found some adequate symbol to express our relationship to a dead master.

But behind this simple wish to honor the dead is a more complex loss that this volume addresses. From one perspective it is foolish to assess Barthes's importance a decade after his death. Barthes cannot participate in the debates and circumstances of the 1990s. He will remain forever part of the period from the Liberation to the end of the Cold War—his texts simply do not reflect the final failure of Soviet planning, the perceived collapse of World War II political settlements, or the renewed importance of nationalism. On the other hand, although he is still very close to us, he appears caught up in yesterday's arguments and priorities; whatever the elegance of his writing (which is always considerable) his texts often seem very dated.

To take only one example, the whole semiological project now seems a historical curio, part of the desperate attempt for the arts to claim equal academic footing with a science triumphant in the aftermath of World War II. There is little doubt that this "datedness" itself will pass—that further developments in our own fields and a clearer view of the real significances of the recent past will enable us to see how much of Barthes will be debated far into the future. But the attempt to force that moment seems doomed to futile failure. If it is a project that attracts us, I am sure it says a great deal about our own situation—that as critics, scholars, intellectuals, we find ourselves increasingly unable to justify our own activities in a crisis of aesthetic value, of the literary tradition, of political action. It may be that the deepest level of our interest in Barthes is an anxiety about our own situation, our own future.

I cannot pretend to have a reading of Barthes that produces a new vision linking literature, the academy, and society in fresh and more productive circuits. However, what Barthes's work does offer, and in this he is still fully contemporary, is a commitment to analysis across—to use an affectionate archaism—the whole range of signifying practices. From *Mythologies* on, Barthes constantly engaged in analysis that covered image and sound, text and performance. There is, to my mind, no doubt that any future cultural criticism of consequence will have to be as wide-ranging as Barthes himself. This is worth stressing because that moment in the 1970s that promised cultural studies ranging from the literary tradition to contemporary media, from high theory to low culture, seems to have given way to an academic compartmentalization in which film and television are granted a legitimate field of study, but since this study is divorced from traditional cultural analysis both are fatally impoverished.

The reasons for this *marche en arrière* are multiple and far beyond the scope of this brief chapter. All I wish to do here is indicate very briefly to what extent Barthes's final work on photography finds in the image arguments that are in direct contradiction with the major theses and themes of his earlier work. I also want to sketch the similarity of the central argument of *Camera Lucida* with the fundamental premise of André Bazin's reflections of the image. My conclusion is at one level no more than an intellectual puzzle that can be simply stated in the form of a question. Why does Barthes make no acknowledgment of his illustrious predecessor? An answer might have to go beyond the crude positivities of intellectual history to see that, whatever their similarities, Barthes's and Bazin's analyses presuppose very different intellectual projects.

Camera Lucida not only dedicates itself to Sartre's *L'Imaginaire* but presupposes as its method a traditional phenomenology in which Barthes takes his own reaction to photographs as the fundamental given of his study. This phenomenology is justified by a prior assessment that it is impossible to separate a photograph from its referent. Barthes makes almost no argument for this. More surprisingly, he simply ignores arguments that refuse the photograph any privileged relation to the referent and instead analyze it within systems of connotation and signification that provide it with its meaning. The surprise stems from the fact that Barthes himself most tellingly articulated such arguments from *Mythologies* onward.

All such arguments are summarily dismissed at the beginning of *Camera Lucida.* After he has stated with admirable brevity that "the referent adheres" (*CL*, 18), Barthes considers the various attempts in the analysis of photography to ignore this basic fact and through either technical or sociological analysis to produce photographs as signifiers or signifieds. His reason for rejecting this form of analysis is personal and affective.

It is with "*agacement*" ("irritation," *CL*, 7) that he realizes that these discourses are completely inadequate to deal with his own relationship to the photos he loves. So affected is he that these analyses put him "en colère" ("furious," *CL*, 7). It is deeply ironic that Barthes's account of his rejection of these discourses reads exactly like the tirades of the enraged humanist when first confronted with a structural or sociological analysis of his or her favorite canonical texts.

The aim of the text becomes a phenomenological analysis of the systematic regularities that unify the photos that touch Barthes, and he advances the twin theses of the *studium* and the *punctum*. The *studium* captures the relation to the referent by placing it within the comprehensible world of objects. The *punctum* indicates that moment at which the referent touches the subject, destroying the world of objects, and the moment of comprehension disclosing the drives that make the world comprehensible. Although the particular analysis in terms of *studium* and *punctum*—itself a reworking of the *plaisir/jouissance* distinction of *The Pleasure of the Text*—are quintessentially Barthesian, the surprising analysis of the photograph in terms of its privileged relation to the referent inevitably recalls the great theme of André Bazin's work. Bazin's single most celebrated essay and, indeed, the first substantial piece he published was "Ontology of the Photographic Image"; in it he argues, in terms and examples that often run very close to Barthes, that photography distinguishes itself from all other arts because of its privileged relation to the real.[1]

Bazin's article analyzes the history of representation in relation to the psychological desire to defy time and death. It is this desire that underlies our efforts to produce imperishable copies of bodies destined for decay and dissolution. All Western art then finds itself (particularly with the development of perspective) caught between its aesthetic function of developing the reality of its own forms and the psychological need to represent reality. Photography liberates painting and sculpture from this contradiction by offering a reproduction of reality with which they cannot compete. The fact that no human agency is involved in the fundamental photographic process marks photography as a genuinely new art and determines that realism is the essential aesthetic of both photography and cinema.

Once one has noticed the parallels between Bazin's and Barthes's theses, it becomes absolutely extraordinary that Barthes makes no mention of Bazin in his bibliography. The absence is all the more startling because Barthes does mention Bazin in passing—but in reference to a theory of the function of the screen in cinema (*CL*, 90). Indeed Barthes's book was originally published in a series edited by *Cahiers du Cinéma*, the magazine founded by Bazin. How then is one to explain this astonishing absence? Does one attribute it to fashion? Bazin's Catholic humanism and realist aesthetic had banished him from the theoretical reading lists of the 1960s and 1970s. But if Barthes was always, as a good Parisian, aware of fashion, he was scarcely its victim. In any case, given that the whole book is written against all the intellectual fashions of the time and that it explicitly takes its cue from Sartre's *L'Imaginaire* (about as unfashionable a book as one could wish for), such an explanation has no plausibility. And it is even less likely that Barthes wished to hide a debt.

It is simply unbelievable that Barthes consciously borrowed from Bazin without attribution. What is clear is that Barthes undertook no systematic reading for what was to be his final book. It seems more than likely that Barthes did read Bazin's essay at a much earlier period of his career and it seems plausible that Bazin's meditation on the relation between photography and death, particularly in relation to family portraits, did leave unconscious traces. Further historical research on Barthes's reading in the late 1940s and a close comparison of the texts might yield interesting results.

Whatever the similarities between Barthes and Bazin—and they are striking—I would like to conclude by signaling the immense differences that divide their texts. Barthes could not have taken full cognizance of the similarity of his position to Bazin's without devoting a great deal of his text to making those distinctions, which would have taken him to a much more significant confrontation with his previous intellectual positions than *Camera Lucida* proposes. Bazin's work is written from a wide anthropological perspective that attempts to situate photography both in relation to the other arts and in relation to the fundamental evolution of the human species. In this context the realism of photography offers a fundamental transformation of humanity's relation to its own history.

Barthes's book is a work of personal mourning for a mother around whom his whole emotional life had revolved. It is no exaggeration to say that the whole text was written as a prolonged analysis of the photograph of his mother as a young girl that he describes at length in the second part of the book. I also have little doubt that this photograph caused Barthes to reject with such uncharacteristic anger the semiological and sociological theories that had occupied so much of his life.

The difference between Bazin and Barthes is that Bazin's analysis of the photograph is the prelude to an analysis of the cinema, which is then conceived as a fundamental transformation of human understanding of the world in which we live. Barthes's analysis from the very first page divorces photography from cinema and isolates it as the area of a realism that is, above all, personal rather than social. In this context it is very significant that the one moment at which Barthes mentions Bazin is when he agrees that photography touches cinema. For Bazin it is crucial that what happens on screen is immediately connected to a reality that exceeds it; the screen is not a frame but a hideout from which the characters step forward into the real world. For Barthes the realism of the photograph mummifies the subject, who is thus removed of the contingencies of action before and after the moment of the photograph. But Barthes agrees that there is a moment when the photograph leads one into the real world of which it is a part—it is the moment of the *punctum* of an erotic photograph, when what is not in the frame of the photograph animates both the photograph and the spectator.

Insofar as the realism of sexuality is annexed to the personal world of the photograph, Barthes effectively constitutes a crucial divide between a public world of codes and a private world of direct reference. Had he chosen to investigate how the real of the mother and of sexuality related to the codes of the public form of cinema, he would have had to confront directly not only his relation to Bazin but also the relation between his sexuality and his past theoretical project.

Note

1. "Ontology of the Photographic Image" was first published in 1945 under the title "Ontologie de l'image photographique" in *Problèmes de la peinture*; reprinted in André Bazin, *Qu'est-ce que le cinéma?* (1st ed. 1958; rev ed. Paris: Cerf, 1975) pp. 9–17. Bazin writes, for instance, "The existence of the photographed object participates of the existence of the model exactly as fingerprints do" (16).

5

Roland Barthes's Obtuse, Sharp Meaning and the Responsibilities of Commentary

Derek Attridge

Searching for a name to give to the excessive, exorbitant meaning he senses in certain Eisenstein stills, Roland Barthes comes upon the Latin word *obtusus*, or perhaps more accurately, it comes to him. He explains why it seems just right:

> *Obtusus* means *blunted, rounded* [. . .] An obtuse angle is greater than a right angle: *an obtuse angle of 100°*, says the dictionary; the third meaning, too, seems to me greater than the pure perpendicular, the trenchant, legal upright of the narrative [. . . .] I even accept, for this obtuse meaning, the word's pejorative connotation: the obtuse meaning seems to extend beyond culture, knowledge, information [. . . .] It belongs to the family of puns, jokes, useless exertions; indifferent to moral or aesthetic categories (the trivial, the futile, the artificial, the parodic), it sides with the carnival aspect of things. *Obtuse* therefore suits my purposes well. ("The Third Meaning," *RF*, 44)[1]

This comes from an essay first published in 1970, in which Barthes posits two "obvious" meanings—the informational or communicational meaning and the symbolic meaning—and the "third meaning," which is not really a meaning at all. A decade later, seeking a name for an element in the photographic image that escapes all the codes of reading governing what he now calls the *studium* of the photograph, he is again struck by a Latin word that seems to have exactly the right connotations:

> This element [. . .] rises from the scene, shoots out of it like an arrow, and pierces me. A Latin word exists to designate this wound, this prick, this mark made by a pointed instrument: the word suits me all the better in that it also refers to the notion of punctuation, and because the photographs I am speaking of are in effect punctuated, sometimes even speckled with these sensitive

points; precisely, these marks, these wounds are so many *points.* This second element which will disturb the *studium* I shall therefore call *punctum*; for *punctum* is also: sting, speck, cut, little hole and also a cast of the dice. A photograph's *punctum* is that accident which pricks me (but also bruises me, is poignant to me). (*CL*, 26–27)

Blunt versus sharp, carnivalesque versus poignant: the metaphorics of these two essays in naming could hardly be more different, even though we feel strongly in each the satisfaction with which Barthes greets the term when it comes to him. ("The word [obtuse] readily comes to mind, and miraculously, upon exploring its etymology, I find it already yields a theory of the supplementary meaning" [TM, 44]; "the word [*punctum*] suits me all the better in that [. . .]" [*CL*, 26].) As he elaborates on the notion of the *punctum* in *Camera Lucida*, Barthes makes no reference back to the "obtuse meaning" of his earlier essay. Furthermore, one essay concentrates on images of actors and emphasizes the question of disguise, the other on portraits and historical referentiality. One examines stills and pursues a definition of the "filmic" (TM, 58); the other examines photographs and seeks to establish the "essence of the Photograph" (*CL*, 73). In "The Third Meaning," Barthes resists the idea that the excessive effect he is discussing arises from the photograph's recording of the real: it cannot be "reduced to the persistence which any human body exerts by merely being present" (TM, 43); it has "a distancing effect with regard to the referent" (TM, 55). In *Camera Lucida*, the recorded presence of the referent becomes crucial.

In spite of these marked differences, many readers have made a connection between the obtuse meaning and the *punctum*, situating both in a series of terms that attempt to capture a moment of breakdown in the codes of signification to whose elucidation Barthes devoted so much effort. The list includes *jouissance* (notably in *The Pleasure of the Text*), haiku and *satori* (discussed in *The Empire of Signs*), and *significance* (in a number of texts).[2] Unlike *obtuse meaning* and *punctum*, however, the other terms in the series are borrowings and inevitably come into Barthes's work with a certain amount of foreign theoretical matter clinging to them. I want to focus on the two coinages, since I believe that—precisely as coinages—they play a special role in Barthes's writings on the image.

Once we examine Barthes's attempts to explain and exemplify the phenomena to which he is responding in these two pieces of writing, we find that the metaphorical opposition between them begins to collapse.[3] The obtuse meaning, he tells us, is not so much "read" as "received" (TM, 42), making us think of the arrow of the *punctum*. It "can be seen as an *accent*, the very form of an emergence, of a fold (even a crease) marking the heavy layer of information and signification" (TM, 56);

this sounds very like the way in which the *studium* is "traversed, lashed, striped" (*CL*, 40) by the *punctum*. The obtuse meaning is even said at one point to be a "penetrating feature" (TM, 48); conversely, it is the *punctum* that "bruises" (*CL*, 27). And the following comments on an instance of the *punctum* seem to invoke something like obtuseness as well as acuity: "The effect is certain but unlocatable, it does not find its sign, its name; it is sharp and yet lands in a vague zone of myself; it is acute yet muffled, it cries out in silence" (*CL*, 52–53).

There are many other similarities between the two accounts. Both phenomena are said to be outside the intention of the artist, and both are described as "supplements" to the primary cultural meaning. Both have a distinctive emotional force, are associated with love and eroticism, and inhere primarily in details. (Barthes identifies a second *punctum* in *Camera Lucida* that does not inhere in details; I shall return to this somewhat different employment of the term.) Although Barthes does not say so, his choice of examples suggests that both are especially likely to be produced by images of the human body's border zone: its material excrescences or its accoutrements (no fewer than three of the examples, one of obtuse meaning and two of the *punctum*, consist of images of human nails; others include hair, teeth, a ring, a bandage on a finger, facial makeup, shoes, and a necklace). Moreover, although most of the account of the obtuse meaning is based on stills involving actors, Barthes adds, as a supplementary example that threatens to cast the entire argument in a new light, a documentary image of Hermann Goering handling a bow and arrow at a Nazi publicity event.

What, then, are we to make of the fact that the names Barthes fixes on—with the entire lexicons of more than one language to choose from—are so contradictory? This is surely connected to another striking fact about the two pieces: that it is normal for readers to finish them without having gained any specific understanding of what obtuse meaning and *punctum* are. I am not denying that we gain a theoretical understanding of the place of obtuse meaning and *punctum* in the account of signification Barthes provides, but the very nature of these phenomena makes such an understanding limited in its usefulness. To understand them in their specificity could only be to *experience* them *in the examples Barthes gives*, since it is a constitutive feature of both of them that they cannot be conveyed in words. ("We cannot describe the obtuse meaning" [TM, 55]; "What I can name cannot really prick me" [*CL*, 51].) Now, when I look at the image of the two courtiers pouring gold over the young tsar's head with which "The Third Meaning" begins, I see what Barthes has pointed out—the contrast between the two faces, one refined, the other coarse, and so on—but it possesses no special affect for me. When I take in the photograph by James Van der Zee titled "Family Portrait" that Barthes reproduces in *Camera Lucida*, I sense a certain pathos in the figure of the sister or daughter deriving from her rather little-girlish outfit, but I do not find the low belt and the strapped pumps piercing me with inexplicable force. I must immediately add that when I look at these images fresh from Barthes's vivid commentary I am likely to experience a kind of aftereffect, temporarily convincing myself that I am indeed feeling what he felt—but even if I do, this experience is exactly what obtuse meaning and *punctum* are not: the product of words.

Clearly the terms *obtuse meaning* and *punctum* themselves have the status of something like obtuse meanings or *puncta* within Barthes's writing. Their emergence in his discourse is not the product of calculation but of something more like a happy accident (that appears "miraculous" to him), and although Barthes devotes much space to accounts of the terms and gives several examples of their operation, their meaning remains obscure and recalcitrant, having to be revised with each new example, and they do not lend themselves to use in new contexts by the reader. They stand out from or cut into the flow of the discourse, which would be only mildly interesting without them. (The discussions of *obvious meaning* and *studium* are not what we remember in these texts.) They thus only masquerade as technical terms, their specificity and Latinity a ruse, preventing generalization rather than facilitating it. They are not the names of concepts but function more like proper names. As with the instances of obtuse meaning and *punctum* in the images, we can understand how the two terms function for Barthes but we cannot share their specific force. (Again, I must qualify this statement: the reader who has been through several pages of Barthes's explanations and paraphrases of these terms may believe that he or she is deriving from them the same mental and affective content Barthes did, but I doubt whether, in most cases, this is a very durable impression.)

We have, then, an explanation for the contradiction between obtuse and sharp, or, rather, we find that it does not require explanation. The rightness of the two names is not, finally, to be explained in terms of etymology and dictionary definitions, but in terms of their special meaningfulness for Roland Barthes at different times of his life and in front of different objects. The contradictions—between the two accounts and within each—indicate that we are not dealing with "obvious meanings," with informational or symbolic codes, with the *studium* of theoretical semiotics, but with a singular response that resists or exceeds what can be discursively conveyed. The quality or qualities to which the two terms refer—a certain kind of thickness that is also a kind of sharpness? or sometimes one and sometimes the other?—cannot be extracted from the discussion in which Barthes elaborates on their meanings. Like that which they name, the terms themselves have a bluntness, resisting hermeneutic procedures with their obstinate quiddity, and an acuity, piercing the flat surface of the prose with their striking foreignness. An obtuse meaning or *punctum* can be named only by a *punctum* or an obtuse name.

The semiotic project of these two texts is therefore impossible. The images Barthes reproduces are provided in order that the reader may have direct access to the experience of the obtuse meaning and the *punctum* (among whose characteristics, we should remember, is the fact that they impose themselves on the reader). However, the nature of the obtuse meaning and the *punctum* is such that Barthes's readers do not experience them by simply looking at the pictures—if they did, the meaning in question would be an instance of the informational or symbolic levels, part of the shared codes that constitute the *studium.* Barthes is obliged to add a commentary, therefore, but here is the paradox: the more successful he is in conveying to the reader in language the special quality of the features that have moved him, the more he shifts them from the realm of obtuse meaning and *punctum* to the realm of the coded and cultural. (To anticipate my argument a little: is this not the difficulty faced by any commentary on a work of art, in any medium?)

Thus the words that Barthes skillfully accumulates in "The Third Meaning" to convey a sense of his response to the two courtiers build, of their own accord, a meaning that is not evanescent or resistant: "There is a certain density of the courtiers' makeup, in one case thick and emphatic, in the other smooth and 'distinguished'; there is the 'stupid' nose on one and the delicate line of the eyelids on the other, his dull blond hair, his wan complexion, the affected smoothness of his hairstyle which suggests a wig, the connection with chalky skin tints, with rice powder" (TM, 42–43). These meanings do not, it is true, contribute to the narrative of *Ivan the Terrible,* but they do contribute to the texture of the representation, and Barthes begins to sketch an interpretation of the features he has just pointed out: one courtier "remote and bored," the other "diligent," the pair signifying that "'*They are simply doing their job as courtiers.*'" To save the obtuse meaning, he has to assert rather lamely that this hermeneutic exercise "does not altogether satisfy me" and that "something in these two faces transcends psychology, anecdote, function, and, in short, meaning" (TM, 43). The other examples in the essay are caught in the same double bind.

Barthes is somewhat cannier in *Camera Lucida* but is still unable to escape the structural predicament his project has placed him in. To take one example, in "Family Portrait" he first identifies the younger woman's belt and strapped pumps as the location of the *punctum,* but later, to illustrate that the *punctum* can unfold after the photograph is no longer in front of him, he revises this to the gold necklace she is wearing. Once more, we are guided toward an understanding of this effect by a commentary:

> It was this same necklace (a slender ribbon of braided gold) which I had seen worn by someone in my own family, and which, once she died, remained shut up in a family box of old jewelry (this sister of my father never married, lived with her mother as an old maid, and I had always been saddened whenever I thought of her dreary life). (*CL*, 53)

This time Barthes makes no attempt to provide an interpretation that the reader can share; the associations of the gold necklace are resolutely private. Nevertheless, he has given us a domestic narrative which, to the extent to which it explains the force of the *punctum* upon Barthes, denies its existence as *punctum*. It becomes part of a recognizable set of codes, including those of psychological associations and gender stereotypes.[4]

Barthes is, of course, aware of the impossibility of his task, even if this awareness is not theoretically articulated. His presentation of examples is studded with remarks that allude to the private nature of his responses, including the frequently repeated phrase "for me." The fact that his readings are presented as narratives of his readings (including, in both texts, narratives of past readings) testifies to their personally and historically determined nature. (Not "This detail means x . . ." but "This detail has, or had, x effect on me . . .") Of the first example of obtuse meaning—the courtiers pouring gold—he says, "I am not certain whether my reading of this third meaning is justified—if it can be generalized" (TM, 43). Later in the essay he draws a touching analogy between his fascination with incommunicable properties of images and Saussure's compulsive search for anagrams:

> The obtuse meaning is not structurally situated, a semantologist would not acknowledge its objective existence (but what is an objective reading?), and if it is evident to me, this is still perhaps (for the moment) because of the same "aberration" which compelled the unfortunate Saussure alone to hear an enigmatic, obsessive, and unoriginated voice, that of the anagram in ancient poetry. (TM, 54–55)[5]

In *Camera Lucida* Barthes stresses the private nature of the *punctum*: "I dismiss all knowledge, all culture, I refuse to inherit anything from another eye than my own" (*CL*, 51)—a gesture that may sound like a classic phenomenological *époche* but in fact has nothing to do with the postulation of a universal subject. And of course, most tellingly of all, he does not reproduce the Winter Garden photograph out of which the whole of Part II arises:

> It exists only for me. For you, it would be nothing but an indifferent picture, one of the thousand manifestations of the "ordinary"; it cannot in any way constitute the visible object of a science; it cannot establish an objectivity, in the positive sense of the term. (*CL*, 73)

The withholding of the picture of his mother is entirely consistent with the logic of the *punctum*; for us, it provides no evidence for the effect, and the affect, he is trying to describe. But the same logic would demand the removal of all the images in which a *punctum* is said to operate. The only point in providing them would be to discuss the *studium*, which we can be expected to share with the author, and in which, at this stage of his life, Barthes is not really interested.

If Barthes is aware of the necessary incommunicability of the effect he is discussing, why does he reproduce images and write commentaries that strive to make us see the obtuse meaning or the *punctum*? Partly, perhaps, because he never gives up the hope that somehow it will be possible to communicate exactly what one of these details makes him feel—for without such communication (even to himself), the experience lacks substance. This hope that somehow, against the logic of absolute singularity that governs the phenomenon he is discussing, a sharing of the experience will be possible emerges overtly at one point in "The Third Meaning":

> If you look at these images I am talking about, you will see the meaning: we can understand each other about it "over the shoulder" or "on the back" of articulated language: thanks to the image [. . .], indeed thanks to what in the image is purely image (and which, to tell the truth, is very little indeed), we do without speech yet continue to understand each other. (55)

This dream of understanding without the mediation of a code is a familiar utopian (or Edenic) fantasy, which does not mean that it can simply be ignored. In *Camera Lucida*, the most potently affecting photograph for Barthes—the one we do not see—generates in him just this utopic experience, which he calls "the impossible knowledge of the unique being" (*CL*, 71).

But it is not just stubborn hope that drives Barthes. One aspect of the experience Barthes is attempting, impossibly, to describe and exemplify is a *demand* for translation: the details that bruise or pierce him call out to be made known, to be transferred from the singular to the general, from the idiosyncratic to the communal.[6] Indeed, it might be said that they are only fully constituted in their incomprehensibility in the necessary attempt to render them comprehensible, that their specificity actually depends on the words (or other codings) by which the viewer acknowledges and attempts to articulate them—in the first place, to himself or herself. They thus appear only in the moment of disappearance. (Think again of the terms *obtusus* and *punctum*: how much of Barthes's elaborate description of the photographic elements they claim to name in fact *derives from* his lexicographic and etymological research?)

We should not, therefore, simply think of Barthes's examples and commentaries as so many manifestations of the failure of his endeavor. His narratives do achieve the signaling of certain effects that are crucial to the affective power of images, and they succeed in doing this precisely through their inability to specify those effects in such a way as to enable others to experience them. Barthes here joins a long tradition of commentary on the arts, or "aesthetic experience" more generally, in which the impossibility of exhausting the power of an image, a text, or an object receives testimony in the failure of commentary to do justice to it. Indeed, the very institution of Western art, as it has existed for centuries, demands that there be some region inaccessible to the calculations of codes and semes. The work cannot sustain its moving power if that power is charted and explained; we are not in general sympathetic to the notion that a sufficiently complex program would allow a computer to produce new artworks as forceful or as touching as those we already value. Almost all of a work's effectiveness may be accounted for by means of cultural codes, as long as there remains a tiny enclave that refuses all accounting. However tiny this reservation, it functions as a supplement in the full Derridean sense: apparently a little extra ingredient beyond the mass of culturally coded material, it is the one thing that the work could not do without. (Recall that both obtuse meaning and *punctum* are called "supplements" by Barthes.)[7]

One response to this long history of the supplementary *je ne sais quoi* or "nameless grace" that becomes the work's animating principle is to undertake a complete demystification—to show that this property of the work always functions culturally, ideologically, psychologically, somatically, or some combination of these, and that its apparent mysteriousness is due only to our ignorance or self-delusion. Hence the projects of structuralism, the sociology of art, much Marxist criticism, some of what is labeled "cultural studies"—and much of Barthes's early work. But the importance of Barthes's oeuvre as a whole is that it demonstrates, in its dogged pursuit of such explanations, both their value and their necessary failure (and the value of that failure). The pursuit is an essential part of the process, since what remains inexplicable can be most fully apprehended through the activity of analyzing what can be explained. Barthes observes in "The Third Meaning":

> We can perceive the filmic [which Barthes has identified with the obtuse meaning] only after having traversed—analytically—the "essential," the "depth," and the "complexity" of the cinematic work—all riches belonging only to articulated language, out of which we constitute that work and believe we exhaust it. (59)

I may seem to have generalized too hastily from Barthes's specific focus on the photographic image to the arts and even more widely to something as vague as "aesthetic experience"; he himself insists at several points on the uniqueness of the photograph in relation to other fields of artistic production. So I must emphasize once more that the supplementary force I am talking about, though its effects are everywhere to be felt, is not a generalizable phenomenon. It inheres in the particular and the contingent; it cannot be programmed or predicted; it arises out of an encounter between a work and a consciousness in a given time and place. Barthes, in these two texts, has described some aspects of the particular form it takes in photography; the sheer materiality of bodily excrescences, for instance, is more likely to play a part in our response to photographs than to other kinds of art or image.

The *punctum* of the photograph is by no means always an apprehension of bodily matter, however; Barthes's examples include a number of other aspects of the image (the comic potential of the Highlander holding Queen Victoria's horse, for instance, or the dirt road of a Central European scene). The fact that there is in *Camera Lucida* "another *punctum*" (*CL*, 96), somewhat different from the first, begins to suggest the plurality of the effects he is discussing. As I have already noted, the two terms I am focusing on exist in a chain of terms that take us well outside the photograph. None of them is interchangeable with any other, necessitating a careful regard for the individuality of each, but all are related to one another.

Let us look for a moment at the second *punctum*, which seems to lead to a more theoretical understanding of the nature of photography. It rests on what Barthes argues (as he had done in earlier essays) is the photograph's unique relation to the referent. The "photographic referent" is "the necessarily real thing which has been placed before the lens, without which there would be no photograph" (*CL*, 76). The photograph says, "*Ça a été*"—"This has been." It is from this sheer contingency, this unmediated reference, as Barthes portrays it, that there arises the "new *punctum*" (*CL*, 96): the intense apprehension of time and what it implies—the actuality of a life that existed and, twisted inseparably with it, the inevitability of the death that lay in wait for it.

The story of Barthes's progression to this moment of recognition is moving and compelling, and once again it is important to stress that it could be told only as a personal history, since it is not essentially a theoretical argument. To respond fully to Barthes's text, however, is to attempt to extend its range and prolong its life by trying to carry over his terms and his thought. We have already seen that neither the instances of obtuse meaning and *punctum* that Barthes puts before us nor the very terms *obtuse meaning* and *punctum*, carry over without loss; this is part of what defines them. Is the same true of the "new *punctum*," of the photographic *ça a été*? The theoretical content is certainly much greater. The argument, not original with Barthes, that the distinctiveness of photography lies in the mechanical and chemical processes that register the real existence of an object, making it, in Peirce's terms, an index rather than an icon or symbol, is sound and helps account for the different reactions we have to paintings and to photographs. However, in a gesture rather similar to those Derrida has traced in a number of writers, Barthes quickly dismisses the apparently marginal cases in which the photograph we see is *not* the unmediated result of light striking a chemically sensitized surface: "The Photograph is indifferent to all intermediaries: it does not invent; it is authentication itself; the (rare) artifices it permits are not probative; they are, on the contrary, trick pictures: the photograph is laborious only when it fakes" (*CL*, 87). (By contrast, his early essay "The Photographic Message" [*RF*, 3–20] devoted a section to "trick effects.")

What, then, if the girl in the Winter Garden photograph was not Barthes's mother but, say, an unknown cousin who looked like her? Would this mean that Barthes's intense apprehension of a truth about his mother (and himself, and photography) was invalid or deceptive? What if that expression of kindness on her face was in fact the result of a speck of dust in the darkroom? Perhaps if Barthes had lived on into the age of digital photographic images, no longer analogically bound to the referent and therefore open to infinite manipulation, he would not have been so ready to assert that photographs are self-authenticating, that "every photograph is a certificate of presence" (*CL*, 87).[8] The photograph, as Derrida might say, can always *not* be the direct effect of the referent on sensitized paper. This fact has to be taken into account in any attempt to say what photography is.

Perhaps Barthes acknowledged this fact in the medium by means of which he presented his "discovery" of the essence of photography. The autobiographical narrative, partaking of the literary as it does, can itself always not be true. (Recall the handwritten epigraph to *Roland Barthes by Roland Barthes*: "It must all be considered as if spoken by a character in a novel.") What if there is, and was, no Winter Garden photograph? Barthes's moving and memorable exploration of the distinctive qualities of photography would not thereby be revealed as vacuous, though we might revise our estimate of the author's practices.[9] Similarly, if it turned out that Barthes was mistaken about the picture he took to be the unmediated image of his mother, this would not disqualify the insights we might have gained from it—unless our reading of *Camera Lucida* took it to be a scientific treatise or a work of philosophy. Barthes's practice thus shows that the referent is not the source of photography's special power—although the referential may indeed be crucial.[10]

I noted earlier that the obtuse meaning and the *punctum* depend on the very codes they resist. The result is a short-circuiting of cause and effect, a thwarting of chronological progression. Although these aspects of the image convey a feeling of priority, this feeling is itself a product of the operation of the primary codes: a place where these codes slip, contradict one another, fissure, fall into an infinite regression. (Barthes himself wrote in many places about these moments in texts.) If human nails, for instance, have a special potency in certain images, it may be not because of the substance of which they are made, recorded on sensitized paper, but because of their liminal status between our categories of live and dead matter. Obtuse meaning and *punctum* thus stage a certain undecidability between activity and passivity, an undecidability that extends to the other terms in the chain, such as *scriptibilité, jouissance,* and *textuality.*[11]

The contingency and referentiality Barthes talks about in photographs is thus an effect—not a controlled and calculated "reality-effect" of the type Barthes himself analyzed so brilliantly, nor a completely random by-product, but the product of something he calls "luck," though it has other names too. Hence *punctum* and *studium* are interrelated and interdependent; contingency and singularity are not separable from codedness and generality; the experience of the wholly private significance would not be possible without the functioning of public meaning. If Barthes does succeed in conveying to his readership one of the *punctum* effects he is discussing, and thereby abolishes it, a transformation in the shared *studium* is produced, opening up possibilities for new *puncta.* The passage of time—and the work of artists, critics, and readers—is thus continually altering the relations of coded meanings and uncoded effects.

Doing justice to a work of art, a family photograph, the performance of a song, an autobiographical essay, a memoir, or a theoretical text involves a response to what is singular and untranslatable in it—the obtuse meaning, the *punctum,* the grain of the voice, the moment of *jouissance,* the supplementary force. Such a response necessarily attempts the impossible: respecting that singularity while generalizing it, turning the other into the same without losing its otherness, making the obtuse obvious while retaining its obtuseness, and making the *punctum studium* without its ceasing to be *punctum.* The impossibility is not because the singularity in question is a hard, resistant, unchanging nugget but, on the contrary, because it is completely open, always answering to the structuring properties of culture and ideology in a particular time and place, always borne on, and born from, the contingency of a particular encounter between an object and a viewer, listener, or reader, and always ready to yield to a codifying procedure that effaces precisely what made it singular. Barthes attempted this impossible task many times and in many different ways, and it seems fitting that his last book is, for many readers, the one that comes closest to fulfilling it, while simultaneously (and I have tried to show that this amounts to the same thing) demonstrating its impossibility.

Notes

1. I refer to "The Third Meaning: Research Notes on Several Eisenstein Stills" (in *RF*, pp. 41–62) as TM in the rest of this chapter. Translations have occasionally been modified.

2. Among the commentators who have linked a number of these terms are Michael Moriarty, *Roland Barthes* (Stanford: Stanford University Press, 1991), pp. 203–4; Tim Clark, "Roland Barthes, Dead and Alive," *Oxford Literary Review* 6 (1983): 104–5; Andrew Brown, *Roland Barthes: The Figures of Writing* (Oxford: Oxford University Press, 1992), pp. 278–80; and Anselm Haverkamp, "The Memory of Pictures: Roland Barthes and Augustine on Photography," *Comparative Literature* 45 (1993): 265 n. 9.

3. The original subtitles also signal by the use of the word *note* that they are not offered as finished theoretical statements: "Notes de recherche sur quelque photogrammes de S. M. Eisenstein"; *Note sur la photographie.* (Only the first of these survives in the translation.) The use of *note* is less an apology on Barthes's part than an indication of the nature of the project itself.

4. It is Barthes who identifies the necklace as a "slender ribbon of braided gold": one cannot see this in the reproduction, where it looks white and rather thick—and identical to the other necklace in the picture, from which no *punctum* shoots. This discrepancy is of no account, however; even if we did see what Barthes describes, we would remain impervious to the *punctum*'s laceration.

5. In "The Grain of the Voice" (in *RF*, pp. 267–77), Barthes also experiences the solitariness of the interpreter of uncodifiable meaning—in this case, the "phonetics" of Panzera's singing—and adduces "Saussure's work on anagrams" (*GV*, 272).

6. Derrida has discussed this demand for translation in "Des Tours de Babel," in *Difference in Translation,* ed. Joseph F. Graham (Ithaca, N.Y.: Cornell University Press, 1985), pp. 165–207.

7. For a discussion of this supplementary logic at work in accounts of literature from the Renaissance onward, see Derek Attridge, *Peculiar Language: Literature as Difference from the Renaissance to James Joyce* (Ithaca, N.Y.: Cornell University Press, 1988).

8. Surprisingly, Barthes appears to take no account of the fact that many of his examples depend on information external to them for their effect. That a

certain portrait is of Lewis Payne before his execution and that another is of William Casby, born a slave, are two such examples. The information, however, could always be false.

9. Diana Knight has suggested that the photograph of Barthes's mother to which he responded so strongly is actually the one reproduced in *Camera Lucida* with the title "The Stock" and that the conservatory setting described by Barthes is a fiction. See her essay in this collection.

10. Derrida effects this subtle but transformative shift in Barthes's argument in a parenthesis in "The Deaths of Roland Barthes," in *Philosophy and Non-Philosophy Since Merleau-Ponty*, ed. Hugh J. Silverman (New York: Routledge, 1988), pp. 259–96. "He first highlighted the absolute irreducibility of the *punctum*, the unicity of the referential as we say (I appeal to this word so as not to have to choose between reference and referent: what adheres in the photograph is perhaps less the referent itself, in the effectiveness of its reality, than the implication in the reference of its having-been-unique)" (285). Derrida produces a more consistent (and more Derridean) Barthes, but one who lacks the force of a desire for unmediated access to the real that animates and complicates Barthes's writing.

11. There is also a sexual dimension to this undecidability, which functions as part of a long sequence of partly concealed, partly overt references in Barthes's work to his homosexuality. We may also note that Barthes describes the obtuse meaning in sexual terms that appear to distinguish it sharply from *jouissance*: "It maintains itself in a state of perpetual erethism; in it desire does not attain that spasm of the signified which usually causes the subject to sink voluptuously into the peace of nomination" (TM, 56).

6

Photographeme

Mythologizing in *Camera Lucida*

Jolanta Wawrzycka

In the process of reading and analyzing Barthes's last book, *Camera Lucida,* I kept experiencing a forking of my sensibilities. On the one hand I was taken by the clever and convincing elucidation of pictures scattered throughout the text, yet on the other hand, I kept resisting the alarmingly reductive "readings" of the photographs, as well as the phenomenological leap of faith I felt invited to perform. But before I elaborate, let me reveal something about my own attitude toward photographs. I do so encouraged by the subtitle to the English-language translation of *Camera Lucida*: "Reflections on Photography."

I remember my very early childhood experience with photographs. When I asked my mother why I had never had grandparents, she replied that of course I had them—everybody did; it was just that mine were dead. She walked to the library shelf and took down a big, leather-bound photo album with silver clasps, browsed through it, and pulled out three rectangular cardboard or plastic-like cards. In one were two brown patches that coincided with the shapes I was so fond of drawing at that time and calling "Mom and Dad"; she said that the patches were *her* mom and dad. "Did you draw them?" "No; they are *zdjęcia*" (the Polish word for "pictures," literally meaning "taking-offs" or "removals"). Two shapes—people—in one photograph were looking in my direction. In the other two "removals," the same people were looking at me more obviously: I had adjusted to recognize the patches as faces. Yet my mind could not hold that adjustment for long. It still perceived the content of the cards as brownish shapes; they could not be Mom's mom and dad, for how could they fit into the rectangle I was holding in my hand? And how could they be there in front of me if they were dead?

Eventually, like all children, I learned how to look at the photographs, but my "learned" behavior never fully displaced those first impressions of photos as flat paper objects with patches on them, with fancifully cut edges and long-expired addresses of photo studios where the "taking off" took place. To this day, as I ponder the Polish word *zdjęcie*, "taking off" or "removal," I keep wondering, Taking off of what, from where? or Removal of what, from where, and where to? I never had that problem with drawings. Like all children who draw, I somehow understood that I was imitating what I saw; I was aware of the process through which pictures I drew came into being—an aspect entirely missing from my relationship to a photograph until I was eleven or so, when I studied optics as part of a science curriculum in physics and the concepts of "camera obscura" and "camera lucida" as part of both physics and "history of ideas" curricula, supplemented by my extracurricular "exposure" to photography.

Given all I have said so far, my rereading of *Camera Lucida* could only cause the epistemological split in me. To be fair, Barthes did occasionally approach a satisfactory—for me—definition of photography, but he also ducked each time. He asserts that photography is never distinguished from its referent, carrying it with itself (*CL*, 5),

> united by an eternal coitus. The Photograph belongs to that class of laminated objects whose two leaves cannot be separated without destroying them both: the windowpane and the landscape [. . .] Good and Evil, desire and its object: dualities we can conceive but not perceive (*I didn't yet know that this stubbornness of the referent in always being there would produce the essence I was looking for*). (*CL*, 6; emphasis added)

Striving to answer the question why certain referents arrest, "puncture," or "prick" him while others leave him close to neutral, Barthes abandons one of those "leaves of laminated objects," the windowpane, and analyzes just the landscape. Ultimately, a photograph emerges as just a mimetic and evocative image. Barthes reads that image as a text and responds to it by employing the apparatus of sensory perceptions, eidetics, and good old interpretation—the tools of the modernist, aesthetic approach to texts, long buried by postmodernists. To me *Camera Lucida* obscures the physicality, the *whatness*, of a photograph, its photosynthetic metareality registered on photosensitive film/paper by a mechanical device of prearranged lenses that trap light rays and trick them into mimesis. My own bias forever prevents me from considering a photograph to be purely mimetic and "thematic." But then, in line with what I demand from my students, I decided to grant Barthes his terms, mainly because the *lisible* was quite apparent to me; it was the *scriptible*, the self-conscious and the resistant in me, that kept interfering.

In analyzing his "photographic 'knowledge' " (*CL*, 9), Barthes explores three practices that result in the final product, the photograph. They are expressed by the infinitives "to do," which involves the Operator or the Photographer; "to look," which engages the Spectator; and "to undergo," which involves the target, or the referent. The "Operator's photograph" is linked to "the vision framed by the keyhole of the *camera obscura*" (*CL*, 10) and to the processes of looking, framing, and perspectivizing. The "Spectator's photograph" descends from the "chemical revelation of the object (from which I receive, by deferred action, the rays) [. . .]" (*CL*, 10). Thus a given photograph is always seen by Barthes as a qualified (appropriated) object resulting from a process and always seen in relation to human perception. The *it*, the nominality (or should I say object-ivity?) of the photograph itself, is absent from this otherwise satisfactory configuration. Barthes analyzes the effects that photographs have on Spectators by introducing the notions of *studium* and *punctum*. Through the photograph's *studium* the Spectator's interest is aroused based on cultural recognition of the photographer's intention (*CL*, 26–27), whereas through its *punctum* the spectator breaks away from the polite interest aroused by the *studium*: "*punctum* is that accident which pricks me (but also bruises me, is poignant to me)" (*CL*, 27). Thus, on the one hand, Barthes's definition of photography coincides with mine, when he asserts that

> Technically, Photography is at the intersection of two quite distinct procedures; one of a chemical order: the action of light on certain substances; the other of the physical order: the formation of the image through an optical device. (*CL*, 10)

On the other hand, however, the object resulting from that intersection —the physical sheet of photographic paper—is overlooked, or rather, looked-through, its referent being so ridden with subjectivity and intentionality that it is here where my epistemological forking begins. Yet it is also at this crossroad that I find myself immersed deeply enough in Barthes's text to want to continue the pleasure of the text and my own process of discovery.

Here is why. Barthes defines the referent as "any *eidolon* emitted by the object which I should like to call the Spectrum of the Photograph, because this word retains, through its root, a relation to 'spectacle' and adds to it that rather terrible thing which is there in every photograph: the return of the dead" (*CL*, 9). This notion of death arrests me. It is so obvious that it actually surprises me. After all, the pedestrian reason why we take pictures is in diametrical opposition to death: pictures immortalize the moment, preserve it for eternity. And here, I suppose, lies the essence of what surprises me: my own insistence on the physicality of a photograph as an object has so far prevented me from realizing the extent to which photographs, for me, always also inscribed Time. I have always been aware that when people talk about their photographs they usually resort to metonymy ("This is X at the seaside . . ." or "This is X and Y in the Alps . . . ," when they really mean "This is a piece of photographic paper *imaging* X or Y . . .). I, on the other hand, usually resort to narration: "This was taken when I was here and there . . ." or "This is what my parents looked like when they got married. . . ." Invariably a story, but always prompted by a "pre-text," an object called a photograph.

I suppose I carried this habit from my native language, in which, although it is correct to say "This is X . . ." when one means a picture, it is more habitual to point to "a picture of X." Chomsky called language "a mental organ." My growing a new organ called English certainly did not eradicate the old organ called Polish, though it might have atrophied it. One of the cells of that Polish mental organ, the concept of photography, has to do first with the physicality of the object called photograph, and only second with the phenomenological dimensions of the subject-turned-object. But it is the latter that preoccupies Barthes when he asserts, "Photography transform[s] subject into object" (*CL*, 13)—a clear and obvious enough assertion, although for me photography also transforms the resulting object (the picture) into subject (of the stories I love to tell as I show my photos to those few interested).

The fact that Barthes sees the notion of death configured into photography reminded me of some older folk from the Poland chapter of my life who would not be photographed if their lives depended on it. In a way it did, for they lived under the spell of superstition that to have one's picture taken meant to die soon. Death, then. Barthes is quite explicit, albeit metaphorical, on the subject of death. He regards a photograph to be "flat death" (*CL*, 92). In one sense, he reflects that whenever he is being photographed, that is, whenever he experiences himself as subject-becoming-an-object, he undergoes a "micro-version of death: [he is] truly becoming a specter [. . .] Death in person" (*CL*, 14). Death is precisely what he seeks in the photograph of himself: "Death is the *eidos* of that Photograph" (*CL*, 15). While viewing photographs of himself, he finds his desire clinging to the sound the camera makes as the photographer's finger triggers the shutter (the finger being a less terrifying organ than his eye):

> For me the *noise of Time is* not sad: I love bells, clocks, watches—and I recall that at first photographic implements were related to the techniques of cabinetmaking and the machinery of precision: cameras, in short, were *clocks for seeing*, and

perhaps in me someone very old still hears in the photographic mechanism the living sound of the wood. (*CL*, 15; emphasis added)

It seems that for Barthes, then, "noise of Time" counterbalances Death encoded in the photograph of himself. For me, the stories triggered by the pictures of my family and me do the same. In this context, Barthes's concepts of *studium* and *punctum* emerge as the "tools" that enable him to view photographs other than those of himself. Rather than as "flat death," he sees them from a variety of points of view: as adventure, as information, according to their ability to paint, surprise, signify, waken desire, or produce *satori.* His method of analysis, "a casual, even cynical phenomenology," is steeped in a paradox of wanting, on the one hand, "to give name to Photography's essence" as an eidetic science and recognizing, on the other hand, that Photography, always a "contingency, singularity, risk" (*CL*, 20), participates in what he calls "banality." Barthes's recognition that "Classical phenomenology [. . .] had never [. . .] spoken of desire or mourning," forces him to abandon "the path of formal ontology" (*CL*, 21) and retain only his desire and grief. Thus he cannot separate the essence of photography "from the 'pathos' of which, from the first glance, it consists." He is interested in Photography only for "sentimental" reasons, as a Spectator who wants "to explore it [. . .] as a wound: I see, I feel, hence I notice, I observe, and I think" (*CL*, 21).

Barthes supplements this affective essence of photography by yet another element, *satori.* He arrives at the notion of *satori* via the agency of *punctum.* Noting the trick of vocabulary in the phrase "to develop a photograph," Barthes points out that "what the chemical action develops is undevelopable, an essence (of a wound) [. . .]" (*CL*, 49). That essence can only be repeated but never transformed. Barthes likens the effect to that of the Haiku: "For the notation of a haiku, too, is undevelopable: everything is given, without provoking a desire for or even a possibility of a rhetorical expansion" (*CL*, 49). This "intense immobility," however, seems to be at odds with the energy implicit in *punctum,* though by linking it with *satori* Barthes comes close to Joyce's notion of epiphanic stasis in *A Portrait of the Artist as a Young Man,* "that cardiac condition which the Italian physiologist Luigi Galvani, using a phrase almost as beautiful as Shelley's, called the enchantment of the heart."[1]

Ultimately *satori* brings Barthes back to the referent of photography: that "*necessarily* real thing which has been placed before the lens, without which there would have been no photograph" (*CL*, 76). He refers to it as the "that-has-been" of photography: its *interfuit.*

What I see has been here, in this place which extends between infinity and the subject (*operator* or *spectator*); it has been here, and yet immediately separated; it has been absolutely, irrefutably present, and yet already deferred. It is all this which the verb *intersum* means. (*CL*, 77)

For Barthes, this is the genius of Photography and its horror: a photograph simultaneously testifies to the presence of a thing at a certain past moment and to its absolute pastness, its death. By attesting that what we see indeed existed, Photography partakes in the economy of death and resurrection (*CL*, 82), and it is in this context that Barthes analyzes the 1898 Winter Garden photograph his mother when she was five years old.

Barthes's goal in looking through the photographs of his mother after she died was to find "the truth of the face" he had loved (*CL*, 67). As he enters the labyrinth of those photographs, he confesses:

I knew that at the center of this labyrinth I would find nothing but this sole picture, fulfilling Nietzsche's prophecy: 'A labyrinthine man never seeks the truth but only his Ariadne'. The Winter Garden Photograph was my Ariadne, not because it would help me discover a secret thing (monster or treasure), but because it would tell me what constituted that thread which drew me toward Photography. I must interrogate the evidence of Photography, not from the viewpoint of pleasure, but in relation to what we romantically call love and death. (*CL*, 73)

Here, photography's banality and pathos are joined by "the melancholy of Photography" (*CL*, 79). The intentional/emotional pursuits of Barthes's quasi-phenomenological investigations cancel out the operation of *studium* and *punctum* that works fairly well when he investigates photographs other than those of himself and his mother. Actually, his phenomenological perspective borders on phenomenological fallacy, so much is it invested in fictionalizing, mythologizing, and spinning the novelistic thread of "love and death" (that parallels the paradigm of life and death he mentions later [*CL*, 92])—which is no different from my fictionalizing, mythologizing, and storytelling prewritten in and by my photographs. All photographs, as Barthes hastens to remind us, are "reduced to a simple click, one separating the initial pose from the final print" (*CL*, 92). And that mythologized print has the capacity to function as Ariadne's thread thanks to the "luminous rays" and the optic of the camera obscura, in other words, thanks to the discovery that "made it possible to recover and print directly the luminous rays emitted by a variously lighted object" (*CL*, 80):

The photograph is literally an emanation of the referent. From a real body, which was there, proceed radiations which ultimately touch me, who am here; the duration of the transmission is insignificant; the photograph of the missing being, as Sontag says, will touch me like the delayed rays of a star. A sort of umbilical cord links the body of the photographed thing to my gaze: light, though impalpable, is here a carnal medium, a skin I share with anyone who has been photographed. (*CL*, 80–81)

The umbilical cord links the "this-will-be" of the referent with the "this-has-been" experienced by the Spectator, leaving the latter always pondering "over a *catastrophe which has already occurred.* Whether or not the subject is already dead," adds Barthes, "every photograph is this catastrophe" (*CL*, 96).

For Barthes, the light that reaches the Spectator literally resurrects the referent from flat death. In photographs of relatives, the rays reveal/confirm the Spectator's resemblance to the referent, thus conforming to the Spectator's notion of the subject's identity: all photographs of my mother's parents look like all other photographs of her parents; all photographs of Barthes's mother look like all other photos of her. Barthes sees the equation between resemblance and identity as "an absurd, purely legal, even penal affair" (*CL*, 102). Skeptical about his mother's likeness, he finds "the splendor of her truth" only in the Winter Garden Photograph, "one which does not look 'like' her," the photograph of a child he never knew (*CL*, 103).

The affective conclusion, disappointingly enough, does not yield any new insights into the nature of that truth about his mother that Barthes has set out to find through this book. The photograph can only authenticate the existence of his mother before he could have possibly known her. The sign of her face undergoes a process of mythologization as he finds in it "something inexpressible: evident (this is the law of the Photograph) yet improbable (I cannot prove it)" (*CL*, 107). To be sure, he also traces what he calls "genetic features" and lineage in the photograph; he discovers "the air," or expression, a look, through which he glimpses her soul, *animula* (*CL*, 109), all of which (a leap of faith by a loving son) contributes to the intentionality-laden affective "myth" of his mother's soul, as it reduces her to a metaphor of his own experience. None of this could possibly have been experienced by any other spectator, who, in viewing the Winter Garden Photograph, would have at best imparted a polite *studium* upon it, a fact only too well realized by Barthes, who, for that very reason, does not reproduce this picture, crucial to his study. Such a built-in *aporia* inherent in the text of *Camera Lucida* is one of the elements that produces desire in the reader who, deprived of the visual illustration of Barthes's point, pursues the textual solution but reaches none—the latter, like the former, relies on the economy of the void.

The flat death of the photograph encodes at once the pastness of the once-present moment and the click that "shot," "removed" that moment into the future from which the spectator can view it as past. For Barthes, the possibility of repetition, that is, the mechanistic reproduction of photographs, translates into resurrection; his mythologizing could be viewed as participating in the economies of death and rebirth or, more poignantly, in rebellion against the inescapability of "flat death." By the same token, my storytelling may, too, be a rebellion against the morbid semantic implications of the Polish word *zdjęcie*, or "removal," and against the colloquial English word *shot*, the latter forever marked for me to the point that I never use the phrase "to take a shot."

Is it because of the family mythology hidden behind those old photographs of my grandparents, those "patches" my mother showed me when I was little? Later I learned that my grandfather was shot in 1946 by the NKVD[2]: he had to be removed since he was an officer in AK, the Polish Home Army, which opposed the invading Red Communist Army and supported the London-based Polish government-in-exile.[3] But it all began on 10 November 1944, the day before my mother's birthday, when my grandfather mysteriously disappeared. Rumor had it that he, along with other officers, had been taken prisoner by the Nazis. For seven months my grandmother made trips to Lublin's Castle, which had been turned into a Nazi prison, to deliver food parcels to her husband. One day late in June 1945 the truck she was riding to the prison was bombed by the retreating Germans. My grandmother, fatally injured, died on Sunday, 1 July 1945. She was thirty-seven. Six months later, on 22 January 1946, my grandfather unexpectedly reappeared. It turned out that all this time he had been in a labor camp in Russia. He managed to escape only to return home and find his wife dead and his two teenage daughters in the care of his wife's mother. Five days later, on Sunday, 27 January 1946 he was removed by the NKVD. My mom found him shot, lying face down in the snow outside the house. He was forty-five.

Whenever I remember this story, the patches on the old photographs evolve into two faces that cease for an instant to represent "flat death." Initially a *studium* for me, the photographs evolve. The luminous rays that emanate from the two faces engender *punctum* in me, not so much by the referents themselves, as by the *interfuit*, the "this-has-beenness" of what I apprehend. My gaze then turns inward—*satori*—and for a fleeting moment I see myself, incredulously, a descendant of those unknown deceased, a living seed of death connected to those faces by the umbilical cords of luminous rays emanating from them. After Roland Barthes, how else could I view these three photographs?

Notes

1. James Joyce, *A Portrait of the Artist as a Young Man* (New York: Viking, 1968), p. 213.
2. NKVD (Narodny Kommissariat Vnutriennikh Del, or People's Commis-

sariat of Internal Affairs) was a Soviet police agency responsible for internal security and corrective labor camps. Concerned mainly with political offenders, the NKVD used its broad investigative and judicial powers to carry out Stalin's massive purges of the 1930s. In March 1946 it became the Ministry of Internal Affairs (*Encyclopaedia Britannica*, 15th ed., s.v. "Poland, History of" p. 652).

3. Polish government-in-exile was formed in France in 1939, based on a 1935 constitution. As a civil and military resistance movement had formed in occupied Poland in September 1939 after the German invasion, the Polish government-in-exile assured the survival of the Polish Republic under the leadership and supreme command of General Sikorski. It moved to the United Kingdom after the defeat of France in 1940.

7

Narrative Liaisons

Roland Barthes and the Dangers of the Photo-Essay

Carol Shloss

This chapter can be located at an intersection of theory, at a place where Roland Barthes's rhetorical analysis of the image meets a method of narratology he first set forth in "Introduction to the Structural Analysis of Narratives." In his earlier work, Barthes spoke primarily about the cultural codes that inform our reading of individual images, suggesting only in passing that images arranged in sequence, like those of a magazine photo-essay, could have a cumulative effect. "Naturally," he said, "several photographs can come together to form a sequence [. . .]; the signifier of connotation is then no longer to be found at the level of any one of the fragments of the sequence but at that—what the linguists would call the suprasegmental level—of the concatenation" ("Rhetoric of the Image," *IMT*, 25). But I wanted to think about the photo-essay as a closely articulated narrative and to understand what Barthes's categories of cardinal function and catalyzer, his way of distinguishing the moments of narrative consequence and risk from those of mere cohesiveness, could reveal about the representations of visual culture. I was especially drawn to *Streetwise*, a series on homeless children in Seattle by Mary Ellen Mark, because the subject pointed to itself as an emblem of the dynamic between risk and social cohesiveness, a drama carried on at the fringes of culture, at a seam, at a place of radical discontinuity where the very ground of culture's ability to regenerate was itself called into question.

One of the first things to take into account in such a venture is the multiplicity of codes that buttress our understanding of Mary Ellen Mark's project.[1] Not only did she photograph vagrant children, but she returned with her husband, Martin Bell, to make a movie of their lives.[2] Her book consists of images, captions, an edited sound track, and a narrative account of how she met the kids and gained their trust. Before we even confront the polysemy of the images, we have to think about a dense texture of intersecting messages that surround them; and I think it is important to notice that unless the captions identify people by their first names, they consist of quotations attributed to the children. Although Barthes usually considered captions to be a verbal intervention that limited or "tied down" the multiple and ambiguous attributes of photographs, these particular captions give us the children's self-understanding so that we can measure their explanations of their experience against our own. In other words, Mary Ellen Mark's book exists as a form of dialogue between the children and the culture that surrounds and encodes them and that is represented to us alternately by their photographed bodies and by the white spaces of the pages themselves.

This circumstance has a particular poignancy, for we see immediately that risk is understood in different terms depending on the perspective that measures it. Kim and Tiny, talking about the pros and cons of prostitution and choosing a "good" pimp, know how to weigh certain dangers while remaining oblivious to others:

> KIM "I just started doing this stuff. I never even thought of 'hoing 'til I got down here. You know Tracy? She used to live with me when she was a home girl, because her parents kicked her out. And she disappeared. She went downtown with Lorna. You know Lorna? And then Lorna came back and said that Tracy's a 'ho now. And then I got really worried about her. I said, 'I can't let her do that stuff.' 'Cause I always heard bad things like white slavery, that she's gonna get beat up and everything. That's what scared me. So I thought, I gotta come down and get her out of there, whether I gotta kidnap her or what. Then I come down here and I see her and she says, 'It's great, man.' So I'm just sittin' there going 'What? I heard that you don't like it down here, that you're getting beat up and raped and everything.' She said, 'I'm making so much money and it's so easy, the money comes so easy. It's great. You gotta do it.' And I sat there and I go, 'How much money do you make?' and she started naming off and I go, 'Wow I think I'd better.'" (*SW*, 63)

Barthes tells us that "for a function to be cardinal, it is enough that the action to which it refers open an alternative that is of direct consequence for the subsequent development of the story" ("Narrative," *IMT*, 93–94). No one, child or reader of the text of the child's life, would disagree that this action inaugurates an uncertainty or that it entails a risk. If we regard the street life of these young girls as a narrative syntagm, no one would doubt that a grammar or a combinatory system would mark the moment of becoming a child prostitute as cardinal: on this decision will rest a string of other lesser actions we can categorize as waiting, approaching, greeting, making a contract—the behaviors that lead up to the "date" and that, in a fictional narrative, would provide areas of relative safety or rest, serving to bind the nuclei—the more dangerous, consequential moments—together.

I can see immediately that there are several problems a photo-essay presents that fictional narrative need not concern itself with, and that these arise from the referential quality of the photo: in none of his early writing about the semiology of images did Barthes confront their status as testament. It was only at the end of his life, searching for the likeness of his dead mother in the Winter Garden photograph, that he could say, "It is reference which is the founding order of Photography" (*CL*, 77) and understand the searing implication of that statement to his own situation as a reader and subject of culture. No longer content to classify the codes that denoted gender, age, or position in what he saw, he pushed forward—some, like Jonathan Culler, would say backward[3]—to name an interior adventure inflected by grief and private agitation: "I am a primitive, a child—or a maniac; I dismiss all knowledge, all culture, I refuse to inherit anything from another eye than my own" (*CL*, 51). I think Barthes would have appreciated my search for the codes of street life and my attempt to name the logic of their presentation, and he would never have disagreed that our reading of photographs is colored by them. But in his final venture into understanding the photograph, he relegated such knowledge to what he called the image's *studium*—a kind of logic of culture that required one to recognize it as though disincarnated, disaffected, and outside—a stance he was no longer willing to take. "I wanted to explore [photography] not as a question (a theme) but as a wound" (*CL*, 21).

In saying this, Barthes was of course proposing to shift the basis for viewing photographs and to experience them with the private urgency engendered by death. But his need to do this, to find the ultimate reaches of communication through images, brought him to a boundary, to a place beyond the ability of culture to mediate. "Cruel, sterile, deficiency: I cannot transform my grief, I cannot let my gaze drift; no culture will help me utter this suffering which I experience entirely on the level of the image's finitude [. . .] when it is painful, nothing in it can transform grief into mourning" (*CL*, 90). That place was the absent referent—the "that-has-been" of photography—the intractability, its subject and its separation in time. "Photography's referent is not the same as the referent of other systems of representation," according to Barthes. "It's not optionally real; it's necessarily real [. . .] Every photograph is somehow co-natural with its referent" (*CL*, 76). For him, this was photography's *punctum* and his private grief; for him, images were death's alibi, the sleight of hand that profferred the excited, living presence of those already and absolutely gone.

This has been a long digression to remind us to avoid being facile about the risks of narrative and the codes of risk. Barthes's most profound writing about photography distinguished clearly between the *studium* and the *punctum*; he saw that "danger" can be read as a logic or it can be experienced as a wound. Though, as I have said, he made this distinction for the spectator, his clarity about the "that-has-beenness" of the photograph implies a similar regard for the subjects of the representation whose experienced wounds he would surely have recognized as commensurate with his own. I extend this observation and return with it to Mary Ellen Mark's photo-essay about streetwise children. For by this detour we can now see that the two "voices" of her book—the images themselves and the voices of the children—correspond in spirit with Barthes's *studium* and *punctum*—one giving us a logic of information and a way of reading its combinatory system and the other rendering the ache of circumstance and the thwarted desire to transform the unspeakable conditions of life. For surely these children are like photographs, their abbreviated lives a fugitive testimony to our inability to imagine "duration, affectively or symbolically." "The age of the photograph," Barthes reminds us, "is also the age of revolutions, contestations, assassinations, explosions, in short, of impatiences, of everything which denies ripening" (*CL*, 93).

So, what does photography know of these impatient, unripe children who seem prematurely to know so much? If we first address this question at the level of codes, we notice that Mary Ellen Mark consistently photographs at a site of loss, which discomforts or unsettles a middle-class spectator's historical, cultural, and psychological assumptions. Barthes tells us that we find photographs intelligible to the extent that we have already learned to recognize signs, whether practical, national, cultural, or aesthetic, and that we can see them in the gestures, attitudes, and expressions of the subjects. In *Streetwise* it seems to me that we read by a kind of sinister, inverted logic. Where we expect to find shelter, we see eviction:

RAT (voice over) "There's this old abandoned hotel and we took all the furniture we could find in all the different rooms and put it into this one room. And we'd carry water up in these gallon jugs, 'cause it didn't have no water or electricity. And we'd just shower down at this place called The Compass on Washington Avenue for fifty cents. And do our laundry in the laundromat and whatever it took. It was pretty easy actually." (*SW*, 61)

Where we anticipate privacy, we discover exposure. Actions that might in other circumstances be considered tender or moving are here subject to arrest:

LULU (shouting) "I just got out of jail not even a month ago. I ain't gettin' in no trouble, punk. I bet you I got a bruise on my arm, guaranteed. And I'm pressing charges on your ass. Punk. 'Cause I hate you and I'm gonna git you for that. [. . .]
SECOND COP "What's the trouble here, young man?"
LULU "I'm not a him. I'm a her. I'm pressing charges. [. . .]
SECOND COP "Will you please calm down?" (*SW*, 71)

The writing of the body is transposed into literal citation. I think it is important for us to notice that Barthes expropriates the language of street life for the description of narrative, making into a system of metaphors—movement, arrest, eviction, citation, shelter, or the lack of it—the very terms that describe the literal situation of these children. For Rat, Tiny, Lulu, and Dewayne—the kids who let Mary Ellen Mark photograph them—there seems to be no inalienable site where, in Barthes's words again, their "image is free" or where they can enact "an interiority which [. . .] is identified with [. . .] truth" (*CL*, 98). These children own so little that not even privacy, which in the West falls under the historical laws of property, is theirs.

The result of such exposure is a prolonged irony. The children are denied access to the symbolic, given few ways to master their fates by the displaced repetitions of culture that Freud and Lacan both considered essential to human development; their lives nonetheless are coded by the symbolic, almost as if their bodies could bear the imprint of what has rejected them and cast them out. I am reminded here of Wilfred Owen's indictment of England during World War I, in which the young poet pitted the bodies of the wounded and dead against the language of the fathers in order to discredit their false romanticism:

If you could hear, at every jolt, the blood
Come gurgling from the froth-corrupted lungs
[. . .] you would not tell with such high zest
[. . .] The Old Lie: Dulce et decorum est
Pro patria mori.[4]

But there are no liars here. Or I am reminded of Franz Kafka's explorer in *The Penal Colony* who was told by the commandant that "Whatever commandment the prisoner has disobeyed is written on his body by the Harrow."[5] "Does he know his sentence?" the explorer asks. "No," he is told, "there would be no point in telling him. He'll learn it on his body" (197). But there are no commandants.

There are simply the signs of dispossession, which are, interestingly, also the signs of mass culture—its T-shirts, its leather, its makeup. Far from being announcements of outlandishness, the getup of these children suggests to us that their lack of homes leaves them defenseless and vulnerable to whatever impressions American culture has available, letting us speculate about how the private realm, the space of shelter in families, can function as a space of resistance to the writing of culture, a beyond of human identity before cultural codes press their stamp on the unsuspecting young.

I am also struck in these photographs by an unexpected disparity of codes—a joining of sign systems that would seem incongruous in other circumstances—the mixing of signs of childhood with those of adult sexuality or responsibility: a thirteen-year-old prostitute holds a rag doll; a young mother holds a child and a stuffed animal, herself young enough to play with the toy. There is also the coupling of middle-class dreams and the sordidness that signals their defeat: "I wanna be really rich [. . .] and live on a farm with a bunch of horses, which is my main best animal [. . .] and have three yachts or more [. . .] and diamonds and jewels and all that stuff" (*SW*, n.p.). The image that most haunts me, as it must have Mary Ellen Mark because she put it on the cover of her book, is "Tiny, Halloween, 1983"—in which a thirteen-year-old's Halloween costume is a hat with a veil, a short black dress, and dark stockings and gloves. She had come to the drop-in center dressed, as she told Mary Ellen, as a French whore, signing herself as an alien version of what she already is.

When we think of *Streetwise* as a narrative, we can see that behavior the kids would never consider to be rule-governed is in fact bound by clear systems of association. The pattern is established by the "trick" and by the dangers that accompany the hunt for it. Either the girls are waiting in aggregate, arranged syntagmatically with each other, or they can be considered hierarchically, each group leading to its pimp, who reveals the hidden paradigmatic relationships of the whole: "I'm goin' to those high schools and get me some fresh ones" (*SW*, 63). Each girl is easily replaceable in the system. Thinking narratively, we can see that cardinal functions far outweigh catalyzers and, in fact, there are few liaisons represented that are not dangerous.

KIM "He said, 'If anybody comes to beat you up and I come and save you, that means you gotta work for me.' I hope he doesn't got somebody to come beat me up. [. . .]"

ERICA "He'll kill you, O.K.? He'll ass-fuck you, fuck you in the ear or anything. I'm serious, don't mess with Patrice. [. . .]"

TINY "He raped me last year, when I first came downtown. [. . .]"
ERICA "He raped me too. And he took my money. Up in that hotel, he came and said he was gonna rob this dude. [. . .]"
KEVIN "People get killed down here, they go to jail down here. Everything happens down here and none of it's good." (*SW*, 63–64)

Apart from the occasional partner—which all the kids seem to want[6]—association is fraught with risk, each encounter an invitation to damage, a violation of innocence and an announcement of the lack of protection and support in their lives. In the last two prints in the series, Mary Ellen Mark shows us the final imprint of this culture. Looking at Dewayne, and then looking at Dewayne in his coffin, we can see clearly the implied signification of the whole essay: death, which had previously remained lurking in the margins, enters the frame, transformed into an explicit image. A child is totally deleted, completing the message of his eviction—the perfect apotheosis of the absence of meaning that is the felt quality, if not the culturally encoded message, of his life. Kim's "Who cares?" is the implicit question that accompanies the whole project.

This image and this sentiment bring us curiously back to the speculations of Roland Barthes at the end of his own life, when, faced with his mother's death, he looked for the essence of photography in her childhood image. Looking at the Winter Garden photograph, he spoke variously of its "thereness"—its presence, its ability to evoke the experience of *satori*—and its horror, its intractable record of death. And he concluded from the puncture, the interior rending of such an experience, that the project of all photography without exception is death:

For Death must be somewhere in a society; if it is no longer (or less intensely) in religion, it must be elsewhere; perhaps in this image which produces Death while trying to preserve life. Contemporary with the withdrawal of rites, Photography may correspond to the intrusion, in our modern society, of an asymbolic Death, outside of religion, outside of ritual [. . .] Life/Death: the paradigm is reduced to a simple click, the one separating the initial pose from the final print. (*CL*, 92)

"Whether or not the subject is already dead," Barthes claimed, "every photograph is this catastrophe" (*CL*, 96). These final reflections have a curious affinity with the interior life of Mary Ellen Mark's photo-essay, for in both cases, as dissimilar and dispossessed as streetwise kids may seem from an aging French intellectual, the absence of mothers provides the constant subtext of their searches for meaning.

KIM "[. . .] And I go 'Mom, I am not [a prostitute]. Just leave.' And she goes 'Fine. Thanks alot. All week long I'm going to remember this. All week I'm going to be thinking about how much you love me.' I don't care. She doesn't care about me. She never did. She doesn't" (*SW*, 62)

RAT (voice over) "And she starts crying alot. [. . .] And I just said, 'Mom, I gotta go' and I hung up on her." (*SW,* 66)

SHADOW (voice over) "Six months were up, nobody could find my mother. A year went up, nobody could find my mother. [. . .] I left." (*SW,* 68)

RAT (voice over) "Let her think what she wants, that I'm dead, whatever she wants to think. But I don't want to listen to her cry [. . .] makin' me feel bad." (*SW,* 66)

When we look at *Camera Lucida,* we can see a similar site of loss, and in fact, I think it is possible for us to conclude that the death of Barthes's mother was the circumstance that brought him, that great codifier of cultural systems, to the absolute limits of those systems.

Faced with her absence, Barthes sought for what could solace him and found nothing: "My photograph [. . .] is without culture: when it is painful, nothing in it can transform grief into mourning" (*CL,* 90). Not only was his mother "out of play" (*CL,* 69), but he found himself beyond coding, at a place where no social behavior could mitigate the singular fortune of a motherless child. Where rhetorical analysis can tame photographs, distancing, sublimating, and pacifying them, no aesthetic or empirical habit can enter that place where images are suspended, that place Barthes referred to, hesitantly and self-consciously, as "the very space of love" (*CL,* 72).

Far from regarding this as sentimental or romantic, I want to relate this recognition with another, which Elaine Scarry makes eloquently in her book *The Body in Pain.*[7] There she observes that "[t]he notion that everyone is alike by having a body and that what differentiates one person from another is the soul or intellect or personality can mislead one into thinking that the body is shared and the other part is private when exactly the opposite is the case" (256). Both she and Barthes were, I think, reflecting on the body's isolate existence and on the extent to which individual sentience remains beyond the power of cultural intervention. We recall here that Barthes opened *Camera Lucida* with the question "What does my *body* [italics added] know of Photography?" (*CL,* 22) and that in *Roland Barthes by Roland Barthes* he identified *corps* as his "mana-word": "a word whose ardent, complex, ineffable, and somehow sacred signification gives the illusion that this word holds an answer to everything" (*RB,* 129). If we use Scarry's description of culture as "perceived-pain-wished-gone," then we must imagine Barthes at the end of his life to be expressing his understanding that in psychological pain, as in physical aversiveness, the collective wishes of culture can remain inadequate to the task of individual rescue. "When it is painful, nothing can transform grief into mourning" (*CL,* 90).

The children in Mary Ellen Mark's book seem to me to know these things. According to Rat, "as soon as you turn around, you got a knife in your back" (*SW*, 65). Lulu saw the treachery of the streets in the body as well: "What's your name? Did somebody hurt you? Really, I won't hurt you. (To the arriving paramedic.) Looks like her jaw is broke" (*SW*, 74). I have argued previously that these children are dispossessed even in the very acts that mark them as trapped by culture, and we see them repeatedly engaging in behaviors that suggest that they experience the streets not as culture's opposite but as its apotheosis. They want to escape from it and can only use other cultural tools to try:

SHADOW "You learn to fight or you disappear. I know how to fight but I like disappearing." (*SW*, n.p.)

RAT "I love to fly [. . .] The only bad part about flying is having to come back down to the fuckin' world." (*SW*, n.p.)

SHADOW "'Why do you want to dye your hair? To change?'" "Not to change. To get away from everything." (*SW*, n.p.)

The limits of their ability to effect transformation is something they consistently have to face.

It took Roland Barthes a lifetime to get to the same place, to walk down an emotional street where personal danger is isolate and inescapable. It is as if he left the activity of recording and analysis, that activity passed on to us as viewers of any photo-essay, and joined the other side of the frame, using the voice of the children in the captions who speak their self-understanding. The point is not whether one can achieve this goal of acculturation, whether a fringe of uncoded existence remains for us to enter, but rather one of consent. Barthes tells us that "culture (from which the *studium* derives) is a contract arrived at between creators and consumers" (*CL*, 28). I would argue that Barthes's withdrawal stems from his realization of culture's ultimate impotence: it exists but it cannot soothe or quiet or make shareable one's grief at the absence or death of a parent. But whatever his motive, and whatever we think of the possibility of achieving the goal, *Camera Lucida* marks Barthes's breaking of his side of the contract: "I am a primitive, a child—or a maniac; I dismiss all knowledge, all culture, I refuse to inherit anything from another eye than my own" (*CL*, 51). It is as if he were telling us that mothers make us streetwise, but the absence of mothers puts us on the street.

Notes

1. See Roland Barthes, "The Death of the Author": "We know now that a text is not a line of words releasing a single 'theological' meaning (the 'message' of the Author-God) but a multi-dimensional space in which a variety of writings,

none of them original, blend and clash. The text is a tissue of quotations drawn from the innumerable centres of culture" (*IMT*, 146).

2. "In late August 1983 Cheryl [McCall], Martin, and I returned to Seattle to make *Streetwise.* [. . .] In October of 1984 we returned to Seattle to show the completed film to the kids. This was the first public showing in this country of *Streetwise,* and it was for all of us the most terrifying. If the kids in the film did not like the film or if they felt betrayed by it then we would have failed. [. . .] By the end of the film many of the children were in tears. One boy approached Martin. 'Are our lives really like this?' he asked. [. . .] The street children of Seattle embraced the film as their own. They felt it was truly their story" (Mary Ellen Mark, *Streetwise* [New York: Aperture, 1983], p. xi). These circumstances tell us that the intention of the author/photographer was to conduct the dialogue of the text as a cohesive one, that is, as a form of speaking in which the self-image of the children accorded with the "signs" of their lives presented by the photographer. Subsequent references to excerpts from *Streetwise* are given in the text with the abbreviation *SW.*

3. See Jonathan Culler, *Roland Barthes* (New York: Oxford University Press, 1983).

4. Wilfred Owen, *The Collected Poems of Wilfred Owen* (New York: New Directions, 1963), p. 55.

5. Franz Kafka, *The Penal Colony* (New York: Schocken, 1948), p. 197.

6. RAT (voice over) "Every person, no matter how big or tough they are, should always have a partner. You never want to go on the streets alone. It's a mistake. It's just you'll get lonely, you'll get upset, you'll get beat up. Because, you never can tell if someone's gonna come up from the front of you and start to get your attention, and this other dude is gonna walk up behind you and bust your fuckin' head. Partners are always better" (*SW,* 69).

7. Elaine Scarry, *The Body in Pain* (New York: Oxford University Press, 1985).

8

Circulating Images

Notes on the Photographic Exchange

Liliane Weissberg

Kafka

A myth, as Roland Barthes insists, is a repetition of images. It is also a message and a system of communication.[1] Which message, however, can be transmitted by a particular photograph? And when and how does photography enter the mythological realm?

In *Camera Lucida*, Barthes tries to decipher this image's message in sketching an archaeology of sight that reaches beyond his native French. Two Latin words serve this task. The term *studium* is used as the "application to a thing, taste for someone, a kind of general, enthusiastic commitment" (*CL*, 26). This contextual application is punctured and disturbed by another factor of Barthes's study, namely the *punctum*, a "sting, speck, cut, little hole" (*CL*, 27), interrupting the continued absorbance, and carried by a striking visual element. The *punctum* fixates the gaze of the viewer on a part of the image that translates it as a whole. Like a fetish, this element—the shoe or dress of a person depicted—expresses and stands for the viewer's desire and, metonymically, for his or her experience of the photograph itself. As a "wound" (*blessure*[2]), the *punctum* provides this experience through an injury that in itself can be fetishized—indeed, it resembles the prime object of a female fetishism, as put forth by Naomi Schor in her reading of George Sand's work.[3]

Photography's *punctum* turns the image into a gendered one: phallic and wounded at once, a desired female body is able to transgress the *logos* of time. *Coupure* and *coup de dés*:[4] Barthes's *punctum* fractures time as well. His search for the meaning of photographs is thus carried by this notion of contingency, a hardly explicable fascination with details that seem not only to supplement but also to undo the *studium*'s task.

Barthes's project is not without precedent. In his "Short History of

Photography," Walter Benjamin focuses on the picture of the photographer Karl Dautheney and his bride, a woman who will not only become the mother of a poet but also meet an early, violent death. Here, too, the camera may have found some sense of future mourning and an invisible space in which "reality" partakes of an image as a rupture and a *punctum* of sorts:

After contemplating a photographic image for some time, one notices how much its contrasts come to touch each other: the most exact technology can offer its products a magic value, such as a painted picture can no longer contain for us. Despite the photographer's skill and the planned posture of his model, the viewer experiences the unresistable desire to find in this picture a tiny spark of chance—Here and Now—by which reality, so to say, has burnt itself into the image's character. He wants to find the invisible place [*unscheinbare Stelle*] in which, in the existence [*Sosein*] of this long past moment, the future rests today, and rests so eloquently, that we can find it looking back.[5]

In Barthes a particular detail like a shoe can evoke the appropriation of the image as memory. He can recall the past. For Benjamin, however, the *unscheinbare Stelle* should draw the photograph into the here and now, give evidence of its present currency. Memory is experienced in these seemingly invisible places not as a reference to the past, moreover, but to the future.

Photographs of children, for example, may tell of such a future by also hinting at their subject's own future. Benjamin selects a particular photograph for discussion. This photograph, which is not reproduced in this essay but in other work documenting Benjamin's personal collection, hints at Benjamin's present and future occupation, his work on Franz Kafka (Figure 8.1):[6]

At that time, studios emerged with their draperies and palm trees, tapestries, and easels, which oscillate ambiguously between execution and representation, torture chamber and throne room and from which a moving testimony is brought to us in the form of an early picture of Kafka. There, a young boy of about six years is standing in a kind of winter garden landscape, dressed in a tight, and, as it were, humbling children's suit that is loaded down with trimmings. Palm leaves are starring in the background. And as if it counts to increase the stickiness and humidity of these upholstered tropics, the model carries a disproportionately big hat with a large rim, just like Spaniards wore, in his left hand. Surely, the model would disappear in this arrangement, if not for his immeasurably sad eyes which dominate this destined landscape.[7]

Kafka's eyes document a sadness other than nostalgia; they capture his life and work and times by clairvoyant means. Benjamin's lucid camera sheds light by offering the mysterious and magical darkness unknown even to the subject himself.

Figure 8.1. Franz Kafka (circa 1888). From the collection of Klaus Wagenbach, Berlin.

Benjamin points at the difference with which the eye of the viewer and the lens of the camera behold their subjects. Man focuses consciously, while the camera may make visible what a person cannot see. This sight can be likened to an unconscious reception, and in referring to the technical possibilities of photographic enlargements or the photograph's simple freezing of time, Benjamin coins a term that integrates this art form with science as well as therapeutic medicine: the optical unconscious. "About this optical unconscious, [the viewer] will only learn from [the camera lens], just as he will learn about the instinctive unconscious from psychoanalysis."[8]

While Benjamin compares the photograph to the psychoanalytic project, Barthes's *Camera Lucida* bears psychoanalytic references like none of his other texts. In her study of the essay, Eilene Hoft-March stresses Barthes's indebtedness to Freudian concepts and Lacanian theory, drawing attention, for example, to the relationship between the *studium* and Lacan's notion of the law and the symbolic.[9] Benjamin's photograph in turn may tell of a successful analytic session; the unconscious is brought to light, even though photography itself documents art's shift from aureatic uniqueness to the modes of technical reproduction. This particular form of repeated image poses the exhibition value (*Ausstellungswert*) over that of cult (*Kultwert*).[10] In this way, Benjamin's photographs tell myths of their own.

Barthes's own desire, not the photograph's value, structures his reflections. His contemplations on photography are a work of mourning, a *Trauerarbeit* by which he contemplates the status of the photograph, trying to recall not just a photographic image but a person. Barthes is in search of photographic authenticity. Written shortly after his mother's death, *Camera Lucida* wants to match a photograph with his own memory of her and to see whether this memory has been or can be captured in a photographic image at all. The photograph, then, is looked upon as a trace that may not only mark his mother's existence, but prolong it by affirming his memory. And, indeed, Barthes is able to find such a photograph. It does not show his mother as he might have known her but as a child, lonely, although standing next to others, photographed like Kafka, in a winter garden room.

Absence/Presence

A winter garden alters the flow of seasons. Reaching out for his mother's photograph, Barthes seems to alter the chronology of time as well, not the least in the sequence of generations. He can look protectively at a child who gave birth to him and whose later life and death he knows about. This is the mother he has known—although he has never known her like this. There is a photograph in *Camera Lucida* from the author's collection that pictures a nameless female child. This picture, titled "The Stock" (*CL*, 104), is marginalized, however, and open to speculation: it may represent the author's family and it may not. The Winter Garden photograph that takes center stage in his discussion is absent, averted from the reader's eyes, and Barthes's private property. Within the series of photographs presented, it has itself become a *punctum*, a curious interruption of visibility.[11] *Camera Lucida* is a book not only about photography but also about an absent photograph, one that is merely described and perhaps wished for. It stands for Barthes's desire itself.

Barthes clearly indicates that he prefers the suggestive and the veiled in contrast to the exposed and pornographic image. Benjamin's camera could expose beyond the human eye; Barthes, in turn, wants to reestablish the eye as the detective, hoping for a process of unveiling that ultimately may provide the revelation of the viewer's self. Self-authenticity is at stake here. Replacing Kafka's image with that of his mother, Barthes can speak more clearly about himself, replace the intellectual with the genealogical tradition, with the history of his own body. This is where the *punctum* may change into an antifetish, as Barthes rejects any ersatz for the experience of desire, the goal and utopia of an imaginary union, and the realm of the imaginary itself. In reverting to the mother-son relationship, Barthes revises the oedipal story into a temporal space that can be wounded and restored.

The reader, learning about Barthes's search and desire for his mother's photograph, can never rival him as a viewer. Blinded, he can only receive the text's allusions. Can this picture's viewer be a woman? Or can the photograph's image be that of a father? The distance provided by time as well as the photograph seems crucial to provide the desire for the family bond. But the absent biological father curiously evokes another father figure, the equally absent but implicitly present Sigmund Freud, a theoretician of the fetish and desire. In *Camera Lucida*, this is the father who guides Barthes's pen and against whom he protests. How can Barthes's search for his mother, and his search for himself, proceed without Freud's image?

There is a play of absence and presence performed in photographs of Freud also. In her essay "Photographie et littérature," Martine Léonard searches for the limit of the biographical project by referring, in a footnote, to the photographs of Edmund Engelman.[12] Shortly before Freud's emigration to England in 1938, Engelman took pictures of Freud's Viennese home and office to document a life and a project that were bound to change if not end (Figure 8.2).[13] Benjamin once described nineteenth-century interiors with their elaborate furnishings as the ideal setting for a crime.[14] Engelman's camera precedes the crime of Freud's expulsion

Figure 8.2. Reproduced from *Berggasse 19: Sigmund Freud's Home and Offices, Vienna 1938/The Photographs of Edmund Engelman* (New York: Basic Books, 1976).

and tries to detect a life and, indeed, the figure of Freud through pictures of his rooms and objects: the couch, the desk, a collection of antiquities. Freud himself does not appear in most of these photographs. Once, the sphinx asked the riddle about human life, and Oedipus, who faced her and discovered the "truth" about his own relationship to his mother and father, deprived himself of any images by blinding himself. Freud's figure of the sphinx, placed in one of his glass cases, tells of Freud's collecting obsession as well as of the material instigation of his oedipal theory.

Freud was not opposed to having his portrait taken. In 1926 Ferdinand Schmutzer did an etching of him (Figure 8.3).[15] K. R. Eissler describes it as a work of art that

> shows Freud as he was becoming known to the world in his gradual rise to fame: an inscrutable face, from which the eyes look out keen, wise and understanding; a face which does not flinch from the tragic eventualities of this world; a face which can never again know fear, and which, despite the expression of sadness, is a stranger to despair; a controlled face, with a slight suggestion of those Olympian features that Goethe so loved to show to the world.[16]

Freud hung two versions of Schmutzer's work in his home, each above a couch, although not his professional one (Figures 8.4 and 8.5). Engelman's camera traces these pictures as well as the photographs of family members, friends, and acquaintances that are tucked away on table corners, placed or pinned on bookshelves, or simply put into and crowding a picture frame (Figure 8.6). Thus, taking pictures as a photographic *mise-en-abîme*, Engelman provides a system of quotations that seems to avoid a direct confrontation with human bodies and the exposed or "pornographic" view of the master himself. In those photographs in which Freud appears, lack is turned into excess, into an overdetermination of the image.

Elsewhere, Freud's physiognomy is well documented. Photographs trace his life from early youth to old age, providing the viewer with a series of emblematic images that can and will have to replace any memory of the person himself. Some of these pictures retain a mysterious essence, as the viewer tries to understand Freud's self-confident posture with cigar (Figure 8.7), and the penetrating glance that would not have seen Napoleon—as Barthes's photographic subject, the emperor's brother Jerome did (*CL*, 3)—but men who thought they were Napoleon.[17] The eyes may, indeed, stand for the optical unconscious itself, the technical instrument of revelation. Who could tell Barthes more about his mother, his wish to see her, his mourning of her—a constant play of *fort* and *da*—and his attempts to know, enlighten, *elucidate*?

Figure 8.3. Sigmund Freud, portrait by Ferdinand Schmutzer (1926). Sigmund Freud copyrights. Mary Evans Picture Library, London.

Figure 8.4. Reproduced from *Berggasse 19: Sigmund Freud's Home and Offices, Vienna 1938/The Photographs of Edmund Engelman* (New York: Basic Books, 1976).

Circulation

In his study on the changing notion and position of the viewer and observer, Jonathan Crary points at the common birth of photography and the capitalist system. "Photography and money become homologous forms of social power in the nineteenth century. They are equally totalizing systems for binding and unifying all subjects within a single global network of valuation and desire," he writes, echoing John Tagg's and Alan Sekula's essays about the relationship between photography

Figure 8.5. Reproduced from *Berggasse 19: Sigmund Freud's Home and Offices, Vienna 1938/The Photographs of Edmund Engelman* (New York: Basic Books, 1976).

and commodity culture.[18] In doubling Schmutzer's etching, Freud has shown his awareness of the technical means of reproduction, and his apartment provided a first space for the circulation of his image. Even more so than etchings, however, photographs can be mechanically produced and exchanged. But they can also, in turn, be transformed into etchings. In 1987, the Austrian National Bank issued a fifty-schilling banknote that bears the image of Sigmund Freud (Figure 8.8). The source of this image was the photograph of Freud in Figure 8.7, taken, according to bank officials, from the book *Sigmund Freud: Sein Leben in*

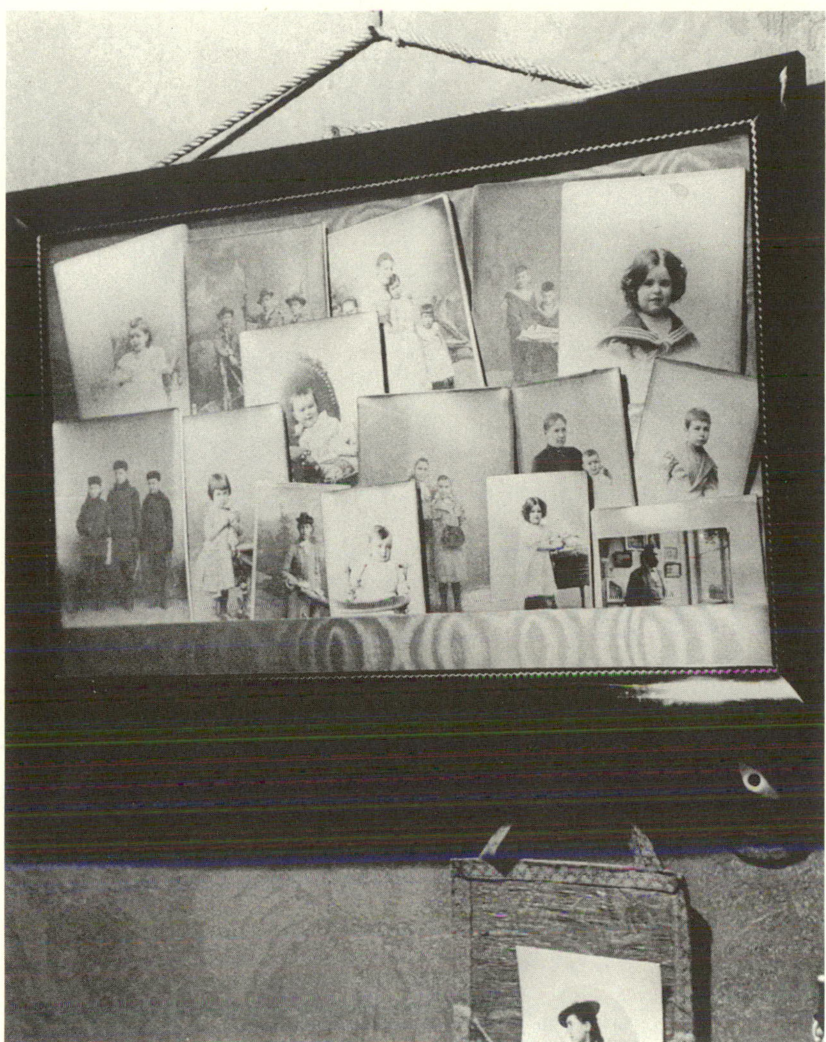

Figure 8.6. Reproduced from *Berggasse 19: Sigmund Freud's Home and Offices, Vienna 1938/The Photographs of Edmund Engelman* (New York: Basic Books, 1976).

Bildern und Texten.[19] *Sigmund Freud* is a pictorial biography, conceived in the tradition of *Andenkenbücher* or memorial books. Such books, providing photographs of the everyday life of German or Eastern Jews before the war, have been very successful, and this particular study combines the tradition of telling the story of a famous person's life with that of a

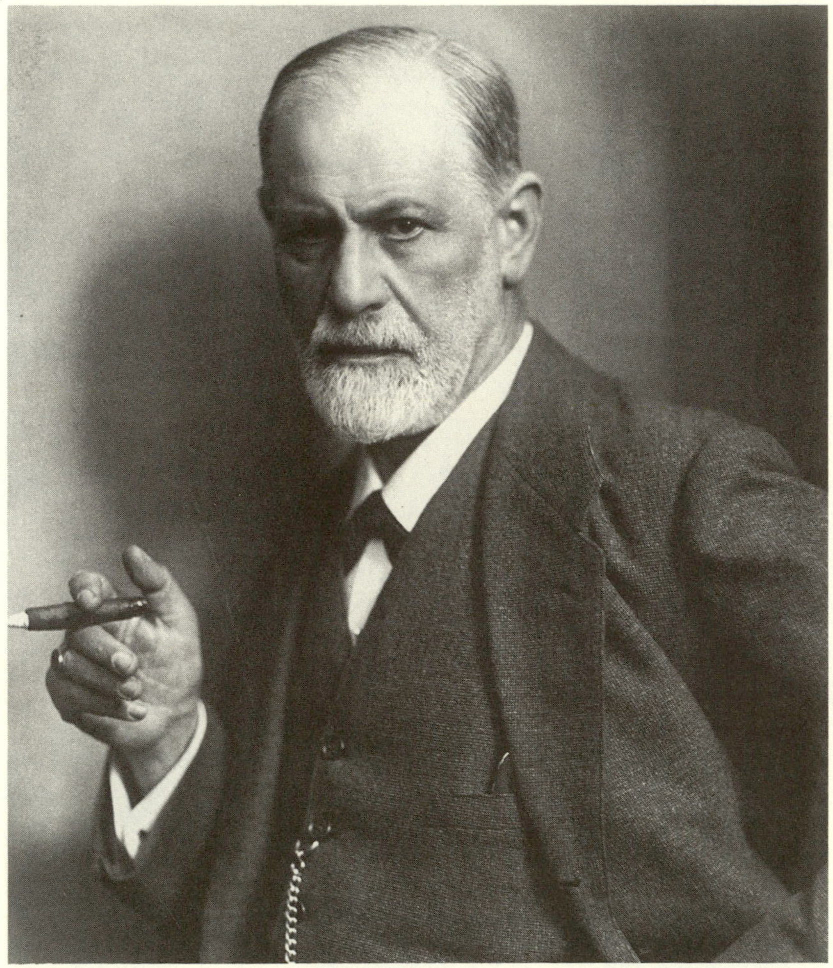

Figure 8.7. Sigmund Freud, photograph by Max Halberstadt (1921). Sigmund Freud copyrights (courtesy of W. E. Freud). Mary Evans Picture Library, London.

community and world lost today. Mourning, controlled by the distance of place and time, turns the private into a public sphere and becomes general nostalgia. The Austrian National Bank insists on depicting only dead personalities on their banknotes and refers with their bill of Freud to this tradition of memorial books.

On the left side of the banknote, facing Freud's portrait, is an abstract

Figure 8.8. Fifty-schilling banknote, Österreichische Nationalbank.

rendering of Freud's sphinx, the emblem of mythology and psychoanalysis. According to the bank's officials, the idea for this motif was taken from the Schwerdtner medal, issued in 1907 on the occasion of Freud's fiftieth birthday; the medal shows Oedipus, not Freud, facing the sphinx.[20] The sphinx depicted on the banknote bears more likeness to Freud's own antiquity, however, as shown in Engelman's photographs.[21] Thus, this Austrian banknote produces a particular play of *fort* and *da*: Engelman's images of absence precede Freud's departure from Vienna. The Austrian banknote turns Freud into an Austrian presence. Among the ambassadors of "Austria's culture, science, and art" represented on the banknote series, he finds, as one of the bank officials confirms, "a well-earned place."[22] Like any ambassador, Freud returned only to have the chance to be sent abroad again, taking this unstable place in the name of the Austrian state.

The word *economy* derives from the Greek *oikos* (home) and *nomos* (law); the latter suggests not just the general law but the law of distribution (*nemein*) as well as sharing. Economy thus implies division or partition (*moira*) as well as distribution, and also "the idea of exchange of circulation, of return."[23] For Jacques Derrida, it is not the story of the sphinx but that of Odysseus that serves as economy's founding tale:

> This motif of circulation can lead one to think that the law of economy is the—circular—return to the point of departure, to the origin, also to the home. So one would have to follow the *odyssean* structure of the economic narrative. *Oikonomia* would always follow the path of Ulysses. The latter returns to the side of his loved ones or to himself; he goes away only in view of *repatriating* himself, in order to return to the home from which [*à partir duquel*] the signal for departure is given and the part assigned, the side chosen [*le parti pris*], the lot divided, destiny commanded (*moira*). The being-next-to-self of the Idea in Absolute Knowledge would be odyssean in this sense, that of an *economy* and a *nostalgia*, a "homesickness," a provisional exile longing for reappropriation. (6–7)

Freud, the exiled scientist, is Oedipus, the solver of riddles, and Odysseus, the seafarer, at once. Claimed as a national treasure, he can stand for the notion of *oikonomia* itself, for a circulation longing for the home.

Safe Transfer

In the banking world, the Austrian fifty-schilling bill gained a particular reputation: it is thought to be the safest banknote in the world. As with all current banknotes, it is illegal to photograph it, but it is also nearly impossible to falsify.[24] Fitted with five different security features, it serves as an example for other currencies.[25] Unlike its photographic source, Freud's eyes on the banknote may follow the viewer further, for one of its safety features is the so-called *Kippeffekt*, a slight change of the image when the banknote is viewed at an angle. Ultimately, Freud's face itself, however, proves to be a safety feature that had determined its selection:

> The person chosen has to be dead, and has to have had a striking [*markantes*] face—this will ease the work of the graphic artists of the National Bank, and make mistaking one banknote for another more difficult. Portraits with wild beards or hair are also increasing the security factor of the money. If the art work on a banknote is more complicated, it will become more difficult to forge them.[26]

Considering Freud's psychoanalytic theory, the rendering of his portrait on a banknote may seem quite ironic. In his essay "Character and Anal Eroticism," Freud was eager to prove the relationship between money and feces, and he described this relationship further in case studies of neurotic behavior, such as his study of the "rat man."[27] The works of mourning (*Trauerarbeit*) and culture (*Kulturarbeit*) are necessary to transform feces into a gift and the gift into money. Freud's genealogy of money and its role in human development was commented on by several of his students, including Sandor Ferenczi, and rarely put into question.[28] But Freud's monetary portrait may also seem ironic given the story of his personal life. Much like Barthes, Freud came from a family with modest means.[29] In his youth and early career, he incurred many debts,[30] and in his choice of medical specialization and choice of patients, Freud was very well aware of financial concerns. In all probability he also knew about the fate of his uncle Josef, who had gone to prison for circulating counterfeit fifty-ruble notes.[31] In his writings on psychoanalytic practice, Freud was eager to stress that treatment had to be paid for to become successful. The current fifty-schilling note would hardly be enough to pay for an analytic session; equaling about four dollars, it is one of Austria's smallest paper denominations.

Culture, science, and art are quoted as the diplomatic expertises of Austria's monetary ambassadors. Freud's writings encompass all three. Politicians and religious leaders seem to be excluded from the series, but Austrian politics and Freud's religious and ethnic origins led to his expulsion from Austria, then part of a greater German state. For the culture, science, and art of this German state, questions of Judaism and money were intricately related. While Freud himself collected jokes on Jewish beggars,[32] the anti-Semitic literature of his time stressed the image of the rich Jew. Since the Middle Ages, moneylending was a "profession" open to Jews, who were excluded from the guilds; the stereotype of Jewish moneylender who deceived the gentile poor has flourished until the twentieth century. In the eighteenth century, German court Jews attained temporary status by having been granted the privilege of coinage (*Hofmünze*); in more dire times, they were asked by the sovereigns to temper the metals, and were decapitated when the court's subjects rebelled. Whether by lending or trading, coinage or theft, by the late eighteenth century, the connection between money and the Jews had been taken for granted and reaffirmed. Descriptions of Jews by Johann Gottfried Herder and others depicted them as strangers without homeland, as representatives of an emergent capitalist economy, and figures of circulation themselves.[33]

Nineteen twenty-one, the year the Freud photograph that served as a model for the banknote's engraving was taken, was also a year of German hyperinflation. That same year, the National Socialist Party begun a propaganda campaign to put the Jew in his place. Party members collected banknotes, imprinted them with caricatures and slogans, and put them into circulation again. The official etching of Freud's portrait is thus preceded, for example, by the inofficial stamp picturing the "Sowjet Jew Radeck," wanted for communist conspiracy (Figure 8.9). Jews, these stamps declared, did not turn German money into a Schmutzer, but into *Schmutz* (Figure 8.10).

Money itself thus stands for German, if not Austrian, culture, science, and art and brings home the political impact of its message. This political impact was surely not lost on Benjamin, who, in a section on "tax advice" in his *One-Way Street*, called for an analysis of government-issued money as cultural artifacts. Remarking on the seeming naïveté of the depicted images, Benjamin asks for an exposition of the head and portrait—*caput*—of capitalism itself, by drawing attention to a winter garden landscape of economic paradise:

> A descriptive analysis of banknotes is needed. The unlimited satirical force of such a book would be equaled only by its objectivity. For nowhere more naively than in these documents does capitalism display itself in solemn earnest. The innocent cupids frolicking about numbers, the goddesses holding tablets of the law, the stalwart heroes sheathing their swords before monetary units, are a world of their own: ornamenting the façade of hell.[34]

Distant Signs

In *S/Z* Barthes, too, writes about money and relates its history to a story by Balzac. Although money was an index and a concrete reference in the past, it seems to represent everything today as an equivalent, as an exchange or sign (*SZ*, 39). This also marks the difference between feudal and bourgeois society:

> the index has an origin, the sign does not: to shift from index to sign is to abolish the last (or first) limit, the origin, the basis, the prop, to enter into the

Figure 8.9. One-thousand-mark banknote with stamp. From the collection of Wolfgang Haney, Berlin.

Figure 8.10. One-thousand-mark banknote with stamp. From the collection of Wolfgang Haney, Berlin.

> limitless process of equivalences, representations that nothing will ever stop, orient, fix, sanction. (*SZ*, 40)

In *Camera Lucida,* Barthes's last work brought into circulation and itself a "[bank-]note sur la photographie," money's power to totalize as well as circulate returns—as Barthes's desire for an index, an authentication of photographs that would stop a process of equivalences and exchange, orient its viewer, and provide him with the knowledge needed. Instead, Barthes has to confront the issue of distance by pursuing his game of *fort* and *da.* Following the sequence of images, searching for his mother and his memory of her, Barthes experiences a separation while insisting on an imaginary realm where mother and son, or father and daughter, would be able to meet. In his *Philosophy of Money,* published in 1900, the very year of Freud's *Interpretation of Dreams,* Georg Simmel describes this distance as money's characteristic, documented not only by the abstractness of paper currency but also by the process of circulation. For Simmel, this distance produces aesthetic value:

> If an object of any kind provides us with great pleasure or advantage we experience a feeling of joy at every later viewing of this object, even if any use or enjoyment is now out of the question. This joy, which resembles an echo, has a unique psychological character determined by the fact that we no longer want anything from the object. In place of the former concrete relationship with the object, it is now mere contemplation that is the source of enjoyable sensation; we leave the being of the object untouched, and our sentiment is attached only to its appearance, not to that which in any sense may be consumed. In short, whereas formerly the object was valuable as a means for our practical and eudaemonistic ends, it has now become an object of contemplation from which we derive pleasure by confronting it with reserve and remoteness.[35]

For Simmel, however, money that provides and stands for this aesthetic value and pleasure has already turned into the sign of modernity itself. Money's concepts of equivalence and exchange are carried by a notion of distance that pervades each object—for example, photographs—and every form of life; indeed, it marks the relationship between people themselves. Here desire comes into play: "Only the deferment of satisfaction through obstacles, the fear of never attaining the object, the tension of struggling for it, brings together the various elements of desire; the intense striving and continuous acquisition" (89). The wish for closeness, then, would be doomed from its very inception. In yearning for his mother and for her authentic photograph, Barthes takes part in an economy of desire that cannot stand still but has to circulate.

Has the mother, then, to remain forever distant? And how does one locate one's father? On the back of the Austrian banknote, one may find a sense of geographical place (Figure 8.11). No winter garden is de-

Figure 8.11. Fifty-schilling banknote, Österreichische Nationalbank.

picted here, but rather the Josephinum building, since 1920 a museum of the history of medicine, and formerly a medical academy that served, by order of Emperor Joseph II, as a military academy for the education of the medical army corps from 1783 to 1920. By the year of Freud's portrait pictured on the banknote, it was already a museum. Freud had no relationship to it, nor to the military institution that preceded it. No relationship, that is, other than the geographical proximity between his own apartment and office in the Berggasse and the institution in the Währinger Straße, likewise located in Vienna's *9. Bezirk.* The power of the military and the state are thus brought together with Freud, and separated from him, like the two sides of a piece of paper, which can never be made to meet.

In his native Freiburg (Pribor) in Moravia, Freud's name can be found on a street sign. Neither in Vienna's ninth district nor in any other part of the city is a street named after Freud. Last November, I had the opportunity to ask a Viennese city official why this is so. He replied with a proud smile. In Freud's case, he indicated, Vienna could offer something much better. He referred to the fifty-schilling note: "Here, Freud is in everybody's hands."

Notes

I would like to express my warmest thanks to Wolfgang Haney, who offered me access to his tremendous collection of German banknotes from the inflation period and gave me permission to reproduce the samples included here. I would also like to thank Ivy Gilbert for her bibliographic assistance.

1. See "Myth Today," in *MY*, p. 109.
2. Roland Barthes, *La Chambre claire: Note sur la photographie* (Paris: Seuil/Gallimard, 1980), p. 49.
3. Naomi Schor, "Female Fetishism: The Case of George Sand," *Poetics Today* 6 (1985): 301–10.
4. Barthes, *La Chambre claire*, p. 49.
5. Walter Benjamin, "Kleine Geschichte der Photographie," in *Gesammelte Schriften*, vol. 2, bk. 1, ed. Rolf Tiedemann and Hermann Schweppenhäuser (Frankfurt am Main: Suhrkamp, 1977), p. 371. Translation is mine.
6. The photograph probably dates from 1888 and is reproduced in Max Brod, *Franz Kafka* (Prague: Heinrich Mercy, 1937), after p. 32. An English translation of the book appeared as *Franz Kafka*, trans. G. Humphreys Roberts and Richard Winston (New York: Schocken, 1947).
7. Benjamin, "Kleine Geschichte," p. 375.
8. Ibid., p. 371.
9. Eilene Hoft-March, "Barthes' Real Mother: The Legacy of *La Chambre claire*," *French Forum* 17 (1992): 61–76.
10. See Walter Benjamin, "Das Kunstwerk im Zeitalter seiner technischen Reproduzierbarkeit," *Gesammelte Schriften*, vol. 1, bk. 2, ed. Rolf Tiedemann and Hermann Schweppenhäuser (Frankfurt am Main: Suhrkamp, 1974), pp. 471–508, especially pp. 482–85. English translation appears as "The Work of Art in

the Age of Mechanical Reproduction," in *Illuminations*, ed. and intro. Hannah Arendt, trans. Harry Zohn (New York: Schocken, 1969), pp. 217–51. See pp. 225–27.

11. See also Ralph Sarkonak, "Roland Barthes and the Spectre of Photography," *L'Esprit Créateur* 22 (Spring 1982): 57.

12. Martine Léonard, "Photographie et littérature: Zola, Breton, Simon (Hommage à Roland Barthes)," *Etudes Françaises* 18 (Fall 1983): 97 n. 6.

13. A selection of these photographs has been published in *Berggasse 19: Sigmund Freud's Home and Offices, Vienna 1938/The Photographs of Edmund Engelman* (New York: Basic Books, 1976).

14. Walter Benjamin, "Hochherrschaftlich möblierte Zehnzimmerwohnung," in *Einbahnstraße, Gesammelte Schriften*, vol. 4, bk. 1, ed. Tillman Rexroth (Frankfurt am Main: Suhrkamp, 1972), pp. 88–89. English translation appears as "Manorially Furnished Ten-Room Apartment," in *Reflections: Essays, Aphorisms, Autobiographical Writings*, ed. and intro. Peter Demetz, trans. Edmund Jephcott (New York: Harcourt Brace Jovanovich, 1978), pp. 64–65.

15. The etching is reproduced and commented on in *Sigmund Freud: Sein Leben in Bildern und Texten*, ed. Ernst Freud, Lucie Freud, and Ilse Gubrich-Simitis, with a biographical essay by K. R. Eissler; designed by Willy Fleckhaus (Frankfurt am Main: Suhrkamp Verlag, 1974), p. 238. The picture appears on p. 239.

16. K. R. Eissler, "Biographische Skizze," in *Sigmund Freud: Sein Leben in Bildern und Texten*, p. 23. I am quoting from the English version, "Biographical Sketch," in *Sigmund Freud: His Life in Pictures and Words*, trans. Christine Trollope (New York: Harcourt Brace Jovanovich, 1978), p. 23.

17. The photograph of Freud with cigar, taken circa 1921, is also reproduced in *Sigmund Freud: Sein Leben in Bildern und Texten*, p. 222.

18. Jonathan Crary, *Techniques of the Observer: On Vision and Modernity in the Nineteenth Century* (Cambridge, Mass.: MIT Press, 1990), p. 13. See also John Tagg, "The Currency of the Photograph," in *Thinking Photography*, ed. Victor Burgin (London: Macmillan, 1982), pp. 110–41, and Allan Sekula, "The Traffic in Photographs," in *Photography Against the Grain: Essays and Photo Works, 1973–1983* (Halifax: Press of the Nova Scotia College of Art and Design, 1984), pp. 94–101. Both essays are also cited in Crary.

19. The banknote was first issued on 19 October 1987. The issue date and the banknotes' sources are referred to in correspondence to me from Mr. Scherz and Mr. Knaur from the Österreichische Nationalbank, Druckerei für Wertpapiere, dated 18 March 1994.

20. Mr. Scherz and Mr. Knaur, correspondence to me, dated 18 March 1994. The sculptor Karl Maria Schwerdtner added text from Sophocles' tragedy to this medal, in English translation: "He who was a powerful man was able to solve the riddle." The image of the medal is reproduced in the pamphlet "Die neue Fünfzig Schilling Note" and in *Sigmund Freud: Sein Leben in Bildern und Texten*, p. 186.

21. Compare also the illustration in Lynn Gamwell and Richard Wells, eds., *Sigmund Freud and Art: His Personal Collection of Antiquities* (Binghamton: State University of New York, 1989), pp. 92–93.

22. Mr. Scherz and Mr. Knaur, correspondence to me, dated 18 March 1994.

23. Jacques Derrida, *Given Time: I, Counterfeit Money*, trans. Peggy Kamuf (Chicago: University of Chicago Press, 1991), p. 6.

24. See Willibald Kranister, director of the Österreichische Nationalbank, interviewed in Michael Kröll, "Die Köpfe auf unserem Geld," F. 7, *Die ganze Woche* 37, 13 September 1990, p. 52. Kranister describes the success rate of copy-

ing the schilling banknotes as "practically equaling zero." Professional counterfeiters therefore prefer other currencies, such as the American dollar bill.

25. See the pamphlet "Die neue Fünfzig Schilling Note," issued by the Österreichische Nationalbank at the time of the publication of the new fifty-schilling bill. The Deutsche Bundesbank, for one, consulted with members of the Österreichische Nationalbank before deciding on their new DM-series, which recently went into effect. I am grateful to Bundesbankamtsrat Edgar Kornübe for this information.

26. Kröll, "Die Köpfe auf unserem Geld," p. 52. Kröll here summarizes his interview with Kranister.

27. Sigmund Freud, "Charakter und Analerotik" [1908], in *Gesammelte Werke,* vol. 7, *Werke aus den Jahren 1906–1909* (Frankfurt am Main: Fischer, 1941), pp. 203–9. English translation appears as "Character and Anal Eroticism," in *The Standard Edition of the Complete Psychological Works of Sigmund Freud,* vol. 9, trans. and ed. James Strachey et al. (London: Hogarth, 1959), pp. 167–75. See also, for example, Eugene Wolfenstein, "Mr. Moneybags Meets the Rat Man: Marx and Freud on the Meaning of Money," *Political Psychology* 14 (1993): 279–308.

28. See Sandor Ferenczi, "The Ontogenesis of the Interest in Money," in *Sex in Psychoanalysis: Contributions to Psychoanalysis,* ed. Ernest Jones (New York: Robert Brunner, 1950), pp. 319–31. The essay was first published in 1914 in German in *Internationale Zeitschrift für ärztliche Psychoanalyse.*

29. See S. L. Warner, "Sigmund Freud and Money," *Journal of the American Academy of Psychoanalysis* 17 (Winter 1989): 609–22, for a discussion of whether Freud's parents were poor, as he often stated.

30. Warner quotes many smaller gifts in the denomination of precisely fifty florins or fifty gulden. See "Sigmund Freud and Money," pp. 615–16.

31. Ibid., pp. 616–17.

32. See Ibid., p. 616, and Elliot Oring, *The Jokes of Sigmund Freud* (Philadelphia: University of Pennsylvania Press, 1984).

33. See Liliane Weissberg, "Hebräer oder Juden? Religiöse und politische Bekehrung bei Herder," in *Johann Gottfried Herder: Geschichte und Kultur,* ed. Martin Bollacher (Würzburg: Königshausen und Neumann, 1994), pp. 191–211.

34. Walter Benjamin, "One-Way Street," in *Reflections: Essays, Aphorisms, Autobiographical Writings,* ed. and intro. Peter Demetz, trans. Edmund Jephcott (New York: Harcourt Brace Jovanovich, 1978), p. 87.

35. Georg Simmel, *The Philosophy of Money,* trans. Tom Bottomore and David Frisby (London: Routledge and Kegan Paul, 1978), p. 73.

9

Roland Barthes, or The Woman Without a Shadow

Diana Knight

In the photo section of *Roland Barthes by Roland Barthes*, Barthes reproduces a nineteenth-century IOU note from his paternal grandfather to his great-great-uncle. In the comment he places beneath this, Barthes contrasts the traditional function of writing as the guarantee of a debt, contract, or representation with its more recent departure toward "text" and "perversion." On the opposite page stands a representation of the "family romance" to which Barthes owes his race and class: a posed family photo of the same grandfather as a young man, surrounded by Barthes's great-grandparents and his great-uncle and great-aunt. Here the comment specifies Barthes's status as a literal incarnation of perversion: "Final stasis of this descent: my body. The last product of the family line is a purposeless being [*un être pour rien*]" (*RB*, 18–19).

When Barthes promotes perversion as a positive textual value of purposeless expenditure, he invariably explains what he means with reference to nonreproductive sexuality.[1] If homosexuality is a perversion that "quite simply, induces happiness" (*RB*, 64), I nevertheless want to explore its relationship to the myth of the Woman Without a Shadow to which Barthes twice refers. For the woman's missing shadow is the visible sign of infertility, and in each of Barthes's references a metaphorical infertility seems to be presented as negative. In the Hofmannsthal libretto of Strauss's opera, the emperor's daughter loses her shadow as a punishment for the choice of nonprocreative sexual pleasure. If she cannot produce a shadow within three days, her husband will be turned to stone. At first she is tempted to steal a shadow from the dyer's wife, at the expense of the fertility of this equally childless couple. When she abandons this selfish path for pity and emotional maturity, both couples regain their shadows amidst a closing chorus of the voices of their unborn children.

In *The Pleasure of the Text*, the Woman Without a Shadow is an image for the sterility of a text that is cut off from all representation and ideology, whereas a small dose of the latter, however stupid, can foster an erotic blush on the cheek of the text. Curiously, Barthes's example is the sticky pronatalism of Zola's late polemical novel, *Fécondité* [Fertility] (*PT*, 31–32). In *Camera Lucida*, the reference to the Woman Without a Shadow is linked to the rebirth of the mother in the Winter Garden photograph (*CL*, 110). If the idea that Barthes himself has reproduced neither the family line nor the human species is omnipresent in the second half of the book, this is obviously linked to the death of his mother and a new awareness of his own mortality. Yet the theme of genealogy and his own lack of issue has appeared before. What is the relationship between the metaphorical and the literal in Barthes's discussions of sterility and fertility? Does it make sense to suggest that fertility is homosexuality's missing shadow?

Barthes's "Deliberation," published in 1979, is normally taken at face value as a meditation on the worth of the private diary as a publishable form (*RL*, 359–73). I see it rather as testing the literary value of a particular content. Of the two sample diary extracts, the first records a month at Urt the summer before his mother's death in 1977 and is full of Barthes's panic in the face of this approaching separation. The second extract, dated 25 April 1979, is obviously the prototype for the staged nightly wanderings of the posthumous "Paris Evenings."[2] Indeed this first "Futile Evening" of 25 April (reproduced in "Deliberation" [*RL*, 367–69]) is suspiciously similar to that of 14 September in "Paris Evenings," which also begins with the words "Futile Evening" (*IN*, 70–72). Both portray Barthes setting out on a cold and wet evening to a bleak area of Paris; in both he escapes from the social chore of a *vernissage* only to launch into a depressing quest for a decent film—this simply to fill in the time before he can return, tired and cold, unwell or afraid that he soon will be, to his home territory, the Café de Flore. If the "Paris Evenings" entry records his rejection, owing to tiredness and lethargy, of two possible homosexual encounters, the "Deliberation" entry (only slightly more discreet) sums up his bad day through its failure to provide him with a single face over which to fantasize.

The similarity in the detail and structure of the two entries suggests that neither is a factual recording of an evening in Barthes's life. Rather, both strike me as literary exercises within Barthes's general project of linking his life and his writing in some new way. On the basis of François Wahl's introduction to *Incidents* it is not clear whether "Paris Evenings" was Barthes's own chosen title or an editorial invention. Certainly "Futile Evenings" (the "Vaines Soirées" used yet again when Barthes lays aside this "diary") is an apt alternative, not least for the

Proustian resonance of *vain* in the sense of futile or fruitless.[3] For like Proust's time which is wasted as well as lost, the manner in which these evenings are idled away could nevertheless form the subject matter of literature. If "Paris Evenings" ends with Barthes dismissing "Olivier G." with the claim that he needs to get on with his work (*IN*, 70), the "Deliberation" entry concludes with a hint that this work might be linked to the lifestyle it claims to replace: "The pathetic failure of the evening persuaded me to try to adopt the changed life style that I've had in mind for a long time. A reform of which this first note is the trace" (*RL*, 368).

In "Paris Evenings" homosexuality, conjured up in the first entry by an allusion to the baron de Charlus (*IN*, 52), occupies most of the text. Explicit reference to the mother takes up far less space than in "Deliberation." Nevertheless, she is indirectly present by her very absence, not least in the most painful moment of the text. Returning by car from a meal with "FW and Severo," Barthes notes that the streets are full of young men. He would like to be dropped off to wander around on his own but is held back by the superego of habit, since his normal practice in this particular company is to be dropped at home: "Returning alone, through a bizarre oversight which distressed me, I climbed the stairs and inadvertently went past my own floor, as if I had been coming home to our apartment on the fifth floor, as in the old days when mother would be waiting up for me" (*IN*, 65). The Paris of "Paris Evenings" is clearly Paris without the mother. In a sort of reversal of the comfort and security called up by Barthes's reading in *Camera Lucida* of the photograph of the Alhambra (*CL*, 39–40), the whole world has lost the *heimlich* qualities associated with the mother. Confronting all the pain of Urt without his mother, Barthes describes himself as "in despair too at never feeling comfortable either in Paris, or here, or when I'm away: no real refuge" (*IN*, 60).

These are the final words of a single diary entry describing an evening at Urt. The entry is sandwiched between two typical Parisian fiascoes: the first, Barthes's account of being stood up by a prostitute whom he paid in advance (*IN*, 59); the second, the sequence that begins with his sexual overtures in a lift to "Darlame." Darlame responds only halfheartedly; when Barthes gets home the music on the radio is unbearable, and the small ads in *Libé* and the *Nouvel Obs* contain nothing for anyone "old" (*IN*, 61). Is there an intended relationship between such moments and the moving evocation of Barthes's sense of loss during the beautiful nightfall at Urt, which builds up to a climax of self-conscious and would-be literary sorrow? "[C]rickets chirping, *as in the old days*: nobility, peace. My heart swelled with sadness, with something like despair; I thought about mother, about the cemetery where she was lying not far away, about 'Life.' I experienced this romantic swelling as a value and felt sad that I could never express it, 'my worth always greater than what I write' (theme of my lecture course)" (*IN*, 60).

I am tempted to suggest that what Barthes needs to convey the value of the heavy heart brought on by "U. without mother" (*IN*, 61) is to turn it into a Romantic song. Music, he claims in 1977, "doesn't derive from a metalanguage, but only from a discourse of value."[4] Although Barthes says that music has an unmediated referent in the human body, thus foreclosing the system of signs and meaning to which the writer is condemned, the points that he makes about Romantic song seem to depend at least partly on its words. For they too lead Barthes straight back to the body: " 'Soul,' 'feeling' and 'heart' are the Romantic names for the body. Everything becomes clearer in the Romantic text if we translate the effusive, moral word by one connected to the body, to the drives" (*RF*, 308). Even more striking, then, is the overlap of vocabulary in Barthes's description of the sorrowful dusk at Urt (his "romantic swelling" and his "heart swollen with sadness") and an earlier radio talk that explicitly sexualizes Romantic song through the metaphor of a male orgasm: "the Romantic 'heart' [. . .] is a powerful organ, pinnacle of the interior body where, simultaneously and as though in a contradictory way, desire and tenderness, the demand for love and the call to jouissance, violently merge: something lifts up my body, swells it, stretches it, carries it to the point of explosion, then immediately, mysteriously, makes it depressed and languid" (*RF*, 289).

Where does the figure of the mother fit in here, given that Schubert's music has the effusiveness, unity, and demand for love associated with a "maternal climate,"[5] and that of Schumann "shelters constantly beneath the luminous shadow of the mother" (*RF*, 298)? In that Barthes so readily merges the discourse of the lover with that of the child (both solitary, lost, or abandoned subjects), he might appear to be conflating the claims of genital desire with need for the mother: "the lover could be defined thus: a child having an erection" (*LD*, 105). But this should not be understood as genital desire *for* the mother, since the imaginary of the lover's discourse is one that accepts the nonunitary subject of the "demand for love" and the "call to jouissance": "I am then two subjects at the same time: I want the maternal and the genital" (*LD*, 104–5). These are explicitly figured as two contradictory embraces, whereby the adult is superimposed upon the child. The maternal embrace is a metaphor for an illusory moment of total and eternal union with the loved person, a regression to a moment (that of the real mother) when desires are abolished because they seem definitively fulfilled. Yet, declares Barthes, in the middle of this childish embrace "the genital never fails to burst through; it breaks up the diffuse sensuality of the incestuous embrace; the logic of desire is set in motion" (*LD*, 104).

The twin claims of the maternal and the genital are figured in two separate photos in *Roland Barthes by Roland Barthes*. The maternal embrace, in which Barthes's mother holds an overgrown infant in her arms, is specifically captioned "The demand for love" (*RB*, 5). The Barthes who clings solemnly to his mother, cheek to cheek, is seven or eight years old. In another photo an older Barthes, with all the awkwardness and indefinable age of the Proustian narrator, stands alone and smiling in his grandparents' garden at Bayonne. It was here, we are told, that some early sexual experiments took place. Curiously, mention is also made of the excessive litters of kittens for which this same part of the garden served as a burial ground. The overfertile mother who offsets Barthes's perverse childhood sexuality is perhaps the very cat, represented on the facing page, clasped on the lap of Barthes's paternal grandmother (*RB*, 10–11).

In the radio broadcasts on "Marcel Proust in Paris" that Barthes made in 1978 with Jean Montalbetti, their perambulations around some of the key sites of Proust's life take them to the *pavillon* in the gardens of the Champs-Elysées.[6] This was the public lavatory in which Proust chose to locate the episode of the grandmother's stroke, on what was to be the narrator's last outing with her. Barthes is clearly intrigued by this choice, linking it both to Proust's own ritualistic visits to his friends' lavatories, and to the development of the narrator's adolescent sexuality, not least his first orgasm while playing with Gilberte, having just accompanied Françoise to the same *pavillon*. In that the grandmother seems to mediate the needs, emotions, and sexuality of both narrator and author, and in that she recurs in Barthes's discussions of Proust, she is a useful focus for the intersection of the maternal and the genital in Barthes's late writing. For example, there could be no better illustration of Barthes's enchanted and immobile maternal embrace than that between the Proustian narrator and his grandmother on his first wretched day in Balbec: "And when I felt my mouth glued to her cheeks, to her brow, I drew from them something so beneficial, so nourishing, that I remained as motionless, as solemn, as calmly gluttonous as a baby at the breast."[7] When the grandmother dies, Proust chooses to locate the narrator's delayed mourning in the volume that also brings him face to face with homosexuality. For *Sodom and Gomorrah* opens with the narrator spying on a primal scene of male homosexuality (the fortuitous "mating" of Charlus and Jupien) and closes with his memory of the lesbian scene at Montjouvain on which he spied in *Combray*. Clearly the mourning is delayed so that the two themes can be juxtaposed in this way.

The involuntary memory in which the narrator, stooping to remove his boots, refinds the face and goodness of his "real grandmother" is an explicit point of reference for Barthes's own narrative of refinding his real mother in the Winter Garden photograph (*CL*, 70). However, I want to suggest that the implicit references to *Sodom and Gomorrah* extend beyond this famous scene. When the narrator paradoxically understands, for the first time, that he has lost his grandmother for ever, all sexual desire deserts him and he shuts himself up in his hotel room to wallow in his grief. If desire slowly returns, it is the suggestion and then the certainty of Albertine's lesbianism that produces his desperate need for her presence—to such an extent that she is declared a necessary part of himself.[8] This quasi-internalization of homosexuality takes the form of a horrible hallucination whereby the scene at Montjouvain, with Albertine in the place of Mlle. Vinteuil's friend, looms up from behind the view from the hotel window at Balbec. In his anguish, the narrator wonders if this is a punishment for having allowed his grandmother to die. Yet it is precisely this melodramatic tussle with homosexuality that motivates the grandmother's second resurrection. As the narrator's long night of misery reaches its climax, dawn breaks over the sea at Balbec. Never, he says, has he seen the dawn "of so beautiful or sorrowful a morning." As the sun bursts through the curtains he hears himself weeping, but "at that moment, to my astonishment, the door opened and, with a throbbing heart, I seemed to see my grandmother standing before me, as in one of those apparitions that had already visited me, but only in my sleep" (*RTP*, 2:1166).

The mystery of this second miraculous resurrection is immediately explained, for the narrator has mistaken his mother for his dead grandmother. The grandmother has borrowed the body of her more than willing daughter, for it is the latter who, separated from the narrator by the same thin partition that had once kept him in touch with his grandmother, has heard his sobs and repeated the grandmother's earlier action of coming in to comfort him: "Her dishevelled hair, whose grey tresses were not hidden and strayed about her troubled eyes, her ageing cheeks, my grandmother's own dressing-gown which she was wearing, all these had for a moment prevented me from recognizing her and had made me uncertain whether I was asleep or whether my grandmother had come back to life" (*RTP*, 2:1166–67).

I do not know whether this particular conflation of homosexuality, the reincarnated grandmother, and the beautiful but desolate dawn is a conscious intertext for the recognition scene at the center of *Camera Lucida.* But I am struck by Barthes's equation of the Winter Garden photograph with Schumann's first *Dawn Song* [*Chant de l'aube*], "which is in such perfect harmony with both my mother's being and my sorrow at her death" (*CL*, 70). Discussing this enigmatic piece of music, to which Barthes says he cannot listen "without a sort of anguish," he declares himself especially moved by the fact that this very late composition, written on the threshold of Schumann's final madness, should have conveyed such a somber entry into the night with a title referring to daybreak.[9] I have already referred to Barthes's placing of Schumann's music under the "luminous shadow of the mother." Now, shut up in his apartment, presumably at night (since he is looking through his mother's photos by the light of a lamp), he finds in this *Dawn Song*, as in the Winter Garden photo itself, the music that precisely captures the value of his sorrow, just as the sunrise at Balbec captures that of Proust's narrator.

Barthes's reference to Schumann's *Dawn Song* is surely related to the Daniel Boudinet polaroid that opens the text of *Camera Lucida*.[10] Barthes must have viewed it for the first time in the middle of writing *Camera Lucida*, when he attended the Boudinet *vernissage* described in "Deliberation." Though Barthes himself gives no details, the polaroid is one of a sequence, *Fragments of a Labyrinth*, taken at night in Boudinet's own apartment between dusk and dawn and using only light entering through the windows.[11] The photo that Barthes identifies as "*Polaroid*, 1979" corresponds to the light of dawn, which gives a blue-green luminosity to the curtains, but is not yet strong enough to illuminate the foreground of the room. However, through an opening low down where the curtains meet, a brighter chink of light falls onto a corner of the bed and the empty pillow. Boudinet's dawn polaroid is certainly an integral part of Barthes's symbolic narrative of refinding his mother in the literal *chambre claire* of the glass conservatory. Just before he relates the discovery of the Winter Garden photo, Barthes refers to the brightness (*clarté*) of his mother's eyes as something that stands out in all her photos: "For the moment it was simply a physical luminosity, the photographic trace of a colour, the blue-green of her pupils" (*CL*, 66). This, he says, is the mediating light that will lead him at last to the essence of her face, a blue-green luminosity which is also that of the Boudinet polaroid.

If Barthes refuses to reproduce the Winter Garden photograph, it cannot be for the reasons given in the bracketed apology (*CL*, 73) that has so often been taken at face value. If *Camera Lucida* recounts a "true story" of Barthes refinding his mother in a photo of her as a child, then the photo must surely be the one reproduced later in the text with the title "The Stock" ("*La Souche*"). If the mother as child is younger than five, and if she and her brother stand with their grandfather (rather than alone in a conservatory), her pose, her expression, and the position of her hands exactly match Barthes's description of the Winter Garden photograph. It is therefore my belief (or my fantasy) that the Winter Garden photo is simply an invention, a transposition of the "real" photo ("The Stock") to a setting that provides Barthes with the symbolism of light and revelation appropriate to a recognition scene and to his inversion of the camera obscura of photography into a *chambre claire*.[12]

If the actual photo of the mother is displaced, its place is taken by what Barthes calls one of the most beautiful photos in the world, Nadar's photo of his mother, "or of his wife, no one knows" (*CL*, 68, 70).[13] The gray tresses of Nadar's mother or wife form a wonderful link with the Proustian hallucination of the grandmother's resurrection at sunrise. For the narrator's "mistake" is largely caused by the gray tresses of his mother's hair, which "were not hidden and strayed about her troubled eyes." Indeed, by splitting the mother figure into mother and grandmother, and by splitting the grieving child into daughter and grandson, Proust also interweaves the theme of the succession and merging of generations. For the earlier involuntary memory had been prolonged, to some extent, by the arrival of the narrator's mother: "as soon as I saw her enter in her crape coat, I realised—something that had escaped me in Paris—that it was no longer my mother that I had before my eyes, but my grandmother." This process of the reincarnation of a mother in her daughter is explained by the image of a male genealogical line of descent in aristocratic families. Just as on the death of the head of the household the son takes the father's title, "so, by an accession of a different order and more profound origin, the dead annex the living who become their replicas and successors, the continuators of their interrupted life" (*RTP*, 2:796–97).

The genealogical theme is thus an interesting link between the Nadar photo and the displaced photo of the mother as child with her brother and grandfather. For *la souche* means both the ancestral founder of the line and the lineage itself. Though the section ends with an assertion of the mysterious differences between members of the same family, not least the child-mother and her monumental grandfather (*CL*, 105), what precedes it is a meditation on the cross-generational genetic links sometimes foregrounded in photographs. Thus, looking at a photo of his maternal grandmother holding his mother's brother as a child, Barthes thinks at first that the grandmother is his mother and the child himself (*CL*, 103). His own link to his father is more visible in photos of his father as a child than as an adult: "certain details, certain features connect his face to my grandmother's and to mine—in a sense over his head" (*CL*, 105).

More indirect still is the genetic link between Barthes and his unmarried aunt: "in one photo, I have the 'face' of my father's sister" (*CL*, 103). If photographic evidence of the continuity of the family line is reassuring ("for the thought of our origins soothes us"), the aunt herself may also conjure up the future that "perturbs us, fills us with anguish" (*CL*, 105). Reproducing her photo as a child in *Roland Barthes by Roland Barthes*, he adds the caption "The father's sister: she was alone all her life" (*RB*, 14). The preceding page shows her as a young woman with her parents, in a family group reminiscent of the black family in Van der Zee's photo in *Camera Lucida* (*RB*, 13; *CL*, 44). The young black woman whom Barthes, in another confusion of generations, identifies as the sister or daughter (*CL*, 43), stands in the same position as his aunt relative to her parents and is linked to the aunt by the supposed retrospective *punctum* of her necklace: "this sister of my father had never married, had lived as an old maid with her mother, and it had always saddened me to think of the dreariness of her provincial life" (*CL*, 53). Of all Barthes's delvings into the past generations of both sides of his family, I am struck by the sympathetic identification with his aunt. If Barthes perceives his lineage as "a disturbing entity" of which he represents the end point (*CL*, 98), his aunt, too, has contributed to the collapse of the paternal line.

When the image of the sterile Woman Without a Shadow is introduced into *Camera Lucida*, it is in the context of Barthes's discussion of the *air*, the "luminous shadow which accompanies the body" and without which the body remains sterile: "It is by this flimsy umbilical cord that the photographer makes the subject come alive; if he fails, either through lack of talent or bad luck, to give the transparent soul its bright shadow, that subject dies for ever" (*CL*, 110). In an earlier chapter the umbilical cord is made up of the light rays that Barthes imagines linking the photographic referent to his gaze: "a flesh and blood medium, a skin I share with the person whose photo has been taken" (*CL*, 81). Barthes represents himself, as he looks through photos of his mother, working his way backward through her life, from her last summer to her childhood. In her final illness this movement has been repeated in reality, his mother becoming his little girl as he cares for her and nourishes her. In a strange moment in his handling of the narrative chronology, Barthes suggests that she has merged with the child of her first photo, even though she has not yet died and he has not yet discovered that photo. Although he has not literally procreated, he has nevertheless engendered his mother as his female child (*CL*, 71–72). One could add that the Winter Garden sequence resurrects her at her literal birthplace of Chennevières-sur-Marne. But are these metaphorical engenderings, which merge in the very fact of writing about his mother so powerfully, enough to produce the mythical shadow?

Somewhat late in the preparation of this chapter, it occurred to me to return to the photo section of *Roland Barthes by Roland Barthes* in search of shadows. I found them, of course. In the very first radiant photo of Barthes's mother crossing a beach, the mother, as she should, casts a clear shadow (*RB*, ii). In a related photo presumably taken on the same occasion, the mother clasps her two sons to her, beneath Barthes's caption, "The family without familyism" (*RB*, 27). The reactionary family ideology so strangely described as contributing to the literary fertility of

Zola's *Fécondité* is not, then, for Barthes's immediate family. For it is clear that this unconventional family, in which Barthes's mother has broken out of her social role of passive reproducer of her husband's line, is positively presented by her first son.[14] Indeed, in "Paris Evenings," it is Barthes's half brother, product of his mother's right to her own desires, who is given the privilege of reincarnating her: "so affectionate, so naive, so sensitive to everything lovely, just as mother was" (*IN*, 60). Here, then, is the idealized image of a very different family structure, whose members, Barthes claims in *Camera Lucida*, are linked by mutual love rather than by their status and function in a patrilinear genealogy: "before us and beyond us, nothing (other than the memory of my grandparents)" (*CL*, 74). Here, surely, is a mother who is presented as projecting her own bright shadow, but without expecting her first son to follow suit. For I have not wished to suggest that there is any element of guilt in Barthes's bringing together his mother and his homosexuality in his late work. Just as the mother herself is allowed an independent genital existence, so I have always taken as acceptance of Barthes's sexuality the example of his mother's goodness read in the Winter Garden photograph: "that she never once, in all our life together, uttered a single 'reproach' " (*CL*, 69).

The photo with which I have chosen to conclude shows a much younger Barthes, tottering across a different beach, "around 1918." If this toddler and his large sun hat cast a fine shadow, it is surely because of Barthes's equally fine caption: "Contemporaries? I was beginning to walk, Proust was still alive, and was finishing the *Recherche*" (*RB*, 22–23). The Proustian intertext echoes, and perhaps resolves, the paradoxes of Barthes's figure of perversion. For the representations of homosexuality that surround the figure of the Proustian grandmother alter the balance of the maternal and the genital once she has died. In the climactic closing scene of *Sodom and Gomorrah* (the sorrowful dawn) the mother acts out the grandmother's role and the narrator takes her in his arms. But this is not to repeat the entranced, static, and appeasing embrace of his grandmother on their first day at Balbec. Rather, it is to tell his mother of his absolute need to marry Albertine (*RTP*, 2:1167–69). At the end of Barthes's elaboration, in *A Lover's Discourse*, of the figure of "Fulfillment" (*Comblement*), Barthes quotes Nietzsche to the effect that "Joy," wanting only the eternal repetition of the same, needs neither heirs nor children. In the same way, says Barthes, the fulfilled lover needs neither "to write, to transmit, nor to reproduce" (*LD*, 56). The wish for everlasting fulfillment in a static maternal embrace is illusory but above all sterile, not least for writing.

Barthes often discusses the mysterious mutation whereby Proust, after toying with the form and content of his work for so many years, in 1909 resolved whatever problem had been holding him back, and launched himself headlong into his novel. Barthes adduces various reasons, ranging from the death of Proust's mother (but this was several years earlier) to the solution of formal problems such as the assumption of the narrative "I."[15] However, according to recent Proust scholarship, it was his interest in the Eulenberg affair, a German homosexual scandal that broke out in 1907, that crystallized Proust's final conception of *A la recherche*, whereby homosexuality in general, and the baron de Charlus in particular, would play a prominent thematic and structural role.[16] Ironically, Barthes seems unaware that this projected inclusion of perversion as content unblocked Proust's creative sterility. Yet without a doubt the homosexual content of *A la recherche* is crucial to Barthes's obsession with Proust.

The protracted metaphor of the orchid and the bumblebee, which introduces *Sodom and Gomorrah*, establishes the mutual fertilization of Jupien and Charlus, despite the biological sterility of their sexual relations. The episode gives way to the narrator's lengthy digression on the resilient descendants of Sodom, a hidden but flourishing race of "inverts" who will come to people Proust's novel. Barthes's playful but bold merging of his own generation with that of Proust, through the "Contemporaries?" of his caption to the toddler photo, provides perhaps a further key to the infamous "Proust and me" of Barthes's 1978 lecture.[17] For the relationship between Barthes and Proust is that of a phantasmic genealogy, whereby an inherited perversion—both literal and literary—projects an exceedingly fertile shadow.

Notes

Page references are to published English translations of Barthes's texts throughout this chapter; I have, however, introduced some modifications.

1. See, for example, the section on "Perversion" in "Twenty Key Words for Roland Barthes," interview with Jean-Jacques Brochier, in *GV*, pp. 231–32.

2. "Soirées de Paris," in *IN*, pp. 49–73. The translator has retained the French title.

3. See François Wahl's preface to the original French edition of *Incidents* (Paris: Seuil, 1987), pp. 7–10, which quotes Barthes's own note at the end of his text, "Arrêté ici (22 sept. 79) les Vaines Soirées" (p. 9, note 3).

4. "Music, Voice, Language," in *RF*, pp. 278–85 (p. 284). Other essays on romantic music quoted below and included in this volume are "Rasch" (1975), pp. 299–312; "The Romantic Song" (1976), pp. 286–92; and "Loving Schumann" (1979), pp. 293–98.

5. Roland Barthes, "Roland Barthes parle de Schubert," *Diapason* 232 (1978): 54.

6. Roland Barthes (with Jean Montalbetti), "Un homme, une ville: Marcel Proust à Paris, III," France Culture, 3 November 1978 (Cassettes Radio France).

7. Marcel Proust, *Remembrance of Things Past,* 3 vols., trans. C. K. Scott Moncrieff and Terence Kilmartin (Harmondsworth: Penguin, 1983), 1: 718. Hereafter cited as *RTP* in the text.

8. For the narrator's involuntary memory and delayed mourning for his grandmother, see "The Intermittences of the Heart," *RTP,* 2:778–809. For the discovery of Albertine's lesbianism and the 'Desolation at sunrise,' see *RTP,* 2:1150–69. The translators' title for *Sodome et Gomorrhe* is *Cities of the Plain.*

9. See the extracts from Claude Maupomé's radio program "Comment l'entendez-vous?" in *Les Nouvelles Littéraires,* 10–17 April 1980, p. 28.

10. This color photograph has been omitted from the English translation. See the original French edition, *La Chambre claire: Note sur la photographie* (Paris: Gallimard/Seuil, 1980), p. 9.

11. See Daniel Boudinet, *Fragments d'un labyrinthe,* in *Daniel Boudinet,* ed. Christian Caujolle, Emmanuelle Decroux, and Claude Vittiglio (Besançon: Editions La Manufacture, 1993), pp. 108–15, and Gianni Burattoni, "La Mort de Daniel Boudinet," *Lettres Françaises* (October 1990): 21.

12. This striking similarity has been noted by Ralph Sarkonak in "Roland Barthes and the Spectre of Photography," *L'Esprit Créateur* 22 (Spring 1982): 56–57, and by Antoine Compagnon in "L'objectif déconcerté," *La Recherche Photographique* 12 (June 1992): 77. Yet neither appears to suggest that the Winter Garden photo could be fictional. Sarkonak comments on the sense of *déjà vu* (and *déjà lu*) when we encounter "The Stock," only to wonder, "Why did this photo not affect Barthes the same way as the one he does describe but does not allow us to see?" (57).

13. On Barthes's "exploitation" of this confusion over the subject of Nadar's portrait, and on its official sources, see Daniel Grojnowski, "Le Mystère de *La Chambre claire,*" *Textuel 33/34,* 15 (1984): 93, 96 n. 2.

14. Barthes's half brother, Michel Salzedo, was born in 1927. See Louis-Jean Calvet, *Roland Barthes* (Paris: Flammarion, 1990), pp. 36–39.

15. See, for example, Roland Barthes, "Ça prend," *Magazine Littéraire* 144 (January 1979): 26–27.

16. See Maurice Bardèche, *Marcel Proust romancier,* 2 vols. (Paris: Les Sept Couleurs, 1971), 1:160–63, and Antoine Compagnon's preface to his edition of Marcel Proust, *Sodome et Gomorrhe* (Paris: Gallimard/Folio, 1989), pp. xiv–xvi.

17. Roland Barthes, "Longtemps je me suis couché de bonne heure . . . ," in *RL,* pp. 277–90 (p. 277). The lecture was given under this title at the Collège de France and as "Proust et moi" at New York University.

10

The Descent of Orpheus

On Reading Barthes and Proust

Beryl Schlossman

> Why, in a text, all this verbal splendor? Does the luxury of language belong to excessive wealth, useless spending, unconditional loss? Does a great oeuvre of pleasure (Proust's for example) participate in the same economy as the pyramids of Egypt?
>
> —Roland Barthes, *Le Plaisir du texte*

> When Orpheus descends toward Eurydice, the night opens through the power of art.
>
> —Maurice Blanchot, *L'Espace littéraire*

Luxury of Language

From the provocative brilliance of *Writing Degree Zero* to the seductive and moving novelistic essay that looks back at us through *Camera Lucida*, Barthes's writing articulates the relations between language and desire. At every turn, the voice of Proust can be heard as Barthes intricately unfolds the origami-style forms of these relations. The often-proclaimed principle of lightness and insignificance that Barthes calls *légèreté* leads him to stage the intricacies of language and desire as a series of effects: *légèreté* is closely linked to the voluptuous "luxury of language." Meaning is conceptualized as the object of a search through the effects of language. Looking for "the design of an intelligence,"[1] Barthes filters through aesthetic appeal, theatrical effects, seduction and "la drague," and the phenomena of love.

Barthes gives several names to the signifiers' effects, perceived through a process of filtration. The supplement of sensual and eroticized perception that Barthes adds to Julia Kristeva's concept of *signifiance* reshapes the concept according to the lightness evoked by Madame de Sévigné. In Proust's novel *Remembrance of Things Past*, Charlus delights the narrator's grandmother with his "delicacies" and "feminine sensibility" when he invokes Sévigné's "Letters" in defense of her love for her daughter. This love produces conversation "that she called 'things so slight that nobody else would notice them but you and I.'"[2]

Barthes's *signifiance* includes enigmatic silences (associated with the interdiction of *jouissance*) and the "frisson de sens" (the shiver or trembling of meaning) associated with the rustle of language: the concept is no longer precisely the same. Barthes's signifiers are as much occupied with producing "insignifiance" as "signifiance." This characteristic mark of contradiction, paradox, and inversion uses an instance of negation to open the space of the desiring subject in literature. Charlus appears in Barthes's texts from time to time, but his reading tacitly informs the whole of Barthesian "lightness." It leads the reader through the critical essays of the 1960s and 1970s—*The Empire of Signs, A Lover's Discourse,* and *Camera Lucida.* In Barthes's last book, the reading of Charlus has gone full circle and returned to the role of the mother: "we supposed, without saying anything of the kind to each other, that the light insignificance of language, the suspension of images, was meant to be the space of love" (*CL*, 72).

The luxury of language (its "efflorescence") is rooted in artifice. Barthes's writing is shaped by two readings of artifice, one from psychoanalysis and the other from literature: (1) Lacan posits the ineradicable difference between the sexual behavior of animals and the symbolic (language-based) vicissitudes of human desire. Lacan's axiom of the nonnaturalness of human eroticism produces something like an unnature. Barthes unfolds the consequences of this unnature, created by language, in semiology, rhetoric, and aesthetics—in his writing about texts, traces, and images—and in the reflexivity of writing about writing itself. (2) An aesthetic of artifice enters French modernity beginning with the hothouse flowers of Baudelaire's *Fleurs du mal.* Baudelaire's poetry is essential to Proust's aesthetic constructions in *Remembrance of Things Past*: its elements include art, love, death, loss, time, and the desire of writing. The artifice of language joins the art form of artifice in Barthes's theory of *jouissance* as the "rustling" of an "erotic machine." At times Japanese or Sadian, at times musicalized or completely literary, the projected utopia of language produces signifiers unfettered by "meaning." The psychoanalytical economy of non-sense includes loss and the division of the subject; the literary economy of erotics is constructed around terms like *élan, discovery,* Bataille's *expenditure, adventure,* and the Baudelairean *Nouveau, the New.* The constant circulation of these terms often leads back to Barthes's reading of Proust.

In Barthes's writing, the luxury (and the artifice) of language coincides with a theater of subjectivity and the staging of desire. Under the double sign of psychoanalysis and literature, Lacan and Proust, Barthes constructs the infinitely plural subject of *A Lover's Discourse.* The first-person amorous subject of Parisian modernity is constructed within a constellation of lovers who move in and out of time and place: they include Proust's Narrator, Goethe's Werther, and the ancient Greeks, especially Socrates in Plato's *Symposium* and the poet Sappho. Their voices resonate through the first-person quasi-fictional account of the search for the elusive object of desire. The object is virtual—it inhabits the subject's imagination. The Proustian search ("à la recherche de . . .") leads into an interior space, constructed in a series of texts and images. Barthes quotes Lacan: "It is not every day that you encounter that which is meant to provide you with precisely the image of your desire." Barthes follows the quotation with a reference to Proust: "scene of the specializing of desire: encounter between Charlus and Jupien in the courtyard of the Hôtel de Guermantes" (*LD,* 20). The artifice of all this luxury includes Barthes's fundamental principle of language as fiction. Its success produces "the truth of the lie" when lightness and style combine to produce a performance of infinite form. Barthes sometimes evokes this performance in the allegorical images of a universe or a galaxy.

An example of the coinciding of lightness and style occurs in "Longtemps, je me suis couché de bonne heure" (in *The Rustle of Language*) in the context of the desire of writing, at the heart of Proust's novel. Barthes's essay is constructed as a first-person account of subjective temporality and the lightness of passage. Barthes articulates a frame for life and writing: at its origin is the figure of Dante, and Proust represents the writing of modern subjectivity. The reference to Proust personalizes Barthes's account: "Dante begins his major work thus: 'Nel mezzo del camin di nostra vita' [. . .] This is a semantic point, the instant, perhaps late, when the call of a new meaning arrives in my life, the desire for a mutation: to change life, break and inaugurate, submit to an initiation, like Dante descending in the dark wood, led by a great initiator, Virgil (and for me, at least for the duration of this lecture, the initiator is Proust)" (*RL,* 284).

"For the duration of this lecture" measures the temporal dimensions of a discourse on life and writing; truth and meaning are subsumed within its parameters. Barthes underlines the fictive quality that is inseparable from language, the purity of its performance. His plan to write something other than essays in criticism fades into the background. The essay urgently solicits the articulation of the following question: what is at stake in the act of writing? And what was Barthes saying about it in the 1950s and 1960s that is still central to his enterprise in 1978 when he reads "Longtemps, je me suis couché de bonne heure" at the Collège de France? One writes through a process of reading; writing is an act; the verb *écrire* is intransitive. The categories of Essay and Novel are subverted, suspended, and blended into a rhapsodic form that Barthes sees as the shape of *Remembrance of Things Past.* He bases it on the disorganization of time, written with the capital letter of Proustian allegory.

Barthes's essay problematizes the intertwined relation of writing and reading in its echo of Proust's "desire of writing." Although "Longtemps" is often interpreted as a kind of credo of the critic turning novelist, its emphasis on silence, the indecision of form, and the fleeting quality of the performance that it stages in the theater of fiction indicate the impossibility of taking the author's statements about writing novels at face value. For this reason, in spite of the differences between Barthes's strategy and the strategy that unfolds in *Allegories of Reading,* "Longtemps, je me suis couché de bonne heure" bears comparison with Paul de Man's essay "On Reading (Proust)." Both critics explore writing as an enterprise that represents and re-creates acts of reading in the disguises, artifices, and fictions of its other worlds.

The Pleasure of the Text

Barthes's lightness has another side, enigmatic and paradoxical as well as "insignificant." It is frightening at times, like the presence-absence of Blanchot's Eurydice in the underworld. The lightness of shades and shadows ("ombres"), specters, "phantoms," and revenants includes unresolved bodies and their baroque effects. They are rendered in Barthes's writings as images of the unsublime, of corruption and darkness. A baroque theatricality shapes Barthes's writings: lightness and clarity combine with images of their dark and obscure counterparts. These images of unresolved bodies haunt the text(s). For Barthes, as Steven Ungar has shown, the power of images goes beyond the role of specific media per se.[3]

Barthes's image always raises the question of the referent: the theater of "effects" also includes the bodies that Barthes complains are missing from cinema. In his writings, the referent is characterized by "lourdeur," the weight of the bodies that pant with pleasure in the Japanese or Sadian erotic machines. In *The Pleasure of the Text,* the "romanesque" is portrayed as an untenable instant of pleasure enjoyed by a libertine. The libertine concludes the machiney of an erotic scenario with the cutting of the cord on which he is hanging; the cord is cut at the moment of his orgasm. In other texts, Barthes seems to locate the "romanesque" quality of this scene in the terms of "duplicity": culture and its destruction, pure language and its death, the consistency of pleasure and the dissolving or fading of *jouissance*. The subject is divided, perverse, fetishistic: the body is like language. It is denatured, rendered unnatural in the break between animal instinct and Eros. The Freudian and Lacanian drives float and push the Barthesian subject along the liquid lines of *The Pleasure of the Text*.

The body in Barthes's writing is filled with desire. It weeps and burns, it thirsts and grows parched like Phèdre in love with her husband's son. It speaks in her voice: "I languished, I dried out, in flames, in tears." The body will die in the real. Speaking through the voices of Dante, Tolstoy, and Proust, Barthes writes: "The middle of life is perhaps never anything more than the moment of the discovery that death is real, and no longer merely awful" (*RL*, 286). For Barthes, the body in and out of writing dissolves into the dust of earth. Like the reflected small image of the subject, it is snapped shut in the mother's rice powder compact.

In Barthes's version of the Lacanian body's "morcellement" (its division into the fragmentary objects of desire), the body is cut apart and displayed. Desired and desiring or dead and mourned, the body that inhabits Barthes's writing is baroque. Barthes portrays it in scenes and images of fetishism, sadomasochistic display, and funereal pomp: Girodet's *Sleep of Endymion* on the cover of *S/Z* is one of its emblems. At the conclusion of an essay on death in Tacitus, Barthes comments: "For perhaps this is what the baroque is: the torment of a finality in profusion. [. . .] Here again, it is the vegetable image which substantiates the baroque: the deaths correspond, but their symmetry is false, spread out in time, subject to a movement, like that of sprouts on the same stalk: [. . .] everything is reproduced and yet nothing is repeated" ("Tacitus and the Funerary Baroque," *CE*, 102). Barthes's comment about death in Tacitus marks a moment that ultimately finalizes the inescapable "weightiness" of the body, the ineradicable referent of his own writing. The body, inseparable from its death, is "undialectical": it provides the resistance to structure that blocks the Proustian system of inversion in "The Names of Proust." Like Proust's novel, Barthes's work depends on the simultaneity of baroque proliferation or "efflorescence" and its blockage. Seen in the light of the difference between the neat designs of structuralism and the troubling intrusion of death that subverts its categories from within, Barthes's work is already "poststructuralist" in *Writing Degree Zero*.

Femininity

The baroque body cannot stop desiring, it will not stop dying, and it never becomes transcendent . . . except perhaps in the Winter Garden photograph, precisely because the materiality of the maternal body hovers beyond the reader's vision. Like the luminous image of the child in 1898, the body of the mother remains invisible for the reader. It is covered by two other images that appear to the reader of *Camera Lucida*.[4]

The first image that hides the maternal body is the voluptuous textured curtain scene of Daniel Boudinet's "Polaroïd." Intimate and yet impersonal, the image of curtains, light, and large cushions on a bed is empty of movement and of human subjects. The curtains are irregular in shape and weave. The impact of their parted shape and the suggestive sensuality of their opening arise from the porous quality of the image: the curtains' translucence allows dazzling light to penetrate a dark interiority that seeps outside itself and dissolves in an upward sweep. The darkness of the image maps out the space of an intimacy with no story; its subjects are absent, and even its dark shade is evanescent. Blue-green like the mother's eyes, Barthes's liminal curtains cover his text and its invisible photograph. After the fact, the text constructs its own version of their allegorical quality. Their split opens slightly to reveal a triangle of clear light: the space of the invisible image is the true centerpiece of Barthes's fictions of the imaginary. Human subjects and objects are conspicuously absent from the scene of the picture. It is constructed and rhapsodized, or sewn together, from the fragments of woven fabrics or texts. These fragments are destined for the intimacies of sleep and sex. Without the markers of proportion, identity, or being, the image hovers beyond meaning, in the airy realm of "insignifiance." The photograph's curtains function like a theater curtain that might rise to reveal an empty stage or perhaps nothing at all. A large expanse of darkness verging on total blackness contrasts with the bright-colored light of the sunlit curtain. Barthes underscores the image's allegorical quality of absence-presence in the context of his book: as a counterpart of the first photograph ever taken, the set table of 1822 by Nicéphore Niepce, "Polaroïd" is the only other image in *Camera Lucida* without a human subject.[5]

In "Amplification: Barthes, Freud, and Paranoia," Mary Lydon[6] connects Daniel Boudinet's mysterious Polaroid curtains with the beating pulse of pleasure: the Barthesian body is a Freudian body. Its subject dwells in a woman's body—or rather, in the body of femininity that Barthes identifies with love. In this context, Barthes seems to assign *amour* and *écriture* respectively to the identifications of the feminine and the masculine. His writings generally subvert that division, however, by emphasizing the opposition between pleasure and *jouissance* in love as well as in writing.

The "subjected subject" of love is feminized—but readers and writers in Barthes are usually masculine, identified by their pronouns. There is a single and singular feminine subject in Barthes; her death haunts his writings from the beginning.[7] In "Longtemps," the mother's death is anticipated in two literary scenes that move Barthes: Bolkonski's death in

War and Peace and especially the grandmother's death in *Remembrance of Things Past* (*RL*, 287). The constantly revived emotion of these scenes implies that the subject's reading takes place in the body. Its imaginary space forms a theater for pleasure and suffering, love and death. Their temporality is also intertwined: "what sort of Lucifer created love and death *at the same time*?" (*RL*, 287).

The body of this singular mother, the present-absent woman walking on the beach, appears in her womanly form in the book entitled *Roland Barthes by Roland Barthes*, but *Camera Lucida* presents her only as an aged and dying child during her final illness. Her son re-creates her as "my feminine child." *Camera Lucida* unveils her absent form in the curtains with their incomparable color and light; it portrays her allegorically in Nadar's beautiful and sensual portrait of a woman with dark eyes and luminous white hair. Barthes wonders aloud if she was the photographer's wife or his mother. He does not ask the reader if she resembles his own mother, obliquely glimpsed at tea with her sons, in a photograph that reveals her to the reader of *Roland Barthes.* Her luxuriant white hair connects her image to the "wife or mother" portrayed by Nadar, Barthes's favorite photographer, and the text on the facing page reinforces the rhetorical power of present-absent images by evoking the Proustian Narrator's experience of his grandmother's death.

Text and Image (or Novel and Photograph) lend their allegorical qualities to Barthes's empty space of light and color, the empty room filled with fabrics, a bed, and some curtains. In Nadar's photograph, the desiring gaze of the subject stares out at the viewer with the strange immediacy of hallucination. Allegory provides a figure of desire and a covering of invisibility: the mother's body is the only one that Barthes takes beyond the borders of pleasure and dying, into the otherworld.

Nadar's photograph is doubly framed by white hair on black velvet and by a lighter ground around the black area. Her desiring and melancholic gaze burns through the image to reach the viewer. Barthes sees her through the optics of his own desire: perhaps he does not want to know that she is not Nadar's mother. The portrait of the Photographer's wife Ernestine, aging and ill in 1890, slips between the pages of *Camera Lucida* to speak for the irretrievably lost physiognomy of Barthes's beloved mother. The image bears the woman's black eyes and white hair, the black velvetlike fabric and her white skin. Nadar combines black mourning and the bright vividness of sensual appetite, indicated in the gesture caught by the camera. The flower that Ernestine holds to her lips lends theatrical eloquence to her silence; it hides her mouth and speaks for her in a metonymy. The dramatic sensuality of her gesture is translucent like the enigmatic curtains of "Polaroïd": Ernestine's flower does not cover up the silences of illness and melancholy that shine through the surface of the image.

The photograph enters an iconography of extremes that ranges from Ophelia's mourning and desire, articulated according to the language of flowers, to Swann's love for Odette, emblematized by the role of chrysanthemums and cattleya orchids. Nadar reinvents the language of flowers in an economy of images and texts, in black and white. Silent and eloquent, the photographer unites the opposition of mourning and desire in the oxymoron of Phèdre's "black light." The portrait of Ernestine Nadar leads in two directions. Her physiognomy anticipates the photograph of Barthes's mother having tea with her sons in *Roland Barthes*; the allegorical resonance of her gestures enters a constellation of mourning and desire that leads the reader to Proust's iconographic images of women and flowers. Proust frames the stages of Swann's love for Odette among chrysanthemums and cattleyas: the Narrator learns from Swann to associate women and flowers in an aesthetic of pleasure. This aesthetic is overdetermined, since the Narrator's perceptions of Gilberte among the hawthorns anticipate Swann's combinations of art and love in the allegorical flowers that gather around Odette. Proust's portrayal of Odette evolves in Time and is altered according to the seasons, but like her theatrical ceremonies for drinking tea and writing letters, her life of seduction, secrets, and display unfolds in an economy of flowers. Even after Swann's love is over, he covers Odette with the flowers of Botticelli's Primavera. The Narrator combines his adoration of Gilberte with an immense admiration for her mother, and flowers provide him with an erotic outlet. He sells antique silverware and some of the furniture inherited from his Tante Léonie to send enormous baskets of orchids to Madame Swann (1: 578); shortly afterward, on the fateful day when the Narrator sees Gilberte walking with a young man in the shadows of the Champs-Elysées, his intended reconciliation with her had induced fantasies of sending her the most beautiful flowers in the world (1: 623). When he imagines that he has lost Gilberte forever, the Narrator immediately adds her mother to his gallery of fascinating women associated with flowers in their spiral journey through Time.

Nadar's photograph of the woman with the flower discretely reminds Barthes of the effects of Time on a figure he has suddenly found in a Winter Garden. The awkwardly posed child of the Winter Garden captivates him; her beauty and gracefulness, her identity itself, are rooted in this image, where they are invisible. Barthes calls on Proust's principles of prefiguration and invisibility, linked to the belatedness of understanding. For Proust's Narrator in *Remembrance of Things Past,* the luxury and voluptuousness of love are prefigured by the obscene gesture of a little girl named Gilberte seen among the flowering hawthorns. Understanding comes many years later, when the Narrator's love for her has disappeared so completely that he can barely remember it, and when the images of the lady in white, Swann, Charlus, and the girl herself have been transformed from their initial mysterious anonymity into the players on the stage of his life. They inhabit a labyrinth of Time that becomes visible in the text of Proust's novel. Lost and found again when it is too late for them, Gilberte and the Narrator recall that when the Narrator first glimpsed Gilberte among the flowering hawthorne, each child was captivated by the image of the other; each one was caught motionless in the act of looking, like the viewer of a painting or a photograph who suddenly mirrors the fixity of the image that absorbs his or her gaze.

The mirroring of viewer and image that characterizes the Narrator's precocious experience of looking at a desirable object is echoed when he goes to the matinée of the Princess de Guermantes in the final episode. He is ravished by an image that others cannot perceive, and it literally stops him in his tracks. At this instant, he descends within himself to look at an interior image. Proust's metaphor owes its rhetorical power to the mystical writings of Augustine and others. At the moment when the subject is stopped in his tracks, the image has begun to take on a life of its own. At the beginning of *Remembrance of Things Past*, Combray emerges from a cup of tea. The novel's first version of the ecstatic experience of lost time freezes the Narrator to the spot: the chills that afflict him are not motivated simply by the weather or by the author's delicate constitution. In a moment of melancholy, loss, and mourning, the Narrator is confronted suddenly by a resurrected world that rises up before him, or inside him, in a virtual space. This space shapes the temporality of the novel; the present tense of the tea drinker fades and becomes static, while the past takes on a newly rejuvenated life in this moment of revelation.

The uncanny reversal of stillness and lively movement is central to the experience of early photography, when the subject was required to remain motionless for many long minutes. Benjamin suggests that this period of stillness intensifies the auratic effect of early photography.[8] Its subjects seem to look back at the viewer, who is absorbed into the stillness of the image. Nadar thematizes this strange reversal in his photograph of the costumed Pierrot playing the Photographer. Standing next to one of Nadar's cameras, Pierrot strikes the photographer's pose: in Nadar's composition, Pierrot and the camera face us from within the centered space of the photographer. Caught by the image and captured by the camera's eye, the spectator suddenly has become the subject of Pierrot's picture-taking venture. Instead of the customary relation between the active viewer (or photographer) examining (or taking) the photograph of a subject who must hold still, Nadar's image instead freezes the viewer in his tracks. At its center, Pierrot displays his traditional whiteface makeup and the white taffeta costume that the commedia dell'arte gave him several centuries before the invention of the daguerreotype. He looks out at the viewer and aims the camera; his mimed picture-taking gives form to the Photographer.

Winter Garden

In "Les Morts de Roland Barthes," Jacques Derrida reads through some of Barthes's images that locate the referent (and reference) at the beginning and end of a life of writing. Derrida skips from the white writing of *Writing Degree Zero* to the *punctum* and the wound of the image in *Camera Lucida*: "Crossing through, overflowing, exploiting the resources of phenomenological as well as structural analysis, Benjamin's essay and Barthes's last essay may well be the two major texts on the question of the Referent in technical modernity."[9] Derrida marks the intersection in Barthes's writings between an act of technical reproduction and a detail ("the *punctum*") that singularizes the image through an act of reading. The *punctum* takes effect on the subject with the knife point of sensibility, the stigmatum of memory and loss, and the stiletto of the reader's investment in style. The reader of texts—written, painted, photographed, filmed—is this Barthesian subject, who theorizes a vantage point that opens new perspectives on art. Barthes's point or *punctum* is outside the intended codes that could reproduce the object of interpretation: the point marks the spot of an act of reading.

Derrida analyzes the detail or *punctum* with the following words: "a point of singularity pierces the surface of the reproduction" (272). He emphasizes the singular effect of Barthes's *punctum*: "If the *punctum* speaks to me, it is in its definition. It is the absolute singularity of the other that speaks to me, of the Referent whose very image I can no longer suspend, while its 'presence' eludes me forever, while it has already plunged into the past" (272). The viewing subject and the referent of the image are caught in a temporal relation. The photographic image persists in its revelation of the singularity of the other; the potentially unlimited technical reproduction of the image, however, seems irreconcilable with the quality of singularity that speaks to the subject. Barthes's *punctum* is the element of the photograph that connects the singularity of the photographic subject with the viewer's experience of looking at it; the instant when the shutter clicked is resurrected in the moment when the viewer gazes at the image. Both instants are fatal: the lingering presence of the referent in the image provides a lesson in mortality to the viewer.

The *punctum* marks the referent's disappearance into the folds of Time. Unlike most painting, photography vividly renders the referent as something that is lost forever; the photographer's unlimited power of technical reproduction flies in the face of Nature as well as Art. Derrida's evocation of Benjamin in the context of *Camera Lucida* raises the question of the status of the referent in the realm of technical reproduction. The invention of photography irrevocably alters the status of objects. The object of art, the cult object, and the "natural" object were once unique: like Eve and Adam, subjected to the demands of reproduction, they lose the paradise of their uniqueness and of their authenticity. In the "Work of Art" essay, Benjamin's understanding of technical reproduction is based on his observation that in modernity "exhibition value" displaces "cult value." The work of art as a product and a commodity displaces the ritual and magical powers that Benjamin links to the practices of tradition.

In 1898, at age five, Barthes's mother is photographed for the future. This photograph takes on the name of its location, the glass-roofed winter garden of the house in Chennevières-sur-Marne where she was born. Barthes describes it as the "true image" he had been seeking; this picture is Photography with a capital letter, "the Winter Garden Photograph" (*CL*, 70). This picture, pale and faded, provides the exemplum for Barthes's reading of photography and its attractions; it also sheds light on the inner workings of the concept of the *punctum*. The Winter Garden Photograph, writes Barthes, is in harmony with both the essence of her being and her son's suffering at her death. The pale and fragile image preserves the uniqueness of the referent and connects it to the suffering of the subject who gazes at it in mourning. In Barthes's text, the effect of this photo produces the sureness of Proustian involuntary memory at the moment when Barthes dismisses the fictional Narrator and attributes to Proust the retrieval of the grandmother's living reality in a chance repetition of gestures. Involuntary memory mediates the connection between the mourner and the lost love object; Barthes quotes Proust and invokes the superlatively beautiful photo by Nadar, seen on the facing page (*CL*, 68).

In the winter garden, Barthes puts out the light on the invisible image of his mother. The unseen photograph that emerges from his writing seems to restore her to the darkness of cult value and magic. *Camera Lucida* presents this darkness as the ultimate product of the camera. The unique being who inhabits Barthes's referent can be named only in the deixis of the demonstrative pronoun, found in other texts in *Roland Barthes by Roland Barthes* and *The Empire of Signs*. The discovery of the photograph leads Barthes to exclaim that the image *is* his lost mother: "Lost in the depth of the winter garden, my mother's face is blurred, pale. My first reaction was to cry out: 'At last, there she is!' " (*CL*, 99). His triumph soon ends in lamentation: the image is without deeper meaning. It is only light and surface and never turns into words. The viewer is caught in a bad dream and holds out his arms toward the beloved who slips back into the Underworld.

In *Camera Lucida*, the childhood photograph of the mother remains invisible. Barthes subtracts its exhibition value and restores it to the cultic realm of ritual and magic. The cult of the mother is a solitary one, modeled on the Proustian Narrator's discovery of Lost Time near the end of *Remembrance of Things Past*. The miracle can take place only when the referent has been distanced: the miracle requires the artifice of the invisible. Barthes's cult of mourning requires the pretext of an absent picture. The camera of "la chambre claire"/"camera lucida" illuminates an empty room; the photographic image of the winter garden blacks out and turns into words. This particular image tells a true story, wrapped in the artifice of Proustian redemption. The story that Barthes hears from it and tells his readers includes a moment of History and a fiction of lost and found. According to Barthes, History is "hysterical"; it can be the object of our gaze only if it excludes us. History, then, is like Photography. The subject who turns on the lights to look at them cannot enter their worlds, nor can History or Photography move over the threshold that separates the dead from the living, Eurydice from the world of Orpheus.

Beginning with the invention of the daguerreotype, technology has reshaped the relationship that once engaged the subject with the image as a singular product of Art or Nature. The referent no longer guarantees the value of the image. On the contrary, the referent is captured by the image of Nature or the Sacred; the referent is absorbed by a new and artificial Life and Death, created by mechanical reproduction. Benjamin's complex articulations of Aura, correspondence, and Nature bear witness to the changed status of the referent as it affects the subject's confrontation with the technical reproduction that inhabits modernity. This confrontation is also at the heart of Barthes's critical enterprise.

Barthes's referent confronts the viewer/reader, the subject. Gazing at the image or the photograph, the subject suddenly encounters the referent. This face-to-face meeting produces the *punctum* when the referent suddenly and unpredictably reaches out to the viewer through a fragment or detail. In the singular subjectivity of the viewer, a chance encounter with a detail of the image takes effect and produces a heterogeneous form of reading that combines essay and novel, theory and memoir. Barthes's concept of the *punctum* simultaneously focuses the reader's attention on the effect of the referent and on the subject's experience of it. The *punctum* articulates a detail that enters the subject in the manner of a secularized stigmatum. In a Proustian image of eroticism and love, the *punctum* pierces the subject's heart; in a Lacanian image of the symptom, it produces an intensity of emotion that takes effect in the Real. The correspondence between Benjamin's writing of modernity and Barthes's dense haunted space of images occurs as a singular event in the moment when the referent slips away forever. The myth of Orpheus captures this moment in the fateful turn, the moment when Orpheus turns to look at Eurydice. Light turns into darkness; the veiled, lightly moving figure of Eurydice is weighted down in the Underworld that she will not escape. The song of Orpheus turns into deep lamentation.

Images of lightness and heaviness enter Barthes's writing in the articulation of Proustian desire, in the words of Charlus and Madame de Sévigné. The terms combine and alternate as figures of materiality; light and darkness mingle in the figures of the photographic image. Both sets of terms seem to inhabit the conceptual opposition between presence and absence that haunts Mallarmé. In the wake of Mallarmé's enterprise, the terms enter some of the critical writings of Blanchot, Barthes, Derrida, and de Man. In "Les Morts de Barthes," Derrida quotes Barthes quoting Blanchot:

> Without showing or hiding. There is what took place. Here, there, the unique other, his mother, appears, i.e. without appearing, since the other can appear only in disappearing. Still the clarity, the "strength of the evidence" he says, of Photography. But it bears presence and absence, it neither shows nor hides. In the passage on the *camera lucida*, he quotes Blanchot: "The essence of the image is to be all on the outside, without intimacy, and yet more inaccessible and mysterious than the interiority of thought; without signification, but calling forth the depth of all possible meaning; unrevealed and yet manifest, endowed with the presence-absence that gives their power of attraction and fascination to the Sirens."[10]

Appearing and disappearing, present and absent, Blanchot's figure of the elusive Sirens resembles his version of Eurydice:

> When Orpheus descends toward Eurydice, the night opens through the power of art. But Orpheus descended toward Eurydice: Eurydice is, for him, the extreme that art may attain; covered by a name that hides her and under a veil that covers her, she is the profoundly obscure point toward which art, desire, death, night appear to reach. In turning toward Eurydice, Orpheus ruins the work, the work is immediately undone, and Eurydice turns back into the shadows. Thus he betrays the work and Eurydice and night. But not to turn toward Eurydice would be no less a betrayal, an infidelity to the power without measure and without prudence of movement, which does not want Eurydice in her diurnal truth and her daily appeal, which wants her in her nocturnal darkness, in

her distance, with her body closed and her face sealed, which wants to see her, not when she is visible but when she is invisible, and not in the intimacy of a familiar life, but in the strangeness of that which excludes intimacy, not to give her life, but to possess in her the living plenitude of her death.[11]

Orpheus is looking back at Eurydice: she is visibly present and forever lost to him at the moment when he turns toward her. Blanchot translates her image into the song of the Sirens, who are simultaneously present and absent to the one who is seduced by their feminine song, in spite of the knowledge that they cannot match it with a human form, a human image. Via the Image, present and absent, Music and Letters combine in the song of the Sirens and in the lyric of Orpheus. Both are already literary in the classical texts that represent their voices to modernity. Both indicate a moment of crisis that shapes and articulates the subject's experience of love and death as well as their transformation and translation in the experience of writing. Caught between the powers of art, love, and death, the figure of Orpheus emerges on the scene of writing.

The undecidable presence-absence that pervades Blanchot's reading of Orpheus speaks throughout Barthes's enterprise; it reads the images produced in art, love, death, writing, photography, and the interpretation of music. It speaks about meaning and nonmeaning, life and death, love and loss. The voice of lightness is also a voice of mourning: Charlus the melancholic turns up at the final matinée as a scandalous and unpleasant lover who cannot recover from his losses. He is a Proustian figure for the "weightiness" that Barthes classifies in *A Lover's Discourse* as the monstrosity of the tyrannical lover: light, fragile, and pitiful, says Barthes, the "subjected subject" is inverted and turned into an odious heavy-handed monster.

Although Barthes often celebrates nostalgia, his turn to the emotional effects of reading Proust moves beyond to something else: in this "other" experience, the subject is moved, as if by a strong wind. In its most extreme form, this other experience appears in Benjamin's allegorical evocation of Paul Klee's *Angelus Novus* as the Angel of History.[12] The angel steps outside the catastrophe that will engulf his allegorist in a nightmare of history from which there is no awakening outside death. Facing the ruins of history, Benjamin's wide-eyed angel renounces the comforts of nostalgia. A stormy wind fills his outspread wings and moves him fatally toward the future even as he turns to look back at the past and its ruins.

Orpheus turns toward Eurydice, and loses her forever to the past. Proust translates this turn in the effects of the grandmother's anticipated death on the Narrator. A modern Orpheus, he calls her on the telephone. Its disembodied voices lead him to the Underworld:

This freedom she was granting me henceforward, and to which I had never dreamed that she would consent, appeared to me suddenly as sad as my freedom of action might be after her death (when I should still love her and she would forever have abandoned me). "Granny!" I cried to her, "Granny!" and I longed to kiss her, but I had beside me only the voice, a phantom as impalpable as the one that would perhaps come back to visit me when my grandmother was dead. [. . .] It seemed to me as though it was already a beloved ghost that I had allowed to lose herself in the ghostly world, and standing alone before the instrument, I went on vainly repeating "Granny! Granny!" as Orpheus, left alone, repeats the name of his dead wife. (2:136–37, Moncrieff-Kilmartin)

The predicament of Orpheus is inscribed in the Narrator's love for his grandmother; his love leads him beyond nostalgia. He frames her loss in the "other" terms of antiquity, the terms of allegory that name her. The connection between love and allegory banishes nostalgia through the strange power of the modern invention, the machine ("appareil") that creates the underworldly and Orphean solitude of the Narrator, who stands before it. Proust provides the evidence for this effect in the single instance when the name that Orpheus calls out in the Underworld is uttered in the novel.

In "Swann in Love," the turning point of Swann's affair with Odette is figured by the naming of Eurydice. One evening, when Swann does not see Odette at the Verdurins' house, he goes into the city to look for her. It grows late, and the artificial nightfall of the lights going out in the restaurants suddenly leads Swann over a new threshold into the unfamiliar "somber kingdom" of shades, phantoms, and dark-desiring bodies. In this Underworld, Swann's relation to Odette is transformed into the suffering of love. Allegory banishes nostalgia and names the shadow of Woman, past and present: Eurydice. Love and death are invented simultaneously, in the harrowing strangeness that Barthes evokes in the name of Lucifer. Through Odette's absence, Proust provides Swann with a singular Eurydice. Unrecognizable in the somber kingdom, shadowy women of the Night ask Swann to take them home. Proust plays on the double meaning of *ramener* when an occasional shade asks Swann/Orpheus to bring her back from the dark kingdom of death:

Meanwhile the restaurants were closing and their lights began to go out. Under the trees of the boulevards there were still a few people strolling, barely distinguishable in the gathering darkness. From time to time the shadowy figure of a woman gliding up to Swann, murmuring a few words in his ear, asking him to take her home, would make him start. Anxiously he brushed past all these dim forms, as though among the phantoms of the dead, in the realms of darkness, he had been searching for a lost Eurydice. (1:252, Moncrieff-Kilmartin)

Notes

I would like to express my gratitude to the Falk Fund and to the Faculty Development Fund at Carnegie Mellon University for supporting the research and writing of this essay.

1. Roland Barthes, "Le bruissement de la langue," in *Le bruissement de la langue* (Paris: Seuil, 1984), p. 96. Translation mine.

2. Marcel Proust, *A la recherche du temps perdu*, 3 vols. (Paris: Gallimard, Bibliothèque de la Pléïade, 1954), 1:763. References to this edition will appear in parentheses in the text. I have also consulted the 1987 Pléïade edition in four volumes. English quotations of the novel are my own, except those marked Moncrieff-Kilmartin, taken from *Remembrance of Things Past*, trans. C. K. Scott Moncrieff and Terence Kilmartin (New York: Random House, 1981).

3. Steven Ungar, "Persistence of the Image: Barthes, Photography, and the Resistance to Film," in *Signs in Culture: Roland Barthes Today*, ed. Steven Ungar and Betty R. McGraw (Iowa City: University of Iowa Press, 1989), pp. 139–56. See also Steven Ungar, *Roland Barthes: The Professor of Desire* (Lincoln: University of Nebraska Press, 1983). In his writings on Barthes's complex relations to different kinds of images, Ungar continues to explore a range of forms, concepts, and texts. His essay on Barthes and Michelet (in this volume) develops the textual role of the image in biography and history.

4. In "'To Philosophize Is to Learn to Die'" (in Ungar and McGraw, *Signs in Culture*, pp. 3–31), Gary Shapiro reads *La Chambre claire* as Barthes's final meditation on death and images. Within the larger project of Shapiro's essay—the exploration of the philosophical economy that shapes Barthes's text—his reading of the Platonic and Nietzschean aspects of this economy is especially pertinent to the questions that concern this essay.

5. Many of the photographs in *La Chambre claire* are taken from Beaumont Newhall, *A History of Photography* (New York: MOMA, 1964). In an essay titled "A Message Without a Code?" (in *Studies in Twentieth-Century Literature: Special Issue on Roland Barthes* 5 [1981]: 147–55), Tom Conley raises some provocative questions about Barthes's use of photography and the absent image of the mother in *La Chambre claire*.

6. Mary Lydon, "Amplification: Barthes, Freud, and Paranoia," in *Signs of Culture: Roland Barthes Today*, ed. Ungar and McGraw, pp. 119–38.

7. See Julia Kristeva, "La Voix de Barthes," *Communications* 36 (1982): 146–49.

8. Walter Benjamin, "Kleine Geschichte der Photographie," in *Gesammelte Schriften* (Frankfurt am Main: Suhrkamp, 1974), vol. 1.

9. Jacques Derrida, "Les Morts de Roland Barthes," *Poétique* 47 (1981): 272. This essay is reprinted in *Psyché: Inventions de l'autre* (Paris: Galilée, 1987).

10. Ibid., p. 279.

11. Maurice Blanchot, "Le Regard d'Orphée," in *L'Espace littéraire* (Paris: Gallimard, 1955), pp. 227–28.

12. Walter Benjamin, "Ueber den Begriff der Geschichte (IX)," translated by Harry Zohn as "Theses on the Philosophy of History," paragraph 9, in *Illuminations*, ed. and intro. Hannah Arendt (New York: Schocken, 1969), p. 257.

II
Seeing Language, Seeing Culture

11

The Imaginary Museum of Jules Michelet

Steven Ungar

"I have a disease. I *see* language" begins a memorable fragment of *Roland Barthes by Roland Barthes.* Cast in the first-person singular, the statement borders on confession understood as the admission of a fault, wrongdoing, or sin. Use of the verb *devoir* in the conditional tense marks the force of a convention or norm that the narrator is presumably unable to meet: "What I should simply hear, a strange pulsion—perverse in that in it desire mistakes its object, reveals it to me as a 'vision,' analogous (all allowances made) to the one Scipio had in his dream of the musical spheres of the world. The primal scene, in which I listen without seeing, is followed by a perverse scene, in which I imagine seeing what I am hearing. Hearing deviates to scopia: I feel myself to be the visionary and the voyeur" (*RB*, 161).[1] What reads as confession derives as well from self-analysis announced by the initial invocation of disease. With the meaning of the passage built on a tension between confession and analysis, it is difficult to determine with certainty the extent to which the capacity to *see* language—a capacity equated by Barthes's narrator with disease—is something to be overcome or otherwise terminated. If, in a strict sense, seeing language is a disease or—more figuratively—a kind of disease, it is one that the narrator seemingly accepts for the insights it provides, perhaps even to the point of pleasure.

"J'ai une maladie: je *vois* le langage." What the first sentence formulates in lapidary syntax with active simple verbs linking grammatical subjects and objects is elaborated in a second paragraph that inscribes the pronominal subject within a more abstract discourse:

According to an initial vision, the image-repertoire [*imaginaire*] is simple: it is the discourse of others *insofar as I see it* (I put it between quotation marks). Then I turn the scopia on myself: I see my language *in so far as it is seen*: I see it *naked*

> (without quotation marks): this is the disgraced, pained phase of the image-repertoire. A third vision then appears: that of infinitely spread-out languages, of parentheses never to be closed: a utopian vision in that it supposes a mobile, plural reader, who nimbly inserts and removes the quotation marks: who begins to write *with me.* (*RB*, 161)[2]

The second part of the fragment invokes terms linked to psychoanalysis and, in particular, the concept of the imaginary associated by Jacques Lacan with those of the symbolic and the real. Yet an emphasis on visuality expressed by terms such as *scopia* and *vision* points as well to models of the self linked to perception in a tradition of phenomenology from Descartes to Husserl. In this sense, the tutor figure of Lacan cannot stand apart from the supplemental tutor figures of Gaston Bachelard and—especially—Jean-Paul Sartre, to whose 1940 study, *L'Imaginaire,* Barthes dedicated his last book, *La Chambre claire.* This semantic density of the term *imaginaire* suggests that instability embodied in the mobile, plural reader referred to above might not necessarily be inadequate in light of a norm of coherence, but understood instead in terms of intermittence and dispersion. As with the earlier equation of the capacity to see language with (a kind of) disease, it remains uncertain that a resolution of instability is more desirable than an intermittence that the self recognizes . . . and accepts.

Especially compelling in this passage from *Roland Barthes by Roland Barthes* is what it suggests about two kinds of instability or—to use Barthes's term—mobility. A first mobility between writing and reading recalls the linkage between readerly and writerly texts that Barthes had posited two years earlier in *The Pleasure of the Text,* as well as that between classical and modern texts set forth in *S/Z.* A second interplay, which obtains from the capacity to see language, asserts the functional priority of the visual as a disclosure of truth over and above the primitive scene in which sight is displaced by hearing. As Barthes's narrator puts it, the primitive scene deviates into perversion that breaks down to a degree where the self hovers between insight (*je me sens visionnaire*) and intrusion (*voyeur*).

I have dwelled at length on this passage from *Roland Barthes by Roland Barthes* in order to redirect what it implies concerning the capacity to see language toward an earlier text by Barthes in which this capacity is performed—that is, shown as well as simply stated. The text I have in mind is the 1954 essay on the historian Jules Michelet (1798–1874) that Barthes was commissioned to write for the same Ecrivains de Toujours series at the Editions du Seuil in which *Roland Barthes by Roland Barthes* appeared twenty-one years later. But where the narrator of the latter text stated that he saw language, I want to explore how the earlier text on Michelet prefigured the capacity to see language invoked in 1975 by performing it—so to speak—*avant la lettre* in extended figures of inversion and crossover.

I take an initial cue from a rare footnote midway through the 1954 monograph in which Barthes remarked that Michelet wrote nothing about anyone without first consulting as many portraits and engravings as he could. "All his life he conducted a systematic interrogation of the faces he passed" (*MI*, 87). Louis-Jean Calvet notes that when Barthes began to read Michelet's histories in the early 1940s, he followed Michelet's example by seeking out as many portraits and photographs of him as possible in the hope that by studying them he might find the man behind the images: "He had been fascinated by Couture's portrait of Michelet sitting at his desk with a slightly disdainful, superior air. He told his friends about the dark flame in Michelet's eyes, his sorcerer's face and demoniacal air and explained that he had decided to work on Michelet because, from his pictures he seemed to be the complete opposite of Barthes himself."[3] As might be expected in light of the passage from *Roland Barthes by Roland Barthes* examined above, this attempt to read clear and stable meaning into the face of Michelet failed. A postcard sent to Barthes in 1945 by his friend Robert David showed a Michelet whose older, rounder face and soft eyes contradicted the mental composite that Barthes had built from other portraits. At this point—Calvet concluded—Barthes no longer knew which was the true Michelet, the good one of the postcard photograph or the demoniac one of the portraits.

While undergoing treatment for tuberculosis in 1942 at the Sanatorium des Etudiants at Saint-Hilaire-du-Touvet, Barthes began to read Michelet's multivolume *Histoire de France.* As he read, he transcribed his notations onto index cards. By January 1945 Barthes was showing these cards—which by then numbered close to a thousand—to others at the Clinique Alexandre in Leysin, Switzerland, by laying them out on a table like stacks of playing cards and contrasting the stacks in various ways. By December 1946 Barthes was back in Paris with a contract to work at the Institut Français in Bucharest, Romania, starting the next fall. (As it turned out, Barthes did not take up his duties in Bucharest until 1948.) In the interim he already thought about expanding his notes into a longer study that, in turn, might later result in a doctoral thesis. Yet once he had completed his readings, the project seemed to collapse—as Calvet puts it—like a house of cards. Over the next five years, Barthes carried the index cards with him as he traveled to Romania and Egypt, arranging them in different combinations in what amounted to an unending game of solitaire. Little surprise, then, that the resulting book published in 1954 resembled nothing so much as "an explosion of index cards, with quotes by Michelet on one side and comments by Michelet on the other."[4]

The interplay of word and image in Barthes's *Michelet* was staged on an opening page that served as a statement of method. Facing an 1856 photo portrait of Michelet by Nadar, Barthes formulated a critical point of departure in which he sought to locate the text that followed apart from or to the side of others in the Ecrivains de Toujours monograph series marked by an evolved *lansonisme* for which biography served a monumental literary history. Understatement (litotes) and double negation—"In this little book, the reader will find neither a history of Michelet's thought nor a history of his life" (*MI*, 3)—combined to ground what Barthes termed a foundational inquiry—"the present work is nothing more than a pre-criticism" (*MI*, 3)—on the basis of which "real critics" such as historians, psychoanalysts, or phenomenologists might proceed toward more systematic analyses. As though to preclude misunderstanding, Barthes reiterated the modest scope of his figure of understatement—"I have sought merely to describe a unity, not to explore its roots in history or in biography"—before specifying that, concerning illustrations—"virtually all the images of Michelet there are" (*MI*, 3)—their choice and placement in the book were inspired by the impassioned gaze which Michelet fastened on any and every historical object. In sum, Barthes concluded, he had chosen several exhibits from what might be called Michelet's *musée imaginaire.* In my reading of the *Michelet* essay, I trace the interplay of word and image in order to explore how Barthes's composite portrait of the historian takes shape as inversion and crossover—chiasmus—that attempts to verbalize the image and visualize the word. In addition, I want to explore how this composite constructed out of word and image extends to a secondary crossover—instability and/or intermittence—involving gender.

The title of the first of *Michelet*'s eight sections, "Michelet, Eater of History," grounded the subject of the composite portrait as an organic entity. For Barthes to propose that Michelet "ate" history was to make the human a subclass of the animal and to imply that the past consumed was capable of sustaining (at least a certain kind of) life. Barthes asserted that Michelet's notorious migraines—often linked to creativity and genius—were brought on by everything from storms, springtime, and even the history he was writing. For Barthes, these historical migraines were to be understood as real and not merely metaphorical:

September 1792, the beginnings of the Convention, the Terror, so many immediate diseases, concrete as toothaches. Michelet is always said to have an excessive sensibility; yes, but above all a sensibility concerted, inflected, directed toward a signification. To be the victim of History not only as a nutriment and as a sacred poison but also as a possessed object; 'historical' migraines have no purpose but to establish Michelet as the manducator, priest, and owner of History. (*MI*, 19)

As eaten by Michelet, history was a complex—that is, mobile and unstable—entity that served a number of functions. Barthes wrote: "History can be an aliment only when it is full as an egg; hence Michelet has filled his, has endowed it with two goals and one direction [. . .]. History is to be *consummated* [*consommée*], i.e., on the one hand, concluded, fulfilled, and, on the other, *consumed* [*consommée*], devoured, ingested, so as to resuscitate the historian" (*MI*, 25). The wordplay that split eating into consummation and consumption was eminently clever. Yet what counted here was, I believe, less a matter of cleverness than of ambiguity. The very expansiveness and volume of Michelet's writings illustrated the difficulty of consummating history, as though the combined body of the man and his works that made up the corpus could be consumed and consummated only by death. History thus fed life to the point of death as it asserted in the form of migraines the materiality of the past reconstituted by the historian who read and wrote. Neither fulfillment as in Hegel's vision of absolute science nor entropy as in recent theorizing of posthistorical *désoeuvrement* accounted adequately for what Barthes saw as an ingestion on the part of Michelet that made the historical mass less a puzzle to reconstitute than what Barthes described as a body to embrace (*MI*, 81).

How literally did Barthes mean for his reader to consider the ingestion of history by Michelet? I raise this question in thinking again of the equation in *Roland Barthes by Roland Barthes* of the capacity to see language with disease and in order to portray Michelet the eater of history as someone for whom words were materialized both as an aliment-nutriment that sustained life and as indices of eventual death. This association of history and death was forcefully staged in word and image when Barthes wrote midway through *Michelet* that since the corruption of bodies was a pledge of their resurrection, the goal of history was to rediscover in each piece of the past's flesh the corruptible element par excellence, not the skeleton but the tissue. In this sense, what Barthes detected in Michelet's writings was less history than anthropology; that is, less a grand narrative of change driven by politics than an account of the essential traits of humankind understood from the perspective of the body:

Michelet's anthropology is an anthropology of humors, not of forms. In historical man we proceed to the most fragile, we leave the expression, the features, and rediscover the corruptible and mortal substance, the color of the blood, the density of the tissues, the texture of the skin, everything which will collapse and subside in the coffin. Let us not expect to find in Michelet's Robespierre or Napoleon men-as-principles: that would be to grant too much to their immortality. In order to be the prey of History, these men must die, and even in their lives they must be marked with an essential and fragile quality, of an entirely sanguine humor, i.e., a humor liable to deterioration, already funereal. All history depends in the last instance upon the human body. (*MI*, 87)[5]

Of particular interest here is what Barthes wrote concerning the fragility that Michelet sought in the flesh of the past embodied in portraits of noted figures. For what was disclosed in these portraits was less the agency of exemplary men and women than the corruptible, mortal substance of the human body that was prey to history. (The passage recalls the scene in Sartre's *La Nausée* in which Roquentin suddenly seized on the artifice that grounded the illusion of calm superiority that the official portraits of illustrious local figures were meant to convey to visitors to the municipal museum of Bouville.) When Barthes wrote that the goal of historical inquiry for Michelet was to find again—Richard Howard writes "rediscover" but I prefer a more literal translation of *retrouver* because it points to something present yet unrecognized—the corruptible element of fragility and corruption, astute readers may identify a prefiguration of the *punctum* that was to draw Barthes to write for twenty-five years on certain photographs in *Camera Lucida* because—much like the central character in Rainer Maria Rilke's *Malte Laurids Brigge*—he sought in them the signs of future death. Reiterating the reduction of the human to the animal and the organic that he had first set forth in the image of Michelet as eater of history, Barthes ended the fragment by invoking the passage in *The German Ideology* in which Marx wrote that because the first presupposition of all human history was the existence of individual living beings, the first state of things to describe was the corporeal organization of these individuals and the relation that this organization gave them with nature.

The emphasis on the essential fragility of bodies moving toward death in the passage described above in *Michelet* also pervaded Barthes's later reflections on photography in *Camera Lucida*. Yet this common concern with the signs of death to come was tempered by irreducible differences of medium and material. A closer look at the passage from *Michelet* reveals how word and image combined to create meaning in which language was to be seen in its graphic materiality and not merely read as though it were transparent. Facing the text of the fragment is a photograph of Michelet's grave at Père Lachaise cemetery. The photo shows a bas-relief of a female figure in a flowing gown hovering above a recumbent male. If the male is meant to represent the historian, does the female represent history or death? If the head covering worn by the female is a kind of Phrygian bonnet, might she be an allegory of the Revolution, a Marianne in mourning?

Rereading the 1954 Barthes of *Michelet* through the 1980 Barthes of *Camera Lucida*, I propose that the *studium* or set of cultural codes at work in this photograph points to conventions of representation related to funereal monument, bas-relief, and allegory in nineteenth-century France. What draws me to the photograph is, however, the female figure and, in particular, the protrusion of the left foot not simply outward from the surface of the stone, but also downward beyond the horizontal lines formed by the top of the coffin and the sarcophagus. Along with the extended right arm and the figure's head turned backward toward the left, this protruding leg forms a diagonal against the perpendicular frame of the bas-relief. The impression of frozen movement resulting from the intersection of the horizontal and perpendicular is enhanced by the gown that is taut across the hips yet billowing behind the head and trailing leg. Finally, I am struck by the *punctum* or detail of affect in the exposed foot whose outward turn recalls the female walker who haunted the narrators of Wilhelm Jensen's "Gradiva" and André Breton's *Nadja*. Starting with the left foot, the diagonal line extends from the calf, thigh, and left arm toward the outstretched right arm and hand near whose fingers is inscribed "L'histoire est une ressuscitation" with the caption "J. Michelet." At first glance, the meaning of the phrase is direct and simple. Yet because the phrase above the right hand is a variant of the first phrase of the fragment that faces it, it is part of a more mobile—that is, "unstable and/or intermittent"—interplay of word and image that stages meaning as a *mise-en-page* in which language is seen in its materiality and read as a transparent medium. On the left (in the photograph) we read that history is a resurrection; on the right, that the corruption of bodies is a pledge of their resurrection. Putting the two sentences together corroborates an implied equivalence of history and the pledge or promise of corruption in the human body. It is this pledge or promise whose signs Barthes seeks out in portraits of historical figures in Michelet's writing of history.

Throughout his 1954 essay, Barthes imitated Michelet's project to discern the "fragile and essential qualities" of the human body that was prey to history through the use of images captioned with passages from Michelet's writings. These portraits fall into two major types, which, for purposes of provocation, I will term flesh and fable. Among the first are portraits of the "pink and milky" Englishman Pitt ("He is red . . . he is a little vulgar . . . everywhere this countenance betrays a certain swollen, choleric childishness" [*MI*, 89]), Louis XVI ("a pale fat king" [*MI*, 91]); Marie-Victoire Sophie de Noailles, Comtesse de Toulouse ("Ripe, pious, sugary, still fresh, plump and lovely" [*MI*, 93]); and Francis II of Austria ("Not a man, not a mask, but a wall of stone from Spielberg" [*MI*, 140]). For the second type, in which the human is reduced to the animal, Barthes proposes Marat-as-Toad (*MI*, 108); Robespierre-as-Cat (*MI*, 113); Danton-as-Bull (*MI*, 181); Man-of-the-Wind Francois I as "living fib, a comedy, a farce, a legend, a fable" (*MI*, 204); and Whale-Man Ruyter as "Gargantua in girth, half whale and half man. His big black eyes protruding from his red face, so proudly colored up, flung forth a rushing stream of life, a fearful good humor, and the contagion of history" (*MI*, 205).

Other images in the essay range from portraits and photos of Michelet and members of his family to paintings of historical scenes and the photograph of an Egyptian sculpture. Where the former extended the thematic of the "fragile and essential qualities" of the human body toward conventional biography, the latter pointed instead to Barthes's sense of unity with respect to the man rather than his life or times. Among the latter, a painting by Piranesi and a bas-relief by Jean Goujoun bore brief captions of passages from Michelet's writings. A reproduction of Dürer's *Melancolia I* was all the more striking because it was one of the few illustrations with a caption by Barthes: "In 1825, Michelet buys a reproduction of Dürer's *Melancholy* for his study. In it, he sees 'all of Faust's thought'" (*MI*, 176). The choice of the Dürer engraving was curious for a number of reasons, including its status as source for the first title of Sartre's 1938 novel published by Gallimard as *La Nausée.* A more substantial function of the engraving related to its placement in *Michelet* at the conclusion of a section, "The Ultra-Sex," devoted to the figure of Woman. (Richard Howard's translation places the Dürer at the very start of the chapter.) Barthes writes:

> Fated to approach Woman as a confidant and not as ravisher, Michelet could only be man and woman both. He does not fail to present a double sex as the ideal one, and androgynous man as the complete one. For Michelet, the two sexes of the mind are nothing but the male force of the idea and the female milieu of instinct. All creation will therefore be divided into two ways of knowledge: that of the mind and that of the heart. For example, there will be male religions (Roman law) and female religions (Christianity), male sciences (history) and female sciences (natural history). Of course, the divorce of the two sexes is disastrous: the nineteenth century, for instance, a dead century had it not discovered Woman, is imperfect insofar as it sets instinct in opposition to reflection. (*MI*, 177)[6]

As with mobility, so with gender. While the seated figure in *Melancolia* is often seen—by Erwin Panofsky, for one—as a self-portrait of Dürer; it is taken to be female.[7] The instability/intermittence invoked in *Roland Barthes by Roland Barthes* with reference to the mobile identity of the reader who also wrote was prefigured in *Michelet* in the "false mixture" of androgyny in which Barthes had identified a preponderance of female qualities. He took this preponderance to be irreducible. In fact, Barthes concluded that Micheletist heroes were, by definition, androgynous: "Without Woman, no masculine genius; but without a little of the male spark, no heroine. The definition of genius is to be man *and* woman" (*MI,* 179, 182). Even more notable in this passage was Barthes's sense that in the Micheletist conjunction of the sexes he termed androgyny, the order of operations was reversed so that reflection did not correct instinct, but intuition gave the idea its complete form. Citing the figure of Joan of Arc as she appeared in volume five of Michelet's *Histoire de France,* Barthes wrote: "It is not her pure femininity which makes her a heroine; it is because, woman that she is, she knows both sexes of the mind, 'common sense in exaltation' " (*MI,* 179).

Barthes concluded *Michelet* with a chronology preceded by an overview of what has been said about Michelet at various times by others. His own composite—titled "Reading Michelet" ["Lecture de Michelet"]—ended with a section on method with emphasis on the Micheletist theme as a critical reality independent from idea, influence, and image. Had *Michelet* been written ten years later and more fully under the sway of structural analysis of the 1960s, Barthes might well have approached the minimal unit on which his composite portrait of Michelet took form. In the early 1950s, however, Barthes approached the theme from the perspective of lived experience. Because Barthes saw the theme as substantial, he held that it resisted history, which in turn could inflect but not change the fixity of recurrent ideas, images, and myths: "The theme is in effect *substantial,* it brings into play an attitude of Michelet's with regard to certain qualities of matter" (*MI,* 202). While Barthes considered the roots of the Micheletist theme as both historical and existential, the latter took clear precedence over the former. As a result, the ambition of a total reading of Michelet invoked by Barthes at the very end of his essay was to be grounded on a capacity to distinguish the themes by linking them to their substantial signification as well as their "relations of dependency and reduction" (*MI,* 203).

Barthes never achieved anything close to this total reading, neither in the 1954 monograph nor in a 1959 text on "La Sorcière." A 1973 contribution, "Aujourd'hui, Michelet," written for a special issue of *L'Arc* did, however, provide a reassessment of sorts. Barthes reiterated that twenty years earlier he had been struck by the thematic insistence of Michelet's writings in which every figure returned bedecked with the same epithets that issued forth from a reading that was both corporeal and moral. In the interim and in light of changes in his conception of the text, what continued to strike him alongside the thematic evidence in Michelet's corpus was a certain discursive disturbance—"un certain trouble de la discursivité"—expressed in holes and gaps: "Toute la scène est pleine de trous: intelligible au niveau de chaque phrase (rien de plus clair que le style de Michelet), elle devient énigmatique au niveau du discours."[8] Michelet's notoriety among other historians was not simply a matter of style, but an excess of the signifier, an excess Barthes found to be legible in the margins of representation ["se lit dans *les marges de la représentation*"].[9]

I believe this excess of the signifier helps explain the interplay between word and image in *Michelet* that prefigures the complexity of the 1975 admission in *Roland Barthes by Roland Barthes* that made the capacity to see language a disease. Yet because I propose that this capacity equated with disease is a condition the Barthes of 1975 accepted to the point of asserting it as pleasurable, I want to end by extending the image in its primacy over the word in *Mythologies* ("Harcourt's Actors," "Garbo's Face," "The Iconography of the Abbé Pierre," "Poujade and Intellectuals,"), *The Empire of Signs, Roland Barthes by Roland Barthes*, and *Camera Lucida* to work back from the 1975 assertion "J'ai une maladie: je *vois* le langage" to the assertion in *Michelet* that the historian spent his life in a systematic interrogation of faces from the past. In so moving backward, I have sought to locate in the earlier text the signs of death that, in an interim text such as Barthes's 1970 essay on Erté, represented death as the absence of face and body. Would this reduction to the letter of death—"M" for *la mort*—then constitute a secondary follow-up to Michelet? That would be the ambition of another *parcours* and another *histoire*.

Notes

1. The original reads: "Ce que je devrais simplement écouter, une drôle de pulsion, perverse en ce que le désir s'y trompe d'objet, me le révèle comme une 'vision' analogue (toutes proportions gardées!) à celle que Scipion eut en songe des sphères musicales du monde. A la scène primitive, où j'écoute sans voir, succède une scène perverse, où j'imagine voir ce que j'écoute. L'écoute dérive en scopie: du langage, je me sens visionnaire et voyeur" (*Roland Barthes par Roland Barthes* [Paris: Seuil, 1975], p. 164).

2. "Selon une première vision, l'imaginaire est simple: c'est le discours de l'autre *en tant que je le vois* (je l'entoure de guillemets). Puis je retourne la scopie sur moi: je vois mon langage en tant qu'il est vu: je le vois *tout nu* (sans guillemets): c'est le temps honteux, douloureux, de l'imaginaire. Une troisième vision se profile alors: celles des langages infiniment échelonnés, des parenthèses, jamais fermées: vision utopique en ce qu'elle suppose un lecteur mobile, pluriel, qui met et enlève les guillemets d'une façon preste: qui se met à écrire avec moi" (*Roland Barthes par Roland Barthes*, p. 164).

3. Louis-Jean Calvet, *Roland Barthes: Une biographie* (Paris: Flammarion, 1990), p. 147. (My translation.)

4. Ibid., p. 146.

5. "L'anthropologie de Michelet est une anthropologie d'humeurs et non de formes. Dans l'homme historique, allons au plus fragile, laissons là l'expression, les traits, et retrouvons la substance corruptible et mortelle, la couleur du sang, la densité des tissus, le grain de la peau, tout ce qui s'effondrera et s'écoulera au cercueil. Qu'on ne s'attende pas à trouver dans le Robespierre ou le Napoléon de Michelet, des hommes-principes: ce serait là trop accorder à leur immortalité; pour être proies de l'Histoire, il faut que ces hommes meurent et que déjà dans leurs vie ils soient marqués d'une qualité essentielle et fragile, d'une humeur toute sanguine, c'est-à-dire altérable, déjà funèbre. Toute l'histoire repose en dernière instance sur le corps humain" (*Michelet,* [Paris: Seuil, 1954] pp. 79–80).

6. "Destiné à approcher la Femme en confident et non en ravisseur, Michelet ne pouvait être qu'à la fois homme et femme. Il n'a pas manqué de donner le sexe double comme le sexe idéal, et l'homme androgyne comme l'homme complet. Pour Michelet, les deux sexes de l'esprit ne sont autres que la force mâle de l'idée et le milieu femelle de l'instinct. Toute la création va donc se diviser en deux voies de connaissance: celle de l'esprit et celle du coeur. Il y aura par exemple des religions mâles (le droit romain) et des religions femelles (le christianisme), des sciences mâles (l'Histoire) et des sciences femelles (l'Histoire naturelle). Evidemment, le divorce des deux sexes est néfaste: le XIXe siècle, par exemple, siècle mort s'il n'avait pas découvert la Femme, est imparfait dans la mesure où il oppose l'instinct à la réflexion" (*Michelet,* p. 153).

7. See Erwin Panofsky, *Dürers "Melencolia I": Eine Quellen und Typengeschichte Untersuchung* (Leipzig: B. G. Teuschner, 1923).

8. Roland Barthes, "Aujourd'hui, Michelet," *L'Arc* 52 (1973): 19. The text was reprinted in *Le Bruissement de la langue* (Paris: Seuil, 1984) and translated by Richard Howard as "Michelet, Today," in *RL,* pp. 195–207 ("The whole scene is full of holes: intelligible on the level of each sentence [nothing clearer than Michelet's style], it becomes enigmatic on the level of discourse," p. 195). The 1959 text on "La Sorcière" was published as a preface for the Club Français du Livre, reprinted in *Essais critiques* (Paris: Seuil, 1964), and translated in *CE.*

9. Ibid., p. 21.

12

Barthes with Marx

Philippe Roger

For a long time, French grade crossings have greeted road travelers with this warning: *Attention! Un train peut en cacher un autre.* (Caution! One train can hide another approaching train.) It is no less true of titles, and mine might well hide another. In fact, the first draft of this chapter announced "Barthes *and* Marx." No matter how slight, the distortion had me worried; somehow, it sounded too much like David and Goliath. Thanks to Jean-Michel Rabaté's diligence, the original *with* has been restored, only to elicit new concerns that the chosen conjunction might be misleading. It is not my intention here to examine Marx's work as a possible source or influence on Barthes. Such a task would not only go against Barthes's constant caveats ("I do not believe in influences"); it would also prove embarrassingly disappointing. Of no greater interest would be an exhaustive recapitulation of Barthes's statements, qualified or not, in favor of Marx or Marxism: no posthumous Barthesian *Pour Marx* will emerge from these wanderings through Barthes's early writings. My *with* was and still is intended to draw attention to the very particular companionship of Barthes (who never was a Marxist fellow traveler *sensu stricto*) with a Marxism of his own. And I would like to explore the riddle of Barthes's relationship with Marxism in connection with theater, his absorbing passion for a decade. A rapture and a political gesture, Barthes's intellectual romance with theater had Marxism for its soundtrack and accompaniment. At the risk of overstretching the metaphor, I would like to describe Roland Barthes in the 1950s as accompanied by Marx, rather than following his teachings. Then my title should be read both ways: "Marx with Barthes" as well as "Barthes with Marx"—which is, after all, consistent with the English version of the same cautionary signal: *Beware! Trains coming both ways.*

Discovering Marxism, with a Twist

There is nothing more misleading than an intellectual biography, except perhaps an intellectual autobiography. "At the time of the Armistice," Barthes confided in 1971 for the benefit of *Tel Quel* readers, "I was a Sartrian and a Marxist"—a statement to be taken with some caution.[1] Edgar Morin, who knew Barthes in the 1950s and remained a lifelong friend, adds more than a nuance, suggesting that Barthes was then basically endorsing the "Marxist Vulgate" typical of those intellectuals who had perhaps read only a few pages of Marx, and even more plausibly only a few pages of Sartre.[2] However, one may agree with Barthes (vintage 1971) on one thing: before 1945 he was neither a Marxist nor a Sartrian. There is no hint of any interest or even awareness of Marxism in his early contributions to *Existences* (1942–44). Before the war, Barthes was certainly not completely apolitical: he took part in a small antifascist student group and welcomed the 1936 Popular Front. But his political involvement remained minimal and his knowledge of Marxism less than minimal. In this respect, Barthes did not differ from the intellectual generation of would-be Normaliens described by Jean-François Sirinelli.[3]

We have no reason, on the other hand, to suspect Barthes's account of his introduction to Marxism late in 1944 through his new friend Georges Fournié, a fellow patient in Switzerland. Fournié, who like Barthes suffered from tuberculosis, had a working-class background and a very different personal history: while still a very young man, he fought in the Spanish civil war. He was a convinced and apparently convincing Marxist. He was also a Trotskyite, a circumstance of particular importance that allowed Barthes to learn of Marxism through a "dissident," a word used at the time for Marxist opponents to Stalinism. Back in Paris, it was through Fournié that Barthes became acquainted with the man who "gave him a start": Maurice Nadeau. Barthes's intellectual closeness to Edgar Morin, who was expelled from the French Communist Party in 1951, has already been mentioned. For Barthes, Fournié, Nadeau, Morin, and Claude Bourdet, the late 1940s were a time of companionship. Barthes shared the excitement of postwar literary and political journalism in *Combat* or *Les Lettres Nouvelles* with these brilliant young men. They also shared a vocabulary. In an article published by *Combat* in June 1951, Barthes referred explicitly and sympathetically to the "dissidents"—meaning the anti-Stalinist, Marxist militants. Commenting on a book by Roger Caillois, *Description du marxisme*, which he found irritating, he sided with those "numerous dissidents, whose individual destiny is still today fecundated by Marxism" and who cannot afford to regard Moscow-style Marxism as a "scandal" (Caillois's word) because they experience it as a "tragedy."[4] Even though Barthes was later acquainted with more orthodox Marxists, particularly within the context of the journal *Théâtre Populaire*, it is important to underline the peculiar way in which he first had access to Marxism before trying to elucidate his somehow perplexing relationship with Marxist politics or theory.

By tracing his professed Marxism as far back as 1945 (or even 1940) in the *Tel Quel* interview, was Barthes antedating it for the edification of his highly politicized interlocutors?[5] Whatever his reasons, chronology here gives away a clue. On the whole, before 1950–51, Barthes's writings offer few Marxist references; when they do, as in some of the *Combat* articles that eventually became *Writing Degree Zero*, ambiguity prevails. In these short essays, and even more so in the book version, scattered references to the division of classes are permanently recoded in a very different language, a language of yearning for a "reconciled world" that strongly evokes Blanchot's "communauté impossible." After 1960, on the other hand, whenever Barthes mentions Marxism, it is clearly from an outsider's viewpoint. In *Roland Barthes by Roland Barthes*, a chronological chart of his intellectual life indicates that the "intertext" named after Marx, Brecht, and Sartre comes to an end after *Mythologies* (1957) and before *Elements of Semiology* (1965). In fact, Barthes's dissociation from Marxism is obvious in his work by 1959–60. As I said before, Roland Barthes had a tendency to overstretch his own "Marxist" period. By reducing it to the years 1950–60, I do not mean to deflate its importance but to emphasize the temporal connection between Barthes's active interest in Marxism and his *passion prédominante*: his extraordinary infatuation with theater. Marxism and theater: these two intellectual attachments have the same life span in Barthes's career. There is nothing accidental in that coincidence.

The Climax of 1955

This is not to say that Barthes was not active in other fields, present on other battlefields. To illustrate his attitude during 1950–60, I will briefly evoke the climatic year of 1955, before coming back to Marx, Brecht, and the question of theater. Three distinct episodes make 1955 especially significant.

First there was Barthes's bitter, final exchange with Albert Camus. I have previously analyzed that quarrel in some detail[6] and here give only a sketchy reminder of its reasons and implications. An enthusiastic commentator of *L'Etranger* in 1942 and again in 1947, Barthes wrote a negative review of *La Peste* in January 1955. The major flaw of the novel in Barthes's view was a symbolism that betrayed Camus's proclaimed intention to depict the reality of anti-Nazi resistance throughout Europe; it was the substitution of a vague and shallow humanism for a much-needed political and historical solidarity. Camus, in his brief answer, displayed his polemical crafts: how could Barthes, who had liked *L'Etranger* so much, deplore such a lack of "solidarity" when it was so clear that *La Peste* bade farewell to the loneliness of *L'Etranger* and opened the way to collective answers to evil in the city? The reason why he, Camus, had chosen symbolism to make his political statement was very simple: he did not believe in "realism in art." If Barthes, on the other hand, found the morality of *La Peste* "insuffisante," could he please tell what other, better "morale" would satisfy him? Thus cornered, Barthes took the plunge: he, Barthes, did believe in "réalisme en art," more precisely in an "art littéral" that would not obliterate the object under the metaphor; and he, Barthes, was indeed speaking in the name of "historical materialism."

Barthes had thus burned his vessels in April. Two months later, an article by Jean Guérin in *Nouvelle NRF* started a new conflagration. Quoting excerpts from *Mythologies*, which since 1951 had appeared in *Esprit* and *Les Lettres Nouvelles*, Jean Guérin was pressing Barthes for an answer: was he a Marxist, and if so, why did he not say so in the first place? He was met with a brutal rebuff: "What difference could it make to Monsieur Guérin?" Barthes answered in the summer issue of the *Lettres Nouvelles*: ". . . that kind of question is normally of no interest to anybody but the McCarthyists." An angry Barthes went on, suggesting that Monsieur Guérin "go and read Marx and decide for himself," adding that "one is not a Marxist by immersion, initiation or declaration" and that his own admission of Marxism would be both irrelevant and arrogant, inasmuch as "that doctrine [Marxism] is very demanding on its partisans."[7]

Interestingly, Barthes's answer duplicated the speech strategy adopted by presumed communists in the United States during the McCarthy era. But its transposition to a distinctly different context was not without irony. In previous years, the French Communist Party had indeed been subjected to some police intimidation: in 1952 its leader, Jacques Duclos, had been briefly arrested on a conspiracy charge, rallying support from Jean-Paul Sartre; in 1953 the communist novelist and journalist André Stil (whose style Barthes derided the same year in *Writing Degree Zero*) had been jailed for his graphic depiction of police violence against strikers. But in 1955 the heat was off. Barthes, on the other hand, was not answering any special committee on un-French activities: his self-styled prosecutor in the *Nouvelle NRF*, writing under the alias of Jean Guérin, was none other than Jean Paulhan, a prominent figure on the literary scene, an *éminence grise* at Gallimard—but hardly the French counterpart to Senator McCarthy.

Before the end of 1955, Barthes was fighting still another battle: this time on the theatrical front, to defend *Nekrassov*, Sartre's satirical play on media manipulation in Western capitalist countries. *Nekrassov* is a farce about a crook passing for a defector from the Soviet Union, with the active complicity of rightist politicians and cynical journalists. Such a topic, in the midst of the Cold War, was sure to be a hotbed of controversy. With very few exceptions, the press (including left-wing Françoise Giroud) knocked down the play as silly, "invraisemblable," and a shallow piece of pro-Moscow propaganda. Barthes, on the contrary, vehemently defended *Nekrassov* as both witty (as witty "as Beaumarchais") and relevant. He accused the press of reacting in selfish self-defense. Finally, he did more than hint at the accuracy of the fabrication charge central to the plot.

Now, only a few years after the "affaire Kravchenko," such a defense would inevitably raise questions. Kravchenko, a defector from the Soviet Union, had been constantly portrayed as an impostor by the communist press and his book, *I Chose Freedom*, denounced as a hoax. In France, the communist campaign had been a success, and Kravchenko's credibility was shaken, if not destroyed, in sectors of the opinion far beyond communist hard-liners. While Sartre's *Nekrassov*, as a play, was not as mediocre as the Parisian critique made it sound, it certainly seemed to give a belated blessing to the disinformation campaign led by the French Communist Party. It suggested, in retrospect, that Kravchenko was no more "real" than the fictitious Nekrassov, a question Barthes addressed in a bizarre, distorted way, as if the reality of Kravchenko were only a matter of literary doctrine. The press having declared the central character in the play to be "invraisemblable," Barthes was quick to return the favor. "The bourgeoisie always had a very tyrannical as well as discriminating notion of reality: the real is what the bourgeoisie sees, not what is actually there; the real is whatever can be directly related to its sole interests: Kravchenko was real, Nekrassov is not."[8] Witty as it was, Sartre's play participated in the general denial among the French left of whatever painful truth from the East could "désespérer Billancourt."[9]

The three episodes of 1955 encapsulate the three facets of Barthes's concerns at the time and illuminate his ideological radicalization during the 1950s. Politically, his choices were unambiguous. He broke with a more and more isolated Camus—isolated because of his unwillingness to support the terrorist activity of the Algerian National Liberation Front. He split with Paulhan and the notoriously anticommunist *Nouvelle NRF*. Finally, he rose in defense of a battered Sartre who had himself rallied in support of the harassed French Communist Party three years earlier, in 1952.

Even more revealing is the intellectual coherence of the three episodes. Barthes turned away from Camus because of what he saw as an aesthetic as well as a political betrayal. "A modern chef-d'oeuvre is impossible," he had warned in *Writing Degree Zero* two years before, but Camus would not listen. At best, what could be done by the modern writer, according to Barthes, was to inscribe the impossibility of a "reconciled," homogenous world: "white writing" was the name and the mark of that inscription. But Camus insisted on the legitimacy of a moral-political statement made through a very conventional fictional form, the novel as "chronicle." Barthes's brutal dissociation from Camus's works, thus, is not only indicative of a more militant political stand; it is also indicative of Barthes's conviction in the 1950s that fiction writing was not the appropriate answer to what he called, with remarkable insistence, "l'évidence de la dure altérité des classes" (1952), "la dure sécession des classes sociales" (1954), or "le durcissement général de la situation historique" (1956).[10]

Narrative fiction had become a sideshow for Roland Barthes in 1955. The "historical situation" called for something else: a "social critique" that would systematically unmask bourgeois ideology, hence the importance given by Barthes to his *petites mythologies*. On a larger scale, it called for a collective form of art and communication capable not only of exposing bourgeois ideology but of tying together all those who "suffer and stifle under the bourgeois evil."[11] This form and art is theater.

Staging Politics

Roland Barthes's involvement with theater is by far the most important aspect of his intellectual life in the 1950s as well as the most pleasurable, the most passionate. Theater for Barthes is no less engaging than *engagé*. For about ten years, he happily devoted himself (in *Théâtre Populaire* and other media) to the transmutation of theater in France. Here again 1955 was a strong moment in this quest, the year of a much-debated special issue of *Théâtre Populaire* on Brecht. But it is clear that Barthes's passion for the stage was overwhelming during the entire decade, ending brutally—as passions should—in 1960. After 1961 Barthes dropped the curtain, ceasing to write on theater, even ceasing altogether to go to the theater.

Barthes's relationship with the stage has been little studied; his theatrical reviews and editorials were not easily available until the 1993 publication of the first volume of his complete works. This may explain in part the common misperception of Barthes as a sole and dogmatic supporter of Brechtian theater. There is no denying the admiration Barthes felt for Brecht; he himself has spoken of his *éblouissement* when confronted for the first time (in 1954) with Brecht as performed by the

Berliner Ensemble. But it is no less important to insist on the complex, far-ranging vision that Barthes entertained about theater—a vision that was his central *projet,* in the Sartrian sense of the word, during the 1950s.

Clearly, Barthes's writings on the theater constitute a coherent body of "interventions," which he intended to republish after revision. Reading them today, one is struck by their scope. To be sure, Barthes deals at length with Brecht and the diffusion of the Brechtian repertoire in France. But he is no less interested in other "revolutionary" attempts, such as Vinaver's in *Aujourd'hui ou les coréens.* He is no less concerned with the actors than the texts, no less with the classics than the avant-garde—a notion he often analyzes and criticizes. He does not content himself with the Parisian stage; he also writes in support of provincial endeavors, like Planchon's in Lyons; he attends and reviews amateur theatrical sessions organized in the suburbs by the Ligue de l'Enseignement. A severe, unbending critic of the productions, he also devotes many pages to criticizing the critique. In short, he leaves aside no aspect of theater, from program to costumes and makeup: "make-up," he writes in 1955, "ultimately is part of the same revolutionary struggle as the text."[12] Barthes's vision encompasses new texts as well as new acting, new staging and, most of all, a new sociology of theatergoers. For the new theatricality he advocates implies and requires a new sociability, paving the way to a renewed citizenry. In this global assessment, Brecht, exemplifying a theater "at the height of our history," is one—but only one—important answer.

Moreover, Barthes's use of Brecht is quite personal, "dissident," so to speak. It has often been said that Barthes's personal brand of Marxism was "Brechtism." Less commented on has been Barthes's paradoxical use of Brecht to distance himself not only from official Marxism but also from the concept of history central to Marx's thought.

"One knows that Brecht was a Marxist," Barthes wrote, tongue in cheek, in 1957, "but it is certain that Brecht's theater, which owes so much to Marxism [. . .] does not directly realize the Marxian idea of an historical theater."[13] Barthes is not content to reassert humorously the preeminence over and autonomy vis-à-vis the political theory of Brecht's works, writing that "it is fair to say also that Marxism owes a lot to Brecht." He devotes the larger part of this important article to demonstrating that Brecht, far from accomplishing Marx's ideal type of historical theater (as expressed in letters to Lassalle on the play *Franz von Sickingen*), did not even "borrow from Marx his conception of History." For Marx and Engels, according to Barthes, "theater must give an accurate, complete account of historical reality at its very roots"—an exhaustive, didactic description of the characters' class status. Barthes disagrees, paradoxically using Brecht as an authority against Marx. "One should not conceive of History as a mere type of causality, like the one Marx is asking for, or the one which is elsewhere [in repertoire historical dramas] caused to disappear under the guise of historical scenery. In reality, *and especially in Brecht* [emphasis added], History is a general category. [. . .] Brecht does not make History into an object, however tyrannical, but into *une exigence générale de la pensée*" (754).

The strange formulation "and especially in Brecht" is revealing. In these pages, Brecht is being used by Barthes, not only to chastise and reform the French stage and not only as a dialectical weapon against both the bourgeois "theater of participation" and "the progressive theater" of "predication." Brecht is also used to construct a notion of history where "historical materialism" would not be denied but kept at a convenient distance from the practitioner and the observer. Brecht thus becomes both an ally and an alibi for that "idea of History" Barthes had already sketched in the 1951 review of Caillois's *Description du marxisme.* In that article, Barthes first made clear his acquiescence in the concept of class struggle, only to develop, in the following paragraphs, an original concept of history as "inalienable and explainable" at the same time: "History is inalienable and nevertheless explainable; such is the dilemma. Marx seems to have seen it well: class struggle, for instance, is not an analogy, but an organizing principle, which does not hurt the nonnegotiable content of each of its episodes."[14] Barthes in 1951 "derived" from Marx exactly what he later gave Brecht credit for: his own notion of history as "principe organisateur" or "catégorie générale." In its Barthesian version, historical materialism, like Epicurus's gods, is somewhere out there—but in such a distant empyrean that the "inalienable character of every historical fact, every historical man"[15] can be preserved. The first, but not the last of Barthes's *détournements,* Brecht would be enrolled under the banner of Barthes's very particular, post-Epicurian and prestructural breed of Marxism.

Returning to Barthes's militant attitude toward theater, one is confronted with a second paradox. Through his eulogy of the Brechtian theater, Barthes's crusade revives a "mythology" deeply embedded in French culture since the eighteenth century: the notion of the stage as a new pulpit and of the actor as "lay preacher"—the "prédicateur laïc," in Diderot's words. His own warnings against a "preaching," progressive theater notwithstanding, Barthes did not hesitate to draw an explicit parallel between Brecht and Diderot, who "have so many traits in common," nor did he shy away from comparing the "tableau brechtien" to Greuze's paintings,[16] a rather unexpected tribute, all the more disconcerting for Barthes's general lack of interest in French Enlightenment writers. Barthes does not bother to elaborate on the "many common traits" that would justify his comparison. One reason might be that his parallel does not so much aim at any specific analogies between Diderot's dramaturgy and the "Brechtian revolution" as it points to their broader concern with redefining theater in civic terms. By associating Diderot and Brecht, Barthes seems to be confessing his belief, shared in the past by the philosophes, in the enlightening powers of theater and its capacity to help shape a new morality and define a new social cohesion. Describing theater in 1954 as an "important civic problem" and a "thoroughly national question"[17] in which the state must participate (not to control the content, of course, but to subsidize low-price theater seats in Paris as well as the provinces), Barthes repeats claims and demands that were Voltaire's, d'Alembert's and Diderot's—not Marx's. Denouncing the bourgeois theater and its expensive seats; smearing the indifferent, narcissistic, snobbish audiences; and accusing the locale itself, "the stage closed like an alcove or a police chamber, where the audience is a passive voyeur,"[18] Barthes suddenly sounds as if he were rewriting Rousseau's *Lettre à d'Alembert sur les spectacles.*

Theater has a "mission": Barthes does not dodge the ideologically laden word, "the majesty of which should not scare us"—although he does italicize it.[19] In the eighteenth-century French tradition of theater-bashing in the name of theater as it should be, Barthes echoes the philosophes' call for a new civic theater capable of the same political effects as the "popular" theaters of the past. If successful, he insists, a Brechtian theater would be the modern equivalent of the ancient Greek or Elizabethan stage: "moral," "bouleversant," and "civiquement justifié."[20] Neither experimental nor avant-garde, such a regenerated theater would not content itself to become a token of modernity in an unchanged landscape. It would have to be part of a global process, implying not only drastic conceptual changes in acting and staging (like the wide-open wind-beaten stage in Avignon) but also and more importantly a sociological shake-up of audiences drawn from workers' unions and local cultural associations. This emphasis on sociology is one of the salient features of Barthes's approach to theater in the 1950s, which led him from a rather skeptical mood toward the Théâtre National Populaire (which he declared in 1953 "populaire plus par ses intentions que par sa sociologie"[21]) to an ever more optimistic perception of a renewed medium with enlarged audiences. Only one year later, he wrote that Jean Vilar's Théâtre National Populaire, was already a revolutionary phenomenon, be it only because of its "ampleur sociologique."[22]

The sociological argument made by Barthes is at the core of his passionate support for stage innovators of the 1950s. It also plays a key role in Barthes's choice to "favor" theater over fictional narratives. Always fond of "binarisme" as an investigative tool, Barthes did not cease for a decade to contrast theater and the novel, in terms of reception and outreach. In an article titled "Petite sociologie du roman français," Barthes insisted on the "division of audiences" typical of the novel, thus concluding, "le roman ne va jamais trouver que *son* public."[23] Published in 1955, such a depiction of the novel as an alienated genre strictly reproducing the "cloisonnements" of French society takes its full paradigmatic value when confronted with Barthes's descriptions of theater audiences as (at least potentially) social melting pots. Sociological evidence concurred with the formal analysis developed in *Writing Degree Zero* to dismiss the novel as an irremediably "compromised" form, whereas a "theater of liberation"[24] is possible here and now.

In the early 1950s, theater had thus become for Barthes what literature could not be. In *Writing Degree Zero,* Barthes had condemned modern literature to exposing only the impasse of a divided society and bearing testimony, through a degraded and compromised language, of its own impotency. Not so with theater. While no new language could be pure enough to quench the writer's thirst, the wind now blowing on the stage would relieve and revive those "Frenchmen like me [R.B.] stifling under the bourgeois evil."[25] When literature could be no more than an "empty sign," theater emerged in Barthes's provisional *Weltanschauung* as the greatest of expectations for mind and body and the collective body of society: for "theater is in advance emasculated if one does not crave it with one's entire body, and if that craving is not shared by an entire community."[26]

"Le théâtre est un acte total,"[27] Barthes wrote in 1953. It presents the viewer with "une évidence *viscérale*" [Barthes's italics] and with his or her own freedom: "in *Mutter Courage,* fatality is on the stage, freedom in the audience."[28] Only theater can be, in the same span of time, the ideal battlefield of politics, the hedonistic arena of physical beauty, and the forum where morality and integrity are put to test: for each evening, on stage, "the impure theater, the theater of complacency, where the degrading themes of money and adultery are put to work," wages war against "the pure theater, the strong theater where what is at stake is man, man at odds with himself, man in the city."[29]

A global experience by nature, a civic medium by tradition, theater and only theater, in Barthes's view, can bring together what bourgeois society has divided: art and politics, classes and languages. Hence Barthes's fascination—and his atypical militant rhetoric. Focusing on theater, Barthes for a decade ceased to be "only" a critic. Reshaping, redeeming French theater, he could feel he was part of that "acte total" and engaged in a praxis that would affect French society itself. If Brecht plays an important part in the Barthesian dramaturgy of theater as politics, it is less for the Marxist "lesson" inscribed in his plays than for the added critical and moral value given to Marxism. "Brecht's theater,"

Barthes wrote significantly in 1956, "is in its major part, and precisely in its most intimate, subjective, psychoanalytical depth, an apocalyptic theater of demystification."[30]

As such, theater appealed to Barthes in the 1950s as a holier, more promising land than literature: while writers according to *Writing Degree Zero* must, like Moses, die without seeing Canaan or, like Orpheus, lose Eurydice when trying to see her, the stage was to be not only the ideal tribune dreamt of by the philosophes, but also the only "situation" where, in bourgeois society, a miraculous unveiling of truth could happily take place. In 1954 Barthes had praised Jean Vilar for the extraordinary achievement of his acting which, he argued, pointed out the "admirable *sociabilité* du langage."[31] A few years later, he ceased expecting anything from either actors or directors, or even from Brecht himself. "Imagine," said Barthes in a 1962 interview, "a mind like Brecht's confronted with life today; that mind would be paralysed by the diversity of life."[32] End game. Barthes's disaffection toward theater, as we said before, was brutal and total. But the disillusionment came neither from Brecht nor from the French stage at the end of the decade. I would suggest that it came from the very success of a popular, political, even civic theater in the 1960s—a success for which André Malraux and the ambitious cultural politics launched with de Gaulle's support after 1958, resulting in the creation of dozens of *maisons de la culture* and *centres dramatiques* in almost every major French city, must be credited. It was a bitter paradox for Barthes to see the despised "régime du Général" realize (or "recuperate") a shared, militant dream of civic regeneration through theater. Barthes's disenchantment with theater after 1960, his move toward other interventions on other signs, has a lot to do with what must have appeared as a misappropriation, but his disappointment would not have been so profound had he not invested theater with a mission he then declared impossible.

Notes

1. Roland Barthes, "Réponses," *Tel Quel* 47 (Fall 1971): 92.

2. Quoted by Louis-Jean Calvet, *Roland Barthes* (Paris: Flammarion, 1990), p. 153.

3. See Jean-François Sirinelli, *Génération intellectuelle: Khâgneux et normaliens dans l'entre-deux guerres* (Paris: Fayard, 1988).

4. "[P]our de nombreux dissidents, dont le marxisme continue de féconder le destin individuel, le dogmatisme moscovite n'est pas un scandale: il est une tragédie, au milieu de laquelle ils essaient pourtant de garder, comme le chœur antique, la conscience du malheur, le goût de l'espoir et la volonté de comprendre" (*Combat*, 21 June 1951; in *OC1*, p. 104).

5. In what sounds very much like a slip, Barthes in "Réponses" spoke of the

Liberation as "l'Armistice." To the classically phrased question, "At the time of the Liberation, where did you stand?" he answered substituting the term *Armistice*, normally used in French in reference to the June 1940 ceasefire, not the end of the World War II.

6. See Philippe Roger, *Roland Barthes, roman* (Paris: Grasset, 1986; Paris: Livre de Poche, 1991), part 4, chapter 4.

7. Roland Barthes, "Suis-je marxiste?" *Lettres Nouvelles* (July–August 1955); in *OC1*, p. 499.

8. "La bourgeoisie a toujours eu une idée très tyrannique mais très sélective de la réalité: est réel ce qu'elle voit, non ce qui est; est réel ce qui a un rapport immédiat avec ses seuls intérêts: Kravchenko était réel, Nekrassov ne l'est pas" ("Nekrassov juge de sa critique," *Théâtre Populaire* 14 [July–August 1955]; in *OC1*, p. 504).

9. "Désespérons Billancourt!" exclaims Georges, alias Nekrassov, repeatedly at the end of the sixth tableau. The phrase "ne pas désespérer Billancourt" has taken a quasi-proverbial meaning in French: it is now used ironically to describe any attempt to keep the people unaware of a demoralizing truth.

10. In, respectively, *L'Observateur*, 27 November 1952; *Théâtre Populaire* 5 (January–February 1954), editorial; *Théâtre Populaire* 17 (March 1956), p. 90.

11. The phrase appears at the end of the Nekrassov article. *Théâtre Populaire* 14 (July–August 1955); in *OC1*, p. 506.

12. "[L]e maquillage est lui aussi un acte politique, sur lequel nous devons prendre parti, et qui, par l'infinie dialectique des effets et des causes, participe finalement du même combat révolutionnaire que le texte" (*Tribune Etudiante*, April 1955; in *OC1*, p. 482).

13. "Brecht, Marx et l'histoire," *Cahiers Renaud-Barrault*, December 1957; in *OC1* p. 754.

14. "L'Histoire est inaliénable et pourtant explicable; tel est le dilemme. Marx semble l'avoir bien vu: la lutte des classes, par exemple, n'est pas une analogie, mais un principe organisateur, qui n'attente en rien au contenu incessible de chacun de ses épisodes." ("A propos d'une métaphore [Le marxisme est-il une église]," *Esprit*, November 1951; in *OC1*, p. 112).

15. "Tout fait historique, tout homme historique est inaliénable" ("Les Révolutions suivent-elles des lois?") *Combat*, 20 July 1950; in *OC1*, p. 86.

16. Préface à B. Brecht, *Mère Courage et ses enfants*," *L'Arche*, 1960; in *OC1*, p. 900 n. 1: "Si l'on veut bien faire abstraction du style et de la qualité, et en considérant seulement le mouvement idéologique (ce qui d'ailleurs ne laisse pas d'être arbitraire, car une œuvre d'art n'est réellement que la rencontre d'une histoire et d'une forme, c'est-à-dire d'une résistance à l'histoire), c'est plutôt à Greuze qu'il faudrait comparer le tableau brechtien, Greuze dont le théoricien, Diderot, a tant de point communs avec Brecht." A dubious adequation, and a bizarre equation, where Barthes would be to Brecht what Diderot was to Greuze. Hence, Barthes = Diderot?

17. "La Question du théâtre populaire est une question franchement nationale," *Théâtre de France*, t.IV, 1954; in *OC1*, p. 442.

18. "Pourquoi Brecht?" *Tribune Etudiante*, April 1955; in *OC1*, p. 481.

19. "Espoirs du théâtre populaire," *France-Observateur*, 5 January 1956; in *OC1*, p. 530.

20. "Théâtre capital," *France-Observateur*, 8 July 1954; in *OC1*, p. 419.

21. "*Le Prince de Hombourg* au T.N.P.," *Lettres Nouvelles*, March 1953; in *OC1*, p. 208.

22. "Ce qui fait l'originalité de son action, c'est son ampleur sociologique. Vilar a su amorcer une véritable révolution dans les normes de consommation du théâtre [. . .] Grâce à l'expérience de Vilar, le théâtre tend à devenir un grand loisir populaire, au même titre que le cinéma et le football" (*Théâtre de France*, t. IV, December 1954; in *OC1*, pp. 444–45).

23. "La société française d'aujourd'hui nous présente des publics de romans fortement personnalisés, mais aussi fortement cloisonnés, isolés les uns des autres, échangeant rarement leur rôle, essentiellement déterminés par la condition sociale de leurs participants [. . .] En somme, le roman ne va jamais trouver que son public, c'est-à-dire un public qui lui ressemble, qui est avec lui dans un rapport étroit d'identité"; "Petite sociologie du roman français," *Documents*, February 1955; in *OC1*, p. 469.

24. "Théâtre capital," *France-Observateur*, 8 July 1954; in *OC1*, p. 419.

25. "Nekrassov juge de sa critique," *Théâtre Populaire* 14 (July–August 1955); in *OC1*, p. 506.

26. "Le théâtre est à l'avance émasculé, si on ne l'attend pas de tout son corps, et si cette attente n'est pas partagée par toute une collectivité" ("Le Grand Robert," *Lettres Nouvelles*, October 1954; in *OC1*, p. 436).

27. "L'Arlésienne du catholicisme," *Lettres Nouvelles*, November 1953; in *OC1*, p. 238.

28. "Théâtre capital," *France-Observateur*, 8 July 1954; in *OC1*, p. 420.

29. "Le théâtre impur, le théâtre complaisant, où l'on met en œuvre les thèmes dégradants de l'argent ou du cocuage [. . .]"; "le théâtre pur, le théâtre fort, où ce qui est en cause est l'homme aux prises avec lui-même, l'homme dans la cité" ("Le théâtre populaire aujourd'hui," in *Théâtre de France*, t.IV, dec. 1954; in *OC1*, p. 443).

30. "Le théâtre de Brecht est en majeure partie, et précisément dans son fond intime, subjectif, psychanalytique, un théâtre apocalyptique de la démystification" ("Note sur *Aujourd'hui* [de Vinaver]," *Travail Théâtral*, April 1956; in *OC1*, p. 542.

31. "Une tragédienne sans public," *France-Observateur*, March 1954; in *OC1*, p. 410.

32. *Le Figaro Littéraire*, 13 October 1962; in *OC1*, p. 980.

13

Beyond Metalanguage

Bathmology

Pierre Force

In his preface to *The Physiology of Taste*, Barthes analyzes Brillat-Savarin's comments on the physiological effects of champagne: first, champagne stimulates you; then, after a while, it makes you drowsy. This example allows Barthes to posit what he calls "one of Modernity's most important formal categories: the gradation of phenomena."[1] This category is so important for Barthes that he does not hesitate to coin a new word to designate it: "Let us call this 'indenting,' this scale of champagne a 'bathmology.' Bathmology would be the field of discourses in so far as degrees come into play."

One finds a similar argument in *Roland Barthes by Roland Barthes*, in which bathmology accedes to the dignity of "a new science: that of the degrees of language" (*RB*, 67). Of course, this kind of programmatic assertion appears frequently in Barthes's writings. Thus the idea of a science of degrees in speech should be taken with a grain of salt. But whatever its scientific merits, bathmology is a concept of the utmost importance because it affords us a direct view of many other important concepts in Barthes's work.

The previously quoted fragment from *Roland Barthes by Roland Barthes*, in which the term *bathmology* is proposed, analyzes the effects of reflexivity in language: "I write: that is the first degree of language. Then, I write that I write: that is language to the second degree. (Already Pascal: 'A thought has escaped: I was trying to write it down: instead I write that it has escaped me')" (*RB*, 66). To the quote from Pascal's *Pensées* we could add another in which Pascal, in a typically Barthesian fashion, shows the kind of dizziness bound to affect the interpreter when the relationship between signifier and signified is taken not only as meaning but also as the signifier of a signified of a higher order:

> Vanity is so firmly anchored in man's heart that a soldier, a rough, a cook or a porter will boast and expect admirers, and even philosophers want them; those who write against them want to enjoy the prestige of having written well, those who read them the prestige of having read them, and perhaps I who write this want the same thing, perhaps my readers . . .[2]

Pascal's fragment ends with an ellipsis suggesting that reflexivity causes a sort of *regressus ad infinitum.* If any relationship between a signifier and its signified can become the signifier of yet another signified, then there is no reason to stop the game of interpretation. This is, I believe, how the fragment titled "When I Played Prisoner's Base" should be understood:

> In the great game of the powers of speech, we also play prisoner's base: one language has only temporary rights over another; all it takes is for a third language to appear from the ranks for the assailant to be forced to retreat: in the conflict of rhetorics, the victory never goes to any but the *third language.* The task of this language is to release the prisoners: to scatter the signifieds, the catechisms. As in prisoner's base, *language upon language,* to infinity, such is the law which governs the logosphere. (*RB,* 50)

There are striking similarities between bathmology, a neologism coined around 1975, and a more familiar notion that Barthes started using in the late 1950s: the distinction between language object and metalanguage.

> Every novelist, every poet, whatever the detours literary theory may take, is presumed to speak of objects and phenomena, even if they are imaginary, exterior and anterior to language: the world exists and the writer speaks: that is literature. The object of criticism is very different: the object of criticism is not "the world" but a discourse, the discourse of someone else: criticism is discourse upon a discourse; it is a second language, or a *metalanguage* (as the logicians would say), which operates on a first language (or *language object*). It follows that the critical language must deal with two kinds of relations: the relation of the critical language to the language of the author studied, and the relation of this language object to the world. It is the friction of these two languages which defines criticism and perhaps gives it a great resemblance to another mental activity, logic, which is also based on the distinction between language object and metalanguage. ("What Is Criticism?" *CE,* 258)

In order to understand the philosophical assumptions behind this argument and especially to understand why Barthes, in 1963, was drawing a comparison between literary criticism and formal logic, it may be useful to refer to *The Infinite Conversation,* a book written by Blanchot between 1953 and 1965 (published in 1969). Blanchot's book puts this distinction between language object and metalanguage under the authority of Bertrand Russell and Ludwig Wittgenstein. In a chapter titled "Wittgenstein's Problem," Blanchot summarizes the problem of Flaubert's writing by saying that it is nothing but the question of the "Other" of speech:

Now, ever since Mallarmé, we have sensed that the other of a language is always posed by this language itself as that by way of which it looks for a way out, an exit to disappear into or an Outside in which to be reflected. Which means not only that the Other is already *part* of this language, but that as soon as this language turns around to respond to its Other, it turns toward another language; a language that, as we ought not ignore, is other, and also has its other. At this point we come very close to Wittgenstein's problem, as corrected by Bertrand Russell: every language has a structure about which we can say nothing *in* this language, but there must be another language that treats the structure of the first and possesses a new structure about which we cannot say anything, except in a third language—and so forth.[3]

If Barthes had needed a philosophical justification for the famous tables one finds in *Mythologies* and *The Fashion System*, he could have found it in Blanchot. What all these tables have in common is a ternary structure, in which the relationship between two elements is taken as a single element that enters a relationship with a new element. For instance, a poet writes "sail" to mean "ship." The reader understands that "sail" means "ship." That is meaning number one. But meaning number one itself becomes a signifier: the fact that "sail" means "ship" means we are reading a poem. The signified of meaning number one *qua* signifier is poetry. This relationship is possible only in a language of a higher order, namely rhetoric. We must add that for Barthes, as well as for Blanchot, any metalanguage can be overtaken by another metalanguage and thus become a language object.

In his conclusion to *The Fashion System*, Barthes comes back to his famous table illustrating the relationship between denotation, connotation, and rhetoric, to add another layer, the analyst's metalanguage (i.e., the language in which this table can be built). This metalanguage, Barthes says, will be taken over by a new metalanguage sooner or later:

This dialectic can again be expressed in formal terms: speaking of the rhetorical signified in his own metalanguage, the analyst inaugurates (or adopts) an infinite science: for if it happens that someone (someone else or himself later on) undertakes the analysis of his writing and attempts to reveal its content, that someone will have to resort to a new metalanguage, which will signal him in its turn: a day will inevitably come when structural analysis will pass to the rank of language object and will be apprehended within a superior language which will in its turn explain it. (*FS*, 294)

Such a conclusion is certainly impressive, and, I might add, almost intimidating, because it seems to anticipate the conditions of its own refutation. Barthes's argument, however, is flawed. If there is such a thing as a metalanguage, then it is not possible for this language to be overtaken by another language. We have seen that Barthes draws a comparison between literary criticism and formal logic. If the comparison makes sense, that is, if one accepts that literary criticism is a metalanguage in the way that formal logic is a metalanguage, then literary criticism cannot be spoken of in a higher language. There is no such thing as a logic of logic, thus there should be no such thing as metacriticism.

The very notion of metalanguage is misleading. Here again Blanchot's argument is very telling. When Blanchot places the paradoxes of metalanguage under the authority of Russell and Wittgenstein he perhaps does not misread Russell, but he certainly misreads Wittgenstein. For Wittgenstein, there is no such thing as the "outside" of language. We, by definition, are always inside, and there can be no distinction between a language object and a metalanguage. This is the conclusion Barthes arrived at a few years after *The Fashion System.* He simply gave up the notion.

Contrary to Barthes's expectations, *The Fashion System* has not been subject to reassessment by languages of a higher order. It has simply been forgotten, abandoned. This is because literary discourse and critical discourse are not subject to the laws of metalanguage but rather to the laws of bathmology. Only a bathmologist can explain how a discourse can give way to another discourse.

How does it happen then? Very simply. A new discourse always emerges as a flat negation of the old:

> *Sed contra.*
>
> Frequently, he starts from the stereotype, from the banal opinion *which is in him.* And it is because he does not want that stereotype (by some aesthetic or individualist reflex) that he looks for something else; habitually, being soon wearied, he halts at the mere contrary opinion, at paradox, at what mechanically denies the prejudice (for example: "There is no science except of the particular"). (*RB*, 162)

The first step a bathmologist makes is always a step into paradox. The starting point is always common opinion, referred to as petit-bourgeois ideology in the writings of the 1950s and as *doxa* in the writings of the 1970s. The paradox, true to etymology, is a reversal of common opinion:

> You suppose that the goal of the wrestling match is to win? No, it is to understand. [. . .] The Martians? They are not invoked to stage the Other (the Alien) but the Same. [. . .] Racine's theater is not a theater of erotic passion but of authoritarian relations, etc.
>
> Such figures of Paradox are countless; they have their logical operator: the

expression *in fact*: strip-tease is not an erotic solicitation, *in fact*, it desexualizes woman, etc. (*RB*, 83)

Of course, this reversal is soon reversed, according to a law of succession that Pascal, in *Pensées*, calls "constant swing from pro to con." When Pascal considers the question "Should persons of high birth be honored?" only two answers are possible: yes or no. However, since there are many different reasons to say yes or no, opinions on the subject are ordered in a five-step gradation:

Cause and effect. Gradation. Ordinary people honour those who are highly born, the half-clever ones despise them, saying that birth is a matter of chance, not personal merit. Really clever men honour them, not for the same reason as ordinary people, but for deeper motives. Pious folk with more zeal than knowledge despise them regardless of the reason which makes clever men honour them, because they judge men in the new light of piety, but perfect Christians honour them because they are guided by a still higher light.

So opinions swing back and forth, from pro to con, according to one's lights.[4]

In Barthes, as in Pascal, the argument goes from *doxa* to paradox, then to a paradox within the paradox, a step forward that may appear as a step back. This swinging back and forth has been described in an illuminating and entertaining fashion by a twentieth-century moralist, Renaud Camus, who considers himself a disciple of Roland Barthes. In a small book he first planned to title *Fragments of Daily Bathmology* but finally called *Buena Vista Park*, Camus gives no fewer than eight reasons why a man who has been sentenced to be shot to death can accept or refuse the blindfold that is offered to him:

1. The condemned man accepts the blindfold, because it is offered to him and he doesn't think of refusing it.
2. The condemned man refuses the blindfold, because he is courageous and wants to look death in the face (Ney, etc.)
3. The condemned man accepts the blindfold because position #2 seems ridiculously banal to him, and the worn-out tradition of the condemned man who refuses the blindfold to show that he is courageous and can look death in the face seems tiresome.
4. The condemned man refuses the blindfold, even though he is in complete agreement with position #3, because he's interested in seeing what's happening.
5. The condemned man accepts the blindfold, because he's afraid that the position he might have tended to adopt, the fourth one, will be confused with the second, and that his simple preference for the absence of a blindfold will pass for a ridiculous (in his eyes) demonstration of codified heroism. . . .[5]

Camus notices that in this succession of opinions not all positions are equivalent. There is a fundamental difference between odd-numbered, affirmative positions and even-numbered, negative positions, which Camus suggests calling "second-degree" positions. These negative positions have two things in common: they are driven by suspicion, and their mode of expression is irony.

As Barthes suggests, a second-degree position is where most intellectuals are to be found:

> Today there is an enormous consumption of this second degree. A good part of our intellectual work consists in casting suspicion on any statement by revealing the disposition of its degrees. [. . .] There is an erotic, an aesthetic of the second degree (kitsch, for example). We can even become maniacs of the second degree: reject denotation, spontaneity, platitude, innocent repetition, tolerate only languages which testify, however frivolously, to a power of dislocation. (*RB*, 89)

This is probably where the source of Barthes's interest in Marxism and psychoanalysis can be found. Both Marxism and psychoanalysis cast suspicion onto the ulterior motives of any speech. For practitioners of these two doctrines, suspicion has become second nature; thus whenever the mind applies itself to something, it does not start at the first but at the second degree. As Renaud Camus writes jokingly, "the three great Jews who have shaped our minds have taught us, thanks to the steadiness of their paranoia, that everything is relative, including truth itself, and that any discourse dissimulates another discourse; thus we wish to spare ourselves the trouble of going through the first layer."[6] In that sense, the pedagogical enterprise Barthes started in the 1950s has been very successful. Today, very few people consume motion pictures or television advertising in the first degree, and the culture industry has adjusted to this evolution in taste: television shows are now using irony, parody, and all other tools of reflexivity systematically. In many ways, suspicion (the mental disposition that used to produce paradox) has acquired the strength and naturalness of prejudice. This is the ultimate proof of how successful a doctrine has been.

This evolution in the culture made it necessary for Barthes to go one step beyond the second degree. Barthes first did that in *S/Z* by going after the rhetorical mark of the second degree, irony. If, in retrospect, we apply bathmological categories to *S/Z* we can say that Barthes defines *écriture* as a discourse of the third degree, in other words, as a discourse that cannot be ironically interpreted:

> The only power the writer has against the dizziness of stereotypes (this dizziness is also that of "silliness" and "vulgarity") is to enter into this dizziness without quotation marks, by producing a text, not a parody. This is what Flaubert

did in *Bouvard et Pécuchet*: these two copyists are code copiers (they are, if you will, silly), but since they are confronted with the class-induced stupidity that surrounds them, the text opens up to a circle in which nobody (not even the author) has power over anybody; such is the function of writing: to render absurd, to annul the power (intimidation) of a language over another, to dissolve any metalanguage in the very moment it constitutes itself.[7]

At this stage in his evolution, Barthes decided to defend writing against metalanguage. This is how he presented his *Lovers' Discourse: Fragments*—as writing, not metalanguage. But one might as well say, from a bathmological point of view, that metalanguage is nothing but a second-degree position that would solidify into a system. From the outside, it is impossible to distinguish between a third-degree position and a first-degree position. Hence, Renaud Camus formalizes a number of paradoxes: "Bathmological subtlety is never a weapon of victory: if you stand on floor 8, for the tenant of floor 7 you will still be on floor 6."[8]

Camus then asks: "On floor 8, are you closer to the tenants of floor 7, whose positions are contrary to yours, or to the tenants of floor 6, whose positions are apparently identical to yours?" Any third-degree position is considered naive by the proponents of the strategy of suspicion. Camus goes on to quote Barthes:

> I was glad I had written (endorsing the apparent silliness of such a statement) that "one writes in order to be loved"; I am told that M. D. finds this sentence idiotic; it is in fact bearable only if it is consumed in the third degree. Being aware that it has been at first touching, then stupid, you finally have the option of finding it to be accurate, perhaps (M. D. has not been able to reach that point).[9]

If suspicion lets us pass from first to second degree, fatigue drives us to step from second to third. Barthes writes: "The stereotype can be evaluated in terms of *fatigue*. The stereotype is what *begins* to fatigue me. Whence the antidote, cited as far back as *Writing Degree Zero*: the *freshness* of language" (*RB*, 92). This remark smacks of dandyism, and one could reply to Barthes that boredom or excitement is irrelevant when assessing the truth of a discourse. Yet this is precisely where the strength and wisdom of Barthes's attitude are to be found. On one hand, it is true that Barthes's role on the intellectual scene has been that of a trendsetter. Some might even say that in some cases he was a trend follower: he had a flair for what was in the air, and his writings both shaped and reflected the opinions of the avant-garde. On the other hand, as he started to think more and more in bathmological terms, Barthes had the wisdom to humbly acknowledge this position. In this respect, there is no difference between intellectual fashion and haute couture. It is very significant that the metalanguage of *The Fashion System* has not been overtaken by a higher metalanguage; what has happened instead is a revenge of fashion. Far from being a language object, fashion has revealed itself a key for understanding all of Roland Barthes's positions since *Writing Degree Zero.*

Metalanguage consists in raising a language against another language. The goal is to dominate, to take prisoners. Bathmology, on the other hand, consists in affirming or not affirming an existing discourse. Thus metalanguage belongs to science, whereas bathmology belongs to both aesthetics and ethics. Semiologists, or more generally, social scientists, to the extent that they use metalanguage, remain exterior to the value judgments they are interpreting. A bathmologist, however, not unlike the existentialist of *Writing Degree Zero,* is *engagé.* But unlike existentialists, a bathmologist believes that one cannot be the author of one's speech. All possible discourses already exist, and there are not that many of them. The difficulty lies in picking the right discourse, and picking it for the right reasons.

Now we can see the continuity between bathmology and the ideas of the early Barthes, who wrote in his preface to *Critical Essays,* "No one can write without passionately taking sides (whatever the apparent detachment of his message) on what is going wrong in the world."[10] Although Blanchot defines literature by reversing Flaubert's judgment "Too many things, too few forms" and saying, "Always too many forms, never enough things," Barthes would say, "Very few things, and very few forms":

> The affectivity which is at the heart of literature includes only an absurdly restricted number of functions: *I desire, I suffer, I am angry, I contest, I love, I want to be loved, I am afraid to die*—out of which we must make an infinite literature. ("Preface," *CE,* xvi–xvii)

In a sense, all writers are similar to the condemned man in *Buena Vista Park.* They have only one thing to say, "I am not—or perhaps I am—afraid to die," and only two ways of saying it: refusing or accepting the blindfold. This is why Barthes, as Pascal did before him, defines literature as a game of combinations: "There are never creators, nothing but combiners, and literature is like the ship Argo whose long history admitted of no creation, nothing but combinations" (*CE,* xvii). This has often been taken as a formalist statement, but in fact, it is just the opposite. Only if one believes that the role of literature is to reveal, to manifest the truth, can one say with Pascal, "Let no one say that I have said nothing new. The arrangement of the materials is new."[11]

Notes

1. Roland Barthes, preface to *Physiologie du goût,* by Brillat-Savarin (Paris: Ed. des Sciences et des Arts, 1975), p. 7. Translation is mine.

2. Pascal, *Pensées,* fr. 627, Lafuma ed., translated by A. J. Krailsheimer (Harmondsworth: Penguin Books, 1966), p. 236.

3. Maurice Blanchot, *L'Entretien infini* (Paris: Gallimard, 1969), p. 495.

4. Pascal, *Pensées,* fr. 90, p. 53.

5. Renaud Camus, *Buena Vista Park* (Paris: Hachette, 1980). This passage was translated by Christopher Rivers in "After the Age of Suspicion: The French Novel Today," *Yale French Studies* (1988): 293. See also Pierre Force and Dominique Jullien, "Renaud Camus," pp. 285–90 in the same issue.

6. Camus, *Buena Vista Park,* p. 20. Translation is mine.

7. Roland Barthes, *S/Z* (Paris: Seuil, 1970), p. 105. Translation is mine.

8. Camus, *Buena Vista Park,* p. 43.

9. Ibid., p. 65.

10. Roland Barthes, *Essais critiques* (Paris: Seuil, 1964), p. 14. Translation is mine.

11. Pascal, *Pensées,* fr. 696, p. 247.

14

Who Is the Real One?

Antoine Compagnon

I have read many different Roland Bartheses; we all have known numerous Roland Bartheses—in succession and perhaps simultaneously. Once one caught up with him, he had already settled, or paused, somewhere else. Raymond Picard, for instance, at the time of the notorious controversy that brought such publicity to the so-called *Nouvelle Critique* around 1965, blamed Barthes for speaking in *On Racine* of the author in spite of his denials, because Barthes considered that all Racine's tragedies constituted a single comprehensive work whose deep, unconscious, determining structure or organization was to be discovered and established.[1] Picard was not altogether wrong: *On Racine*, when reread today, unquestionably recalls and belongs to the paradigm of phenomenological criticism devoted to the analysis and interpretation of a transcendental ego. Husserl's intentionality served as a transition between the traditional identification of meaning with authorial intention and the death of the author—soon proclaimed by poststructuralism. On the first page of *Michelet*, Barthes spoke plainly of restoring "to this man his coherence," of describing "a unity" by recovering "the structure of an existence," identified as an "organized network of obsessions" (*MI*, 3). *On Racine*, whose method presupposed a hidden and implicit consciousness or inner self as a principle of unity within the complete works of Racine, remained undecided and ambivalent.

However, when Barthes replied to Picard in *Criticism and Truth* a year or so later, he behaved as if the question had been resolved long ago, settled once and for all, as if the author had been dead for a long time (although the body was still warm). The author certainly was neither absent nor extinct in *On Racine*. And why would he have been? Humanism was not yet obscene in the early 1960s. Marxism, existentialism—a self-proclaimed humanism—phenomenology preserved or even praised man.

The case is at any rate rather characteristic: Barthes had already moved away; he no longer stated the problem in the same terms. As a result, however, he did not feel that he had the duty—either ethical or epistemological—to answer objections to positions he formerly held: such complaints no longer regarded him, made no more sense to him. But he did not consider either that he should have explicitly distanced himself from an essay that no longer corresponded to his views. Between *On Racine* and *Criticism and Truth*, the text had been invented and commanded his whole attention. Textuality became a fixation that should have compelled universal recognition and silenced all critics. Intertextuality followed, then pleasure, then a certain return of the author, and so on. For a few years, things changed so fast in the French—or Parisian—intellectual landscape that nobody felt responsible: the death of the author was practiced and performed before being certified. At the time, one spoke of *paradigms* to refer to dominant models or fashions and their rapid rotation. There was a psychoanalytical paradigm, a linguistic paradigm, a Marxist paradigm. We were all running, but Barthes was leading the race. He was first, the avant-garde, impossible to catch up with.

Now I wonder what he was running after, why he had to give up any position he had just conquered, as though the best, or only, defense were to run away, radicalize and overturn his views on the spot. *On Racine* was far from indefensible, but Barthes chose not to come back to it and professed a critical system different from the one under attack. After Althusser, we had grown accustomed to claiming that there had been a young Marx and an old Marx, with a break, a rupture, in between. About Freud, we knew that there had been a "second topic," and therefore that there must have been a first one. This is more or less the scheme that American commentators copied in order to distinguish a break—unheard of in France—between structuralism and poststructuralism in Barthes or Foucault. But each of their books is in fact a new school or paradigm by itself, and Foucault answered no more than Barthes to criticisms expressed against *The Order of Things* or *History of Sexuality* at the time. To do so would have seemed old hat, positivistic, philological. There is no young Barthes and no second Barthes, such as the Barthes of system and then the Barthes of pleasure, because *On Racine* and semiology do not embody the same system at all: there are as many Barthes as projects on which he embarked, each one giving way to the next. One can perhaps be content with noticing this instability, but it is not a very satisfying remark, however postmodern we deeply feel. Who was Barthes after all? Which was the real one? Possibly none. As we go on asking if Baudelaire was a charlatan or a mystic, we still do not know. Both most likely.

Barthes, it was often perceived, made curious use of the term *fascism*, which according to his views had a very broad, extended meaning. Capitalism and the bourgeoisie were tendentiously fascist; fascism was *in posse* always and everywhere, but particularly here and now. Intellectuals were designated victims of ordinary fascism. In France, the word *bourgeois* still has an eminently and universally negative meaning, in memory of the bourgeoisie's hostility toward art and literature under the Second Empire. Barthes called Homais, the bourgeois of Flaubert, a fascist without qualms. In his inaugural lesson at the Collège de France, he went further and crossed a taboo in applying the adjective *fascist* to language itself, which would be fascist because it forces to speak.[2] This paradox scandalized in the same way as Derrida, when he professed that writing had precedence—logical and chronological—over speech, or Foucault, when he substituted institutional incitation to desire for its repression by society: "Language is legislation, *langue* is its code. We do not see power in language, because we forget that all language is a classification, and that all classifications are oppressive. [. . .] Speaking and, all the more so, discoursing, is not communicating, as it is repeated too often, it is subjecting, forcing" ("Inaugural Lecture," *BR*, 460; translation modified).

At the bottom of this extraordinary indictment of language, there probably resides an ambiguity or misunderstanding about the meaning of the word *code.* Saussure said that language is a code, and all French structuralists in the wake of Lévi-Strauss imagined that other symbolic systems function like language, on the basis of a code. But is it not playing with words to assimilate language with a legislation, a civil code, and even a penal code? Other terms in Saussure entailed similar confusion, like *value.* Saussure called the differential relationships between signs *value.* He could have given them a different name. But the simultaneous cutting-out of the sheet of sound and the sheet of meaning into discrete units that Saussure fancied at the origins of language becomes with Barthes an ideological and even political assigning. Any language, as a system of values, constitutes an oppressive ideology. For Barthes, there is no longer any difference between language and ideology: individuals are not free to change language by themselves; language is therefore fascist. A third Saussurean vulgar word confirms this fatal implication: the term *arbitrary.* Saussure simply emphasized that linguistic signs are not motivated, but for Barthes *arbitrary* becomes synonymous with *totalitarian.* Language is a code, language is a system of values, language is arbitrary: in each case the other term of the dichotomy—message, signification, motivation—is suppressed; *code, value, arbitrary* forfeit their relational aspect within a differential system and become hypostatized as evil essences. How could one doubt after all these coincidences that language is irretrievably fascist? It follows without difficulty from there that any discourse, any system, any theory is a servitude or an unbearable prison from which one should promptly shake free.

I put together these two sides of Roland Barthes's thinking—his breathless race after the new and his deep suspicion of language—and propose their rapprochement because they seem to consolidate and clarify each other, at least to me. Barthes, judging them irrelevant, did not respond to the observations made regarding his books. He moved unceasingly and at great speed from one stand to the next; he changed his angle after each book because any method, any language that he had set going, immediately froze into a stereotype, became an instrument of servitude and submission, for himself as well as others. Once he reached the Collège de France, it became important to claim high and loud that the king was naked, that all language was oppressive, and that no language would be imposed here, no knowledge, no system.

But observing and describing this attitude is not explaining and interpreting it. Why should one make such a tragedy of our condition within language? Why should one forsake successive codes and methods instead of making them more complicated, sophisticated, elaborate? Why should one constantly start from scratch, with the risk of rediscovering lightning? These questions are all the more unavoidable since Barthes demonstrated an obvious linguistic playfulness and poetic cheerfulness throughout his career. Language did not compel him. If it does not tyrannize fatally, if it emancipates as much as it subjugates, it is because of its openness and polysemy; one can play endlessly with its homonyms, make love with language, transform and revolutionize it. This is precisely the case with the words *code*, *value*, and *arbitrary*, by which Barthes meant things that Saussure certainly did not intend. Why regret a code's arbitrariness, in the sense of its tyranny, if codes, values, and arbitrariness are so easygoing that they let us manipulate them—themselves and not just any words—in defiance of their proper meanings and original contexts? What can the fascism of language mean when language can be treated as Barthes treats it when he calls it fascist? One cannot have it both ways. Language is fascist, but this epithet itself is, it seems to me, in contradiction with its utterance. Language is not fascist if I can say it is. Calling language fascist is showing that it is not.

The true question is the following: why does Barthes not see, why can he not see, or why does he not want to see the paradox in his pronouncement on the fascism of language, and, as a consequence, of any system functioning like language? Where does this radical, essential, absolute suspicion regarding language, so contradictory with the freedom of his own wordplays and language-acts, originate? This question remains an enigma to me. I would not say that the Barthes who played with words, signs, and letters, the one who entitled a book *S/Z* for instance, is truer, more authentic than the one who calls language Nazi or Stalinist, but I still would like to understand what awful experience with language and its classifications, its labels and slurs, led to his formidable and probably untenable ruling. "Je vois le langage," Barthes wrote, "I see language." He called this voyeuristic condition a disease.

Happily, we have literature, says Barthes, which cheats with language, which cheats language and undermines its intrinsic fascism. But what is literature? Is it not again an arbitrary word and repressive category, something like value par excellence? Who could ever parcel out, among all usages of language, those that are literary and others? No definition of literature, today of literariness, ever held water. Literature is what we call literature here and now. If language is fascist and literature is not, but we cannot say where language ends and literature begins, is the fascism of language not a fantasy? Language is no more fascist than literature. Barthes, who loved language, must have suffered immensely from it. It was his passion, most likely his truest passion.

Notes

1. For a good account of this famous controversy, see Philip Thody, *Roland Barthes: A Conservative Estimate* (London: Macmillan, 1977) pp. 54–68.
2. See "Inaugural Lecture, Collège de France," in *BR*, pp. 457–78.

15

The Art of Being Sparse, Porous, Scattered

Marjorie Welish

Neither an art historian nor an art critic, Roland Barthes writes so rarely on painting that when he does we anticipate his commitment to something else. This is the case when we discover that Barthes wrote on the art of Cy Twombly—not once but twice. The question immediately presents itself: what urgency or scintillation does this art possess for him, a *littérateur* of cultural scope? Answers may strike us with peculiarly vivid force if we regard Barthes's literary interpretation of Twombly from the perspective of art history, because from the vantage of art history the semiology Barthes pursues is literary in its peculiar emphasis on literariness as well as in its assumptions of the verbal grounding of visual things. From the perspective of art history—art history, moreover, occasioned by the constraints of the catalog essay—the norms lie elsewhere.

Whereas the catalog essay is typically bound to honor its function of describing art rather than criticizing it, the catalog essay specifically occasioned by a retrospective is further bound to review the entire career of works on display. Since time is here an epistemological factor, if not a factor of style, sense must be made of the art through a compelling temporal order that demonstrates and proves the content the art historian believes is significantly integral to the work. The art essay of some intellectual heft meanwhile treats the artist's stylistic history as it engages cultural history in significantly conjunct or disjunct ways. In other words, whatever else it is, the catalog essay is a species of dependent beauty. Its constraints are demonstrably those of occasion, function, and social purpose, the last tied to educating a public.

Any audience already familiar with Roland Barthes has already guessed that he would have exploited the occasion otherwise. Commissioned by the Whitney Museum of American Art to accompany a midcareer retrospective of Cy Twombly's art spanning 1954–77, Barthes wrote "The Wisdom of Art."[1] Cheerfully frustrating the curatorial and educational staff in the process, he pretended to acquit himself with this essay of extravagantly "free" beauty.

Barthes's literary representation of visuality flaunts poetic over historical narrative. He delights in the perversity of doing antinarrative antihistory when professional decorum would suggest otherwise. Barthes indeed exercises the option to be literary accorded to *hommes de lettres* when commissioned to write catalog essays. Topics freely adapted from Aristotelian poetics, announced at the outset, become the mobilized nodal points under phenomenological consideration. A fact, a coincidence, an outcome, a surprise, an action—these are the terms of interest.

Material facts are noted. Elements prior to art—pencil scratches, brown smudges—are "as stubborn substances whose obstinacy in 'being there' nothing (no subsequent meaning) can destroy." The pencil line has come to usurp the place of the brush stroke but is not noted as such.[2] Rather, in Barthes's schema, pencil is less an instrument and more a residue comparable to *materia prima*.[3] Barthes has found a visual analogue to the verbal "prelinguistic" utterances remarked by Julia Kristeva.

Graphic elements receive a provisional taxonomy: scratching, smudging, staining, and smearing. Then the written elements are mentioned, and these names—Virgil, Orpheus, The Italians, as in the paintings by Twombly—lose their "nominalist glory" in having been written clumsily. Even so, this clumsiness of application "confers on all these names the lack of skill of someone who is trying to write; and from this, once again, the truth of the Name appears all the better."[4]

Barthes next entertains chance under the aspect of inspiration. The material smudges and stains seemingly thrown across the canvas, separated in space, produce in Barthes "what the philosopher Bachelard called an 'ascensional' imagination: I float in the sky, I breathe in the air."

Up to this point Barthes has cited works from the early 1960s. *Mars and the Artist,* a work on paper from 1975, prompts a passage contemplating symbolic composition featuring furious lines at the top and a contour forming a flower, accompanied by the artist's name below. Figurative and graphic elements combine to raise the issue of representation again. "It is never naive [. . .] to ask oneself before a painting *what it represents,*" he says. People want meaning from a painting and are frustrated if it—Barthes returns to *The Italians* (1961)—does not give them the understanding they seek. This is especially so since viewers seek meaning from the title of the image they see. Looking at *The Italians,* people are bound to ask, "Where are the Italians? Where is the Sahara?" Even so, Barthes maintains, the viewer intimates a proper solution or outcome consonant with the painting at hand and perceives "what Twombly's paintings produce [. . .]: an effect." And explaining that his word choice derives from the French literary usage from the *Parnasse* to *symbolisme* to "suggest an impression, sensuous usually visual," *effect* is the very word that for him captures the airy qualities in such early paintings as *The Italians* or *The Bay of Naples*, suggestive of the Mediterranean.[5] It is a Mediterranean effect "into which [Twombly] introduces the surprise of incongruity, derision, deflation, as if the humanist turgescence was suddenly pricked." Through such deflationary pricks and clumsiness, there arises the experience of *satori*.

Finally, the drama of it all registers. A doing integral to "a kind of representation of culture" not through "depiction" but through "the power of the Name" animates these paintings. The name that stands in for the subject in classical painting presents the topic in these paintings as well: that question of rhetoric reflecting what is being talked about. And what is being talked about in the painting as subject falls back on the subject who painted it? Twombly himself.[6]

If a historical narrative may be defined as a temporal ordering of events happening under the aegis of an intellectually predetermined scheme, then a poetic nonnarrative may be said to propose a simultaneity arrived at contingently, where events that might have happened breathe with life.[7] History whose causal or logical temporality has relaxed serves the ascendancy of the lyrical narrative. At least since Wittgenstein, theories of interpretation have displaced explanation as valid and have built on the long-standing contention between the human sciences' reliance on meaning and intention and the analytical sciences' reliance on logic and necessity for what constitutes explanation in history.

Barthes's interpretative performance puts such history on notice, particularly that sort of docile unfolding of fact and biography associated with the norm of historical narrative appropriate for the museological occasion. A declared symbolist bias aids and abets Barthes's phenomenological reading of Twombly. Sensation as such is all-important. That Barthes searches out the tangible effect of emotion shows a predisposition to view Twombly as Baudelaire viewed Delacroix.[8] But Barthes's assumption that poetic effect and sensation are synonymous (revealing a bias the surrealist poet Paul Eluard will come to reinforce) leads Barthes to overestimate this content: he neglects or otherwise discounts the cognitive component in Twombly's visual discourse. Even though in a subsequent piece on Twombly Barthes notes that gesture conveys intellection, this is mere mention compared with the weight given to intuited sensation with resultant *satori*, which puts analytic intention at a clear disadvantage.[9] A manifested spirit-within-matter is Barthes's interpretive choice.

In Barthes's scheme of things, values centering on epitome give privilege to paintings and essentialize sense and significance. Selective attention paid to early work establishes a core stylistic identity for Twombly, which accords with Barthes's own. For when Barthes wrote this first essay for Cy Twombly's retrospective in 1979, he chose to concentrate on the paintings created in 1960 or thereabout, relatively early in the artist's career. This presents an occasion to examine the significance of Barthes's selective attention as a historical representation of the artist and as a stylistic representation of himself.

Discarded by Barthes are various alternative emplotments of an artist's retrospective career. Among the art-historical discourses not assumed by him is, least interestingly, the chronological account typical of catalog essays of the 1950s and 1960s in the United States and often still obligatory. As the discursive yet redundant form of the listed biography otherwise placed in the back pages, this chronicle of a life unfairly stigmatizes all art history—as though chronology and history were synonymous, despite the fact that history is a universal term covering any number of particular temporal emplotments and that, in the allowable decorum governing catalog practice, most approaches, ranging from formalist to cultural, are practiced simultaneously.

Attention paid to chronology in the Twombly catalog is indeed abbreviated:

> Cy Twombly was born April 25, 1928, in Lexington, Virginia, studied at Washington and Lee University in Lexington, Boston Museum School in Boston, Massachusetts, and Art Students League in New York. In 1951 he studied at Black Mountain College, North Carolina. Between 1951 and 1953 he traveled and lived in North Africa, Spain and Italy. In 1957 he moved to Rome where he still lives.

This is the entire biographical text, printed in back alongside a chronology of exhibitions following reproductions of Twombly's work. Ever since *Sade/Fourier/Loyola* we have come to expect this inverted priority of fact and interpretation from Barthes, and here it is again. But independently of this, many artists of Twombly's generation—especially those raised on avant-garde formalism as well as those in color-field painting belatedly joining in the formalist rhetoric—disallow anecdote, incident, and other signs of the personal biography adored by editors of glossy art magazines. Twombly has long distanced himself from public appetite. In this sense, the intentionalist fallacy will be defended wherever catalogs devoted to him appear, and as with the catalog copy for this retrospective, biography is similarly perfunctory elsewhere.

Chronology, by no means the only normative historical approach for catalog writing, may occasionally even prove strategic.[10] Yet social history may be the preferred mode of choice when treating entire art movements or when plotting artistic interventions such as those by Palladio or Tatlin or Man Ray, whose functionally dependent art and career are inextricable from milieu and cultural context. In fact, a culturally contextual approach to art writing is more commonly employed than is readily acknowledged by those who want to stereotype the historical enterprise by limiting the scope and resourcefulness of its instrumentality.

Although intellectual antagonists, formalism and social history coexist in educating the public. One need only remember the debate in the 1930s between the formalist Alfred Barr—the first director of the Museum of Modern Art, who in 1929 coined the term *abstract expressionism* to refer to Kandinsky—and the social art historian Meyer Schapiro over the meaning of abstract art. The subsequent emergence of the New York School provoked rival histories and comment by the art historians Meyer Schapiro and Robert Goldwater; the formalist Clement Greenberg and the humanist Harold Rosenberg, both cultural critics; and the formalist chronicler Irving Sandler and the cultural critic Dore Ashton.

Essays by critical historians or semioticians are prevalent in certain museological enclaves: much depends on the intellectual and administrative freedom given museum staffs by their board. By the 1970s and sporadically thereafter, when Roland Barthes was approached by the Whitney Museum of American Art, critical paradigms applied to catalog essays were quite variously creative. Recall, for instance, Lawrence Alloway's applied communication theory and semiotic overlay on American pop art for the Whitney Museum after decades of writing about the subject he had initially defined and traced in Britain and the United States.

These days, however, the thematic approach favored more and more in an era of nonspecialist audiences is also ironically most amenable to the *littérateur*, for, of all typologies, this requires the least scholarly specialization or comprehension. The thematic approach lends itself to lay percipience, expressed in the aperçu and in the impressionistic criticism of poets writing on art. Together with Meyer Schapiro and Rudolf Arnheim, poets—and artists—were conscripted by editor Thomas Hess to review in *Art News*, covering abstract expressionism in the 1950s when such painting was shunned almost everywhere else. This was how the poet and lawyer Harold Rosenberg, who had published vorticist poems in *Poetry* magazine in the early 1940s, found a forum for his metaphoric art criticism mobilizing enthusiasm for action painting. Relative to the sociolinguistic practice of our times, when an avid appetite for simplistic popularization in the press assumes reception made queasy if confronted with art history, intellectual history, or criticism, Barthes's playful interpretation of Twombly supplies what the public wants, yet elusively. As sensuous impression, Barthes's art writing is meanwhile consistent with a tradition of the belletristic liberal construing of his object.

Since, after all, a retrospective raises the question of style across time, let us review Cy Twombly's career by decade to ascertain the interpretive spin Barthes put on the matter. Although ignored by Barthes, the 1950s were indeed represented in the retrospective exhibition and catalog. A formalist would have taken note that in Twombly's work *matière* and tactility, registering the artist's allegiance with art brut (and Jean Dubuffet in particular), give way to attenuated expression. Reliance on line is conspicuous. If style is "patterned selection of possibility afforded by forms,"[11] these early works reveal Twombly's interest in exploiting reduction for expressive possibility. Yet given the variety of expressionist tendencies keeping pace with the stylistic milieu of the period, Twombly's personal style, it may be guessed, continues to form in response to the period style.

Given the emphasis abstract expressionism placed on Nietzsche—an antiaesthetic archaism, the anteriority of which was already a commonplace by the time the craze for Nietzsche reached the United States—we might assume Barthes would have laid even more emphasis on expressions of the philosopher's Dionysiac archaism made lean.[12] Neither children's art nor the art of the insane—whose grammatical and lexical forms are writ large in Twombly's work (as they are in European and Europeanized art of the 1950s)—figures in Barthes's discussion, except through the attribute of clumsiness. Were he to have mentioned the aesthetics of children's art, as he did in his second article, "Cy Twombly: Works on Paper," then his interpretation of Twombly at this stage would have had to be reformulated. It would have to consider the sensorimotor handicap Twombly deliberately undertook when drawing with his left hand to place himself at a disadvantage to acculturation.

Drawing the graphic equivalent of the prelinguistic utterance and so sacrificing linguistic competence by reducing one's means: such was decidedly part of the ethos of authencity inscribed in Twombly's aesthetic. Because of this it is tempting to wonder why Barthes laid so much emphasis on *satori* if the Greek concept of vulnerability "which is essential to the manner in which the excellent man conducts himself" was culturally closer at hand.[13] The answer might be that once Barthes classified Twombly a symbolist, surprise—and ironic surprise especially—lent the notion he needed to fill out his scheme. To return to the phenomenological without delineating the historical era associated with it may be Barthes's implicit purpose.

Although literary critics and art historians alike do tend to disregard the stray, idiosyncratic, or occasional manner as intellectual noise irrelevant to the style of art unfolding before them, art historians more readily accept the deviation because their commitment is to an unruly universe of experiential findings even at the expense of the rational principles they hold to be true. Barthes's adherence to an original grammar of style located in those values deemed representative of the artist's work centers on works from the early 1960s, the years when the artist came into his own. Given this selective attention to the early 1960s, the grammar of dispersal, disposing of lexical smudge and smear, is adequate to interpret Twombly at this moment. It accounts for the highly articulable range of material properties a painterly mark can manifest. Not merely various, Twombly's mark-making unsystematically encapsulates a set of intensely sensuous and expressive reductions[14]—and Barthes gets a good grip on this heterogeneous material anatomy even if, semantically, he could have noted that a fully formed lexicon is implicit at this early, so-called primitive stage.

The consensual cultural reading reinforces Barthes's interpretation. The milieu at Black Mountain College, where John Cage, Merce Cunningham, and Robert Rauschenberg brought fruitful anarchy to disciplined yet pragmatically oriented *technè* brought there by Josef Albers, Anni Albers, and other exiles from the Bauhaus, fostered radical experiments with materials and craft. It also gave rise to radical renovations of definition. For instance, music now construed to be anything derived from the principle of sound is answered by the notion that dance incorporated all kinesis. Anecdotally, this assumption of art as materially and formally comprehensive extends to Twombly, who, only a few years ago, wondered aloud whether he would ever again hear "a certain Futurist music entitled *Veil of Orpheus*," which he had heard long before. Fortunately, I too had heard Pierre Henry's *Veil of Orpheus* and could supply Twombly with a cassette of this *musique concrète* of 1953, which is largely percussive thanks to its object-generated sounds and so provides an aurally dispersed lexicon of timbre and rhythm (that, by the way, still sounds new, unlike so many experiments that have attained a quaint status as period pieces). Twombly's effort to realize the phenomenal visual analogue to aural sound structures remains underappreciated because naive viewers (including the more discerning Barthes) perceive, at best, a rarified sensibility.

Further issues of signification arise even where Barthes is strongest. *The Italians* (Figure 15.1) seizes his attention as a painting whose title finds no objective or subjective representation on canvas; the relation of signifying title to signified subject remains tantalizingly abstract. "Where are the Italians? Where is the Sahara?" he asks in vain. Yet even as the nonreferential title underscores the abstract nature of painting

Figure 15.1. Cy Twombly, *The Italians* (1961). Oil, pencil, and crayon on canvas, 6′ $6\frac{5}{8}$″ × 8′ $6\frac{1}{4}$″ (199.5 × 259.6 cm). The Museum of Modern Art, New York. Blanchette Rockefeller Fund. Photograph copyright 1996, The Museum of Modern Art, New York.

itself, symbolist traces abound, if only to manifest the content of this style, which animates nothing providently. And given the chromaticism and wet-in-wet pigment decidedly present in *The Bay of Naples* and *Empire of Flora*, for instance, more needs to be done to elucidate content than Barthes's hedonist impulse will allow. Barthes may even have suppressed the latent historical content suggested by his questions that only a few years ago he might well have allowed himself to recall.[15] Another mention of *The Italians* confidently asserts its allusion to the classical spirit, but, if anything, Twombly's calligraphic mark serves the Nietzschean barbaric revitalization of that classical spirit.

Perhaps because pursuing the Mediterranean effect under the aegis of French grace, Barthes ignored the consensual interpretation that could reinforce his own sensualist bias.[16] As though unfamiliar with

André Breton's writings on Arshile Gorky—not to mention the painterly antecedent to Twombly in Gorky—Barthes disregards both the surrealist gynecological vernacular and the scatological corollary to *matière* deposited on canvas. Nor in his mention of the Mediterranean effect does Barthes take into account that this very surrealist content prevented Twombly from being accepted as an abstract expressionist when lines of aesthetic and ideological battle were being drawn up, and that Twombly's removal to Italy in 1957 was in large measure because of pressures to become a purist when the impure state of throwing figural and abstract gestures and signs together in a condition of contested agony was his abiding interest. These very vestiges of surrealism, not to mention figuration as such, were prejudicially received by the formalist critic Clement Greenberg. The decidedly formalist and materialist artistic climate in the 1950s and 1960s promoted color-field painting, then minimalist objects. Europe, not America, remained more hospitable to art nurtured in the legacy of symbolism. Barthes does not rehearse this critical face-off, so he does not exploit the situation debated within painting—Twombly's painting—itself.

Even early on, Twombly's paintings take up the issue of radical aesthetic purity. In the 1961 painting *The School of Athens*, and with determined frequency thereafter, a structuralist discourse conflating expressively and rationally coded painterliness dramatizes the possibility of synthesis. Today, there are no slides of this painting with its schematic rectilinear dais engaging vehement gesture, as *The School of Athens* and the New York School play out their destinies jointly.[17] Nor is there a slide of *Leda and the Swan*, the necessary thematic antagonism of which throws together a formalized expressionism, although both works were on view in the retrospective. Deservedly well known are the paintings by Twombly that treat mathematical and rational discourse as felt ideas. In a deceptively simple formal conversion, what was white is black and what was black, white; and the field of sensation has become a didactic field of operational thought.

On Twombly's "blackboards," the semantic range of the mark has been reduced to almost sheer uniformity: some feature a single line read as measurement—the notion of measurement—by virtue of a number placed above, where convention would mandate. Since syntax as operational thought is more elaborate elsewhere, campaigns or topology become the elusive subject of a serial accumulation of line, heavily qualified by trial and error—or at least the apparition of trial and error inscribed, erased, and reinscribed. In consequence, the quarantining of poetic from scientific discourse advocated by the New Critics is synthesized in Twombly's calligraphic compositions from this phase. The field of thought seems equally creative and critical, expressively self-forgetful and empirically inquiring. But while in some canvases the dialectical process seems to have intervened at the point of origin, in others, isolating poetic from scientific vocabulary seems more clear-cut. In any event, Twombly's analytical intention is in the foreground.

Jasper Johns owns a painting by Twombly in which the calligraphy has achieved the perfect neutrality and uniformity earlier paintings had barred from their surfaces. This, of course, is not a consequence of development, for Twombly's skill—indeed, virtuouso *technè*—was evident all along in the pictorial intelligence, as Barthes noted, wherever one looked. Here, rather, is captured the antithesis of the prelinguistic sign seen in abundance earlier on developmentally, this evidence of motor control revealed through the Palmer method of calligraphic training for children proves the code of acculturation and mastery. It is, further, the symbolic code for prose. Barthes ignores this phase of Twombly's art almost entirely, perhaps since its style might seem to refute that which he had identified as recently his own. In evoking the authority of the poetic mark, then, Barthes may be reluctant to acknowledge the full spectrum of Twombly's discursive intentionality.

Barthes's selective attention to the originary phase in Twombly's art treats the oeuvre as an enactment of Barthes's own late poetics. Aphoristic impressions, willfully literary, not historical, stand for Barthes's declared representation of Twombly's history on the occasion of the retrospective. What it leaves out is cultural context in the panorama of stylistic milieus in which Twombly moved, and to which his embedded rhetoric gave witness. The mid-1970s saw a relatively conservative historicism in art. Neoexpressionism purported to recuperate meaning, yet with few exceptions artists recuperated only illustrative and familiar ambivalences to nationalist themes. Against this postmodernist reaction, Twombly's reinvestment in figural imagery seems more continuous with his own poetics than appropriated from without.

The retrospective featured a few of these efforts and included canvases and drawings penciled with single mythic names, or, rather, a penciled name together with a reductive graphic symbol serving as attribute: "Virgil" is erased through the application of paint smearing the graphite; "Dionysus" rides a phallus; "Orpheus" is set above a launched strong diagonal in awkward cursive script. In light of work soon to follow, propulsive gestures organizing themselves into a nearly pacific image in *Mars and the Artist* may dramatize the motivated sign as well.

Twombly's so-called return to figuration is symbolic—a virtue or quality enacting a name. With a modernist clarity and universality of poetic signs treating topics, Twombly himself seems to be insisting on the structuralist phase of Barthes's early rhetoric. Free variants on a thematic constant abound. Here, then, are early modernist ideograms whose formalist reductions function equally as sign system and as reference. Although beyond the scope of the retrospective, the epic *Fifty Days at Ilium* (Figure 15.2) was available for viewing, courtesy of the Dia Foundation, at the same time, and might well have existed in transparencies for Barthes to see. A single painting comprising ten canvases now on permanent view at the Philadelphia Museum of Art, Twombly's *Fifty Days at Ilium* is truly a major work from his career.

Poetry ignores writing as a figure of history in styles, according to Annette Lavers.[18] But Twombly's thematic inscription of epic into a lyrical mode compels attention paid to this implication of history, if only to lend myth the experiential "feeling" of history. Meanwhile taking a linguistic approach to structure, Twombly seems to "omit what is accidental or contingent [. . .] and gives imaginative expression to the essential type,"[19] for he utilizes style and schema alike to encapsulate the drama of Apollonian and Dionysiac crisis. Note, then, the evolving or devolving image concept.[20] Whether single or manifold, each image is precisely that, Alois Riegl would argue, because condensed by virtue of enfolding motivic transformations:

Shield of Achilles
Heroes of the Achaeans
The Vengeance of Achilles
Achaeans in Battle
The Fire That Consumes All Before It
Shades of Achilles, Patroclus, and Hector
House of Priam
Ilians in Battle
Shades of Eternal Night
Heroes of the Ilians

Action painting, having accrued libido and animus, subsides into gesture; gesture subsides into contour. Remember the myth of Flora memorializing the destiny of warriors who, when they die, undergo a transformation and metamorphose into flowers. Having painted this symbol early on (in vivid chroma), Twombly in midlife continued to grant the heart or flowering heart or passionate flower accord in the schema of the rosette: a funerary remembrance.

Note a conversion from the diachronic story into a structure featuring transposition and reflection. Where in Homer's myth the empowering shield had been placed centrally in the narrative, Twombly's retelling has the shield initiate the action. Occupying the center of Twombly's narrative is the scheme of rosettes symbolizing the shades of Achilles, Patroclus, and Hector, and in reflection on either side images of victory

Figure 15.2. Cy Twombly, *Gallery 1691—Installation View of Cy Twombly's* Fifty Days at Ilium (1977–78). A painting in 10 parts, 300 × 2582 cm. Oil, oil crayon, pencil on paper. Philadelphia Museum of Art. Photograph by Graydon Wood, 1989.

and defeat, passion and reason—that represent, left and right respectively, the houses of the Achaeans and Ilians. Painting and drawing administer the contesting forces of passion and reason in the synchronic epic Twombly has constructed for his *Fifty Days at Ilium.* The question remains, Why did this not appeal to Barthes, the once master structuralist? It might have, had Barthes not years before disavowed this structuralist possibility for himself. If the catalog essay on Twombly demonstrates anything, it is a stylistic representation of Barthes himself in a post-structuralist phase acknowledging that the validity of the artist might be enacted in a form and manner compatible with his own beliefs.[21]

The ahistorical aspect of structuralism could be said to be expressed by treating a retrospective study of art thematically, on a sample of work meant to suffice for the entirety. In this sense, the Aristotelian categories Barthes imputes to Twombly's work emerge not only through the suggestive link with actual text on canvas but also through the adoptive myth located in mythic time which Twombly desires for his archaic modernity, a mythic time to which Barthes willingly subscribes. At least for the duration of the catalog essay, Barthes treats those Aristotelian terms as though they were *churinga* of European vintage: verbal objects symbolic representation removed from the depths of a cave to be verbally caressed and prayed over, and then returned to their proper archival setting once the connection between the present and mythic past has been made. (Refelt and thus remade, as George Poulet might advise, the terms may now be said to embody the essences to which they refer.) This ahistorical metaphor for history is not incompatible with Barthes's synchronic approach to Twombly's style: a thematic appreciation of symbolic events, acts, and effects more connected to a mythic saturation than to its modern and contemporary histories that contextualize conditions and intentions.

But it is the poststructuralist scatter and dissemination to which Barthes returns at the end of his essay that give emphasis to his own intentions. Having inverted the intellectual hierarchy by which the structure of history culminates as a sequence of contextual approaches to an event, the event of Twombly's particular paintings, Barthes distributes free variants of key terms throughout the essay, the sensuous effects of terms scattered throughout constituting a field of *écriture* closer to art appreciation than to art criticism. The significance of Barthes's impressionistic and selective attention, then, is meant to reinforce Barthes's own late style of transfigured dissolution. The columns he wrote for *Le Nouvel Observateur* from December 1978 to April 1979 reveal this post-structural rationale for style, in which the particular, the occasional, moment at hand is historically embedded in life, as much as his late books do. This is as much of a claim to structuring history as Barthes wishes to make. Toward the close of his catalog essay on Twombly, he writes:

> Thus this morning of 31 December 1978, it is still dark, it is raining, all is silent when I sit down again at my worktable. I look at *Herodiade* (1960) and have really nothing to say about it except the same platitude: that I like it. But suddenly there arises something new, a desire: that of *doing the same thing* (no longer that for writing), to choose colors, to paint and draw. In fact, the question of painting is: "Do you feel like imitating Twombly?"[22]

And so Barthes, a transient figure inscribed as Proust inscribes himself within a text, closes his essay considering the topic of production and the drama of doing that initiates Twombly's art and essentially permeates it.

Notes

1. Unless otherwise stated, all quotes by Roland Barthes derive from this essay. Translated by Annette Lavers, for *Cy Twombly: Paintings and Drawings, 1954–1977,* Whitney Museum of American Art, 10 April–10 June 1979. The essay reappears in Richard Howard's translation in *RF,* pp. 177–94.

2. Marjorie Welish, "A Discourse on Twombly," *Art in America* 67, no. 5 (September 1979): 81.

3. In phenomenologically keyed interpretations, Barthes takes pains to record primordial experiences for primordial forms.

4. Barthes dwells on the issue of names. Preoccupying Barthes, I believe, is not only the painting *The Italians* but "The Italians," for as a name it recalls "Italianicity," from earlier writings on advertisements in which the name suggests inflated value and cultural priority. Italy as connotative of cultural priority over the French haunts Barthes still, even as the uncertain calligraphy of Twombly's inscription of the name deflates its "nominalist glory" and calls into question its "pure" value.

5. The unmotivated signifier of the title throws the abstract nature of the composition into relief. Beyond the scope of this chapter is a discussion of "possible worlds" that names in Twombly's art evoke. The mythological or legendary status of certain names is particularly provocative: "Homer" represents that cultural entity indicating the collectively authored oral epic poem *The Iliad* recited over time. Barthes, fascinated with designation as well as meaning, might well have been drawn to Twombly's art for the enigmatic modal logic of naming as much as for the codes inscribed in the gestural calligraphy.

6. As Annette Lavers reminds us, style for Barthes is the instrumentality of the imagination, not of the social sphere. *Roland Barthes: Structuralism and After* (Cambridge, Mass.: Harvard University Press, 1982).

7. During Twombly's formative years, the idea of history advanced in the United States by New Critic Kenneth Burke was a metaphoric notion of dramatism, crucial to advancing the aesthetic and ethos of action painting. Antithetical to New Critical practice, the revered Chicago Aristotelian Richard McKeon developed thematic typologies for philosophy, history, rhetoric, and poetry.

8. Discussed at length by Lee McKay Johnson in "Baudelaire and Delacroix:

Tangible Language," in *The Metaphor of Painting* (Ann Arbor: UMI Research Press, 1980).

9. See "Cy Twombly: Works on Paper," in *RF*, p. 160.

10. *Picasso and Braque: Pioneering Cubism*, organized by William Rubin for the Museum of Modern Art in 1989, depended on an almost forensic patience for day-by-day evidence of the collaborative effort in evolving the cubist style. Temporal and material positivism here proves strategic.

11. Seymour Chatman, "The Styles of Narrative Codes," in *The Concept of Style*, ed. Berel Lang (Ithaca, N.Y.: Cornell University Press, 1979, 1987), p. 239.

12. Placing creative expression at the putative poetic origin of human utterance is a cultural phenomenon that Barthes ignores, but in the 1940s Vico's translated writings encouraged the identification of behavioral and evolutionary linguistic development in primitive vocal practices.

13. Martha Nussbaum, *The Fragility of Goodness* (New York: Cambridge University Press, 1986), p. 20.

14. Marjorie Welish, untitled catalog essay, in *Cy Twombly: Paintings* (New York: Stephen Mazoh Gallery, 19 April–27 May 1983), unpaginated.

15. The history that may have subconsciously formulated these "random" questions possibly centers on Mussolini's advance on Africa. My thanks to Joseph Masheck for the suggestion.

16. Welish, "A Discourse on Twombly," p. 81.

17. Ibid., p. 83. See also the catalog essay for Stephen Mazoh. Reviewing the latter exhibition for the *New York Times*, art critic John Russell denied the possibility of ratiocinative processes and intentions in the "intuitive" art of Cy Twombly. His response is typical.

18. Lavers, *Roland Barthes*, pp. 42–43.

19. Richard McKeon, *Thought, Action, and Passion* (Chicago: University of Chicago Press, 1954, 1974), p. 204. Expression of essences throughout Twombly's art from the 1960s on would seem to cast it in this vein. Meanwhile, as Twombly's figural manipulations simplified, Barthes's were growing more complicated. Gérard Genette had already noted in 1964 that Barthes was preparing to deal with free variants of constants ("The Obverse of Signs," in *Figures of Literary Discourse* [New York: Columbia University Press, 1982], pp. 27–44).

20. Lavers notes Barthes's admiration for Bachelard's defining an image as a set of potential transformations (*Roland Barthes*, p. 37).

21. Once "postulating (after Hjelmslev) that any *process* presupposes a *system*," Barthes would seem to now believe any system presupposes process (Lavers, *Roland Barthes*, p. 52). Whereas once "the effects" of happenings were doomed to trivialize confrontational dialectic, Barthes now prefers the former for its non-authoritarian stance. See Lavers, *Roland Barthes*, p. 79.

22. Barthes's writerly symbolist correspondence to Twombly's style recalls a similar impulse not so long ago in the art criticism on behalf of action painting. Well known is the fact that in 1952, when support for abstraction was at best a precarious matter even among the well-intentioned art public in New York, Harold Rosenberg tried to mobilize the public with passionate partisanship inspired by Baudelaire in essays on European abstraction in exile. "The American Action Painters," notorious then, has subsequently moved through the status of celebration back to notoriety, as younger critics, siding with Greenberg's color-field formalism declared Rosenberg's essay both ill-conceived and unreadable. What is less well known, yet which I maintain elsewhere ("Harold Rosenberg: Transforming the Earth," *Art Criticism* 2 [1985]: 10–28), is that the charge of

Rosenberg's having "made up" the term *action* so that artists would rally around him is ignorant of the tradition of romanticism and of revolutionary activism, both of which informed Rosenberg's choice of slogan. At the very least, the spirit of vorticism informing Rosenberg's first and only book of poetry, *Trance Above the Streets,* published a decade prior to his art essay, shows the poet-critic promoting a culturally embedded metaphor wrested from Aristotelian poetics and reconfigured "dramatistically" for a variety of modernisms. As for being unreadable, "The American Action Painters" is, like Barthes's essay on Twombly, an enactment in the style of the message he is advocating. As such, in its aphoristic performative mode, it is perfectly readable—this last point remaining undetected even by the progressive wing of art writers who profess to advocate style as content.

16

Genetic Criticism in the Wake of Barthes

Daniel Ferrer

This is a story that we should be able to tell in the historical past, the simple past (French *passé simple*), the tense that has been so sharply analyzed and demystified by Barthes in *Writing Degree Zero* and that he himself used as the basis of the subtle rhetoric of *Camera Lucida*. The story translated into English, and in a much shortened version, would run more or less like this:

> During the 1960s, traditional philology and literary history, which prevailed in the field of literary studies in spite of existentialist inroads, were superseded by structuralism, which was then replaced by its poststructuralist variant. Then genetic criticism, reviving an interest in the historical dimension of the text and combining it with a modern conception of textuality, took its turn as the most dynamic critical movement in the field.

As Barthes has shown, the point of such narratives is that they are neatly ordered, self-sufficient, safely distanced, in no way relevant to the present situation of enunciation. Unfortunately—or fortunately—I do not feel in a position to tell such a story. Barthes cannot be safely distanced, he is still relevant to us; the mourning period is not over, and I do not see any sign that it is coming to an end.

By calling this paper "Genetic Criticism in the Wake of Barthes," I did not mean to convey the idea that genetic critics were post-Barthesian epigones, nor that Barthes, bearing the brunt of the theoretical storm, flattened the rougher waves so that we now have a smooth sea before us. Rather than a nautical metaphor, the image of an Irish wake is perhaps more appropriate: genetic criticism is sitting at its place in the circle of mourners, moaning and singing, passing around the whiskey, vaguely entertaining the hope that, as in *Finnegans Wake*, the smell of the liquor may wake up the sleeping giant. Or perhaps one should think of more primitive rites, in which the body of the deceased is carved out in the hope that those who partake of it will incorporate his virtues. So this will be a rereading (and sometimes a deliberate misreading) of some aspects of Barthes, in the light of the present preoccupations of genetic criticism. In other words, I will be staking my claim for some bits that I have picked out because they seem particularly appetizing at this moment.

Retrospectively, it does not seem impossible that Barthes himself, in one of his notoriously unpredictable shifts of direction, could have become the initiator of genetic criticism. Many signs in his work seem to point in that direction. First of all, it would be a complete mistake to think that Barthes was not keenly aware of the diachronic dimension of writing and creation (although this awareness is, of course, more conspicuous in his early, prestructuralist work).

A Stubborn Afterimage

In *Writing Degree Zero*, having noted parenthetically that "structure is the residual deposit of duration" (12), Barthes develops at length the idea of an inertia of written traces, a persistence of past states of writing:

> It is under the pressure of History and Tradition that the possible modes of writing for a given writer are established; there is a History of Writing. But this History is dual: at the very moment when general History proposes—or imposes—new problematics of the literary language, *writing still remains full of the recollection of previous usage,* for language is never innocent: *words have a second-order memory which mysteriously persists in the midst of new meanings.* Writing is precisely this *compromise between freedom and remembrance,* it is this freedom which remembers and is free only in the gesture of choice, but is no longer so within duration. True, I can today select such and such a mode of writing, and in so doing assert my freedom, aspire to the freshness of novelty or to a tradition, but it is impossible to develop it within duration without gradually becoming a prisoner of someone else's words and even of my own. *A stubborn after-image, which comes from all the previous modes of writing and even from the past of my own, drowns the sound of my present words. Any written trace precipitates, as inside a chemical at first transparent, innocent and neutral, mere duration gradually reveals in suspension a whole past of increasing density, like a cryptogram.* (*WDZ,* 16–17; *OC1,* 148; emphasis added)

Barthes is referring primarily to an external, historic, dialogism but also to an inner dialogism, involving the development of an individual work and thus resulting in a kind of genetic inertia.

Traumatic Criticism

In a strange paper called "Les 'Unités traumatiques' au cinéma" (1960), Barthes confesses his embarrassment with film because its temporal dimension cannot be evaded ("the film image is pure genetic matter") and seems in direct opposition to a structuralist point of view. The contrast between disturbing genetic process and reassuring structure is reminiscent of Barthes's version of Michelet as a historian strangely uneasy with narrative and rejoicing in diagrams ("aporie du Récit . . . euphorie du Tableau" [*OC1*, 92]). As occurs very often in *Michelet*, the personal note is unmistakable. But here Barthes openly confronts his embarrassment and turns it into a stimulus to theoretical progress (although the program was never implemented):

> One could say that the film image is pure genetic matter, as opposed to current structural research that implies, at least in its mode of exposition, a stabilization and a kind of timelessness of the functions it discovers. But it is precisely because the gap between genesis and structure, process and diagram, is still profoundly puzzling for modern epistemology that one must not hesitate to confront it.[1]

Nevermore

Ten years later, in "The Old Rhetoric," Barthes emphasizes a fundamental genetic problem: the conflicting time sequences of the writing and the written.

> The relation between the *order of invention* (*dispositio*) and the *order of presentation* (*ordo*), and notably the gap in the orientation (contradiction, inversion) of the two parallel orders, always has a theoretical bearing: it is a whole conception of literature which is at stake each time, as is evidenced by Poe's exemplary analysis of his own poem "The Raven": starting, in order to write the work, from the *last thing apparently received* by the reader (received as "ornament"), i.e., the melancholy effect of the word *nevermore* (*e/o*), then tracing back from this to the invention of the story and of the metrical form. (*SC*, 49–50)

Saussure

Again in 1973, Barthes notes the ideological nature of Saussure's "profound hostility to geneticism" ("Saussure, the Sign, Democracy," *SC*, 151–56) and distances himself from it.

We could multiply the examples of Barthes's awareness of and interest in the genetic dimension, but one might wonder why Barthes, given those premises, never seemed to become aware of what could be gained by studying the actual genesis of the text. In many directions that he opened, genetics would seem to be the logical next step.

Commutation

Barthes writes that we must use systematic commutation to fight against the closure of the text, against its obviousness:

> In analyzing a text, we must constantly react against the impression of obviousness, against the it-goes-without-saying aspect of what is written. Every statement, however trivial and normal it appears, must be evaluated in terms of structure by a mental test of commutation. Confronting a statement, a sentence-fragment, we must always think of what would happen if the feature were not noted or if it were different. (*SC*, 227)

In this context it seems strange that he did not consider that the best possible commutation for this purpose is the commutation between the text and the "avant-texte": There we can find out exactly what happens when the feature is not noted or when it is different from its canonical form.

Bathmology

In the case of "bathmology," one of Barthes's most exciting ideas (see Pierre Force, "Beyond Language: Bathmology" in this volume), one might also expect genetic developments. Bathmological analysis, concerned with "one of the forms of time," is always at least virtually genetic: a statement is taken as subsuming one (or several) previous statements. Should this virtuality not be actualized, whenever possible?

If we admit that bathmology is not something that surfaced with *Roland Barthes by Roland Barthes* or "Brillat-Savarin" but constantly preoccupied Barthes, we can illustrate this point with Barthes's analysis of personal pronouns in fiction in *Writing Degree Zero.* Grammar and tradition allow for only two possibilities: writing in the first and in the third person. But Barthes shows that the same sign takes on a very different meaning according to the stance of the work within a general or individual history. There is a first person to the first degree ("the most obvious solution"), a first person to the second degree, and presumably, to the third, fourth, and so on. The same can be said of the third person (suitable for the simple conformist as well as for the sophisticated seeker of novelty through convention). Understanding the passage from one to the other requires a true grammatical genesis (history as conjugation):

> The "I" [. . .] is at the same time the most obvious solution, when the narration remains on this side of convention (Proust's work, for instance, purports to be a mere introduction to Literature), and the most sophisticated, when the "I" takes its place beyond convention and attempts to destroy it, by conferring on the narrative the spurious naturalness of taking the reader into its confidence

[. . .]. In the same way the use of the "he" in a novel involves two opposed systems of ethics: since it represents an unquestioned convention, it attracts the most conformist and the least dissatisfied, as well as those others who have decided that, finally, this convention is necessary to the novelty of their work. [. . .] In many modern novelists the history of the man is identified with the course of the conjugation: starting from an "I" which is still the form which expresses anonymity most faithfully, man and author little by little win the right to the third person, in proportion as existence becomes fate, and soliloquy becomes a Novel. (*WDZ*, 35, 36–37)

But a less abstract treatment might be more satisfactory. Obviously presenting Proust's work as "a mere introduction to Literature" whose "narration remains on this side of convention" does not do justice to Proust's use of the first person. It would seem necessary, in this context, to mention that Proust's first person is the result of a transformation of a third person (as evidenced in the unpublished *Jean Santeuil*).

Complex Graph

We can wonder how a critic, who in his "Inaugural Lecture" at the Collège de France defined literature as "the complex graph of the traces of a practice, the practice of writing" (*BR*, 462), could be so incurious about the actual traces of that practice, the materiality of the complex graph that can be found on the manuscript page.

Barthes was certainly not insensible to the materiality of handwriting. In a well-known interview ("Un rapport presque maniaque avec les instruments graphiques"), he insisted that the material aspects of writing were "heavily charged with significance." In a much lesser-known preface to an encyclopedia of writing and typography (*La Civilisation de l'écriture*), Barthes comments on the historical dimension of writing (in the material, manual sense, not in the way it is understood in *Writing Degree Zero*), but also on the bodily process of inscription on the page:

While thinking of what to write (as I am doing at this very moment), I feel my hand acting, turning, connecting, diving, rising, and very often, through the interplay of corrections, canceling or expanding the line, opening up space as far as the margin, thereby constructing from an array of tiny and apparently functional marks (the letters) a space which is quite simply the space of art: I am the artist, not in that I represent an object, but more fundamentally because in writing, my body takes pleasure in tracing, in rhythmically incising a virgin surface (the virgin being the infinitely possible).

[. . .] the human desire to incise (with a point, a reed, a stylus, a pen) or to caress (with a brush, a felt-tip pen) has undergone many transformations which have concealed the specifically corporal origins of writing; but it is enough that from time to time a painter (such as, today, Masson or Twombly) incorporates graphical forms into his work for us to be reminded of the evidence that writing is not only a technical activity, it is also a physically pleasurable practice.[2]

Barthes acknowledges the materiality of the space of writing, its artistic nature. He is fully aware that manuscript words generate a space that is equivalent to the space of painting—but apparently shows no desire to make it an object of research.

Barthes does study the intrusion of the practice of writing in painting and makes illuminating remarks on this occasion, but he never studies this practice in its natural locus (the manuscript). About Twombly, for instance, he shows that the "reader" must regress from the trace to the tracing, from the line to the movement of the hand, from the product to the production: "His work does not derive from a concept (*mark*) but from an activity (*marking*); or, better still, from a field (the sheet of paper), insofar as an activity is deployed there" ("Cy Twombly: Works on Paper," *RF*, 173). The product is devalued, denounced ("betrayed as imaginary," which is a derogatory term in the critical idiom of the 1970s), and production is promoted.

> This œuvre conducts TW's reader (I am saying: *reader*, though there is nothing to decipher) to a certain philosophy of time: he must retrospectively see a movement, what was the hand's *becoming*; but then—a salutary revolution—the product (any product?) appears as a kind of bait: all art, insofar as it is accumulated, acknowledged, published, is betrayed as *imaginary*; what is real, to which TW's work continuously recalls you, is producing: at each stroke, TW blows up the Museum. (*RF*, 172)

However, no critical consequences (such as moving from a study of the work to a study of the writing process) are drawn from this aesthetic revolution.

Flasher

In "To the Seminar" Barthes suggests, "let us write in the present, let us produce in the others' presence and sometimes with them a book *in process* [*parfois avec eux en train de se faire*]; let us show ourselves in the speech act [*en état d'énonciation*]" (*RL*, 339–40). There is an obvious play between "exposing ourselves in a state of enunciation," and a state of erection, but this writerly exhibitionism never seems to correspond to an equivalent voyeurism. Barthes never seems curious to peep at others in a state of enunciation, to catch a glimpse of books in the making as they can be observed in genetic documents.

Philological

As far as I know, the only time Barthes mentions an author's manuscript and compares it to the published text, in *Michelet*, he makes a very traditional and purely philological use of it, as a repository of the truth, of the author's genuine intention, falsified in the text as it was published by Michelet's wife (*OC1*, 359).[3]

But I would like to suggest that in his ultimate book, *Camera Lucida*, ostensibly about photography, Barthes is indirectly dealing with a much more constant preoccupation of his, enunciation,[4] and, in this indirect way, presenting us with a genetic view of enunciation—or at least to suggest that it is possible to read the text as an extreme example of that kind of indirection Barthes called "la figure Moussu."[5]

Crusoe's Footprint and Balzac's Coffee Stain

It is remarkable that, compared with other students of signs, Barthes always privileged a semiology of the signal over a semiotics of the index. The reason for this might be his fascination with enunciation. Only signals open the "abyss" of enunciation behind them. Only signals have an enunciator. But paradoxically, enunciation cannot be signaled (without becoming enounced, "de l'énoncé"); it can only be decoded from signals through a process of inference that turns them over and changes them into indices.

To my knowledge, Barthes never discussed this phenomenon explicitly, but at last in *Camera Lucida*, he came to grips with the indexical nature of photography and thus raised a problem that was apparently entirely different from all those he had encountered (but sounds nevertheless vaguely familiar to the Barthesian reader):

> The image, says phenomenology, is an object-as-nothing. Now, in the Photograph, what I posit is not only the absence of the object; it is also, by one and the same movement, on equal terms, the fact that this object has indeed existed and that it has been there where I see it. Here is where the madness is, for until this day no representation could assure me of the past of a thing except by intermediaries; but with the Photograph, my certainty is immediate: no one in the world can undeceive me. The Photograph then becomes a bizarre *medium*, a new form of hallucination: false on the level of perception, true on the level of time. (*CL*, 115)

"Here is where the madness is," "a new form of hallucination," or again: "The *noeme* of Photography is simple, banal; no depth: 'that has been.' [. . .] [S]uch evidence[6] can be a sibling of madness" (*CL*, 115). This insistent invocation of madness should remind us of a fragment of *Roland Barthes by Roland Barthes* (the same that introduces the idea of "bathmology") in which enunciation is called the "abyss opened by each word," "the madness of language." It is "evident" that enunciation is "madness" because, in the same way as photography, it implies presence and absence "by one and the same movement."

Enunciation and photography both belong inside the general semiotic category of imprints. In his much less emotional analysis of such motivated heteromaterial metaphoro-metonymical expressions, Umberto Eco took as an example the solitary footprint discovered by Robinson Crusoe on his island, and remarked that it could be translated as "a man passed here,"[7] which we can take as another form of the photographic "that-has-been." But it should be noted that in Defoe's novel this paradigmatic footprint is the starting point of a short episode of madness, a short but intense moment that shakes the roots of Robinson Crusoe's well-ordered universe (whereas the actual appearance of the cannibals leaves him perfectly composed).

Another example brings us closer to our point. On some of Balzac's manuscripts, we find brownish circles, obviously the imprints of his famous coffee cup. This is certainly as striking to the beholder as a photograph of Balzac—it carries the kind of hallucinatory, mediumistic power described by Barthes. The strokes of Balzac's pen on the page are a slightly different kind of imprint, but they have a similar status. It is easy to see that they carry a much more complex signification of the same order because, to take up Barthes's terminology, the writer, in this very peculiar photographic process, is at the same time the operator (he is using pen and paper to take a kind of picture) and the spectrum (the surface of the paper records an image—perhaps even a film—of him in the process of writing), but also the spectator (the author's gaze on his own manuscript is encapsulated in his revisions and deletions).

The first page of *Camera Lucida* expresses Barthes's amazement in front of the portrait of Jerome Bonaparte: "I am looking at the eyes that looked at the Emperor" (3). The power of the manuscript is similar: Balzac (or Flaubert or Joyce) has seen this page. My eyes meet theirs on the page. Balzac is looking at me through those large, brownish eyes of the coffee marks, as well as through every line and every erasure on the page.[8]

The Particular and the Genetic

Another bridge between Barthes's conception of photography and the "avant-texte" is their common relation to the Aristotelian "Tuché":

> What the Photograph reproduces to infinity has occurred only once: the Photograph mechanically repeats what could never be repeated existentially. In the Photograph, the event is never transcended for the sake of something else: the Photograph always leads the corpus I need back to the body I see; it is the absolute Particular, the sovereign Contingency, matte and somehow stupid, the *This* (this photograph, and not Photography), in short, what Lacan calls the *Tuché,* the Occasion, the Encounter, the Real, in its indefatigable expression. (*CL,* 4)

This is particularly interesting if we read it as an indirect reference to the iterability of the text, as opposed to the unicity of the utterance, which translates itself, at another level, as the difference between the a posteriori necessity of the text and the radical contingency of enunciation as it can be grasped in the manuscript.

This radical contingency does not mean that nothing can be said about photographs or manuscripts, that no law can be posited, that we can never go beyond the *mathesis singularis* that Barthes imagines in his last book. For beyond the individual, according to Barthes, there is precisely the genetic:

> the Photograph sometimes makes appear what we never see in a real face (or in a face reflected in a mirror): a genetic feature, the fragment of oneself or of a relative which comes from some ancestor. [. . .] The Photograph gives a little truth, on condition that it parcels out the body. But this truth is not that of the individual, who remains irreducible; it is the truth of lineage. (*CL*, 103)

Or,

> *Lineage* reveals an identity stronger, more interesting than legal status—more reassuring as well, for the thought of origins soothes us, whereas that of the future disturbs us, agonizes us; but this discovery disappoints us because even while it asserts a permanence (which is the truth of the race, not my own), it bares the mysterious difference of beings issuing from one and the same family: what relation can there be between my mother and her ancestor, so formidable, so monumental, so Hugolian, so much the incarnation of the inhuman distance of the Stock. (*CL*, 105)

"Truth of lineage," "genetic essence," "difference of beings issuing from one and the same family": no transposition is necessary here to apply this to manuscripts, versions, related drafts of a text.

Dupin's Flaw

In his "Introduction to the Structural Analysis of Narratives," Barthes offers what he calls a kind of fable based on Poe's "The Purloined Letter" and the failure of the Paris police chief to find the letter:

> He [the police chief] "saturated" the level of "search"; but in order to find the letter—protected by its conspicuousness—it was essential to pass to another level, to substitute the concealer's pertinence for that of the policeman. In the same way, complete as the "search" performed on a horizontal group of narrative relations may be, in order to be effective it must also be oriented "vertically": meaning is not "at the end" of narrative, it traverses it; quite as conspicuous as the *purloined letter*, it similarly escapes any unilateral exploration. (*SC*, 102)

The two dimensions of investigation appear as complementary to each other, but there is another possibility that neither Dupin nor the chief of police seems to have imagined: that the minister might have chosen to conceal the letter in a different room every day. Since the rooms are thoroughly searched one by one by the police, this would have been a perfect method of concealment. It is a possibility that Barthes did not consider either, at least until his last book, in which he wrote that "in the Photograph, what I posit is not only the absence of the object, it is also, by one and the same movement, on equal terms, the fact that this object has indeed existed and that it has been there where I see it" (*CL*, 115); or, more generally, when he considered the juxtaposition of different temporalities "under the instance of 'reality'."

This possibility (the possibility of a mobile configuration, of a historicization of presence) opens up a third dimension, which cuts across the text; is neither horizontal nor vertical, or rather is one and the other, since it is of a paradigmatic order (and thus vertical); and yet is oriented, vectorialized. It is precisely in that dimension that genetic criticism dwells and meets the final Barthes.

Notes

1. Translation is mine. The original French reads: "On pourrait dire que l'image filmique est du génétique pur, face à une recherche structurale qui implique précisément, du moins dans son exposé, une stabilisation, et comme une atemporalité des fonctions repérées. Mais c'est précisément parce que le hiatus entre genèse et structure, procès et tableau, embarasse encore profondément l'épistémologie moderne, qu'il ne faut pas hésiter à s'y attaquer de front" (*OC1*, 875).

2. My translation. "Écrire," preface to *La Civilisation de l'écriture* by Roger Duret and Herman Grégorie (1976), *OC3*, 422–423.

3. This is very close to the attitude denounced in *Criticism and Truth*: "We are generally inclined, at least today, to believe that that author can lay a claim to the meaning of his work and can himself make that its legal meaning; from this notion flows the unreasonable interrogation directed by the critic at the dead writer, at his life, at the traces of his intentions, so that he himself can guarantee the meaning of his work" (*CT*, 75–76).

4. As elsewhere in this paper, I am using "enunciation" to translate the French *énonciation.* "Speech act," used in the official translations, often seems misleading.

5. See Philippe Roger's analysis of this typical Barthesian trope in *Roland Barthes, roman* (Paris: Grasset, 1986), pp. 142–46.

6. "Obviousness" would be a more accurate translation of *évidence,* but the forensic connotation of "evidence" is welcome in this context.

7. Umberto Eco, *A Theory of Semiotics* (Bloomington: Indiana University Press, 1979), 222 n.

8. In this matter, the gaze should not be confused with the eye, and the photographic representation of the human eye is not the crucial point. Barthes

himself refuted such an identification as soon as he had posited it about film, in which, as opposed to photography, looking at the camera is strictly forbidden: "[I]t is forbidden for an actor to look at the camera, i.e., at the spectator. I am not far from considering this ban as the cinema's distinctive feature. This art *severs* the gaze: one of us gazes at the other, does only that: it is my right and my duty to gaze; the other never gazes; he gazes at everything, except me. If a single gaze from the screen came to rest on me, the whole film would be lost. But this is only the literal truth. For it can happen that, on another, invisible level, the screen [. . .] does not cease gazing at me" (*RF*, 242).

17

Roland Barthes Abroad

Dalia Kandiyoti

In a 1977 interview for the *Nouvel Observateur*, Bernard-Henry Lévy asked Roland Barthes about his much criticized acceptance of a lunch invitation from Giscard d'Estaing. Barthes began his reply, "[A] myth-hunter, as you know, must hunt everywhere" (*GV*, 269). Barthes, as semiologist, linguist, cultural critic, and literary theorist, disseminated himself in the landscape of myths, left and right, high and low. I argue that texts he wrote in the late 1960s and 1970s—*The Empire of Signs*, the preface to Pierre Loti's 1879 *Aziyadé*, *Alors la Chine?*,[1] and "Incidents"—remythify, in however Barthesian a manner, the difficulties of travel and representation. Formulated as an escape from the old myths, Barthes's travel writing partly effects a remystification that stands on the shoulders of one of the most irrepressible mythmaking modes of reading, that is, of exoticism. As a particular way of perceiving and representing difference, exoticism is far from being an antediluvian literary practice, but very much on the current agenda not only in terms of its extant forms in the domain of popular culture and mythologies but also in the domain of the theory and practice of cross-cultural discourse. I present some of the most characteristic features of fin-de-siècle exoticism, which seems to have had the most lasting effect on our century, through an introduction to Pierre Loti as a backdrop to Barthes's travel writings and through Barthes's essay on Loti.[2]

The glowing preface Barthes writes is for the 1971 reprinting of Pierre Loti's "Turkish novel," *Aziyadé*. Who is this "minor, *démodé* author" (*NCE*, 18) Barthes admires so much? The unspeakable Pierre Loti (pen name for Julien Viaud), was a high-placed career officer in the French navy as well as a Turcophile, diplomat, dandy, and, most important, author of numerous works largely perceived to epitomize nineteenth-century exoticism. His admirers were many and quite diverse: Proust could recite whole passages of *Aziyadé* by heart;[3] Henry James wrote rhapsodic prefaces to his novels. Anatole France and Alphonse Daudet were friends and supporters, as was Edmond de Goncourt. Not all of his fans were literary or even armchair travelers. About a century ago, the majority of French Naval School entry candidates named their readings of Jules Verne and Pierre Loti as their chief inspiration for naval careers.[4]

As an influential officer of the French navy, Loti was a diplomatic negotiator, especially on behalf of the Ottoman cause. After becoming a Turcophile on his very first visit (*Aziyadé* being the trace of the trip), he published many volumes and pamphlets in which he deplored the European appetite for Ottoman lands. However, loyal to his vision of the Orient as the space of constancy, he was at the same time strongly opposed to the contemporary attempts to infuse the Ottoman monarchy with democracy. He always acted in the interests of France, advocating a return of the Ottoman Empire, in its traditional albeit disintegrating state, back to the sphere of French influence, away from the British. Pierre Loti, a servant of empire, belongs firmly in the tradition of colonial literature.

Exemplifying the coupling of writing and empire in the colonial context, Loti's vocation was always double. A member of the French Academy at an exceptionally young age, Loti was also a glorified personification of the sailor myth: disembarkation at a foreign port, the inevitable sensuous encounter(s), tattoos, and the return. But Loti's other vocation was *writing* about his *dépaysement*, his conquests, his multiple displacements into "native" modes of being. Like contemporary tourists, he despised tourists and lamented the monocultural turn the world was taking, but unlike most of them he immersed himself completely in the native culture at every port, adopting local dress, habits, language, and women. Ottoman Turkey was his favorite habitat, but he slipped in and out of Arab, Southeast Asian, African, Far Eastern, and Pacific-island life in a Zelig-like fashion.

Although, like every travel writer, Loti supplied his readers with descriptions of local ways, he did not engage in conscious pseudo-ethnography as did, for example, Lafcadio Hearn in his turn-of-the-century books on Japan. Like Barthes, Pierre Loti chose not to be a cultural translator but to personalize boldly his own experience of the traveled space. His fragmented narratives remain at the level of personal impressions and reminiscences and rarely emulate the authoritative, realistic travel accounts masquerading as ethnography, whose aim is "objective" representation. Defying genre boundaries, blurring the categories of fact and fiction, each of Loti's narratives is a mélange of autobiography, travel writing, and diary form.

In these writings, the *ailleurs* is completely codified. Despite locational differences, Loti, the literary machine, churns out the same story each and every time. Traveling only puts him in a *situation d'écriture* and his discourse, in the best colonizer tradition, "turns on the recognition and disavowal of racial/cultural/historical differences."[5] The mechanical reproduction of identical *mise-en-scènes* in novel after novel in which the white man meets, loves, and leaves the woman of color—or the woman of difference—allows the colonial (colonizing) writer to project himself onto the conquerable and interchangeable landscapes. The writer and protagonist infiltrate the traveled space by going native, by a thorough immersion in the local cultures and the adoption of local dress and lifestyles. In Istanbul, Loti becomes a Turk whom no Turk can tell from a real one. "Passing," whether for Turkish, Japanese, or Tahitian, seems to be the penetrating drive of travel and writing. The identification required in passing also excuses the objectification of the other. The traveler becomes one of "them," so that he can command, study, or write from within, with both a good conscience and intimate knowledge of the insider.

In addition to a privileged vantage point, going native allows the traveler to indulge in a mourning of what one has destroyed. This is a "particular kind of nostalgia, often found under imperialism, where people mourn the passing of what they themselves have transformed. Imperialist nostalgia thus revolves around a paradox: a person kills somebody and then mourns his or her victim."[6] Pierre Loti is a master mourner. As a temporary "native," he is able to take both a melancholy and critical stance toward Westernization in Turkey or in Japan for destroying difference, for leaving nothing to penetrate. His work is full of apostrophes and lamentations expressing his imperialist nostalgia as the original passes away in favor of inauthenticity and mimicry.

Thus, the encounter with the other is essentially a mimetic one in which self and other collapse. In the colonial chamber of mirrors,[7] the adventure of difference comes home to narcissistic self-projection. And of course, Barthes's utopian project involves an escape from precisely this collapse of difference. But the flip side of exoticism involves an extreme estrangement and alienation from the other, the necessary tactic of subjugation. An embodiment of threatening alterity, the colonized subject becomes, as Abdul JanMohammed has written, "no more than a recipient of the negative elements of the self that the European projects onto him."[8]

For the most part, Loti's 1887 *Madame Chrysanthème*, his "Japanese" novel, dutifully obeys the Pierre Loti script. As expected, once he meets a Japanese woman through a "temporary marriage" broker whom he pays handsomely, the writer/sailor immediately acclimatizes. Loti and his "wife" live in a traditionally furnished Japanese house in a Japanese neighborhood, wear only Japanese clothing, eat Japanese food, and amuse themselves with Japanese activities. If, in Michel de Certeau's words, the travel text "is the witness of the other,"[9] it is, in Loti's case, a witness of oneself *as* the other. With his various props—local woman, house, dress, all punctuated with a tattoo—Loti writes himself Japanese. According to Mario Praz, "the real exoticist gives primary importance to pageantry,"[10] and pageantry for Loti is requisite for happiness abroad and at home.[11] Loti loves pomp and circumstance and, above all, costume. Perhaps, his military career was an extension of a technology of the self expressed in serious dressing up (naval costume) and dressing down (in the native mode). His self-grooming was always meticulous, and he took care to keep up a fit and athletic look. Richard Sieburth once said that he may have been "the first bodybuilder in French literature."

In spite of the fulfillment of his desire for "authentic" staging, Loti is malcontent in Japan. The country to him is all form and no feeling, all decoration and no substance, indeed a dollhouse. The people are cold and ridiculous in their smallness. He finds Japan devoid of meaning, composed of purely aesthetic objects that he sometimes appreciates and mostly ridicules. But, with his love of pageantry, costume, decorative objects, and going fully native, it is of course Loti who aestheticizes the *ailleurs.*

Loti's last act in this vigorous consumption of signs is the inscription of a tiny symbol of Japan onto his body—a tattoo. Just as a *récit de voyage* serves as a trace of the trip, so does the tattoo.[12] His body, which is the site of many other tattoos, in memory of Aziyadé, of Rarahu, is like a well-worn passport marked by many exit stamps. The tattoo is a memento, an unperishable Japanese signifier, a curio. Loti treats the world as an exotic flea market, collecting signs without reading them.

The double movement, typical of exoticism, of rendering the exotic place as familiar, predictable, and interchangeable with others while simultaneously perceiving it as incomprehensible and unaccountably different (and in Loti's case, sinister) occurs in *Aziyadé* as well as in *Madame Chrysanthème.* In the preface to *Aziyadé,* Barthes brackets both the exoticist and colonialist context of Loti's work. The preface is an essay in which the *démodé* turns into modernist writing and a campy nineteenth-century author becomes an innovator. In Barthes's rereading of *Aziyadé,* a mirroring effect between Barthes and Loti takes place. Barthes calls Loti a *démodé* author, and this is the word he uses to refer to his own life: "Subtracted from the book, his life was continuously a *démodé* subject" (*RB,* 125). Barthes detaches Loti's novel from its received association with colonialist representation and places it in the quintessentially Barthesian realm of in-betweenness, that of the drift, or *dérive.* According to Barthes, floating indeterminately between ambiguous positions, Pierre Loti writes out a pure signifier of displacement. The novel's hero, Loti, is neither Pierre Loti the author nor Julien Viaud the officer. The identity of the narrator is often blurred but not identical with the identity and history of the author. As to whether he is a tourist or resident, Loti's status is both and neither. Despite his adoption of Ottoman dress and language, he retains a psychic distance. Moreover, as others besides Barthes point out,[13] Loti's is an ambiguous sexuality on tour: implicit homosexual yearnings accompany explicit heterosexual affairs. Barthes determinedly brings out the implicit; in effect he brilliantly queers *Aziyadé*.[14] He points to the novel's subtext of gay desire between the hero Loti and his Ottoman sidekicks: "A motif appears here—which is visible in other places as well: no, *Aziyadé* is not altogether a novel for well-brought up girls, it is also a minor Sodomite epic, studded with allusions to *something unheard-of and shadowy*" (*NCE*, 111).

Ambivalence and plotless writing of the nonevent are coupled in *Aziyadé*, as they are in *Madame Chrysanthème*: "In other words, *nothing* happens. Yet this *nothing* must be said" (*NCE*, 108). For Roland Barthes, the business of *écriture* is establishing a discourse without referring to anything (and this is accomplished by saying *nothing* [*NCE*, 109]). A fragmentation of meaning takes place through the writing of "not an adventure, but *incidents*" (*NCE*, 108), Barthes writes, echoing his own future text. A fragmentation of the self occurs in Loti's lust for passing, his Ottoman masquerade. In what he calls Loti's transvestism, his adoption of local "costumes" and blending into local color like a "native," Barthes sees "a subject [who] dissolves himself [. . .] by participation in a proportion, in a combination system" (*NCE*, 116). Loti's propensity for self-dissolution strikes at the heart of what one critic called Barthes's quest "to effect multiple displacements which generate self-dispersion and a movement toward ontological emptiness."[15] This is especially true of *Roland Barthes by Roland Barthes*, in which the playful move between subject and object positions is most pronounced.

Barthes clearly reads Loti backward from himself. Leaving aside the obvious biographical mirroring between the two authors (both of them Protestant, lovers of men), his preface shows us that what Barthes sees in *Aziyadé* are echoes, prefigurings of Barthesian writing. The most important of these are the notions of the drift, self-displacement, the fragment, the play of signifiers, and the writing of the nothing. Yet, as we have seen, the much-desired inscription of the *rien* takes its cues from a colonial project. Where one might see in Loti's *Aziyadé* an Orient that is the space of a "sick man" and death, a woman who is nothing but a blank space, a wish for a picturesque, static despotism, Barthes sees the writing of nothing. Where one might see a colonial officer gone native yet retaining a psychic outsiderness that affords him both the insider and the dominating outsider roles, Barthes sees an ambiguous subjectivity, floating between mimesis and alterity, refusing to choose between positions until forced to do so.

But is Loti effecting a transvestism or a masquerade? The difference between the two concepts has been discussed, in relation to femininity, by the early twentieth-century analyst Joan Riviere[16] and recent feminist film theory. Transvestism is an oscillation between subject positions. It signifies mobility between femininity and masculinity and, in our case, self and the cultural other. A masquerade, however, goes against the grain of transvestism, in that what is paraded (exaggerated femininity or, here, cultural otherness) is acknowledged to be a mask. By performing, exhibiting an excess of cultural otherness, otherness is held far away. In the feminist film theorist Mary Ann Doane's words, "to masquerade is to manufacture a lack in the form of a certain distance between oneself and one's image."[17] So, the identification staged in going native plays out its opposite, alienation. And in fact, despite his full native getup and authentically local lifestyle, Loti is always estranged from his milieu. In all his novels, there are endless passages written in purple prose about a melancholic sense of detachment and alienation, which usually results in a perception of the traveled space as alien, sinister, and inferior.

For Barthes, however, desire, not domination, is the central axis of *Aziyadé*. It illuminates Loti's relation to the political and the historical: "desire always proceeds toward an extreme archaism, where the greatest historical distance assures the greatest unreality, there where desire finds its pure form: that of an impossible return, that of the Impossible (but in writing it, this regression will disappear)" (*NCE*, 117). But how exactly will the regression disappear through the sheer feat of writing? The archaizing nature of (Loti's) desire has been the motor of too many narratives of orientalism and exoticism. Barthes writes that *Aziyadé* is "the novel of Drift" because of "the notion that desire is a force adrift" (*NCE*, 119). Detaching it from any moorings, Barthes disengages desire from grounding and turns his critical gaze away from the political vulgarity of *Aziyadé*.

Reading the preface to Loti's novel along with *The Empire of Signs* (the two texts were written very close in time), we witness an unfolding of the same kind of poetics of liquidation. Given "our incognizance of Asia by means of certain known languages (the Orient of Voltaire, of the *Revue Asiatique*, of Pierre Loti, or of Air France)" (*ES*, 4), writes Barthes, "an enormous labor of *knowledge* is and will be necessary." However, in this text he will leave aside the "vast regions of darkness (capitalist Japan, American acculturation, technological development)" and occupy himself with flashes of light, the rupture of the symbolic, with a Zen-like "exemption from meaning" (*ES*, 4). The Orient is a space of liquidation—of meaning, intelligibility, the signified.

One of the most fundamental satisfactions of travel in Japan is the loss of meaning, the unintelligibility that not knowing a language affords. In the same interview with Lévy, Barthes says, "It's a very restful thing, not to understand a language. All vulgarity is eliminated, all stupidity, all aggression" (*GV*, 264). Barthes's trip has been mapped by several critics (Higgins, Porter, Lowe) in terms of an inward return, an attempt toward a reconquest of the infantile, imaginary, prelinguistic state of being, the "state of infancy (infans: incapable of speech)".[18] The trip is equated with the infancy and the maternal, afforded by not knowing a language.

The most graphemic culture he has encountered, Japan unravels itself and opens up to Barthes like a beautifully wrapped, inscribed, layered package that contains nothing. Japan is truly the land of vacation, of *vacare*, emptying.[19] There are no binary oppositions, which plague Western thought, no center (upside down, a room looks the same, the city center is a void), no content (women carry empty bags on their backs; the gift is in the wrapping). Culture is a compendium of, in Lynn Higgins's words, an "esthetics of gesture" (167). Barthes inscribes a landscape of empty signs. His voyage constitutes an escape from an essentializing mode of perception into a mode of unintelligibility, a celebration of signs without content, a retreat into form and gesture.

Barthes's Japan does not exist outside the covers of the beautiful Skira edition. Compromising no "real country by [his] fantasy," Barthes "can isolate somewhere in the world . . . a certain number of features, and out of these features deliberately form a system" (*ES*, 3). In *The Empire of Signs*, Japan is in quotation marks; it is an invention, a construct. *The Empire of Signs* is a journey away from the facts, or even a knowledge of Japan, toward a fiction. This fiction is without a story; it is composed of a string of elements that Barthes would call the "novelistic" (*le romanesque*)—unstructured, unstoried fragments featuring the handpicked signifiers of Japanese culture.

But why are all the signs of which Barthes so joyously writes "politically innocent" ones? Barthes's highly selective eye is fixated on "traditional" aspects of Japanese culture. From theater, food, clothing, social forms, religion, poetry, the "indigenous" is privileged to be a part of Barthes's Japan. With the exception of the game *pachinko*, most elements of Japanese life Barthes engages are "age-old." Modern Japanese customs, cuisine, literature, economic and political systems—all of which carry indelible traces of the West—are absent. In his fiction of Japan, there is a quasi erasure of the contemporary in favor of an Ur-Japan, as it can be imagined before foreign contamination (and the subsequent collapse of difference). One of the chief features of exoticism is the experience of the *ailleurs* as a static realm beyond history, forever playing out an originary scenario.

Stripped of their present and historical context, Japanese cultural productions are easily transformed into exclusively aesthetic objects. Aestheticism of the other is a factor in mythifying the experience of the *ailleurs*. It is a practice of which Loti is a master. To him all is a cadre, costume, the staging of a beautiful tableau. The self-orchestrated absence of Western constructs is an occasion for joy and enchantment for Barthes. An extended process of naming (without classifying) accompanies Barthes's trip. We fully savor the words *Kabuki, sashimi, Mu, Ku, pachinko, Bunraku, tempura.*[20] Japan is a garden of delights.

In the discourse of fin-de-siècle exoticism, Japan was a mythical, fairyland-like country in the imagination of most Westerners.[21] Clean, delicate, subtle, Japan was otherworldly—a storybook kingdom. Rudyard Kipling, who visited Japan in the late 1880s, (appreciatively) calls Japan a "Fairyland" numerous times in his collection of travel writings. Despite his journalistic bent, he scarcely touches on the political developments in a Japan that was at the time busily adjusting to Western-style capitalism and cultivating imperialistic ambitions in the area. Kipling opposes Japan's adoption of democratic procedure and writes that Japan has swapped its soul for a constitution. He believes this land of "clean, capable, dainty, designful people" should not be a part of messy world affairs but that it would be better to put the whole empire in a glass case and mark it "'*Hors concours*,' Exhibit A."[22] Loti also wholly ignores a Japan under radical transformation and consumes ageless Japanese signs.

Barthes's treatment of Japan, whether in quotes or not, harks back to a fairytale treatment of the country. In *The Empire of Signs*, where Barthes, as I quoted above, will "leave aside vast regions of darkness" and concentrate instead on the flashes of light, his poetics of liquidation is expressed in the exoticizing binarism of light and dark. For Barthes, it is the Western-influenced elements of Japan that are in the realm of darkness. The "slender thread of light" (*ES*, 4) seeks and finds the uncontaminated Japan.

The euphoric emphasis on the ahistorical,[23] unadulterated aspects of Japanese culture that form "his" Japan is bound up with an old exoticism that assumes an absolute difference and denies hybridity. (The one exception to this denial of hybridity is the picture of himself "Japanned.") The strict opposition between inside and outside, native and foreigner, that Barthes draws on to establish his position in Japan seems to keep binarisms intact. He is an outsider and therefore will not comment. As Homi Bhabha has written, "In order to understand the productivity of colonial power it is crucial to construct its regime of truth, not to subject its representations to a normalizing judgment. Only then does it become possible to understand the *productive* ambivalence of the object of colonial discourse—that 'otherness' which is at once an object of desire and derision, an articulation of difference contained within the fantasy of origin and identity."[24] The search for a happy alterity, unadulterated by the oppressive weight of Western meaning systems, an "us" as opposed to "them" discourse, falls back into a quest for authenticity and results in an erasure of *métissage* that represses all (historical) mediation.

I am arguing here for a partial representational continuity in time, an intersection between the projects of Barthes and of exoticism, not an identity. After all, Barthes is aware of the long-standing narcissism of the self-mirroring languages "of Voltaire, Loti, or Air France," that is, of exoticism. In *The Empire of Signs,* there is no identification with the "local," no mourning for the death of the other, no transvestism or going native. Whereas Loti and Kipling infantilize the native other, Barthes infantilizes only himself in the other space, though Japan does become, as Abdelkebir Khatibi has written, "a space of play."[25] Instead of knowing the other, an impossibility, Barthes allows otherness to write itself onto him: this is exemplified in his glee at the altering of his features, at having been "Japanned," in a Japanese newspaper illustration he reproduces in *The Empire of Signs.* Delighting in this metamorphosis, this fulfillment of his drive toward a "loss of self" of the 1970s, Barthes enjoys "passing," but his passing is not a penetrating, self-constructed one.

In *Nous et les autres* (1989), Todorov suggests that exoticism is more a formulation of an ideal than a critique of the real. But in constructing a utopia of absolute difference, based on liquidation and absence—of representation, of meaning, of plenitude—the repressed returns: through the aesthetics of the void, Barthes flirts with an exoticism of reverie and potentially alienating difference.

Although *Alors la Chine?* is also an account of a void, of nothing, in it we find that the 1974 Chinese trip fails to inspire in Barthes the enchanted writing pleasure he had found in Japan and Morocco. Flat like its countryside, China affords little passion. Lévy asks him why he wrote hardly anything after he returned from China. Barthes replies: "I wrote very little, but I saw and listened to everything with close attention and interest. Writing demands something else, however, some kind of piquancy in addition to what is seen and heard, something that I didn't find in China" (*GV,* 265). Lacking "some kind of piquancy" (in French, "un sel quelconque"), China for him is uniform (as in the dress of its inhabitants) and bland. Not only is it tasteless, but the country is also colorless: "China is not colorful. The countryside is flat [. . .] no historical object interrupts it; in the distance two gray oxen, a tractor

[. . .] a group of workers dressed in blue, that is all [. . .]," and further "[I have hallucinated] China as an object situated beyond color, beyond strong taste and brutal sense" (*Alors*, 9, 14). In contrast to the eminently savory Japan, China does not create for him the same link between *savoir* and *saveur*. As with Japan, China is also a staging of the nothing to Barthes: "in one sense, we come back (outside of the political response) with nothing" (*Alors*, 7). But this "nothing" is not shot through with the pleasures of signs, with desire. For Barthes, the writing of travel has to be grounded in desire. He tells Lévy, "Signs in themselves are never enough for me, I must have the desire to read them [. . .] In China, I found absolutely no possibility of erotic, sensual, or amorous interest or investment" (*GV*, 265).

Barthes avoids a writing of "local color," a chief feature of exoticist texts. But from these few pages, China emerges, as does Japan in *The Empire of Signs*, as the site of absolute difference. In *Critical Terrains*, Lisa Lowe argues that Barthes's observation that China is not colorful "posits China *in opposition* to the pervasive and overdetermined Occidental systems of signification." "[China is not colorful] is a manner of saying that China is not 'colonized' [. . .] and therefore offers to the western subject one pure, irreducible site from which western ideologies can be criticized."[26] Here, as in Japan, Barthes revels in the loss of meaning and in the capacity of China to arouse in him the feminine and the mother.

This China, which is "eminently prosaic," has a political text that is omnipresent, that speaks only one language. The idiom of a cultural revolution pervades China, and there is no other. "China is peaceful," Barthes writes (*Alors*, 10). "Is not peace [. . .] this region, utopian for us, where the war of meaning is abolished?" Again, a utopian project enters into writing about the traveled space.[27] In *The Pleasure of the Text*, under the section "Guerre" (war), Barthes describes the competition among languages using the vocabulary of bellicosity that reminded me of the "war of meaning" he refers to in *Alors la Chine?*: "we are all caught up in the truth of languages [. . .] each jargon fights for hegemony, if power is on its side, it spreads everywhere [. . .] it becomes doxa [. . .] but even out of power, even when power is against it, the rivalry is reborn, the jargons are split and struggle among themselves. A ruthless *topic* rules the life of language: language always comes from some place, it is a warrior *topos*" (*Alors*, 28). China, for Barthes, is peaceful because there is only one political language. But to what other place have the other languages gone? To what end? The desire for a political utopia results in an evasion of existing oppositional discourses and therefore, once again, of political realities. China's "texte politique" is "everywhere [. . .] in the discourses we heard, Nature (the natural, the eternal) speaks no longer." This monolingual space, in which mythologizing Nature cannot rear its ugly head, is not enthralling or arousing to Barthes. However boring or colorless, it still appeals to a pacific, utopian vision that runs parallel with exoticizing discourse in that it eliminates complexity, resistance, and difference within the language, within the political text of China.[28]

The risky enterprise of utopian discourse seems to be absent from "Incidents," the essay that appeared in 1987 in the eponymous volume published amid considerable controversy. "Incidents" is a text Barthes scholars have by and large avoided until very recently.[29] With its bland account of his homoerotic *rencontres* with young Moroccan men and untroubled awareness of the politics of mutual exploitation embedded in sexual tourism, "Incidents" seems to some to be all too personal and private for the public eye. Yet François Wahl's introduction tells us that Barthes wished to publish his Moroccan diary in *Tel Quel*.

In *Roland Barthes by Roland Barthes* there is a reference to "white writing, exempt from any literary theater" in a list of "Figures of the Neutral." "Displacement" appears in that same list along with "drifting" and "jouissance" (*RB*, 132). This diary, written in fragments of usually not more than two sentences, seems to be an exercise in blandness, a feat of neutral writing. I mentioned before that among the encomiums of *Aziyadé*, Barthes counts the writing of *incidents*. I see another doubling, another mirroring effect between Barthes and another writer in Barthes's 1979 preface to Renaud Camus's *Tricks*, which Barthes says "speak[s], and bluntly, about sex, about homosexuality" (*RL*, 291). He admires the simplicity, the sparseness, the neutrality of the writing of *Tricks*: "Our period interprets a great deal, but Renaud Camus's narratives are neutral, they do not participate in the game of interpretation. They are surfaces without shadows, without *ulterior motives*" (*RL*, 292). What Barthes says is the haikuesque "asceticism of form" (we hear the modernist nausea regarding ornamentation if we think back to Adolf Loos and Barthes's own essay, "Ornamental Cooking" [in *Mythologies*], in which ornament is deceptive, mythical), the hedonism, the lack of depth, applies not only to Camus's *Tricks* but also to "Incidents."

To compose these bare writings in degree zero, Barthes, like Loti, conceives of the traveled space in terms of the possibility of sensuous adventure, of erotic opportunity. In Morocco, Barthes is not the pilgrim he was in Japan. Here, there is no semiofetishism; no Moroccan cultural signifiers leap up at him, enveloping his body. Here, the erotics of the "third world" are most prominent. Sparse and crisp, the fragments relate a politics of the gaze, a touristic being there that is fully aware of objectifying and being objectified: "Chella park: a tall youth with straight hair, dressed all in white, ankle boots under the white jeans, accompanied by his two veiled sisters, stares hard at me and spits: rejection or contingency?" (*IN*, 27). Barthes writes himself as a trick and a john. The sheer anonymity, the absence of the critical trace in these fragments, delivers a surprise.

"Incidents" appears in *Roland Barthes by Roland Barthes* as one of his "book projects": "*Incidents* (mini-textes, haikus, one-liners, puns, everything that falls like a leaf)." Among the other planned books is a "*Compilation of Visual Stereotypes*" (*IN*, 150). Indeed, in reading "Incidents," I was struck by the way in which "local color" is provided mostly through haiku-like renderings of the young Moroccan men. As much as it is a travel diary, "Incidents" is also a book of physiognomies. Local color is provided, not by spatial descriptions of Morocco but by the faces and bodies of the "local coloreds." The country is not even a backdrop. Whatever glimpses of Morocco we get are mostly from the words and bodies of Abdelkebir, Driss, Mustafa, and many others. Unlike in China and Japan, the local people are highly visible, displayed here at their most sensuous and mercenary. Extremely frank about the constant transactions and exchanges of money and sex, Barthes seems to be flinging stereotypes right in our face: "The little Marrakech schoolteacher: 'I'll do whatever you want,' he says, effusively, his eyes filled with kindness and complicity. Which means: *I'll fuck you*, and that's all." In this text, which perhaps we might call his own "blue" guide to Morocco,[30] it is taken for granted that the occidental tourist pays for his roving desire: "I'm afraid I'm falling in love with you. It's a problem. What should I do?—Give me your address" (*IN*, 27). Occasionally, the fulfillment of stereotypes results in a boredom marked by a cruel indifference. He writes: "A girl begging: 'My father's dead. It's to buy a notebook,' etc. (The nasty part of mendicancy is the tedium of stereotypes)."

As a possible intertext for "Incidents," Gide's 1906 *Amyntas* seems very appropriate, although it is comprised of the journals of Gide's travels in Tunisia and Algeria, rather than in Morocco.[31] In a preface to this work, Gide states that he originally wanted to write a "serious book" on North Africa, concerned with economic, ethnological, geographical questions. Instead, he offers a body of spontaneous writings, random jottings, in which the narrator—a *flâneur*—floats ambiguously between exoticism and what Richard Howard calls in the afterword of his translation of the book "disenchanted scrutiny" and "disintoxication" (157–58). In Gide's text, languor, emptiness, and desire figure as prominently as in Barthes's "Incidents." Instead of mastery, both Gide and Barthes thematize a distance.

Most of all, however, reading *Amyntas* along with "Incidents" helps to think about Barthes's text as a work in the pastoral genre. Howard tells us Amyntas is a "name borrowed from the Theocritan canon, later assigned by Virgil to a shepherd of enterprising but melancholy eros" (157). Virgil is a refuge for Gide: "This morning I feel a tremendous resentment against this country, and I withdraw from it desperately [. . . .] Finally [when turning to music fails], I take a copy of Virgil out of my bag and reread the Eclogue to Pollio" (81). Can we read "Incidents" as a version of pastoral, the description of an imaginary universe emptied of politics? Avoiding a sociohistorical contextualization of travel in the colonized space, Barthes's accounts of meetings with the locals are stripped to the bare bones of man-to-man (almost always) encounter orchestrated by the mutual gaze. Barthes temporarily distances himself from the violence of social and political expenditure, and once again being *ailleurs*, incognizant of the language(s), affords him to do just that.

The journey, fragmented and dismembered, is written in atheatrical patches. "With the alibi of a pulverized discourse, a dissertation destroyed, one arrives at the regular practice of the fragment, then from the fragment, one slips into the 'journal' " (*RB*, 95). A way of returning to his first love (his first work was on Gide) the journal may also afford him not only the comfort of the "initial text" but also the *frisson*, once again, of the *démodé*: "The (autobiographical) 'journal' is, nowadays, discredited" (*RB*, 95). The journal is passé, *démodé*, and Barthes will dare to take it up, perhaps because he believes the writer in contemporary culture is a phantasm, someone unimaginable separately from his or her work. For him, "the writer as we can see him in his private diary [is] *the writer minus his work*: the supreme form of the sacred: the mark and the void" (*RB*, 82, his emphasis). It is precisely this phantasmic quality as a writer that he enacts in "Incidents," his memorable indiscretion, which offers the dual presence of both the familiar Barthesian trace and its disaffected withdrawal, the void. In similar moves witnessed in *The Empire of Signs* and *Alors la Chine?* Barthes teases us with intimations of *démodé*, Lotiesque tourism, now turning exoticism on its head and then reveling in its discontents.

Notes

A small portion of this essay overlaps with my article, "Exoticism Then and Now: The Travels of Pierre Loti and Roland Barthes in Japan," *History of European Ideas* 20 (January 1995): 391–97. I would like to express my gratitude to Richard Sieburth for his invaluable comments and suggestions on earlier drafts.

1. Roland Barthes, *Alors la Chine?* (Paris: Christian Bourgeois, 1975). Hereafter cited in the text as *Alors.*

2. The main texts I allude to are Pierre Loti, *Aziyadé* and *Madame Chrysanthème,* in *Pierre Loti* (Paris: Presses de la Cité, 1989); *Japoneries d'automne* (Paris: Calmann-Lévy, 1889); and *La Troisième jeunesse de Madame Prune* (Paris: Calmann-Lévy, 1905).

3. See Leslie Blanch, *Pierre Loti: The Legendary Romantic* (New York: Carroll and Graf, 1985).

4. Alec G. Hargreaves, *The Colonial Experience in French Fiction: A Study of Pierre Loti, Ernest Psichari, and Pierre Mille* (London: Macmillan, 1981), p. 82.

5. Homi K. Bhabha, "The Other Question: Stereotype, Discrimination, and the Discourse of Colonialism," in *The Location of Culture* (London and New York: Routledge, 1994), p. 70.

6. Renato Rosaldo, "Imperialist Nostalgia," *Representations* 26 (1989): 109.

7. Tzvetan Todorov, *Nous et les autres: La Refléxion française sur la diversité humaine* (Paris: Seuil, 1989).

8. Abdul R. JanMohammed, "The Economy of Manichean Allegory: The Function of Racial Difference in Colonialist Literature," in *Race, Writing, and Difference*, ed. Henry Louis Gates, Jr. (Chicago: University of Chicago Press, 1985), p. 86.

9. Michel de Certeau, *Heterologies: "Discourse on the Other,"* trans. Brian Massumi (Minneapolis: University of Minnesota Press, 1986), p. 69.

10. Mario Praz, *The Romantic Agony*, trans. Angus Davidson (1933; Oxford: Oxford University Press, 1970), p. 285.

11. In *Japoneries d'automne* (1889), Loti recounts how he is mesmerized by the parade of the empress and her entourage on a holiday, when the nobility is dressed up in medieval splendor and pageantry is at its most impressive. To complete his devotion to exoticism, Loti later installed himself in his maternal home, decorating his own part of it in the style of his favorite destinations. During his frequent off-duty visits, he hardly left the house but received guests and admirers (ranging from Sarah Bernhardt to diplomatic figures) in these rarified and sumptuous "Turkish," "Moroccan," and "Japanese" quarters (see Blanch, *Pierre Loti*). One can imagine him moving between these rooms, now in his kimono in the Japanese room, now in his Turkish outfit praying in the mosque he had built, changing identities and memories along with the pageantry.

12. Michel Butor, "Travel Writing," trans. John Powers and K. Lisket, *Mosaic* 8 (1974): 15.

13. Clive Wake, *The Novels of Pierre Loti* (The Hague: Mouton, 1974) and Blanch, *Pierre Loti.*

14. In an article published after I wrote this essay, Emily Apter explores some of the themes I have examined in relation to Loti ("Acting out Orientalism: Sapphic Theatricality in Turn-of-the-Century Paris," *L'Espirit Créateur* 34, no. 2 [1994]: 102–16). She also refers to Barthes's queering and bringing out of Loti, and sees in Barthes's move an outing of himself as well as of Loti. Moreover, Apter writes, as I have, of the importance of passing to Loti's work in her examination of *Aziyadé*, arguing that "the theatrics of passing [are] crucial to the performance of national and sexual identity" (108). Apter sees an important relation between performing the "oriental" and the outing of the lesbian or gay self.

15. Lawrence D. Kritzman, "Barthesian Free Play," *Yale French Studies* 66 (1986): 203. See also Diana Knight, "Barthes and Orientalism," *New Literary History* 24 (1993): 617–33.

16. Joan Riviere, "Womanliness as a Masquerade," in *Formations of Fantasy*, ed. Victor Burgin et al. (London: Methuen, 1986), pp. 35–44.

17. Mary Ann Doane, "Film and the Masquerade: Theorizing the Female Spectator," *Screen* 23 (1982): 25–26.

18. Lynn A. Higgins, "Barthes's Imaginary Voyages," *Studies in Twentieth-Century Literature* 5 (1981): 163. See also Roy Porter, *Haunted Journeys: Desire and Transgression in European Travel Writing* (Princeton, N.J.: Princeton University Press, 1991), and Lisa Lowe, *Critical Terrains: French and British Orientalisms* (Ithaca, N.Y. and London: Cornell University Press, 1991).

19. Higgins, "Barthes's Imaginary Voyages," p. 161.

20. Hwa Yol Jung observes the way *savoir* and *saveur* go hand in hand in *The*

Empire of Signs in "The Joy of Textualizing Japan: A Metacommentary on Roland Barthes's *Empire of Signs*," *Bucknell Review* 30 (1988): 144–67.

21. Because of its insularity, it was difficult to collect facts on Japan. Many of the sixty-three articles concerning Japan in Diderot's *Encyclopédie* contained misinformation and were largely based on travelers' accounts of previous centuries. For a comparison of the claims of the *Encyclopédie* and Japanese "reality," see Hisayasu Nakagawa, "Encyclopédie de Diderot et le Japon," in *Colloque International Diderot (1713–1784)*, ed. Anne-Marie Chouillet (Paris: Aux Amateurs de Livres, 1985), pp. 411–21.

22. Rudyard Kipling, *From Sea to Sea and Other Sketches: Letters of Travel* (New York: Doubleday, 1925 [c. 1907]), p. 312.

23. In *Mythologies*, Barthes wrote that the fundamental justification of exoticism is to deny any identification by history (*MY*, 96).

24. Bhabha, "The Other Question," p. 67.

25. Abdelkebir Khatibi, "Le Japon de Barthes," in *Figures de l'étranger dans la littérature française* (Paris: Denoël, 1987), p. 71.

26. Lowe, *Critical Terrains*, p. 167.

27. Ibid., pp. 165–66.

28. Ibid., pp. 162–65.

29. Interestingly, D. A. Miller's study of the slim volume (*Bringing out Roland Barthes* (Berkeley: University of California Press, 1992) does not include any reference to its "Moroccan" portion. While "bringing out" the gay Barthes, Miller closets Barthes the sexual tourist. Two recent articles that do examine "Incidents" and provide more extensive treatment than I have space for here came to my attention after the completion of this article. Diana Knight, who also investigates the utopian aspect of Barthes's Japan, locates "Incidents" within Barthes's orientalist framework, having argued that "Barthes's theoretical and more creative writing was stimulated in various ways by his experience of this so-called Orient," ("Barthes and Orientalism," p. 618) which includes Japan and Morocco. For Knight, as for Ross Chambers ("Pointless Stories, Storyless Points: Roland Barthes Between 'Soirées de Paris' and 'Incidents,'" *L'Esprit Créateur* 34 [1994]: 12–30), there is a link between sexual and (post)colonial politics. Situating "Incidents" within the gay male genre of cruising, Chambers explores the (anti)narrative properties of this writing, focusing on its episodic, catalog-like nature as well as its omissions and forgetting. For Chambers, what is pointedly forgotten and repressed in Barthes's "Incidents" is the colonial story, which puts cruising in Morocco in an altogether different light than cruising in the metropolitan capital, of which Barthes writes in his "Soirées de Paris" journal entries collected in *Incidents*. See also Khatibi, "Le Japon de Barthes."

30. Here I make an allusion not only to the eroticism of travel and Barthes's own essay in *Mythologies* about the *Blue Guide*, but also to Barthes's own ideal of a travel guide, which we find in *ES*, reproduced in handwriting: "Open a travel guide: Usually you find a brief lexicon which strangely enough concerns only certain boring and useless things: customs, mail, the hotel, the barber, the doctor, prices. Yet what is traveling? Meetings. The only lexicon that counts is the one which refers to the rendezvous" (13).

31. André Gide, *Amyntas* [1906], trans. Richard Howard (New York: Ecco Press, 1988).

18

Un-Scriptible

Arkady Plotnitsky

Roland Barthes's *S/Z* has a long-standing reputation, amply confirmed by its continuous circulation ever since its appearance about a quarter of a century ago. Persistence of circulation is, however, a complex and often problematic criterion, as Barthes knew very well and as the opening elaborations of *S/Z* suggest. The special position of the book, however, as marking—and, in many ways, enacting—a transition from structuralism to poststructuralism has, by now, been well established and productively used in many recent discussions.[1] *S/Z* appears to have successfully entered the post-poststructuralist and post-postmodernist landscape as well. A number of recent works explore different theoretical, cultural, and sociopolitical trajectories of the book and of Barthes's discourse in general. Both have been used, positioned, and historicized (or narrativized and allegorized) with remarkable diversity. This chapter suggests some of the lesser-explored reasons for *S/Z*'s significance to the intellectual and cultural landscape of the last two decades, a landscape often defined via the signifier *post*—poststructuralist, postmodern, postmodernist, and so forth. This landscape itself, as *S/Z* shows, is also, and perhaps primarily, a landscape of signifiers, and of an overabundance of signifiers. We still inhabit this landscape—or rather we still thus view the landscape we inhabit—even though this same landscape and our view of it have transformed considerably during the two decades of poststructuralism and "after poststructuralism"—after Roland Barthes. Perhaps not for much longer, however; and it is conceivable that by 1970 *S/Z* and other (even earlier) texts to be discussed here signaled the possibility of such a departure and a transformation that could no longer be contained within this landscape or circulation—within, to use a phrase of Jacques Derrida (one of the key figures in this landscape), the postal economy of the signifier *post*.[2] I develop my argument here by following several significant connections between *S/Z* and certain key ideas of

Derrida and Bataille, and by exploring some of the philosophical implications of these connections. I realize that applying the term *philosophical* to Barthes and Bataille—or even to Derrida, who is of course a philosopher—may be complicated. But then, is it not possible and, at a certain juncture, even necessary to see Barthes's *A Lover's Discourse: Fragments* as a rereading and rewriting of Plato's *Symposium* or *Phaedrus* (or both)? Although not my thesis—the philosophy at stake no longer permits theses—this is my contribution to this tribute to Barthes: in addition to everything else he is and to many other positions (and transitions) he occupies, *voilà*—Roland Barthes, the philosopher. I can easily imagine him saying, almost hear his voice, *la voix scriptible de Roland Barthes,* "La philosophie? C'est moi," or depending on which philosophy is in question, "La philosophie? Jamais!"

First, I revisit Barthes's concepts of *scriptible* and *lisible,* centering on *scriptible.* Then, I indicate the connections between these concepts and Derrida's matrix and suggest that Barthes's *lisible* may be seen as the practice of reading under the conditions of writing—*écriture*—in Derrida's sense of the term. Finally, I discuss Bataille, whom I see as the main source of Barthes's concept of *scriptible,* and several related radical philosophical ideas.

My title reflects the difficulty of forming a grammatical negative in French of Barthes's term *scriptible,* introduced in *S/Z* and usually translated as "writerly," in keeping with "readerly" for Barthes's *lisible.* Except the loss of the rhythm of the pair "readerly, writerly," I see no reason not to translate *scriptible* as "scriptible." The signifier or grapheme—or *scripteme*—"scriptible" can then be related to the grapheme "writing" in English similarly to the way that Barthes's *scriptible* relates to *écriture* in French. My title thus relates to the question of translation—its possibility and impossibility, or both, simultaneously. Much of what is at stake in *S/Z* can be processed through or translated into the thematics of translation, beginning with the relationships between the readerly and the scriptible. Thus, the readerly can be defined as that which is more or less translatable; the scriptible, as that which is more or less untranslatable, including into the ostensibly original language of a given text. Scriptible texts are written neither in a native nor in a foreign language, or in both simultaneously; and one may in turn need to apply the operators "neither . . . nor" and "both" simultaneously here. The grapheme, or *scripteme,* "un-*scriptible*" is thus written in at least a double language—French and English—perhaps neither English nor French, possibly Latin, or, as will be seen, even Greek or Russian.

One can relate Barthes's *scriptible* to a certain un-writing—non-*écriture*—even, and in particular, if writing is understood in Derrida's sense, the most general and the most radical sense of writing available hitherto.

My introduction of the un-*scriptible* does not imply, however, a return to Derrida's economy of writing or, even less so, to a pre-Derridean understanding of writing or signification. Instead, I argue that in order to relate to the un-*scriptible* (or in order to approach the impossibility of relating to this alterity), one might need a certain scriptible text or nontext that can no longer be contained by the Derridean economy of writing. As I discuss in more detail later, one must use that (perhaps Hegelian) double negative that does not return to the original positive.

The genealogies of Barthes's *scriptible* extend to Bataille, Blanchot, and Derrida, among others. Derrida's economy of writing is, I argue, primarily that of the interactions between the readerly and the scriptible in Barthes's sense. By contrast, what is at stake in both Bataille and Blanchot is the scriptible without the readerly, leading to an economy of writing—or of a certain un-writing—different from Derrida's. Barthes's *scriptible* itself corresponds more closely to and possibly derives from Bataille's concept of literature or poetry.[3] It is true that the latter may be related to Derrida's writing as well, as Derrida himself argues in his reading of Bataille in "From Restricted to General Economy: A Hegelianism Without Reserve."[4] I would argue, however, that Bataille's concept of literature may not thereby be subsumed but entails a (scriptible) non-*écriture* to be considered here. Bataille, as Derrida acknowledges, speaks of poetic speech—*voix*—and juxtaposes it to *écriture.* I take seriously Barthes's passing reference to Bataille as one of his sources and see Bataille's ideas, rather than only his reference to Balzac's *Sarrasine,* as a major reason for Barthes's choice of text and the development of his overall matrix (*SZ,* 16). Indeed, Barthes's reference is not so incidental. *S/Z* concludes by citing Bataille as a kind of a posterior epigraph, a posteriorgraph, that moves from writing—*écriture*—to the un-writing of the scriptible and finally to the un-scriptible. The un-scriptible may be the main, if hidden, limit at stake in *S/Z* and elsewhere in Barthes's writing, especially insofar as his writing itself enters the region of the scriptible rather than the readerly and, as such, can no longer quite be read either.

S/Z appears to be mainly a theory of the readerly and the practice of reading readerly texts, as opposed to the scriptible and the reading of scriptible texts, about which, Barthes says, "there may be nothing to say." Nor are scriptible texts available to reading, even the plural reading entailed and enabled by the readerly. One can argue, however—and I do so here—that the scriptible is the most crucial concept and contribution of *S/Z.* According to Barthes himself, the scriptible constitutes the primary value in the overall economy of textual production, and for profound reasons (although Barthes's propositions to that effect require further qualification). After saying that scriptible texts are "certainly not [found] in reading," Barthes adds a parenthesis indicating that some scriptible texts may be found in reading after all—"by chance, fleetingly and obliquely, in certain limit-works" (*SZ*, 4–6). The search for the scriptible may well be the ultimate goal of all Barthes's readings, including *S/Z*. The latter is, even if against itself, in pursuit of the scriptible in the readerly (rather than, as it overtly claims, of the readerly alone), and to become the scriptible and to reach the limit of the scriptible in the un-scriptible may even be the goal of Barthes's own writing. This pursuit reaches its goal or, more precisely, encounters the unreachable—the impossible—in the very last word, or unword, of the text.

This movement from the known to the unknown and finally the unknowable, from the possible to the impossible—from what is possible to "an experience at the limit of the possible" and finally to the encounter with the impossible—defines literature for Bataille.[5] I argue here that, via Bataille, a similar view of literature emerges in *S/Z*. *S/Z* begins by establishing the difference between and the hierarchy of the scriptible and the readerly:

> Our evaluation can be linked only to a practice, and this practice is that of writing [*écriture*]. On the one hand, there is what is possible to write, and on the other what is no longer possible to write: what is within the practice of the writer and what has left it: which texts would I consent to write (to re-write), to desire, to put forth as a force in this world of mine? What evaluation finds is precisely this value: what can be written (re-written) today: the *scriptible*. Why is scriptible our value? Because the goal of literary work (of literature as work) is to make the reader no longer a consumer, but a producer of a text. Our literature is marked by the pitiless divorce which the literary institution maintains between the producer of the text and its user, between its owner and its customer, between its author and its reader. This reader is thereby plunged into a kind of idleness—he is intransitive; he is, in short, *serious*: instead of functioning himself, instead of gaining access to the magic of the signifier, to the pleasure of writing, he is left with no more than the meager freedom of either to accept or reject the text: reading is nothing more than a *referendum*. Opposite the scriptible text, then, is its countervalue, its negative, reactive value: what can be read, but not written: the *readerly*. We can call any readerly text a classic text. (*SZ*, 3–4; translation modified)

At stake is a fundamental evaluation, albeit—and this is important—specific to a certain culture, within which Barthes's discourse operates: each text or encounter with a given work, language, or system is defined by this difference. It may be suggested, more generally, that both the scriptible and the readerly connote in fact, or in effect, situations, economies, or acts of reading or writing, or, in Derrida's phrase, acts of literature and acts of reading. These concepts refer to engagements (and the impossibility thereof) with texts and, thereby, always to certain *constructions*—or constructions/deconstructions—of texts. Derrida's concept of writing or text in general can be seen as involving this process; the same may be said about the textual economy introduced and enacted by *S/Z*. One might argue (as several critics have, both approvingly and critically) that both (the plural of) the readerly and, especially, the scriptible are modeled on the contemporary avant-garde texts or texts of high modernism in general. (I am not sure that Barthes himself would subscribe to this argument; while not irrelevant, it does appear limited.) The possibility, however, of Barthes's reading of *Sarrasine*—and conceivably of reading any given text—as a readerly text or unreading it as a scriptible one would indicate that these terms relate to the economy of reading as just indicated, rather than to the text itself—that is, a text existing by and in itself (outside a given economy of reading). The latter concept is, in fact, no longer possible under these conditions.[6] These qualifications are assumed throughout the present discussion and must be kept in mind whenever I refer to the readerly or the scriptible.

Next, Barthes elaborates on the scriptible, for the last time in the book, as he turns to the readerly. The readerly or *reading* the readerly—what Barthes calls "interpretation (in the Nietzschean sense)"—is juxtaposed to what Barthes sees as consumer value. As he writes:

> [Readerly texts] are products (and not productions), they make up the enormous mass of our literature. How to differentiate this mass once again? Here, we require a second operation, consequent upon the evaluation which has separated the texts, more refined [*plus fine*] than that evaluation, based upon the appreciation of a certain quantity—of the *more or less* each text can mobilize. This new operation is *interpretation* (in the Nietzschean sense of the word). To interpret a text is not to give it a (more or less justified, more or less free) meaning, but on the contrary to appreciate the *plural* that constitutes it. Let us first posit the image of a triumphant plural, unimpoverished by any constraint of representation (of imitation). In this ideal text, the networks are many and interact, without any one of them being able to surpass the rest; this text is a galaxy of signifiers, not a structure of signifieds; it has no beginning; it is reversible; we gain access to it by several entrances, none of which can be authoritatively declared to be the main one; the codes it mobilizes extend *as far as the eye can reach*, they are indeterminable (meaning here is never subject to a principle of determination, unless by throwing dice); the systems of meaning can take over this absolutely plural text, but their number is never closed, based as it is on the infinity of language. The interpretation demanded by a specific text, in its plurality, is in no way liberal; it is not a question of conceding some meanings; of magnanimously acknowledging that each one has its share of truth; it is a question, against all in-difference, of asserting the very existence of plurality, which is not that of the true, the probable or even possible. This necessary assertion is difficult, however, for, as nothing exists outside the text, there is never a *totality* of the text (which would by reversion form an internal order, a reconciliation of complementary parts, under the paternal eye of the representative Model): the text must simultaneously be distinguished from its exterior or from its totality. All of which comes down to saying that for the plural text, there cannot be a

narrative structure, a grammar, or a logic; thus, if one or another of these are sometimes permitted to come forward, it is in *proposition* (giving this expression its full quantitative value) as we are dealing with incompletely plural texts, the texts whose plural is more or less parsimonious. (*SZ*, 5–6; translation modified)

Barthes's allusion to Nietzsche is very much to the point here. "Interpretation" thus conceived—as a plural reading of the plural of the readerly—is much closer to Derrida's, de Man's, and related concepts of reading (which can in turn be traced to Nietzsche) than to the more standard use of the term *interpretation*, connoting more strictly parsimonious or strictly univocal or denotative readings. The latter are complicit with what Barthes sees as consumerist practices and politics of reading. By contrast, reading the readerly offers the possibility of a nonconsumer response. As Barthes makes clear in his subsequent elaborations, the readerly is actually the condition of consumer readings as well (*SZ*, 5–11). That is, consumer readings are simultaneously constituted and dislocated by the readerly. As will be seen presently, the readerly itself is, analogously, both constituted and dislocated by the scriptible. A consumer reading or any restricted form of reading emerges as a certain solidification—or even mortification—within the more liquid and more playful plurality enacted by the readerly, even though this plurality is never fully available to any given reading. In practice, there is no reading—or, again, no situation or economy of reading—without parsimony. In this sense, the readerly, too, while it can no longer be written or rewritten, can never be fully read, but unlike the scriptible it can be read. Thus, as Barthes stresses, his own attempt to explore—or to play out—the plural of the readerly in Balzac's *Sarrasine* is subject to a certain parsimonious, restricted economy (*SZ*, 6–11). This term, and Barthes's usage of the term *restricted* in general, can also be used here in the sense of, and traced to, Bataille's concepts of and distinction between restricted and general economy (in the sense of theories or frameworks), understood as dealing respectively with controlled or parsimonious and more plural or excessive configurations of meaning.[7] Barthes's reading of *Sarrasine* is thus inserted into or, more precisely, derives from the play—and the interplay—of the plural and the parsimonious, the excessive and the limited, the playful and the controlled. At many levels the economy (in whatever sense) of Barthes's reading often (and often deliberately) mirrors the various economies of *Sarrasine*.[8]

This (inter)play is, actually, a general structure or economy, which defines both the theory and practice of *S/Z* and is one of its most significant (although not always noticed) contributions. Various classical structures and regimes—whether defined or governed by (privileging) denotation, connotation, signifier, signified, code, and so forth—are never simply negated or suspended but rethought and reinscribed as effects of the plural, the playful, and, to introduce a new word, the chanceful. At stake is an interaction, often extremely subtle, of various economies of reading—or meaning, in general—rather than unequivocal distinction. In fact, the secondary distinction between consumer and nonconsumer reading is a finer, more subtle one than the primary evaluation between the scriptible and the readerly in part because both occur within the regime of the readerly and can be confused or, indeed, confuse themselves in the practice of reading: they may pass into each other at certain points. At different points, or sometimes even simultaneously, one is subject to both regimes of reading, regardless of one's desire or agenda in this respect. It does not follow, of course, that the differences of that type between practices or outcomes of reading are erased. It does follow, however, that the outcome of such reading or, especially, of the readings of such readings—for example, of readings of Barthes's reading of *Sarrasine*—cannot be certain or determined in advance. Both in the practice of literary culture and mirroring it, in the structure of *S/Z*, the turn to the readerly or again to reading is an abandonment of the scriptible—a perhaps necessary abandonment of the perhaps inaccessible scriptible. At the same time—and this is not paradoxical—the scriptible continues to make the readerly possible, and not only in the obvious sense that it was, at one time, possible to write (or rewrite) now readerly texts, but also, and more important, because the scriptible continues to subsist alongside and is in fact the efficacity of—the dynamics producing—the readerly. As Barthes writes:

> Of scriptible texts there may be nothing to say. First of all, where can we find them? Certainly not in reading (or at least very rarely: by chance, fleetingly and obliquely, in certain limit-works): the scriptible text is not a thing, we would hardly find it in a bookstore. Moreover, its model being the productive (and no longer the representative), it abolishes any criticism which, once produced, would commingle with it: to rewrite [*ré-écrire*] the scriptible text would consist only in disseminating it, in dispersing it within the field of infinite difference. The scriptible text is a perpetual present, upon which no *consequent* utterance [parole] can be superimposed (which would inevitably make it past); the scriptible text is *we ourselves in the process of writing* [*c'est nous en train d'écrire*], before the infinite play of the world (the world as play) is traversed, intersected, arrested, plasticised by some singular system (Ideology, Genre, Criticism) which cuts off the plurality of entrances, the opening of networks, the infinity of languages. The scriptible is the novelistic without the novel, poetry without the poem, the essay without the dissertation, writing without style, production without product, structuration without structure. (*SZ*, 5–6; translation modified)

This passage and surrounding elaborations can easily be linked and may be indebted to Derrida, along with several others. Although in style indisputably Barthes's own, giving it characteristic elegance and flair, the idiom of the book derives from Nietzsche, Bataille, Deleuze, Derrida, Irigaray, and other figures defining the intellectual landscape we have been trying hard to abandon during the last decade or so. Some of the propositions just cited—for example, separating the scriptible and criticism—while not strictly counter-Derridean, would be difficult to unequivocally associate with Derrida's thought. The association of the scriptible with presence—with "a perpetual present"—is closer to Bataille and Blanchot than to Derrida, although one must not confuse this appeal to "presence" with what Derrida calls the metaphysics of presence. By contrast, Derrida would, in the context of writing, speak of the past that has never been present, which is in fact a defining aspect of his matrix of trace, *différance*, writing, and so forth.[9]

It is conceivable, however, that Derrida's main ideas affected *S/Z* more immediately than others at the time (between 1968 and 1970); and one might argue that Barthes grasped these ideas perhaps more perceptibly, subtly, and profoundly than most other readers of Derrida at the time, including many of those who are customarily associated (and who associate themselves) with deconstruction. It would indeed be difficult to think of a contemporary author to whom the matrix of *S/Z* could be related more pointedly, even though—and there is no contradiction here—*S/Z* also reflects a more plural and interactive nature of the idiom and the problematics that, in the United States, are associated almost exclusively with Derrida, or at least are linked to his work in one way or another.[10] This idiom was brilliantly fused by Barthes and, in the process of this fusion, takes over those of structuralism, although, as I have indicated, the juncture itself remains crucial to Barthes's work in *S/Z* and elsewhere. Thus Barthes's proposition, in the passage on the readerly cited earlier—"for, as nothing exists outside the text, there is never a *totality* of the text (which would by reversion form an internal order, a reconciliation of complementary parts, under the paternal eye of the representative model)"—both reflects Derrida's famous "there is nothing outside of the text [*il n'y a pas de hors texte*]" in *Of Grammatology* and offers a subtle qualification, distinguishing Barthes's reading from many misunderstandings of Derrida's maxim, which has been and remains even more misunderstood than it is famous. The opening passages of *S/Z* can be read as a succinct and elegant, if at times elegantly superficial, rendition of the Derridean matrix, both in its constructive and deconstructive aspects, and in its applications to the question of reading. The plural reading of the readerly becomes more or less the reading of that which is *written* in Derrida's sense, as opposed to classical modes of interpretation—denotative, connotative, or other—which *S/Z* dismantles or deconstructs, without simply dismissing them, both by the theory it offers and by the critical practice it pursues. Links to Derrida can be found throughout *S/Z*. Some Derridean themes emerging there include: the general emphasis on writing and textuality; the deconstruction of classical schemes of signification, such as in Saussure, Hjelmslev, and Husserl (see especially *SZ*, 6–7); more generally, interconnections between linguistics and philosophy, especially structuralism and phenomenology, and their common appurtenance in what Derrida calls the metaphysics of presence, which commonality or complicity necessitates and enables the deconstruction of both, sometimes using them against each other; the question of metaphor or catachresis and its connection to the question of writing, on one hand, and to the questions of the feminine, on the other;[11] the question of the (en)closure of Western philosophy, somewhat less prominent in recent discussions but central to Derrida, especially in his earlier works (*SZ*, 7);[12] and finally, the question of translation and its relation to writing and textuality.

I can only acknowledge these connections here without considering them in more detail, and move instead to Bataille—in part in spite (and in part also because) of these connections, Barthes is, in my view, ultimately closer to Bataille or Blanchot than to Derrida. For, if *S/Z* begins with Derrida, without mentioning his name, inscribed in the signifying or graphematic—or conceivably even scriptematic—texture of the book, it ends by citing Bataille, who writes in his preface to *Le Bleu du ciel* [*The Blue of Noon*]:

"To a greater or lesser degree every man is suspended upon narratives [*récits*], on *novels*, which reveal to him the multiplicity of life. Only these narratives, often read in a trance, situate him before his fate. So we ought to seek passionately to find what *narratives* might be.

"How to orient the effort through which the *novel* renews, or, better, perpetuates itself.

"The concern for various techniques which cope with the satiety of familiar forms does occupy the mind. But I am putting it badly—if we want to know *what a novel can be*—that a basis should first be perceived and well marked. The narrative that reveals the possibilities of life does not necessarily appeal. But it reveals a moment of *rage*, without which its author would be blind to its excessive possibilities. I believe this: only suffocating, impossible trial provides the author with the means of attaining the distant vision the reader is seeking, tired of the tight limitations that conventions impose.

"How can we linger over books to which obviously the author was not *constrained*?

"I want to formulate the principle. I will not argue it.

"I shall confine myself to giving some titles that respond to my statement (some titles . . . I could give others, but disorder is the measure of my intent): *Wuthering Heights*, *The Trial*, *Remembrance of Things Past*, *The Red and the Black*, *Eugénie de Franval*, *L'Arrêt de Mort*, *Sarrazine* [*sic*], *The Idiot* . . . ." (*SZ*, 267; translation modified)[13]

Even leaving aside for the moment the general significance, near uncircumventability, of Bataille's thought on the contemporary French intellectual scene and Barthes's own more sustained engagements with it, direct allusions to this passage in *S/Z* and Bataille's understanding—clearly shared by Barthes—of narrative would suggest that Bataille's thought is far from accidental to *S/Z*. Many of Bataille's major themes—loss, excess, consumption and expenditure, eroticism (and the conjunction of eroticism and death), and so forth—permeate the book, both its theoretical framework and its reading of *Sarrasine*. Indeed, Barthes's reading may be seen as Balzac's text processed through Bataille's economy. Bataille's "How to orient the effort through which the *novel* renews, or, better, perpetuates itself" in the passage cited above is the question *S/Z* attempts to address; and the perpetual—nonpresent, Heraclitean, or Nietzschean—presence of the scriptible is Barthes's response to Bataille. As I indicated, *S/Z* may even be "read" as an attempt to make Balzac's text unreaderly once again and return it to the experience of reading and writing evoked by Bataille. This returns it to the scriptible on the way to the experience of the un-scriptible, to an encounter with the impossible, which defines the experience (production and reception) of literature for Bataille. *Sarrasine*, then, would no longer be a pensive text—*le texte pensif*—that classically, pensively, suspends meaning, but a violent transgression of the very possibility of all meaning—of all reading and perhaps all writing, even Derrida's *écriture*, even the non-*écriture* of Bataille's literature and Barthes's *scriptible*. It would also make us rethink—with or against Balzac, Bataille, Derrida, and Barthes—the pensive economy of the feminine—"*Et la marquise resta pensive*"—closing *Sarrasine* and Barthes's reading in *S/Z*.

Sarrasine is twice misspelled by Bataille, who substitutes "z" for the second "s," as the male version of the name would be spelled. Proust does the same in *Sodome et Gomorrhe* when he or, rather (which makes it even more interesting in the context of Balzac's text and Barthes's work), Charlus lists *Sarrasine* among Balzac's great works. By so doing, Bataille, or Proust, offers Barthes another gift, his famous signifier "S/Z," a signifier about the impossibility of all classical (and perhaps any) signification. The cluster of title-signifiers at the end of the Bataille passage just cited would require long analysis. It would take one several pages to sort out the titles alone, from *Wuthering Heights* to *The Idiot*, via *Sarrasine* and *L'Arrêt de mort*—from vertigo to the limit of reason and madness, via the violent eroticism of *Sarrasine* and a death sentence—death as a sentence, and the death of the sentence, the death of all reading and of all writing, *écriture* and *le scriptible*. Vertigo, violence, eroticism, madness, and death are, once again, Bataille's central themes. Neither titles nor the works themselves are a random selection even though, and because, *disorder* is, and must be, one's *measure,* as Bataille says—a disorder conceived more radically than ever, as suggested by Bataille's concept of chance that has nothing to do with the calculus of probabilities. The titles assembled by Bataille form a cluster of mutual influences and contain numerous allusions to each other. They are subtly alluded to in Bataille's passage itself. Thus, the "suffocating, impossible trial" clearly refers to Kafka's *The Trial,* mentioned at crucial junctures of Bataille's works, and of course Kafka is an equally important figure for Blanchot.

I cannot consider the remarkable and extraordinarily rich network of connections here, which, along with Bataille's works, are all part of the massive—and massively parallel—program (in either sense: plan or agenda and software) Barthes and we designate now as *S/Z* and of the "space of literature" at stake there. I instead conclude, as Barthes does, by turning to the final grapheme or scripteme of Barthes's text—"the idiot." *Idiot* is one of the few words, perhaps the only word in Barthes's text, that needs no translation—it is the same in all languages involved here—even though, and again because, it is an ultimately untranslatable, unreaderly word, an irreducibly scriptible text, a scripteme. This scripteme may moreover be read as defining the very scriptibility of the scriptible. It is now forever linked to Dostoyevsky's novel, certainly in Bataille and Barthes. Especially if read alongside "the death sentence," through the juncture of death and madness and their "suffocating impossible trial" (phrases with multiple resonances, as well as connections to Stendhal, in Dostoyevsky's novel, and of course in Stendhal himself), this scripteme defines the irreducible idiosyncrasy of the scriptible that cannot be read—any more than anyone, within or outside the text, can read Dostoyevsky's hero, Prince Leo Myshkin, the idiot, either in his reason or in his madness.

Finally, the scripteme "idiot" *speaks,* with great voices—Dostoyevsky's, Nietzsche's, Bataille's—of the un-scriptible which can never be written or unwritten, nor, of course, spoken. It cannot "be," to begin with, in any conceivable ontological sense; and neither a Heideggerian nor perhaps even a Derridean erasure of Being may suffice to designate or undesignate this un-being. This is not to say that this un-scriptible does not "exist" and does not make us feel the effects of its suffocating, impossible trials, such as death or madness, or reason. It is just that there is no classical, or perhaps any, ontology—or phenomenology, or any other "philosophology"—to approach this existence. We cannot, Bataille says, speak of this unknowable, but only experience its effects. Scriptematically, in the movement that constituted the very definition of literature for Bataille, Barthes's text ends with an ellipsis. By doing so, especially following the grapheme "idiot," it connotes the end of signification in either sense—as referring to the nonsignifiable (either by means of a signified or by means of signifier, as in Lacan) and as announcing the end of the epoch of the signified and signifier, perhaps even of writing in Derrida's sense, and their enclosure. It opens the space of the unknown, and finally the unknowable—the un-scriptible, which is not only a "nonwriting" but "non-nonwriting," and it redefines the space of literature by this movement.

I use this rather idiosyncratic term, *non-nonwriting* in the manner of Hegel's double negative, in which the second negative does not return to the original positive but moves toward a more radical difference from both the positive and the first negative. The negative at stake here would negate or double-negate Hegel as well. Hegel, that great thinker, *penseur,* of the pensive (who, however, sometimes believed himself going mad, a circumstance to which Bataille alludes on several occasions), returns the double negative to Spirit [*Geist*], to its power to confront and overcome both death and madness and their irreducible idiosyncrasy, as he says in the famous passage of his *Phenomenology,* to which both Bataille and Blanchot continuously return in their writing, as do most other major readers of Hegel. Hegel—but following Nietzsche, not Bataille, the grand demolisher of the pensive and the grand affirmer of the irreducible idiosyncratic.

S/Z thus has two last words—one in the main text, the same as the last word of Balzac's *Sarrasine*—"pensive"—the other, via Dostoyevsky and Bataille, an appended last word—"idiot." This second last word opens the space of the un-scriptible—non-non-*écriture*—and idiosyncrasy or madness—the night of madness or, to return to Blanchot's title, the madness of the day—rather than arresting the readerly or even the scriptible by a kind of death sentence. This closure also makes all "last words"—all final and unique words, and all absolute closures or enclosures—structurally impossible.

What I have to say by way of conclusion may be difficult, perhaps impossible to say in an abbreviated fashion. Let me venture it, however, for it contains what I believe to be the radical philosophy implied by *S/Z,* a philosophy of that "un-nameable" (unnameable even as *unnameable*) which may finally be inaccessible to philosophy or criticism—that is, reading—or indeed in a certain sense to anything. It appears that for Barthes, as for Bataille and Blanchot, a certain literature may bring us into a certain proximity to this "un-nameable" or "un-scriptible." It is not and perhaps, by definition, it may not be possible to know how close such a proximity, or how distant such a distance, can be. It is conceivable, as Nietzsche (who, or rather Zarathustra, urged us to love that which is most distant) realized, that distance is the only way to approach this unknowable or impossible, although, as Nietzsche also realized, these concepts or any concept may again be fundamentally—structurally, irreducibly—insufficient here. The "alterity"—or nonalterity, or again non-nonalterity—of what I call the un-scriptible, which is at stake in Bataille, Blanchot, and Barthes's scriptible, may no longer conform to any available or even conceivable concept of alterity, exteriority, or difference; or to any concept or conceptual or interpretive formation—for example, Derrida's neither-a-word-nor-a-concept, such as *différance*—that is or will ever be available to us. That especially includes the concept of absolute alterity, such as that of Kant's things-in-themselves, which, as Nietzsche understood, would be no more sufficient than Hegel's dialectic.

This non-nonalterity may not conform to anything that can be approached through any terms—whether terms of being or becoming, or nothingness, beginning or end, difference or alterity, or exteriority (or, of course, identity, sameness, or interiority), finitude or infinity, unity or multiplicity, continuity or discontinuity, time or space, matter or spirit; the Lacanian Real; *différance* and other Derridean operators; or even the alterity at stake in Bataille or Barthes, or the alterity of the un-scriptible suggested here. Nor do the considerations just given suggest nihilistically that the process(es) and relation(s) at issue here relate to nothingness. What they relate to may be no more "nothing" than "something," or any other thing; no more *is* than is *not*, while producing the effects of nothingness or "somethingness," or "thingness." At issue is a "relation" of neither absolute (or potentially any) alterity, difference, exteriority, or disconnection—which, being absolute, is never radical enough—nor of absolute (or potentially any) connectability, or anything within or, conceivably, outside any form of conceptual or interpretive enclosure within which we must function. The latter formulation, of course, also suggests a form of relation and, as such, may be equally inapplicable. It follows, in fact, that *all* propositions offered at the moment may be equally inapplicable here. All our "relations" to this non-nonalterity are subject to the same economy. We may not be able to unite or dissociate, either connect or disconnect ourselves with or from this alterity through any interpretation, theory, or technology that is or ever will be available to us, if these terms, like others used here, are applicable. The very concept of the impossibility of relating this non-nonalterity to any interpretation may, again, be applicable; and the last proposition—or the present proposition, or again any other negative or qualifying proposition of that type—may need to be negated or double-negated in turn, without returning to what it negates.

Is it possible, then, to conceive of something that neither connects nor disconnects; is neither connected nor disconnected; is, indeed, neither conceivable nor inconceivable; is never fully, or even in any way, inside or outside any enclosure, as all such questions are themselves the products of enclosures, beyond some of which one must move and within others of which one must remain in order to approach this radically, but never absolutely, unrepresentable? It may or may not be possible, for the very concepts of conception, representation, or possibility may need to be further scrutinized, transformed, or abandoned. What Bataille calls "interior experience" and, by implication, literature—writing and reading (although these terms may no longer be applicable)—is an experience at the limit of this possibility or impossibility, an encounter with the unreachable, or again—to double negate without return to the positive—the un-unreachable. The question itself, as the question of the un-scriptible, is posed by or at least after Barthes's scriptible, in all three senses of the word *after*: following or in the style of, pursuing, and leaving behind Roland Barthes. Perhaps none or any combined sense of all three is strictly possible: the text is too scriptible and what is at stake is too un-scriptible for these and other classical—readerly or even scriptible—concepts, or neither words nor concepts. One might say that we need other concepts after Roland Barthes, except that this proposition itself still remains within our contemporary—that is to say, old, classical—enclosure, which can only be dislocated by a text or nontext very different than the one presented here.

There is no single name or cluster, or galaxy of names—whether signifiers, graphemes, or scriptemes—that could govern such a text, perhaps no name at all for such a text, including, and perhaps especially, the name *text*. On this occasion, however, it may be appropriate to suggest that such a non-*écriture* may prove to be something "after—à là—Roland Barthes." In order to do so, however, this non-*écriture* and the philosophy it entails would have to be something altogether different from—something untranslatable, unwritable, un-scriptible into—the text and philosophy of Barthes himself. For it is only about a text and philosophy irreducibly different from his own that Barthes, the author of his own *Symposium—A Lover's Discourse*—could have possibly said, "Oui, c'est moi."

Notes

1. For Barthes's own relevant assessment of *S/Z* as a "textual" rather than "structural" analysis, see his "The Struggle with an Angel" (1971), in *IMT*, p. 137 n. 1.

2. I refer to *La Carte postale: De Socrate à Freud et au-delà* (Paris: Flammarion, 1980); *The Post Card: From Socrates to Freud and Beyond*, trans. Alan Bass (Chicago: University of Chicago Press, 1987). See also, however, "Some Statements and Truisms About Neologisms, Newisms, Postisms, Parasitisms, and Other Small Seismisms," in *The States of Theory*, ed. David Carroll (New York: Columbia University Press, 1989).

3. The relationships between these two terms are in turn complicated in Bataille. I cannot consider these nuances here, and speak of literature, although "poetry" is used by Bataille more often and less ambivalently in this context.

4. In *L'Ecriture et la différence* (Paris: Seuil, 1967); *Writing and Difference*, trans. Alan Bass (Chicago: University of Chicago Press, 1978).

5. I refer especially to Bataille's elaboration in *Inner Experience*, trans. Leslie Anne Boldt (Albany: State University of New York Press, 1980) and its companions in what Bataille at some point conceived of as *la somme athéologique. Guilty*, trans. Bruce Boon (Venice, Calif.: Lapis Press, 1988) and *On Nietzsche*, trans. Bruce Boon (New York: Paragon, 1990). For the French editions of these and other works referred to here see Georges Bataille, *Oeuvres complètes* (Paris: Gallimard, 1970–).

6. An interesting and important question (which cannot be addressed within the limits of this essay) is that of the transformations of such values within—or their translations between—different cultural or (in the broad sense) political economies, both at the macro- and microlevels of cultural processing and stratification. Barthes's work occupies a complex and often ambivalent position or, indeed, a spectrum of positions in this respect—whether one speaks of political (or geopolitical, as between Anglo-American and French cultures), sexual, academic, literary, or other economies of writing and reading. For some of these questions around Barthes and specifically *S/Z* in the context of the contemporary American scene, see Jay Clayton's recent *The Pleasure of Babel: Contemporary American Literature and Theory* (New York and Oxford: Oxford University Press, 1993), pp. 35–40.

7. I refer most specifically to *The Accursed Share*, 3 vols., trans. Robert Hurley (New York: Zone, 1988–90), although the concepts involved are crucial throughout Bataille's writing. It is important to keep in mind that the term *economy* refers here primarily to theory or science, as in "political economy," and in this sense one may indeed speak of different "economics" of meaning. Economic thematics themselves—consumption, expenditure, excess, waste, and so forth—at various and interactive levels (whether sexual, interpretive, political, or monetary) are, of course, just as central to Balzac's *Sarrasine* and Barthes's reading of it as they are to Bataille and Derrida.

8. Cf. Gregory Ulmer's discussion of this type of mirroring in terms of codes (rather than economies) in *Teletheory: Grammatology in the Age of Video* (New York: Routledge, 1989), pp. 79–81.

9. See *Of Grammatology*, trans. Gayatri C. Spivak (Baltimore: Johns Hopkins Press, 1974), pp. 66–67, and "*Différance*" (in *Margins of Philosophy*, trans. Alan Bass [Chicago: University of Chicago Press, 1980], p. 21).

10. It is true that by now a somewhat more diverse picture of this landscape and of deconstruction has emerged (in fact, at times even bypassing, if not repressing, Derrida's role). It would not be possible here to sketch this landscape around (the figure of) Roland Barthes, or even begin to list relevant works, which are numerous. Obviously, Barthes's work in turn has implications for, even if it did not have a major influence on, Derrida's work, perhaps especially in the context of the visual arts (and the question of vision), as in *Mémoires d'aveugle: L'autoportrait et autres ruines* (Paris: Editions de la Réunion des musées nationaux, 1990); *The Memoirs of the Blind: The Self-Portrait and Other Ruins*, trans. Pascale-Ann Brault and Michael Naas (Chicago: University of Chicago Press, 1993). See also Derrida's "The Deaths of Roland Barthes," in *Philosophy and Non-Philosophy Since Merleau-Ponty*, ed. Hugh J. Silverman (New York: Routledge, 1988), pp.

259–97, which is also interesting in the context of the volume (philosophy and nonphilosophy) and of the present argument concerning the philosophical significance of Barthes's work. It is also interesting, but, of course, not surprising that in *The Memoirs of the Blind* (p. 17 n. 10) Derrida links Bataille and Barthes, via Bataille's *The Story of the Eye* and Barthes's earlier commentary on this text, "La Métaphore de l'oeil," *Critique* (August–September 1963). Many key aspects of the argument offered in the present essay can in fact be processed through the question and metaphor of vision, blindness, sight and insight, and so forth. The thematics at issue here are, in fact, processed or coprocessed in both Bataille and Barthes, or of course Derrida—or indeed most figures mentioned here, such as Nietzsche, Blanchot, and de Man.

11. See *SZ*, pp. 32–34. These themes are elaborated in Derrida's *Of Grammatology*; "White Mythology" (in *Margins*); *Spurs: Nietzsche's Style*, trans. Barbara Harlow (Chicago: University of Chicago Press, 1979); and "The Law of Genre" (in *Acts of Literature*, ed. Derek Attridge [New York: Routledge, 1992]), the latter two conceivably influenced by Barthes.

12. I have considered the question of (en)closure in detail in *Reconfigurations: Critical Theory and General Economy* (Gainesville: University Press of Florida, 1993), and *Complementarity: Anti-Epistemology After Bohr and Derrida* (Durham, N.C.: Duke University Press, 1994).

13. Georges Bataille, *Le Bleu du ciel* (Paris: J.-J. Pauvert, 1957), p. 7. (This is the edition cited by Barthes.)

Conclusion: A False Account of Talking with Frank O'Hara and Roland Barthes in Philadelphia

Bob Perelman

And don't worry about your lineage, poetic or natural
—Frank O'Hara

I really shouldn't have been doing it. I had a book to write, poems that needed care and breaking apart and confidence, I wasn't getting much exercise, and of course there was real life, family, teaching, the out-of-date inspection sticker on the Honda . . . Anyway, in spite of all this, and because of it too, no doubt, I found myself in front of the tube, in a curious state of wakeful paralysis. Never had the remote control felt more present, not exactly flesh of my flesh, but anticipatory, fateful, quirky. I noticed that it had many more buttons than I was used to. I had just been glancing through another boring human interest piece about "The Information Highway" ten minutes previously: 500 channels soon, marketing conundrums, visionary entrepreneurs. Then I put two and two together. I was dreaming. I didn't need to count the buttons: there would be five hundred.

This was nice. I never, or say very rarely, get to control my dreams. But here was the vaguely magic clicker and here I was too, on the couch in the den. Things might be a little deterministic finally, but it was better than nothing. I pushed #136.

The title of this chapter refers to O'Hara's "A True Account of Talking to the Sun on Fire Island." A previous version of this chapter has been published as chapter 9 of Bob Perelman, *The Marginalization of Poetry* copyright © by Princeton University Press. Used with permission.

Well, life is full of nonsurprises, even in dreams. 136 was an ad for Roy Rogers flame-broiled burgers. A young, vaguely Italian-American but mostly nondescript male model had just come up an escalator into a space of uniform brightness and lots of carbon-dioxide smoke. It was tacky; it *had* to be tacky or it would have caused Fundamentalist-Trouble to use the afterlife for commercial purposes—such blatant ones, that is. Escalators connoting not just painless and progressive death but automatic heavenly transcendence as well. Hadn't this stage set been used recently in some movie? I'd seen the trailers, so I knew they used white suits, slight overexposure, soft focus, and smoke: heaven was personalized, caring technology that led the simple soul to mild corporate advancement. This particular Roy Rogers ad I'd seen a couple of times already. They were about to work in something about open-flame broiling and hell. It was all meant to be disarmingly goofy, but virtuously neutral and tasty.

I pushed 137. At first I thought I hadn't. The buttons were quite close together and the screen looked basically the same: same escalator, same space full of soft white billows. But the next second I saw that this was something else entirely: there were Roland Barthes and Frank O'Hara. They both had pencil-thin William Powell mustaches. The rhythm was diffuse; in fact, nothing was happening. This was no ad. Wait. They were talking, strolling slowly along, stirring up the white smoke just a bit, the camera following them, keeping them centered. What camera? Never mind. I couldn't quite hear. I pushed the volume.

"A dune buggy brought you here."

"And a laundry truck for you."

"And I see you have one of these as well," Barthes gestured to the halo of white smoke above his head, touching it lightly as if he were touching his hair after he'd combed it. "Oh god," said O'Hara. "That." He waved his hand over his head, trying to shoo away an annoyance. His halo re-formed. It was pencil-thin. "At least we aren't wearing togas or something." They were both dressed in slacks and alligator shirts. I pushed the volume up some more. They looked toward me a second, then back at each other.

"So. We're supposed to read," O'Hara said.

"Yes. A pity we never heard of one another. A curator and a poet, interesting combination. Although, Frank, I think it's just as well we never met. You would have found my circle a bit boring, perhaps. I did eventually, I'm afraid. We had a little power, but not all that much money."

"Would you have minded this, I wonder? Shall I?" O'Hara held a sheet of typing paper.

"Please."

"The Critic. I cannot possibly think of you other than you are: the assassin of my orchards." O'Hara looked up from the page: "It's early work."

"It's quite alright, Frank, early work is charming when it's light enough."

"You lurk there in the shadows, meting out conversation like Eve's first confusion between penises and snakes."

"You know, my students used to mix up penises and phalluses: It got tiresome."

"Oh be droll, be jolly, and be temperate! Do not frighten me more than you have to! I must live forever."

Barthes waited.

"That's it," O'Hara said. "For that one."

"But the poem gives me no offense: you must know, I was never 'The Critic.' Go ahead, live forever! You must admit, it's slightly comic. And anyway, you were flirting there more than attacking, am I right? Another thing: you were a bit of the prophet. I was 'droll, jolly, and temperate'—at least on the good days—and those were the days I wrote." He scuffed his foot in the smoke: it billowed up to his white-clad knee. "Jolly? No, not jolly. And not really droll, either. But, temperate, yes."

"Ah, Sir Roland, when I write it, you mustn't take 'jolly' to mean jolly. But perhaps your appetite for falseness was different than mine. All my words were as false as false eyelashes, but of course I'm looking directly at you when I say them. So you'll have to kiss semiology goodbye. On the eyelashes, of course. Zukofsky, a poet I never read, Louis Zukofsky. He was a formalist like even you wouldn't have believed, a formalist and, finally, a bit of a whiner—but don't you think all formalists, deep down, are whiners?"

Barthes shrugged. "Ah yes, but there's spontaneous whining as well."

O'Hara went on. "Zukofsky believed in the words themselves: yawn—now that's a 'word,' isn't it? As if going to bed with the dictionary was a joy forever, or even for the first five minutes. He wrote one nice thing, though. He tells a joke in a poem, it's only a few lines, and even there he's too coy, but, still, it's a good joke: the sailor's on the operating table, for a hernia or something. The surgeon sees his cock—Zukofsky calls it something else of course—and when the sailor comes to, the surgeon comments on the graceful message he had read tattooed on the sailor's phallus—is that what you called it in those seminars?"

"No, no: penis, penis. Phallus points to the universal ineffability around which all the differential structures of language, the social hierarchies . . . But, please, get to the punchline."

"So the surgeon comments on the graceful message he had read tattooed on the sailor's *penis*—what's with 'phallus' then? Sorry, onward to the punchline: the graceful message on the sailor's penis, the word SWAN. The sailor says, 'SWAN? SWAN? What SWAN? No, that was SASKATCHEWAN.' Well, all my pretty swans are Saskatchewans, if you know what I mean."

"So you liked the pretty falsenesses that lead directly to the body's outrageous truths. Then, I wonder; you might have agreed with this: may I?" Barthes opened a paperback.

"Please."

"Contemporary poetry is a *regressive semiological system.* We talked like that too. At least in the seminars . . . . It tries to transform the sign back into meaning: its ideal, ultimately, would be to reach not the meaning of words, but the meaning of things themselves. . . . Hence the essentialist ambitions of poetry. . . . of all those who use speech, poets are the least . . ."

"Wait! How about this? We join the animals not when we fuck or shit not when tear drops but when staring into the light . . ." O'Hara inserted a thin pause. ". . . we think. Oh, I don't know. I don't buy it myself. David Smith made me say it."

"What can I say, Frank? We said a lot of things when we got enthused. I'll continue. Of all those who use speech—should I have said, 'of all animals who use speech'?—poets are the least formalist, for they are the only ones who believe that the meaning of the words is only a form, with which they, being realists, cannot be content. This is why our modern poetry always asserts itself as a murder of language."

"Thanks a lot."

"I know. A murder of language, a kind of spatial, tangible analogue of silence—I'm afraid we were a bit overfond of those poetic phrases. Poetry occupies a position which is the reverse of myth: myth is a semiological system which has the pretension of transcending itself into a factual system; poetry is a semiological system which has the pretension of contracting itself into an essential system. That was in *Mythologies.* It, also, was early work."

"Well, I'll tell you. What I was aiming to make direct contact with was not the *meaning* of things but bodies—very particular ones. I hated poetic phrases, by the way. Here, how about this? Here's from 'Personism: A Manifesto.' May I?" The typing paper was folded in half, with a number of circular stains on it from bottoms of glasses. O'Hara unfolded it.

"Please."

"I don't believe in god—and I still don't." O'Hara kicked at the smoke. "This smoke is *cheap.* I know I wasn't Fred Astaire, or Balanchine, or even Gene Kelly, for god's sake, but, still, I always appreciated genuine surfaces. Well, what is one to do?—*now,* I mean. As I was saying. I don't believe in god, so I don't have to make elaborately sounded structures. But Zukofsky didn't believe in god either, so maybe I was wrong. Well, it sounded good when I said it. He's a little scary, Zukofsky. I don't even like rhythm, assonance, all that stuff. You just go on your nerve. I'll skip a bunch. His dreaming angel," he nodded at me, "has only moderately fast handwriting.

"How can you really care whether anyone gets it, or gets what it means, or if it improves them. Improves them for what? For death? I'm skipping, skipping. As for measure and other technical apparatus, that's just common sense: if you're going to buy a pair of pants you want them to be tight enough so everyone will want to go to bed with you. I still can't skip that. Personism has nothing to do with philosophy, it's all art. Skipping. To give you a vague idea, one of its minimal aspects is to address itself to one person (other than the poet himself), thus evoking overtones of love without destroying love's life-giving vulgarity. It puts the poem squarely between the poet and the person, Lucky Pierre style, and the poem is correspondingly gratified. The poem is at last between two persons instead of two pages. In all modesty I confess that it may be the death of literature as we know it. Although now that I'm here—*this* is the death of literature as I knew it."

"But we can talk," said Barthes, "and we have this frozen dreaming worthy on his couch here to write it down for us."

I tried to interrupt him and say that I could talk, that it was *my* dream anyway and not him at all, that I wanted to make a point about the differences between a career made of writing with the stuff of everyday life and one built around reading it—suggestively, authoritatively—but fading finally through growing paralysis of desire stilled in the middle of overly legible maps. But it was one of those dreams where your vocal chords are helpless. I stared at him without gesture. My left hand felt the clicker. My right hand, I noticed, was forming letters with a pen.

"That's an old trick," Barthes said, "saying that you can't say something but saying what it is you can't say. I like those old tricks. There would hardly be any literature without them. And not much writing, either, to tell the truth. Isn't that a distinction you're trying to keep in focus? No, no writing at all, really, without such sleights of time. Foreshortenings, nostalgias, longings. With every letter, almost. One might say that they are the heart of the joke. Don't worry, I won't tell anyone."

"When you say *myth*," said O'Hara, "—you didn't read Duncan or Olson, did you? Robert Duncan, Charles Olson? God, you couldn't read two lines of those guys without Venus or Osiris coming on to you. Wagner was *okay*, I suppose, but after a very little while . . ."

"No, I certainly didn't mean the gods. Myth is this." And he kicked the carbon dioxide smoke. "And especially that," pointing over to the smoke and escalator of #136. "The heavenly Roy Rogers flame-broiled burger: as tasty a myth as I could imagine. Shall I be ponderous—as ponderous as one can be in all this smoke—and define: the bourgeois myth of a natural world? And what's more natural than the supernatural made totally consumable? But Charles Olson, Robert Duncan? I'm afraid American poetry never caught my attention, though those two sound interesting, actually. I heard about the Beats, Allen Ginsberg, Kerouac. Were you . . . ?"

"Give me a break, I was never a beatnik. Maybe the best minds of Allen's generation were destroyed, what can I say? If you had to have a *movement* so you could experience life, that's a problem, wouldn't you say?"

"But an individual life is little more than a punchline."

"Maybe. Maybe not. Allen was sweet when he wasn't being the Poet. I was never the Poet, either, if that's what you were thinking of when you wrote *Mythologies*. No, you really must know my work. May I?"

"But of course." Barthes reached down and scooped up some smoke. He let it flow through his fingers and watched it carefully while O'Hara read from sheets of typing paper.

"A Step Away from Them. It's my lunch hour, so I go for a walk among the hum-colored cabs."

"I'm sorry?"

"Hum-colored cabs."

"For a moment, I thought it was 'ham.'"

"Hum-colored. First, down the sidewalk where laborers feed their dirty glistening torsos sandwiches and Coca-Cola, with yellow helmets on."

"Do you miss food—cooking I should say—?"

"Not really. First, down the sidewalk where laborers feed their dirty glistening torsos sandwiches and Coca-Cola, with yellow helmets on. They protect them from falling bricks, I guess. Then onto the avenues where skirts are flipping above heels and blow up over grates. The sun is hot, but the cabs stir up the air. I look at bargains in wristwatches. There are cats playing in sawdust. On to Times Square, where the sign blows smoke over my head, and higher the waterfall pours lightly. A Negro stands in a doorway with a toothpick, languorously agitating."

"Languorously agitating. Frank, I detect a poetic phrase—even an elaborately sounded structure."

"It is nice, isn't it? Languorously agitating. A blonde chorus girl clicks: he smiles and rubs his chin. Everything suddenly honks: it is 12:40 of a Thursday. Neon in daylight is a great pleasure, as Edwin Denby would write, as are light bulbs in daylight. I stop for a cheeseburger at JULIET'S CORNER. Giulietta Masina, wife of Federico Fellini, *è bell' attrice.* And chocolate malted. A lady in foxes on such a day puts her poodle in a cab. There are several Puerto Ricans on the avenue, which makes it beautiful and warm."

Barthes suddenly clenched his fist. Smoke squirted from between his fingers. "Ah, Mr. American Imperial Artist, you were so happy in your walks, in your world."

"Well, I don't know: First Bunny died, then John Latouche, then Jackson Pollock. But is the earth as full as life was full, of them?"

"And you believed in art triumphing over death!"

"Of course. It has so far, hasn't it? And one has eaten and one walks, past the posters for BULLFIGHT and the Manhattan Storage Warehouse, which they'll soon tear down. I used to think they had the Armory Show there. A glass of papaya juice and back to work. My heart is in my pocket, it is Poems by Pierre Reverdy."

"How did that last part go?"

"First Bunny died, then John Latouche, then Jackson Pollock. But is the earth as full as life was full, of them?"

"Bunny?"

"And one has eaten and one walks . . . Bunny Lang. Violet R. Lang, Poets Theatre, Cambridge, Massachusetts."

"Bunny, and not Jack?"

"Nobody called him Jack. 'Jack Pollock.' It has a certain ring, but it's the wrong ring."

"Were you writing there as curator or poet?"

"Neither."

"You can't really say that."

"I did, though. And one walks past the posters for BULLFIGHT and the Manhattan Storage Warehouse, which they'll soon tear down. I used to think they had the Armory Show there. A glass of papaya juice and back to work. My heart is in my pocket, it is Poems by Pierre Reverdy."

"Lucky man! Lucky Pierre I guess you say! When was that? 60? 62?"

"1956."

"1956. Even luckier—for you, that is. We'd been in Indo-China, Algiers. You could aim to live in a world without other countries except Europe and simply be cosmopolitan. Curatorial without having to worry about grants or wall space. Cabs, Puerto Ricans, Negroes, chocolate malteds, Jackson Pollocks, weather, time: perfectly innocent appetite, spiced by the view into the abyss of death. You trigger my melancholy. Listen, this was me, walking in my world. If, for instance, I take a walk in Spain—you never walked under an 'If, for instance,' am I right? Well, I always did. It gained me a big audience, but so many of them were *students*, finally. If, for instance, I take a walk in Spain, in the Basque country, I may well notice in the houses an architectural unity, a common style, which leads me to acknowledge the Basque house as a definite ethnic product. . . . It does not provoke me into naming it, except if I think to insert it into a vast picture of a rural habitat. But if I am in the Paris region and I catch a glimpse, at the end of the rue Gambetta or the rue Jean-Jaurès, of a natty white chalet with red tiles, dark brown half-timbering, an asymmetrical roof and a wattle-and-daub front, I feel as if I were personally receiving an imperious injunction to name this object a Basque chalet, or even better, to see it as the very essence of *basquity*. . . . And the adhomination is so frank that I feel this chalet has just been created on the spot, *for me* . . . without any trace of the history which has caused it.

"For this interpellant speech is at the same time a frozen speech. At the moment of reaching me, it suspends itself, turns away, and assumes the look of a generality: it stiffens, it makes itself look neutral and innocent. . . . This is a kind of *arrest*, in both the physical and legal sense of the term. I hated being called like that. The details became so clear after a while. Imagine reading where you know the sense *perfectly*."

"That's why I liked the movies and Balanchine and de Kooning and my friends. And Rachmaninoff."

"Reading got to be such a chore, Frank. After I got perfect at it, I liked to read perversely: 'the obtuse meaning,' I called it. But I really wanted it to stop altogether. It was very restful not to know a language. All codes are vulgar. I did get it to a certain point—here. No codes here at all." He sighed as he showed O'Hara a small picture. "My mother as a small child. You haven't seen her here, have you?"

"No, I've only seen you, as a matter of fact. But, you know, I liked walking under a—what did you say—under a 'for instance.' Here's another one about the Manhattan Storage Warehouse: 'Une Journée de Juillet.'" The top half of the page was torn. "Damn! I never memorized anything. Let's see: it was hot, sweaty, sticky tar underfoot. Reflected sun shining in my face. Okay, here: The sun licks my feet through my moccasins as I feel my way along the asphalt. The sun beams on my buttocks as I outdistance the crowd. For a moment I enter the cavernous vault and its deadish cold."

"I understand the cavernous vault you entered; I entered it myself every time I read something, and most especially every time I looked at a photograph. Life consisted of these little touches of solitude."

"That's only the setup. I suck off every man in the Manhattan Storage & Warehouse Co. Then, refreshed, again to the streets! to the generous sun and the vigorous heat of the city—July 12, 1955."

"But . . . May I ask you a personal question?"

"They're the only kind I like."

"Perhaps he should mute the volume, don't you think?"

"Oh let him hear. I *want* him to. He's just making all this up anyway. We're both perfectly safe—which is a drag. All that gets left are our *works*; the moments are missing." A white smoke tear drifted down his cheek. "Okay! Okay! So it's smoke." O'Hara glared upward. He took his typescripts and fanned the air above his head vigorously, dispersing the smoke of his halo. But it kept re-forming.

Barthes sighed. "I suppose you're right: we're safe. Well, don't let this sound naive. But the referent itself?"

"Those men in there, you mean? The Manhattan Storage Warehouse?"

"There is—sorry, there was—a science of the single body that I tried all my life to write. The pleasure of the text. Society was a vast code and one could stir the grids with one's sentences, but I wanted to be able to write a body exactly. You seem to have had pleasure and then to have written. Or to have written in anticipation of pleasure. But you wrote in the present, not *as* the present. You didn't try to make writing *be* pleasure, did you? You didn't try to *write* pleasure."

"I was happy and I wrote. I stopped, you know."

"I wrote to be happy. I couldn't stop. I never was."

The smoke had grown thicker. As they reached this broken symmetry, the screen grew totally white a moment.

"That's such an easy ending. It's like this damn smoke. Contemporary cultural information has to be *challenged*: just reading it or celebrating one's navigation among its shoals won't do." I heard myself saying this.

They waved a window in the center of the smoke and peered out. "This is all *fiction*, isn't it?" They were speaking in unison now. They had their arms over one another's shoulder and were looking right out at me. They had italicized "fiction."

Barthes went on, "And not all that perfect fiction, either: the verbs of saying, the physical props. Not to mention the plot."

"Perhaps he needs to *revise*," O'Hara said. They laughed.

I felt the buttons of the remote control were less under my control. There weren't as many as I had thought. The smoke settled back down to knee-height. "Neither of us *ever* resorted to fiction, let alone allegorical fiction. That's why we're heroic—you for the poets, Frank—" said Barthes.

"—and you for the critics, Roland," said O'Hara.

"That's why both your careers came to the impasses that they did," I said. "That's why neither of you were language writers."

"Please, do not play the goat," said Barthes. "I'd hardly call our careers 'impasses.' You must remember that you're asleep so anything you say is more or less upside down. You'd never possibly say anything like that when you were awake. *Mille sabords!* Language writers hate fiction. Even we know that much."

"Come on, he's not sleeping," O'Hara said. "Look at him looking out the window thinking what to write next. 'What are those fuzzy things out there—*trees*? Well, I'm tired of them.'" He turned to Barthes. "I'm quoting Williams's grandmother. Sort of."

"No, *I'm* quoting Williams's grandmother," I said. "Williams, I mean."

"You can *quote* it, but you can only *say* that when you're dead or dying."

"Williams didn't."

"You Americans are obsessed with self-fashioned lineage, aren't you?" Barthes said. "It must be the New World." Then he mused, "'Language writing,' 'Roy Rogers flame-broiled burgers'—why privilege any one bead of the necklace? It's beautiful, but it can choke." He was wearing a long necklace of smoke beads. He grabbed it and started twirling it in front of his chest. The smoke beads shot off slowly, dispersing. He tried to eat one of the detached enlarging beads. O'Hara elbowed him and shot him a look that said, "It won't be satisfying."

O'Hara gestured out of the screen. "He wants to conjure up the birth of language writing from personism and the heroic decodings of taste—god knows why."

"That means he *is* asleep. Upside down."

"He's drawn us out of his narrow cathexes—500 channels, my eye. So now, Croque Monsieur, you've got to put in the date, just like I did. May 13, I still keep track of these things, 1994—lucky *dog*. *Touch* those keys—Friday, the whole schmear: 2:30 P.M., right?"

"Tonnerre de Brest! What if he rewrites? Hegel, et cetera, et cetera. It will be much later. The accuracy will go."

"Let him."

"I predict—though I'm in no position to—he aims for 'an elaborately sounded structure.'"

"Let him try."

Bibliography

I. Works by Roland Barthes

Book selections of available English translations of Barthes's writings are listed in alphabetical order. Each title is followed by the abbreviation used throughout this volume.

Two notes on recent editions: since 1989, most of the Hill and Wang titles have been reissued by the University of California Press without any changes in pagination. Second, at the time most of the essays for the 1994 conference "After Barthes" were written, the first volume of the three-volume *Œuvres complètes* had just appeared. The subsequent publication of volumes 2 and 3—unavailable to the authors at the time—has provided substantially new material for further reflection on Barthes's sustained meditation on the image and the visual arts.

A Barthes Reader [*BR*]. Ed. Susan Sontag. New York: Farrar, Straus, Giroux, 1982.

Camera Lucida: Reflections on Photography [*CL*]. Trans. Richard Howard. New York: Hill and Wang, 1981.

Critical Essays [*CE*]. Trans. Richard Howard. Evanston, Ill.: Northwestern University Press, 1972.

Criticism and Truth [*CT*]. Trans. Katrine Pilcher Keuneman. Minneapolis: University of Minnesota Press, 1987.

The Eiffel Tower and Other Mythologies [*ET*]. Trans. Richard Howard. New York: Hill and Wang, 1979.

Elements of Semiology [*EL*]. Trans. Annette Lavers and Colin Smith. New York: Hill and Wang, 1973.

The Empire of Signs [*ES*]. Trans. Richard Howard. New York: Hill and Wang, 1982.

The Fashion System [*FS*]. Trans. Matthew Ward and Richard Howard. New York: Hill and Wang, 1983.

The Grain of the Voice: Interviews, 1962–1980 [*GV*]. Trans. Linda Coverdale. New York: Hill and Wang, 1985.

Image-Music-Text [*IMT*]. Trans. Stephen Heath. New York: Hill and Wang, 1977.

Incidents [*IN*]. Trans. Richard Howard. Berkeley and Los Angeles: University of California Press, 1992.

A Lover's Discourse: Fragments [*LD*]. Trans. Richard Howard. New York: Hill and Wang, 1978.

Michelet [*MI*]. Trans. Richard Howard. New York: Hill and Wang, 1987.
Mythologies [*MY*]. Sel. and trans. Annette Lavers. New York: Hill and Wang, 1973.
New Critical Essays [*NCE*]. Trans. Richard Howard. New York: Hill and Wang, 1980.
Œuvres complètes [*OC1, OC2, OC3*]. 3 vols. Ed. Eric Marty. Paris: Seuil, 1993, 1994, and 1995.
On Racine [*OR*]. Trans. Richard Howard. New York: Hill and Wang, 1964.
The Pleasure of the Text [*PT*]. Trans. Richard Miller. New York: Hill and Wang, 1975.
The Responsibility of Forms: Critical Essays on Music, Art, and Representation [*RF*]. Trans. Richard Howard. New York: Hill and Wang, 1985.
Roland Barthes by Roland Barthes [*RB*]. Trans. Richard Howard. New York: Hill and Wang, 1977.
The Rustle of Language [*RL*]. Trans. Richard Howard. New York: Farrar, Straus, Giroux, 1986.
Sade/Fourier/Loyola [*SFL*]. Trans. Richard Miller. New York: Hill and Wang, 1976.
The Semiotic Challenge [*SC*]. Trans. Richard Howard. New York: Farrar, Straus, Giroux, 1988.
S/Z [*SZ*]. Trans. Richard Miller. New York: Hill and Wang, 1975.
Writer Sollers [*WS*]. Trans. Philip Thody. Minneapolis: University of Minnesota Press, 1987.
Writing Degree Zero [*WDZ*]. Trans. Annette Lavers and Colin Smith. New York: Hill and Wang, 1968.

II. General Works

Apter, Emily. "Acting out Orientalism: Sapphic Theatricality in Turn-of-the-Century Paris." *L'Esprit Créateur* 34 (1994): 102–16.
Attridge, Derek. *Peculiar Language: Literature as Difference from the Renaissance to James Joyce.* Ithaca, N.Y.: Cornell University Press, 1988.
Balzac, Honoré de. *The Works of Honoré de Balzac.* Vol. 11. 1901. Reprint, Freeport, N.Y.: Books for Libraries Press, 1971.
Bardèche, Maurice. *Marcel Proust romancier.* 2 vols. Paris: Les Sept Couleurs, 1971.
Bataille, Georges. *The Accursed Share.* 3 vols. Trans. Robert Hurley. New York: Zone, 1988–90.
———. *Le Bleu du Ciel,* Paris: Pauvert, 1957.
———. *Guilty.* Trans. Bruce Boon. Venice, Calif.: Lapis Press, 1988.
———. *Inner Experience.* Trans. Leslie Anne Boldt. Albany: State University of New York Press, 1980.
———. *Oeuvres complètes.* Paris: Gallimard, 1970– .
———. *On Nietzsche.* Trans. Bruce Boon. New York: Paragon, 1990.
Baudelaire, Charles. "The Painter of Modern Life." In *The Painter of Modern Life and Other Essays.* New York: Garland, 1978.
Bazin, André. "Ontology of the Photographic Image." In *Qu'est-ce que le cinéma?* Paris: Cerf, 1975.
Bellos, David. *Georges Perec: A Life in Words.* Boston: David Godine, 1993.
Benjamin, Walter. "Hochherrschaftlich möblierte Zehnzimmerwohnung." In *Einbahnstraße, Gesammelte Schriften.* Vol. 4, bk. 1. Ed. Tillman Rexroth. Frankfurt am Main: Suhrkamp, 1972. Trans. Edmund Jephcott under the title "Mano-

rially Furnished Ten-Room Apartment" (in *Reflections: Essays, Aphorisms, Autobiographical Writings*, ed. and intro. Peter Demetz [New York: Harcourt Brace Jovanovich, 1978]).

———. "Kleine Geschichte der Photographie." In *Gesammelte Schriften*. Vol. 2, bk. 1. Ed. Rolf Tiedemann and Hermann Schweppenhäuser. Frankfurt am Main: Suhrkamp, 1977.

———. "Das Kunstwerk im Zeitalter seiner technischen Reproduzierbarkeit." In *Gesammelte Schriften*. Vol. 1, bk. 2. Ed. Rolf Tiedemann and Hermann Schweppenhäuser. Frankfurt am Main: Suhrkamp, 1974. Trans. Harry Zohn under the title "The Work of Art in the Age of Mechanical Reproduction" (in *Illuminations*, ed. and intro. Hannah Arendt [New York: Schocken, 1969]).

———. "Theses on the Philosophy of History." In *Illuminations*. Trans. Harry Zohn, ed. and intro. Hannah Arendt. New York: Schocken, 1969.

Bergala, Alain. Note on *La Paresse*. *Cahiers du Cinéma: Godard, trente ans depuis* special issue (1990): 114.

Berggasse 19: Sigmund Freud's Home and Offices, Vienna 1938/The Photographs of Edmund Engelman. New York: Basic Books, 1976.

Bhabha, Homi K. "The Other Question: Stereotype, Discrimination, and the Discourse of Colonialism." In *The Location of Culture* London and New York: Routledge, 1994.

Blanch, Leslie. *Pierre Loti: The Legendary Romantic*. New York: Carroll and Graf, 1985.

Blanchot, Maurice. "Le Regard d'Orphée." In *L'Espace littéraire*. Paris: Gallimard, 1955.

Boudinet, Daniel. *Fragments d'un labyrinthe*. In *Daniel Boudinet*. Ed. Christian Caujolle, Emmanuelle Decroux, and Claude Vittiglio. Besançon: Editions La Manufacture, 1993.

Brod, Max. *Franz Kafka*. Prague: Heinrich Mercy, 1937. Trans. G. Humphreys Roberts and Richard Winston under the title *Franz Kafka* (New York: Schocken, 1947).

Brown, Andrew. *Roland Barthes: The Figures of Writing*. Oxford: Oxford University Press, 1992.

Bruno, Giuliana. *Streetwalking on a Ruined Map: Cultural Theory and the City Films of Elvira Notari*. Princeton, N.J.: Princeton University Press, 1993.

Burattoni, Gianni. "La Mort de Daniel Boudinet." *Lettres Françaises* (October 1990): 21.

Burgin, Victor. *The End of Art Theory: Criticism and Postmodernity*. London: Macmillan, 1986.

Burgin, Victor, ed. *Thinking Photography*. London: Macmillan, 1982.

Butor, Michel. "Travel Writing." Trans. John Powers and K. Lisket. *Mosaic* 8 (1974): 1–16.

Caillois, Roger. *Méduse et Cie*. Paris: Gallimard, 1960.

Calvet, Louis-Jean. *Roland Barthes*. Paris: Flammarion, 1990.

Camus, Renaud. *Buena Vista Park*. Paris: Hachette, 1980.

Certeau, Michel de. *Heterologies: "Discourse on the Other."* Trans. Brian Massumi. Minneapolis: University of Minnesota Press, 1986.

Chambers, Ross. "Pointless Stories, Storyless Points: Roland Barthes Between 'Soirées de Paris' and 'Incidents.'" *L'Esprit Créateur* 34 (1994): 12–30.

Chatman, Seymour. "The Styles of Narrative Codes." In *The Concept of Style*. Ed. Berel Lang. Ithaca, N.Y.: Cornell University Press, 1979, 1987.

Christian Boltanski: Catalogue, Books, Printed Matter, Ephemera, 1966–91. Ed. Jennifer Flay, with commentaries by Günter Metken. Cologne: Walther König, 1992.

Clark, Tim. "Roland Barthes, Dead and Alive." *Oxford Literary Review* 6 (1983): 97–107.

Clayton, Jay. *The Pleasure of Babel: Contemporary American Literature and Theory.* New York and Oxford: Oxford University Press, 1993.

Compagnon, Antoine. "L'objectif déconcerté." *La Recherche Photographique* (June 1992): 72–77.

———. Preface to *Sodom et Gomorrhe,* by Marcel Proust. Paris: Gallimard/Folio, 1989.

Compagnon, Antoine, ed. *Contexte: Roland Barthes.* Paris: 10/18/Union générale d'éditions, 1978.

Conley, Tom. "A Message Without a Code?" *Studies in Twentieth-Century Literature: Special Issue on Roland Barthes* 5 (1981): 147–55.

Crary, Jonathan. *Techniques of the Observer: On Vision and Modernity in the Nineteenth Century.* Cambridge, Mass.: MIT Press, 1990.

Culler, Jonathan. *Roland Barthes.* New York: Oxford University Press, 1983.

Derrida, Jacques. *La Carte postale: De Socrate à Freud et au-delà.* Paris: Flammarion, 1980. Trans. Alan Bass under the title *The Post Card: From Socrates to Freud and Beyond* (Chicago: University of Chicago Press, 1987).

———. "The Deaths of Roland Barthes." In *Philosophy and Non-Philosophy Since Merleau-Ponty,* Ed. Hugh J. Silverman. New York: Routledge, 1988.

———. "Des Tours de Babel." In *Difference in Translation.* Ed. Joseph F. Graham. Ithaca, N.Y.: Cornell University Press, 1985.

———. "*Différance.*" In *Margins of Philosophy.* Trans. Alan Bass. Chicago: University of Chicago Press, 1980.

———. *L'Ecriture et la différence.* Paris: Seuil, 1967. Trans. Alan Bass under the title *Writing and Difference* (Chicago: University of Chicago Press, 1978).

———. *Given Time: I, Counterfeit Money.* Trans. Peggy Kamuf. Chicago: University of Chicago Press, 1991.

———. "The Law of Genre." In *Acts of Literature.* Ed. Derek Attridge. New York: Routledge, 1992.

———. *Mémoires d'aveugle: L'autoportrait et autres ruines.* Paris: Editions de la Réunion des musées nationaux, 1990. Trans. Pascale-Ann Brault and Michael Naas under the title *The Memoirs of the Blind: The Self-Portrait and Other Ruins* (Chicago: University of Chicago Press, 1993).

———. *Of Grammatology.* Trans. G. C. Spivak. Baltimore: Johns Hopkins University Press, 1974.

———. "Some Statements and Truisms About Neo-logisms, Newisms, Postisms, Parasitisms, and Other Small Seismisms." In *The States of Theory.* Ed. David Carroll. New York: Columbia University Press, 1989.

———. *Spurs: Nietzsche's Style.* Trans. Barbara Harlow. Chicago: University of Chicago Press, 1979.

Doane, Mary Ann. "Film and the Masquerade: Theorizing the Female Spectator." *Screen* 23 (1982): 74–87.

Eco, Umberto. *A Theory of Semiotics.* Bloomington: Indiana University Press, 1979.

Eissler, K. R. "Biographical Sketch." In *Sigmund Freud: His Life in Pictures and Words.* Trans. Christine Trollope. New York: Harcourt Brace Jovanovich, 1978.

Ferenczi, Sandor. "The Ontogenesis of the Interest in Money." In *Sex in Psycho-*

analysis: Contributions to Psychoanalysis. Ed. Ernest Jones. New York: Robert Brunner, 1950.

Force, Pierre, and Dominique Jullien. "Renaud Camus." *Yale French Studies* special issue (1988): 285–90.

Frampton, Hollis. "For a Metahistory of Film: Commonplace Notes and Hypotheses" [1971]. In *Circles of Confusion: Film, Photography, Video, Texts, 1968–1980.* Rochester, N.Y.: Visual Studies Workshop, 1983.

Freud, Sigmund. *The Standard Edition of the Complete Psychological Works of Sigmund Freud.* London: Hogarth, 1955–74.

Gamwell, Lynn, and Richard Wells, eds. *Sigmund Freud and Art: His Personal Collection of Antiquities.* Binghamton: State University of New York, 1989.

Genette, Gérard. "The Obverse of Signs." In *Figures of Literary Discourse.* New York: Columbia University Press, 1982.

Gide, André. *Amyntas* [1906]. Trans. Richard Howard. New York: Ecco Press, 1988.

Grojnowski, Daniel. "Le Mystère de *La Chambre claire.*" *Textuel 33/34* 15 (1984): 91–96.

Gumpert, Lynn. "The Life and Death of Christian Boltanski." In *Christian Boltanski: Lessons of Darkness.* Ed. L. Gumpert and Mary Jane Jacob. Chicago: Museum of Contemporary Art, 1988.

Hargreaves, Alec G. *The Colonial Experience in French Fiction: A Study of Pierre Loti, Ernest Psichari, and Pierre Mille.* London: Macmillan, 1981.

Haverkamp, Anselm. "The Memory of Pictures: Roland Barthes and Augustine on Photography." *Comparative Literature* 45 (1993): 258–79.

Higgins, Lynn A. "Barthes's Imaginary Voyages." *Studies in Twentieth-Century Literature: Special Issue on Roland Barthes* 5 (1981): 157–76.

Hoft-March, Eilene. "Barthes' Real Mother: The Legacy of *La Chambre claire.*" *French Forum* 17 (1992): 61–76.

JanMohammed, Abdul R. "The Economy of Manichean Allegory: The Function of Racial Difference in Colonialist Literature." In *Race, Writing, and Difference.* Ed. Henry Louis Gates. Chicago: University of Chicago Press, 1985.

Johnson, Lee McKay. "Baudelaire and Delacroix." In *The Metaphor of Painting.* Ann Arbor: UMI Research Press, 1980.

Joyce, James. *A Portrait of the Artist as a Young Man.* New York: Viking, 1968.

Jung, Hwa Yol. "The Joy of Textualizing Japan: A Metacommentary on Roland Barthes's *Empire of Signs.*" *Bucknell Review* 30 (1988): 144–67.

Kafka, Franz. *The Penal Colony.* New York: Schocken, 1948.

Kandiyoti, Dalia. "Exoticism Then and Now: The Travels of Pierre Loti and Roland Barthes in Japan." In *The History of European Ideas.* Vol. 20, 1995, pp. 391–97.

Khatibi, Abdelkebir. "Le Japon de Barthes." In *Figures de l'étranger dans la littérature française.* Paris: Denoël, 1987.

Kingston, Maxine Hong. *The Woman Warrior: Memoirs of a Girlhood Among Ghosts.* New York: Alfred A. Knopf, 1990.

Kipling, Rudyard. *From Sea to Sea and other sketches.* New York: Doubleday, 1925.

Knight, Diana. "Barthes and Orientalism." *New Literary History* 24 (1993): 617–33.

Kristeva, Julia. "La Voix de Barthes." *Communications* 36 (1982): 146–49.

Kritzman, Lawrence D. "Barthesian Free Play." *Yale French Studies* 66 (1986): 189–210.

Lacan, Jacques. *Le Séminaire.* Livre 11, *Les Quatre concepts fondamentaux de la psychanalyse.* Paris: Seuil, 1964.

Lavers, Annette. *Roland Barthes: Structuralism and After.* Cambridge, Mass.: Harvard University Press, 1982.

Léonard, Martine. "Photographie et littérature: Zola, Breton, Simon (Hommage à Roland Barthes)." *Etudes Françaises* 18 (fall 1983): 93–108.

Lombardo, Patrizia. *The Three Paradoxes of Roland Barthes.* Athens: University of Georgia Press, 1989.

Loti, Pierre. *Aziyadé.* In *Pierre Loti.* Paris: Presses de la Cité, 1989.

———. *Japoneries d'automne.* Paris: Calmann-Lévy, 1889.

———. *Madame Chrysanthème.* In *Pierre Loti.* Paris: Presses de la Cité, 1989.

———. *La Troisième jeunesse de Madame Prune.* Paris: Calmann-Lévy, 1905.

Lowe, Lisa. *Critical Terrains: French and British Orientalisms.* Ithaca, N.Y. and London: Cornell University Press, 1991.

Lydon, Mary. "Amplification: Barthes, Freud, and Paranoia." In *Signs in Culture: Roland Barthes Today.* Ed. Steven Ungar and Betty R. McGraw. Iowa City: University of Iowa Press, 1989.

Mark, Mary Ellen. *Streetwise.* New York: Aperture, 1983.

Marsh, Georgia. "The White and the Black: An Interview with Christian Boltanski." *Parkett* 22 (1989): 33–39.

McKeon, Richard. *Thought, Action, and Passion.* Chicago: University of Chicago Press, 1954, 1974.

Metz, Christian. "Le Film de fiction et son spectateur." *Communications* 23 "Psychanalyse et Cinéma" (1975): 108–35.

Miller, D. A. *Bringing out Roland Barthes.* Berkeley: University of California Press, 1992.

Moriarty, Michael. *Roland Barthes.* Stanford: Stanford University Press, 1991.

Nakagawa, Hisayasu. "Encyclopédie de Diderot et le Japon." In *Colloque International Diderot (1713–1784).* Ed. Anne-Marie Chouillet. Paris: Aux Amateurs de Livres, 1985.

Newhall, Beaumont. *A History of Photography.* New York: MOMA, 1964.

Nussbaum, Martha. *The Fragility of Goodness.* New York: Cambridge University Press, 1986.

Oring, Elliot. *The Jokes of Sigmund Freud.* Philadelphia: University of Pennsylvania Press, 1984.

Owen, Wilfred. *The Collected Poems.* New York: New Directions, 1963.

Panofsky, Erwin. *Dürers "Melencolia I": Eine Quellen und Typengeschichte Untersuchung.* Leipzig: B. G. Teuschner, 1923.

Perec, Georges. *W or the Memory of Childhood* [1975]. Trans. David Bellos. Boston: David Godine, 1988.

Plotnitsky, Arkady. *Complementarity: Anti-Epistemology After Bohr and Derrida.* Durham, N.C.: Duke University Press, 1994.

———. *Reconfigurations: Critical Theory and General Economy.* Gainesville: University Press of Florida, 1993.

Porter, Roy. *Haunted Journeys: Desire and Transgression in European Travel Writing.* Princeton, N.J.: Princeton University Press, 1991.

Praz, Mario. *The Romantic Agony* [1933]. Trans. Angus Davidson. Oxford: Oxford University Press, 1970.

Proust, Marcel. *A la recherche du temps perdu.* 3 vols. Paris: Gallimard, Bibliothèque de la Pléïade, 1954. Trans. C. K. Scott Moncrieff and Terence Kilmartin under the title *Remembrance of Things Past* (New York: Random House, 1981; Harmondsworth: Penguin, 1983).

Rabaté, Jean-Michel. *The Ghosts of Modernity*. Gainesville: University Press of Florida, 1996.

———. *La Pénultième est morte*. Seyssel: Champ-Vallon, 1993.

Renard, Delphine. "Entretien avec Christian Boltanski." In *Boltanski*. Paris: Centre Georges Pompidou, 1984.

Rivers, Christopher. "The French Novel Today." *Yale French Studies* special issue (1988): 291–315.

Riviere, Joan. "Womanliness as a Masquerade." In *Formations of Fantasy*. Ed. Victor Burgin et al. London: Methuen, 1986.

Roger, Philippe. *Roland Barthes, roman*. Paris: Grasset, 1986; Paris: Livre de Poche, 1991.

Rosaldo, Renato. "Imperialist Nostalgia." *Representations* 26 (1989): 107–22.

Sarkonak, Ralph. "Roland Barthes and the Spectre of Photography." *L'Esprit Créateur* 22 (spring 1982): 48–68.

Sartre, Jean-Paul. *L'Imaginaire: Psychologie phénoménologique de l'imagination* [1940]. Rev. A. Elkaïm-sartre. Paris: Gallimard, 1986.

Scarry, Elaine. *The Body in Pain*. New York: Oxford University Press, 1985.

Schor, Naomi. "Female Fetishism: The Case of George Sand." *Poetics Today* 6 (1985): 301–10.

Sekula, Allan. "The Traffic in Photographs." In *Photography Against the Grain: Essays and Photo Works, 1973–1983*. Halifax: Press of the Nova Scotia College of Art and Design, 1984.

Shapiro, Gary. " 'To Philosophize Is to Learn to Die.' " In *Signs in Culture: Roland Barthes Today*. Ed. Steven Ungar and Betty R. McGraw. Iowa City: University of Iowa Press, 1989.

Shawcross, Nancy. *Roland Barthes on Photography: The Critical Tradition in Perspective*. Gainesville: University of Florida Press, 1997.

Shloss, Carol. *Gentlemen Photographers*. Boston: Northeastern University Press, 1987.

———. *In Visible Light: Photography and the American Writer*. Oxford: Oxford University Press, 1987.

Sigmund Freud: Sein Leben in Bildern und Texten. Ed. Ernst Freud, Lucie Freud, and Ilse Gubrich-Simitis, with a biographical essay by K. R. Eissler; designed by Willy Fleckhaus. Frankfurt am Main: Suhrkamp Verlag, 1974. Trans. Christine Trollope under the title *Sigmund Freud: His Life in Pictures and Words* (New York: Harcourt Brace Jovanovich, 1978).

Simmel, Georg. *The Philosophy of Money*. Trans. Tom Bottomore and David Frisby. London: Routledge and Kegan Paul, 1978.

Sirinelli, Jean-François. *Génération intellectuelle: Khâgneux et normaliens dans l'entre-deux guerres*. Paris: Fayard, 1988.

Sontag, Susan. "Against Interpretation" (1964). In *Against Interpretation*. New York: Doubleday, 1990.

Tagg, John. "The Currency of the Photograph." In *Thinking Photography*. Ed. Victor Burgin. London: Macmillan, 1982.

Thody, Philip. *Roland Barthes: A Conservative Estimate*. London: Macmillan, 1977.

Todorov, Tzvetan. *Nous et les autres: La Réflexion française sur la diversité humaine*. Paris: Seuil, 1989.

Ulmer, Gregory. *Teletheory: Grammatology in the Age of Video*. New York: Routledge, 1989.

Ungar, Steven. *Roland Barthes: The Professor of Desire.* Lincoln: University of Nebraska Press, 1983.
Ungar, Steven, and Betty R. McGraw, eds. *Signs in Culture: Roland Barthes Today.* Iowa City: University of Iowa Press, 1989.
Wake, Clive. *The Novels of Pierre Loti.* The Hague: Mouton, 1974.
Warner, S. L. "Sigmund Freud and Money." *Journal of the American Academy of Psychoanalysis* 17 (winter 1989): 609–22.
Weissberg, Liliane. "Hebräer oder Juden? Religiöse und politische Bekehrung bei Herder." In *Johann Gottfried Herder: Geschichte und Kultur.* Ed. Martin Bollacher. Würzburg: Königshausen und Neumann, 1994.
Welish, Marjorie. "A Discourse on Twombly." *Art in America* 67, no. 5 (September 1979): 79–90.
———. "Harold Rosenberg: Transforming the Earth." *Art Criticism* 2 (1985): 10–28.
———. Untitled catalog essay. In *Cy Twombly: Paintings.* New York: Stephen Mazoh Gallery, 19 April–27 May 1983.
Wenzel, Siegfried. *The Sin of Sloth: Acedia in Medieval Thought and Literature.* Chapel Hill: University of North Carolina Press, 1960.
Wiseman, Mary Bittner. *The Ecstasies of Roland Barthes.* New York: Routledge, 1989.
Wolfstein, Eugene. "Mr. Moneybags Meets the Rat Man: Marx and Freud on the Meaning of Money." *Political Psychology* 14 (1993): 279–308.

Contributors

Editor: *Jean-Michel Rabaté*, professor of English and Comparative Literature at the University of Pennsylvania, is the author of books on Ezra Pound, James Joyce, Thomas Bernhard, literary theory, psychoanalysis, and modernism. He has edited or coedited collections of essays on Samuel Beckett, Ezra Pound, Jacques Derrida, psychoanalysis, and genetic criticism. He has recently published *The Ghosts of Modernity* (1996).

Derek Attridge is a professor of English at Rutgers University. His books include *Peculiar Language: Literature as Difference from the Renaissance to James Joyce* (1988) and *Poetic Rhythm: An Introduction* (1995). He edited *The Cambridge Companion to James Joyce* (1990) and a collection of essays by Jacques Derrida, *Acts of Literature* (1992). He is currently coediting a collection of essays on recent South African writing.

Victor Burgin is a professor on the Board of Studies in History of Consciousness at the University of California, Santa Cruz. His books include *In/Different Spaces: Place and Memory in Visual Culture* (1996), *Some Cities* (1996), *The End of Art Theory: Criticism and Postmodernity* (1986), and *Between* (1986).

Antoine Compagnon is Blanche W. Knopf Professor of French and Comparative Literature at Columbia University and professor of French literature at the University of Paris-IV Sorbonne. In addition to *La Seconde/Main* (1979), his recent books include *Proust Between Two Centuries* (1992) and *The Five Paradoxes of Modernity* (1994).

Daniel Ferrer is director of the Institut des Textes et Manuscrits Modernes (ITEM-CNRS, Paris) and editor of the journal *Genesis*. The books he has written or coedited include *Post-Structuralist Joyce* (1984); *L'Écriture et ses doubles: Genèse et variation textuelle* (1991); *Ulysse à l'article/Joyce aux marges du roman* (1992); *Genèse du roman contemporain: Incipit et entrée en écriture* (1993); and *Virginia Woolf and the Madness of Language* (1990). He is now working on the theory of genetic criticism and on the hypertextual representation of Joyce's drafts.

Pierre Force taught at Yale and Johns Hopkins universities before joining Columbia University, where he is now an associate professor. A former fellow of the Ecole Normale Supérieure, he received his doctorate and *habilitation* from the Sorbonne. His publications include *Le Problème herméneutique chez Pascal* (1989) and *Molière ou le Prix des Choses* (1994).

Dalia Kandiyoti is currently a Ph.D. candidate in comparative literature at New York University. She is completing a thesis on the representation of space in narratives of displacement in the Americas and has published on Huysmans and Paris in *Nineteenth-Century French Studies.*

Diana Knight is a professor of French at the University of Nottingham and the author of *Flaubert's Characters* (1985) and many articles on nineteenth-century French fiction. Her book on Barthes, *Barthes and Utopia,* is forthcoming from Oxford University Press.

Colin MacCabe is a professor of English at the University of Pittsburgh and production director at the British Film Institute. He has published *James Joyce and the Revolution of the Word* (1978) and *Godard: Images, Sounds, Politics* (1980), and edited many collections of essays, including *The Talking Cure* (1981), *James Joyce: New Perspectives* (1982), *High Theory/Low Culture* (1986), and *White Screens, Black Images* (1994).

Bob Perelman is a Language Writing and Literary History professor in the English department of the University of Pennsylvania. He has published nine volumes of poetry, most recently *Virtual Reality* (1993). He has also published two critical studies, *The Trouble with Genius* (1994) and *The Marginalization of Poetry: Language Writing and Literary History* (1996).

Marjorie Perloff is Sadie Dernham Patek Professor of Humanities at Stanford. Her most recent books include *Radical Artifice: Writing Poetry in the Age of Media* (1992) and *Wittgenstein's Ladder: Poetic Language and the Strangeness of the Ordinary* (1996). She has edited *John Cage: Composed in America* (1994) with Charles Junkerman.

Arkady Plotnitsky has written extensively on critical theory, continental philosophy, British and European romanticism, and connections among literature, philosophy, and science. His recent books include *In the Shadow of Hegel* (1993), *Complementarity: Anti-Epistemology After Bohr and Derrida* (1994), and a collection of essays that he coedited with Barbara H. Smith, *Mathematics, Science, and Postclassic Theory* (1996). He is currently completing a study of Shelley, *Physis, Noas, Eros: Shelley and Scientific Modernity.* He is a visiting associate professor in the Literature Program and a fellow at the Center for Interdisciplinary Studies in Science and Cultural Theory at Duke University.

Philippe Roger is director of the Research Center on French Literature and Language in the seventeenth and eighteenth centuries of the CNRS (Paris) and the Sorbonne (Paris-IV) and also director of studies at the Ecole des Hautes Etudes en Sciences Humaines. He is the author of several books, including *Roland Barthes, roman* (1981). He is currently the editor of the French cultural journal *Critique.*

Beryl Schlossman is an associate professor of modern languages at Carnegie Mellon University. She is the author of *Joyce's Catholic Comedy of Language* (1985) and *The Orient of Style: Modernist Allegories of Conversion* (1991). She has published a book of poems in French, *Angelus Novus* (1995), and is currently working on a study of Baudelaire and Benjamin.

Nancy M. Shawcross teaches comparative literature at the University of Pennsylvania and serves as Curator of Manuscripts in the Department of Special Collections. Her book *Roland Barthes on Photography: The Critical Tradition in Perspective* was published by the University Press of Florida in 1997.

Carol Shloss is a professor of English at West Chester University. Her books include *Flannery O'Connor's Dark Comedies* (1980), *In Visible Light: Photography and the American Writer* (1987), and *Gentlemen Photographers* (1987). She is currently completing a critical trilogy about the daughters of modernism. The first volume, *To Dance in the Wake,* will be about James Joyce and his daughter Lucia.

Steven Ungar is a professor of French and comparative literature at the University of Iowa and the author of *Roland Barthes: The Professor of Desire* (1983) and *Scandal and Aftereffect: Blanchot and France Since 1930* (1995). He has coedited *Signs in Culture: Roland Barthes Today* (1989) with Betty McGraw and *Identity Papers: Contested Nationhood in Twentieth-Century France* (1996) with Tom Conley. He is completing a study with Dudley Andrew on literature, publishing, and film in Popular-Front France.

Jolanta Wawrzycka is an associate professor of English at Radford University in Virginia. She has published articles on James Joyce, Milan Kundera, and theories of translation. She has translated Roman Ingarden into English and is the editor of *Gender and Joyce,* forthcoming from the University Press of Florida.

Liliane Weissberg is a professor of German and chair of the Program in Comparative Literature and Literary Theory at the University of Pennsylvania. She is the author and editor of numerous publications in the fields of eighteenth- and nineteenth-century literature and literary theory, among them *Geistersprache: Philosophischer und literarischer Diskurs im späten achtzehnten Jahrhundert* (1990), *Edgar Allan Poe* (1991), and *Weiblichkeit als Maskerade* (1994). She is currently working on a project on paper money and the circulation of ideology.

Marjorie Welish, poet, painter, and art critic, has recently taught on contemporary art and contemporary poetry at Brown University and the

Pratt Institute. She is the author of four collections of poems, among them *The Windows Flew Open* (1991) and *Casting Sequences* (1993), and of several essays on Cy Twombly. Her catalog essay on the art of Rauschenberg was commissioned by the Modern Art Museum of Fort Worth, Texas, in 1995.

Index

Numbers in boldface refer to the author's chapter in this volume.